Arendt, Levinas and a Politics of Relationality

Reframing the Boundaries: Thinking the Political

Series editors: Alison Assiter and Evert van der Zweerde

This series aims to mine the rich resources of philosophers in the 'continental' tradition for their contributions to thinking the political. It fills a gap in the literature by suggesting that the work of a wider range of philosophers than those normally associated with this sphere of work can be of relevance to the political.

Titles in the Series

Kierkegaard and the Matter of Philosophy, Michael O'Neill Burns

Arendt, Levinas and a Politics of Relationality, Anya Topolski

Arendt, Levinas and a Politics of Relationality

Anya Topolski

ROWMAN &
LITTLEFIELD
INTERNATIONAL
London • New York

Published by Rowman & Littlefield International, Ltd.
Unit A, Whitacre Mews, 26-34 Stannary Street, London SE11 4AB
www.rowmaninternational.com

Rowman & Littlefield International, Ltd. is an affiliate of Rowman & Littlefield
4501 Forbes Boulevard, Suite 200, Lanham, Maryland 20706, USA
With additional offices in Boulder, New York, Toronto (Canada), and London (UK)
www.rowman.com

British Library Cataloguing in Publication Information Available
A catalogue record for this book is available from the British Library

ISBN: HB 978-1-7834-8341-9
ISBN: PB 978-1-7834-8342-6

Library of Congress Cataloging-in-Publication Data

Topolski, Anya, 1976–
Arendt, Levinas and a politics of relationality / Anya Topolski.
pages cm. — (Reframing the Boundaries)
Includes bibliographical references and index.
ISBN 978-1-78348-341-9 (cloth : alk. paper) — ISBN 978-1-78348-342-6 (paper : alk. paper) — ISBN 978-1-78348-343-3 (electronic) 1. Political ethics. 2. Political science—Philosophy. 3. Arendt, Hannah, 1906–1975. 4. Levinas, Emmanuel—Political and social views. I. Title.
JA79.T66 2015
172—dc23
2015005063

∞™ The paper used in this publication meets the minimum requirements of American National Standard for Information Sciences Permanence of Paper for Printed Library Materials, ANSI/NISO Z39.48-1992.

Printed in the United States of America

For my daughter Hannah Aliyah Rahela,
a gift of pure joy taken after just two short years on the earth,
leaving a space in my heart and in the world never to be filled.

Contents

Acknowledgements

I first began researching the contents of this book in 2004. In its original form as my doctoral dissertation, it was successfully defended at the end of 2008. By now it is 2014, a decade has passed, and in this time much has changed in the shared world as well as in my own personal life. Let me tell my own story and the story of this work by interweaving them into the changing political context within which they took place.

Born into a nonpracticing Jewish family of Eastern European descent, my world was one of survivors and refugees. The former the generation of my grandparents, the latter the generation of my parents, who were forced to leave Poland in March 1968 during a less known history of Jewish persecution behind the Iron Curtain. Questions of identity, inclusion and exclusion, anti-Semitism and prejudice were never foreign to my thinking, even though as a resident of Canada, they were foreign to my lived experience. All this changed when I moved to Europe to study philosophy. Having lived in many parts of the globe, I never expected culture shock to manifest itself so strongly in the continent my parents had never ceased to speak about as our home, in terms of beings both Jews and Poles.

In post-9/11, 7/7, and 11-M Europe, and most evidently in the decade in which this work has been written, there has been a resurgence of support for politicians, and their ideas, that I would define in Levinasian terms as espousing the 'same hatred of the other man', a form of racism often connected to religion, race or economics. While Europeans, and certainly those caught up in the project of the European Union, talk a great deal about having founded a Europe that will never repeat the wars and genocide that disgrace the history of the twentieth century, what I have observed greatly concerns me. The gap between rhetoric and reality is immense. I have seen Muslim women violently disrobed and shamed much like Jews were in the 1930s. I have seen mosques burning. These images differ only from those I have seen of synagogues burning in the 1930s because they are in colour, digital and often taken by cameras on cell phones of observers. Worst of all, I have seen too many bystanders keep walking and remain silent.

While there are undoubtedly many differences between the histories of Jews and Muslims in Europe, the inspiration for my dissertation and my further research is motivated by a need to signal the alarm bells. In this vein, I see a politics of relationality as a contribution towards an alternative model of politics in which plurality and inclusion are prioritized over economics, control and unity. Arendt and Levinas are, in my esteem, the best guides for this endeavour, having both survived the Shoah and reflected upon its relation to European philosophy. While this research has never been purely theoretical, its importance grew beyond what I could have previously imagined as my family grew. In 2006 I had my first child, who was exposed to philosophy at the wee age of one month when I dragged him (sleeping) to a conference on Levinas. It was during his first few years of life that I realized how much I wanted him, and all other children, to grow up in a world without this 'hatred of the other man'. My second son, born three weeks after I defended my PhD, inspired me to transform my academic endeavour into a book to be shared beyond the ivory tower. As anyone who has engaged in such an academic endeavour knows, this is a slow and difficult process. In my case, finding a means to juggle further research and a growing family significantly decelerated this process.

When my daughter Hannah was born in 2011 the book was almost complete. When she died tragically and unexpectedly, I fell apart. While I had felt that we were all living in politically dark times for quite some time, I had never personally experienced such despair and loneliness. A changed person, it took a long time for me to come back to this project and to the world. This agonizing journey has been my own, but would have not been possible without the immense support of my family, my friends, my faith and my profession. The life of an academic, for all its barriers, is a treasure for those who love to think and talk, listen and learn.[1]

NOTE

1. In this regard, I am very grateful for the opportunity to teach a seminar on this book as it was being prepared for press. I would especially like to acknowledge students of mine who took the time to read parts of the unpublished manuscript and offer me their honest feedback: Teus de Koning, Thijs Van Reekum, Anna Pylypchuk and Henk Ophoff. I would also like to thank Michael Deckard for his support, keen editor's eye and philosophical spirit.

Key Abbreviations for Works by Hannah Arendt and Emmanuel Levinas

See "Works Cited" for complete bibliographical information.

WORKS BY HANNAH ARENDT

BPF	*Between Past and Future: Six Exercises in Political Thought*
CR	*Crises of the Republic: Lying in Politics; Civil Disobedience; On Violence; Thoughts on Politics and Revolution*
EJ	*Eichmann in Jerusalem: A Report on the Banality of Evil*
EU	*Essays in Understanding, 1930–1954: Formation, Exile, and Totalitarianism*
HC	*The Human Condition*
JW	*The Jewish Writings*
KL	*Lectures on Kant's Political Philosophy*
LM	*The Life of the Mind*
MDT	*Men in Dark Times*
OR	*On Revolution*
OT	*The Origins of Totalitarianism*
PhP	'Philosophy and Politics'
PP	*The Promise of Politics*
RJ	*Responsibility and Judgment*

WORKS BY EMMANUEL LEVINAS

AT	*Alterity and Transcendence*
BPW	*Basic Philosophical Writings*
BV	*Beyond the Verse: Talmudic Readings and Lectures*
DF	*Difficult Freedom: Essays on Judaism*
EI	*Ethics and Infinity: Conversations with Philippe Nemo*
HO	*Humanism of the Other*
NTR	*Nine Talmudic Readings*
OB	*Otherwise Than Being: Or Beyond Essence*
OS	*Outside the Subject*
TI	*Totality and Infinity: An Essay on Exteriority*
TN	*In the Time of the Nations*
TO	*Time and the Other*
UH	*Unforeseen History*

Introduction

In Search of a Politics of Relationality

Why are seemingly so few people interested in politics? Why don't people believe that politics can improve our shared world? Why have so many forgotten how quickly a democratic political system can turn into a totalitarian nightmare? These questions have preoccupied me from the day I first heard about the Shoah.[1] Some answers are to be found in public opinion polls and confirmed by informal conversations. People aren't interested in politics because they feel that their voice makes no difference or that politics is disconnected from their actual lives. In addition, there is a widespread view that politics, and more specifically politicians, cannot be trusted and have no ethics. My search for a politics of relationality arose in response to this contemporary reality, to this lack of interest and general disdain for politics among citizens in 'democratic' nations, especially among those of my generation. While I recognize and often share these pessimistic views, I also firmly believe that only by means of an active collective public commitment is there any hope of creating a shared world in which the words 'never again'[2] might have meaning.

This hope led me to search for an approach to the political that was inspirational enough to awaken societies from their political slumber by empowering agency, participation and responsibility, as well as an approach to the political that related to 'others' as gifts rather than threats. As I will argue by turning to their respective oeuvres, I found the former in the thought of Hannah Arendt and the latter in the thought of Emmanuel Levinas. Next I was faced with a much more difficult task: Could the two intersect? While there are certain evident connections, such as their respective Heideggerian-inspired phenomenological approaches, their shared need to understand and respond to the horrors of the Shoah and their shared Jewish roots, there were also many seemingly serious obstacles to such a project. Arendt was a political thinker who seemingly belittled ethics, and Levinas, the foremost ethical thinker of the post-Shoah generation, disdained politics.

The search for a politics of relationality is the attempt to stage a discussion between these two thinkers, a discussion that unfortunately never took place while they were alive. As a substitute, after first developing their respective projects in relation to both politics and ethics, I confront their central claims in order to consider the political promise of this fictitious encounter. The product of this search is the politics of relationality presented in the final chapters. After engaging with both thinkers separately, with a particular focus on Arendt's notion of plurality as the condition of the political and Levinas's notion of alterity as the basis of ethics, the potential for a rapprochement of their respective projects no longer seemed imprudent; on the contrary, it struck me as absolutely essential given our current political climate. For this reason, I was surprised that the writings of Hannah Arendt and Emmanuel Levinas had never been brought into conversation. Without trying to gloss over the differences, my interest is in considering what each can add to the other's thinking. This is my main motivation in staging a dialogue between them. What I have discovered in this speculative encounter is what I define as relationality. While this term has appeared in several different academic contexts in the past decade,[3] in my usage it refers specifically to a model developed from Arendt's notion of plurality and Levinas's ethics of alterity. The notions of plurality and alterity, as I will demonstrate in what follows, both inhabit an ambiguous space between the self and other and have the potential to inhabit the space of alterity within the self. While Arendt and Levinas often speak of *intersubjectivity* with its phenomenological connotations, each revises this concept in her or his respective projects. When using the term *relationality* in the final chapters, I move beyond intersubjectivity, which still gives ontological and epistemological priority to the subject.

Validation of my bold claim that a politics of relationality has the capacity to oppose the current growing political malaise will be bracketed until the conclusion; nonetheless, I now offer a few signs of the path I am pursuing. While the market of ideas is flooded by political models, the vast majority of these models—whether liberal, republican or communitarian—approach the political in terms of either individuals or collectives; the actual relationship between individuals that form collectives has often been overlooked. Approaches often labelled as liberal start from distinct subjects, frequently assumed to be 'at home' in the private sphere, and move towards the public in order to understand the 'we'. Unfortunately the 'we' is commonly seen as subordinate and certainly not constitutive of the 'I'. Other approaches, those commonly presented as either republican or communitarian, move from a particular kind of 'we' towards the individual 'I'; the problem often encountered by these approaches is that it is difficult to respect the distinction and dignity of individual subjects. Relationality avoids these pitfalls by refusing to choose between an 'I' or a 'we'. Instead relationality takes the alterity that constitutes the self and the plurality of the human world as its starting point. 'If being oneself is simultaneously belonging, with others, to a community, the analysis of this simultaneity might reveal some truth[s] about the unity of individuality and community'.[4] Relationality thus offers a new starting point from which to understand and appreciate the political that speaks directly to a paradoxical need to belong to a community while also knowing that our voice is unique.

Although an apt definition of relationality can only properly be developed after a thorough analysis of the Arendtian notion of plurality and the Levinasian notion of alterity, let us consider the following as a 'working definition': relationality is a form of post-foundational politics rooted in plurality, within which an immanent nonabsolute ethics of alterity is performed. In this vein relationality is a type of political ethics, an ethics that arises from within the *polis* rather than being given to the *polis* in the form of a law or categorical imperative. Relationality seeks to (1) strengthen the political by prioritizing alterity—the cornerstone of plurality—and in so doing acts as an extra precaution against nondemocratic political alternatives; (2) creates an ethos of openness and 'equality' (without denying that power dynamics are inherent to all human interactions) necessary for a basic trust to develop between people; and (3) redefines politics such that each person—in her individuality and distinction—has something vital to contribute to the collective, making each voice significant. It is by building this conceptual bridge between plurality and alterity that I develop the claim that a politics of relationality can revitalize trust, participation and interest in politics.

I begin in part I by highlighting intersections between the biographical and philosophical stories of Hannah Arendt and Emmanuel Levinas. After narrating their respective biographies, which intersect at a few peculiar moments, I explore four significant philosophical parallels: the shock of the Shoah, the importance of the phenomenological tradition, Heidegger's influence, and the significance of their Jewish heritage for Arendt's and Levinas's thought. While there are undoubtedly other parallels, I devote significant time to these, as they support the rapprochement I seek to develop between alterity and plurality in relation to my own politics of relationality.

Second, in chapter 2 I consider the intellectual obstacles that might prevent the fruitful staging of their encounter. I briefly consider some of the differences in their respective projects that I do not attend to further in this book. Again, as a systematic and comprehensive list of such differences would call for a separate volume, I try to focus on those that are most problematic in terms of my imagined dialogue, which are also those I return to when sketching a politics of relationality. After considering some of these differences, I focus on the most significant obstacle: the disciplinary division between ethics and the political. What I show is that while one cannot ignore this disciplinary divide, one must also be careful not to apply it too quickly to the work of either Arendt or Levinas, both of whom were not conventional thinkers in any sense of the term. In this vein, I provide a first definition of the political, according to Arendt, and of ethics, according to Levinas, which already sets the stage for their rapprochement and the basis of an alternative political ethics.

If, as I contend, Hannah Arendt and Emmanuel Levinas were reacting to the same thinkers and events and their answers were not in entirely different registers (as one might originally assume), it is precisely because the answer—for Arendt—is to be found in the notion of plurality as a new principle for the political. The goal of part II is thus to explore the notion of plurality, in all its dimensions. But this is not the only goal. In reaction to the depoliticization of the world, it has been of central importance to my endeavour to seek an approach to the political that challenges the view that politics is for the elite, the wealthy, or the 1 percent, that is, who see democracy as a hierarchical project of managing citizens. Hannah Arendt, who describes her own approach as political in opposition to the philosophical,[5] introduces a bottom-up empowering approach to the political by focusing on its meaning and the experience of political action and agency. It is my intention to make clear why it is important that we consider what Arendt can bring to our current depoliticized democracies. In a letter to Jaspers, dated 6 August 1955, she wrote:

> I would like to bring the wide world to you this time. I've begun so late, really only in recent years, to truly love the world, that I shall be able to do that now. Out of gratitude, I want to call my book on political theories '*Amor Mundi*' [this was the original title of *The Human Condition*].[6]

Plurality, the principle of the political, is the key to her approach to the public realm, a space of debate, difference, particularity and participation. The principle of plurality is, as Arendt herself recognizes, marked by a paradox. 'Human plurality is the paradoxical plurality of unique beings' (HC 176). It is thus my goal in part II to develop Arendt's original approach to the political as rooted in plurality.

In parts II and III, I recreate the imagined conversation between Arendt and Levinas that unfolded as I read their work. I begin with Hannah Arendt because of her explicitly political aim. While I disagree with readings of Arendt that define her work as opposed to ethics, it is clear that her concern—certainly before the Eichmann trial—is primarily political. I focus on what I take to be central and most valuable to Arendt's conception of the political and how it developed in response to her analysis of totalitarianism. Throughout my reading of Arendt, I include both explicit and tangential (the latter usually by means of endnotes) discussions with Levinas. One of the first arguments I make is that her writings need to be read as a narrative, as having an implicit red thread. Many of her readers do not explicitly connect her analysis of totalitarianism to her political project on the human condition and later to her work on Kant. Next I re-read her account of totalitarianism, focusing on what I see as its most original and important aspect for today, her phenomenological reading of loneliness. She acutely appreciates how the loss of the political is equally a loss of a sense of belonging, of being part of a community and at home in the world. Without such a web-of-relations, it is almost impossible to be empowered or inspired to participate in the political realm. It is my contention that our current neo-liberal regime, much like totalitarianism in Arendt's times, intentionally produces 'lonely' subjects, as they are easier to manage or control. Her response to such dark times is plurality, which I argue is the principle of the political Arendt sought in *Origins*. It is for this reason that I focus on plurality in her work and as central to a politics of relationality.

In the second chapter on Arendt, I turn to the question of ethics: Is her politics hospitable to an ethics, and if so, what kind of ethics? Along the lines of Canovan's reading, I demonstrate that there is an implicit ethics in the notion of plurality and yet, I do not think it is sufficient for a post-foundational politics.[7] While Arendt rejects all foundational ethics, taking Kant's moral philosophy as exemplary of such an ethics, she by no means fails to appreciate the importance of ethics for the human condition. In this vein, I argue that Arendt seeks a type of post-foundational ethics. It is my contention that such an ethics is developed in the writings of Levinas. To help pave the path for this claim, I include an analysis of the often-overlooked notion of alterity in Arendt's work in this chapter.

In part III, I turn to the thought of Emmanuel Levinas. Chapter 5 offers a reading of the development of Levinas's ethics, from a critique of ontology and Heidegger to ethics as first philosophy and the notion of alterity. While there are several dozen excellent books that offer such a reading of Levinas's turn away from ontology towards ethics, many fail to consider the so-called Jewish writings. It is my contention that limiting oneself to the so-called philosophical texts leads to an incomplete understanding of Levinas's motivation for this turn as well as many of the questions that appear in his later writings. In addition, by reading both the so-called Jewish and philosophical writings in dialogue, the imagined conversation with Arendt is greatly enhanced. This enables me, throughout the chapter, to draw connections to Arendt's project. One important resonance explored here is the notion of responsibility that highlights the intersection of Heidegger, the Shoah, and Judaism in their respective analyses.

In analogy to chapter 4, in which I explore Arendt's ethics, chapter 6 is the exploration of Levinas's politics. Once again, partially due to the neglect of Levinas's so-called nonphilosophical writings, he has been classified as an ethical thinker who either opposed politics or was not interested in politics. For this reason, I once again consider the entirety of his opus in my analysis of his politics. Inasmuch as knowledge of Levinas's ethics enabled me to appreciate Arendt's pursuit of a nonfoundational ethics, Arendt's notion of plurality helps one to understand Levinas's critique of and difficulty with conventional politics. In this chapter I show how Arendt shares Levinas's aversion to hierarchical politics, although she expresses it in terms of a rejection of political philosophy rooted in singularity. I also try to combat the view that Levinas never dealt with the nitty-gritty of politics by looking at pieces that speak directly to political events of his time. To do so, I focus on his discussion of justice, 'the third' (this is how Levinas refers to additional persons who interrupt the self-other relation) and human rights. While it is clear that Levinas both addresses political topics and has a politics, he is greatly limited by his assumption that ethics and politics ought to be compatible—most evident in his notion of justice. This view leads to readings of Levinas that are very Kantian, which is problematic for any model of post-foundational politics. For this reason, I conclude this section on Levinas with a critique of his politics.

Part IV aims to highlight the most important elements of the staged dialogue between Arendt and Levinas while at the same time serving as an introduction to a politics of relationality. I begin by returning to the philosophical parallels (Shoah, phenomenology, Heidegger, and the Judaic) to show how they contribute to the notion of relationality. Second, I develop an often-depreciated resonance, the Judaic contribution, in order to show its role in the notion of relationality. This contribution is distinct from the less controversial and common claim, an indisputable fact, that both Arendt and Levinas were Jewish, which makes no claims about the influence of this heritage on their respective projects. In terms of the Judaic I consider three points: the philosophical anthropology of hope, the importance of responsibility and the relational approach. In the third section I connect Arendt's notion of plurality and Levinas's notion of alterity and show how relationality positions itself in terms of the notion of a self and post-foundationalism.

In the final chapter I try to bring together all the different aspects of relationality in order to show both its promise and its pitfalls. I also consider the importance of the notion of relationality for today and its application in terms of a model of politics. While this does not, to be sure, amount to a comprehensive political doctrine, it points towards a new empowering and life-affirming perspective on the political in light of a relational understanding of the human condition with regard to our responsibility for others and the shared world. It is the latter perspective that has the potential to speak to the lack of interest and engagement in contemporary democratic politics.

NOTES

1. 'Holocaust', which is the more common term for Shoah, has an etymology and meaning that is troubling for many Jews, as it is Greek for 'burnt offering' and was often used in the content of the Christian liturgy. The term *Shoah* means calamity or destruction in Hebrew and is thus less offensive. For more on this see James Carroll,

Constantine's Sword: The Church and the Jews, a History (Boston: Mariner Books, 2002), 11.

2. 'According to the great historian of the Holocaust, Raul Hilberg, the phrase "Never Again" first appeared on handmade signs put up by inmates at Buchenwald in April, 1945, shortly after the camp had been liberated by U.S. forces. . . . Since then, "Never Again" has become kind of shorthand for the remembrance of the Shoah'. David Rieff, 'The Persistence of Genocide', *Policy Review*, no. 165 (March 2011): 29.

3. Judith Butler, *Parting Ways: Jewishness and the Critique of Zionism* (New York: Columbia University Press, 2012); Hilary Bradbury and Benyamin M. Bergmann Lichtenstein, 'Relationality in Organizational Research: Exploring *The Space Between*', *Organization Science* 11, no. 5 (October 2000): 551–564, doi:10.1287/orsc.11.5.551.15203; Susan Stanford Friedman, 'Beyond White and Other: Relationality and Narratives of Race in Feminist Discourse', *Signs* 21, no. 1 (1 October 1995): 1–49; Stephen A. Mitchell, *Relationality: From Attachment to Intersubjectivity*, Relational Perspectives Book Series vol. 20 (Mahwah, N.J.: Analytic Press, 2000); F. LeRon Shults, *Reforming Theological Anthropology: After the Philosophical Turn to Relationality* (Grand Rapids, MI: Wm. B. Eerdmans, 2003).

4. Adriaan T. Peperzak, 'Intersubjectivity and Community', in *Phenomenology of the Political*, edited by Kevin Thompson and Lester Embree, 55, Contributions to Phenomenology 38 (Dordrecht, Netherlands: Springer Netherlands, 2000), link.springer.com/chapter/10.1007/978-94-017-2606-1_5.

5. 'Our tradition of political philosophy, unhappily and fatefully, from its very beginning, has deprived political affairs . . . of all dignity of their own. . . . From the blow which philosophy dealt to politics at the very beginning of our tradition, political philosophy never recovered. . . . Our philosophical tradition of political thought beginning with Parmenides and Plato was found explicitly in opposition to the *polis* and citizenship' (PP 82).

6. Hannah Arendt and Karl Jaspers, *Correspondence 1926–1969* (San Diego: Mariner Books, 1993), 264.

7. Andrew Schaap argues that there is a certain ethical, as opposed to moral (which he associates with liberalism), significance to political conflict, or agonism in Arendt's writings. He argues this point by presenting three examples of agonistic theorists: Chantal Mouffe, Hannah Arendt and Michael Walzer. Another author who sees conflict as a source for community is Derek Edyvane in 'A Back-Turning Harmony: Conflict as a Source of Political Community', *Res Publica* 11 (2005). I agree with his claim that disagreement, or difference, which I will interpret in a Levinasian sense, can bring people together to engage in dialogue and that this difference can be the basis for understanding the dignity of the other. Specifically in the case of Arendt, he identifies the fact that conflict has the ability to disclose a shared world to those in dialogue. It is worth noting that agonistic alterity is not the same as an allergic reaction to alterity, as agonism is rooted in the principle of plurality; it understands that we need this difference and does not seek to eliminate it by means of unity.

I

Bridges and Breaks

ONE

Biographical and Philosophical Intersections

Take a moment to consider these accounts of the twentieth century.

> Two world wars in one generation, separated by an uninterrupted chain of local wars and revolutions, followed by no peace treaty for the vanquished and no respite for the victor, have ended in the anticipation of a third World War between the two remaining world powers. This moment of anticipation is like the calm that settles after all hopes have died. Under the most diverse conditions and disparate circumstances, we watch the development of the same phenomena—homelessness on an unprecedented scale, rootlessness to an unprecedented depth. Never has our future been more unpredictable, never have we depended so much on political forces that cannot be trusted. (OT vii)

> That history of a peace, a freedom and well-being promised on the basis of a light that a universal knowledge projected on the world and human society—even unto the religious messages that sought justification for themselves in the truths of knowledge—that history is not recognizable in its millennia of fratricidal struggles, political or bloody, of imperialism, scorn, exploitation of the human being, down to our century of world wars, the genocides of the Holocaust and terrorism; unemployment and continual desperate poverty of the Third World; ruthless doctrines and cruelty of fascism and national socialism, right down to the supreme paradox of the defence of man and his rights being perverted into Stalinism. (AT 32)

These accounts were not written by the same person; the first was written by Hannah Arendt (1906–1975) and the second by Emmanuel Levinas (1906–1995). Both are highly personal, political and philosophical accounts of the horrors that marked their lives and the world in the twentieth century. One might wonder how they would have described our current reality; are we no longer dealing with the problems of homelessness, rootlessness, imperialism, exploitation or genocide? Are we not still constantly bombarded by such accounts, but respond by donning an emotionally resistant raincoat in order to simply 'make it through the day'? If we allowed the weight of their words or our reality to have its full impact, would we be able to wake up every morning, to do our jobs, or to enjoy life? Is it not our responsibility, as citizens of the world, to divest ourselves of this emotional resistance if only for a brief, albeit unbearable, moment? Both Arendt and Levinas appealed to their readers not to retreat from reality and from the world but rather to take up our difficult freedom and weighty responsibility in order to ensure that the future never again repeats the horrors of the past.

With this in mind, take a moment to re-read their accounts of the reality in which they lived. What strikes me is how meaningless life must have seemed after such an experience, how little hope they must have had. Yet neither of these thinkers succumbed to these emotions, neither wallowed in depression nor was overcome by hate. This fact alone is striking. They could have decided that life after Auschwitz was simply too much to bear. Many did. They could have declared that humanity could never recover its 'soul' in the aftermath of the Nazi genocide. But they didn't. It is this inspirational choice to believe in humanity's potential—against all odds—that motivated their writings and guides this project. The question I ask of both thinkers is what we can do to bring us a step closer, even if it is only a small one, to fulfilling the promise 'never again'[1] made by many of those who survived.

Never Again. These two words convey the shared inspiration of Arendt's and Levinas's thought. While their ethical and political contributions cannot and should not be reduced to responses to the Shoah, the significance of this event changed their lives to such a degree that neither could continue the intellectual pursuits she or he had commenced prior to the war. While for Levinas this meant going *beyond being* towards ethics and the Talmud,[2] for Arendt it meant leaving theology and the singularity of philosophy (by redefining the meaning of the political[3]) towards the plurality created between human beings in the *polis*. While their thought takes divergent, and often conflicting, paths, Arendt and Levinas are connected by their fundamental commitment to this promise and in their shared hope in humanity's ability to fulfil it. In addition, as I will argue, the fact that both situate their projects as a critique of Western philosophy's prioritization of singularity, or the same, and seek a new 'foundation' in alterity and plurality—that is, in the between of intersubjectivity—is not happenstance. Yet before I begin to explore the respective philosophical paths each took in response to this promise, let us take a closer look at their life stories, which helps to situate their respective responses to the thinkers, philosophical methodologies and events of their times.

LIFE STORIES

Born in 1906, Levinas on January 12 in Kaunas (Lithuania) and Arendt on October 14 in Hannover (Germany), their early years were marked by the religious, cultural and political heritage of the Pale of the Settlement where so many Jews had settled, most often as a result of war and displacement (as was the case for much of European Jewry after 1492 or any one of the many other pogroms in Western Europe between the sixteenth and eighteenth centuries). The Pale was the limited geographic region of Imperial Russia where Jews were legally permitted to reside (it included Lithuania, Poland, Ukraine, Prussia and parts of the Austro-Hungarian Empire). Levinas's family fled their home in 1914, in the wake of the First World War, finding temporary refuge in Ukraine, only to return to Lithuania six years later. What is interesting about Levinas's two childhood homes is that each was a centre of an opposing school of Orthodox Judaism (although Levinas was not properly acquainted with either tradition until after the war, when he studied under the tutelage of Monsieur Chouchani). Lithuania was renowned for its hospitality to the thought of the *Vilna Gaon*, the founder of the *Mitnagdim*, a Jewish tradition that sought answers through study and thus required a high level of literacy. By contrast, Ukraine was the centre of the Hasidic movement, founded by the *Baal Shem Tov*, who argued that Judaism's wisdom was nonintellectual and arose from spirituality sought through song and dance. Given the poverty and violence of life in the Pale of the Settlement, and the lack of educational opportunities, it is no surprise that the latter was much more popular.

Hasidism's popularity was certainly not strong in Königsberg (East Prussia, presently Kaliningrad, Russia), where Arendt's family moved in 1909. Although many of the rabbis in her city would deny this non-Jewish influence, it is clear that Kant and German idealism had had a great impact on many young Jewish thinkers at the start of the twentieth century. Having studied in Marburg (Germany), Arendt was very familiar with the thought of Herman Cohen (neo-Kantian) as well as that of Moses Mendelssohn (whom she cites in her book on Rahel Varnhagen), both of whose writings were instrumental in the formation of Reform Judaism (a response to the dominant Orthodox Judaism of much of the Pale of the Settlement). It is rather difficult to put into words the role Judaism played for her family; suffice it to say that they considered themselves first and foremost Prussian (or German) and yet were all too often reminded, by others, that they were, and would always be, first and foremost Jews. The language and culture of these families was that of the country they lived in, yet their laws and literature were often other than that of their land of residence. While according to Arendt's diary she was exposed to very little blatant anti-Semitism, it was somehow always present within the ethos of these Western European cities. It was the latter subtler differences that played an important role in Arendt's upbringing. She often described her childhood feelings by claiming, 'I was different but it is difficult to determine the difference'.[4] By contrast Levinas was much more at home with his Jewish identity, which he described felt 'as natural as having eyes and ears'. Nonetheless, he was no stranger to the feeling of being different than the majority population, a feeling of being both the same and different that many young Jews shared and sought to understand both prior to, and more consciously after, the Shoah.

In 1924 both Arendt and Levinas made a major decision to travel 'West'—literally and figuratively, to pursue an atypical academic career for Jews. This choice to go to Berlin (and then Marburg and Heidelberg) and Strasbourg respectively was the first step that eventually led both to develop an interest in philosophy. While Levinas considered studying in Germany, he seemed to have thought that France was more 'European' and thus a better place to study the classics (as well as psychology and sociology). Likewise, Arendt chose first to follow courses in the classics and Christian theology at the University of Berlin. Their decision to study classics may not strike one as out of the ordinary, yet it was quite exceptional for Jews at the time. Within a few years both developed an enthusiasm for the new phenomenological tradition, an enthusiasm fortified by their time studying in Marburg with Husserl and Heidegger. Arendt left Marburg for Heidelberg in 1926, two years before Levinas arrived as an exchange student in 1928. She completed her dissertation, entitled '*Der Liebesbegriff bei Augustin*',[5] under the guidance of Karl Jaspers, an existential or humanist phenomenologist, in 1929. Both of them were drawn more to Heidegger's existential or ontological phenomenology than to Husserl's more scientific phenomenology. For Levinas, who 'went to Freiburg because of Husserl, but discovered Heidegger', his time in Germany—a country which he refused to ever step foot in after the war—and his early infatuation with Heidegger—evidenced by his performance in a satirical soirée at Davos—seem to have been a later source of shame. While Arendt's infatuation with Heidegger took another form, it is clear from her writings, especially in her final book *The Life of the Mind*, that she viewed Heidegger as one of the greatest thinkers of his time. While there is a great deal written about each of their personal relationships to Heidegger, what is significant is the fact that both Levinas and Arendt were trained in the phenomenological tradition as championed by Heidegger. In the following section, this point will be expanded upon in terms of the second and third philosophical parallels between Arendt and Levinas.

In addition, it relates directly to that parallel—the rise of totalitarianism and the Shoah. Neither was prepared for Heidegger's public support of Nazism in the early 1930s or the events that followed. It is due to these events, and specifically Heidegger's speeches and writings from this period, that led both to question their own personal, philosophical and political presuppositions. For Arendt, Heidegger's rectoral address was a symbolic betrayal of their shared love for thinking. Furthermore, it was also representative of the growing anti-Semitism of many of the leading thinkers of the academy. Levinas also defended his thesis in 1929 on Husserl's phenomenology and thereafter accepted a position at the Alliance Israélite Universelle in Paris.[6] He continued to study philosophy and translated many of Husserl's works into French, notably the section of *Cartesian Mediations* dealing with intersubjectivity. Interspersed with his writings on Husserl, he began to write about Heidegger and the ontological tradition,[7] which he gave up in 1933 after Heidegger delivered his rectoral address. This event was certainly the turning point for Arendt and Levinas as well as many others of Heidegger's Jewish students.[8]

Unlike Arendt, who seemingly forgave Heidegger publicly, at his eightieth birthday celebrations, Levinas chose never to do so. What is interesting about this difference is that both prioritize forgiveness in their writings and associate it with ethics. Levinas, a practicing Jew, was much more aware of the meaning of forgiveness in a Judaic context (*teshuvah*). In line with *teshuvah*, Heidegger could not be forgiven because he had never asked to be (which would require that he first admit his error). Arendt was also familiar with this Judaic concept (JW 42), yet she clearly did not feel that it was necessary for Heidegger to make a public apology for what she chose to interpret as a private affair. While Heidegger's political failure had an immense impact on Arendt and Levinas, neither abandoned the phenomenological method. Nonetheless there is a marked change in their writings on Heidegger after this period.[9] For Levinas, this change is both a clear distanciation from Heidegger's ontological project and an intellectual turn towards the Judaic. Levinas, with the help of his mysterious teacher, Monsieur Chouchani, dedicated himself to studying Judaism—and specifically the Talmudic tradition, in the years directly after World War II. While Arendt also began to study and write about Judaism, and specifically Israel, with the help of her close friend Walter Benjamin, he did not live to complete her education. Nonetheless, 'Arendt was abruptly estranged from this tradition [of German idealism as taught by Heidegger, Jaspers and Husserl] by the rise of Nazism. She first became politicized by Zionism and by the quest for Jewish national identity',[10] quickly coming to appreciate that 'if one is attacked as a Jew, one must defend oneself as a Jew. Not as a German, not as a world-citizen, not as an upholder of the Rights of Man' (EU 11–12).[11] Thus for Arendt, who was forced to flee Germany in 1933, the political path her writings took was very much a response to the events of her life that brought her Judaism and the political reality she was confronted by into conflict, a conflict that was made much more personal and painful by Heidegger's actions.

Both thinkers thus found themselves in Paris in the 1930s, surrounded by many other Jewish intellectuals from across Europe. As odd as it was that they did not meet in Germany while studying phenomenology, the fact that they never met in Paris, where both mingled within similar Jewish and intellectual circles, is rather surprising. The reality of the rising anti-Semitism across Europe, but most severely in Germany, and the impending tensions that preceded the onset of World War II led both Arendt and Levinas to consider what, if any, philosophical connection needed to be drawn between Heidegger's ontological project and the legal and political exclusion of Jews in Nazi Germany. After his studies in Germany, Levinas had made his home in Paris, marrying Raïssa Levin in 1930, and implicitly explores this connection in his 1934 essay, 'Reflections on the Philosophy of Hitlerism',[12] an essay that eerily foreshadows the Shoah, and in his 1935 essay 'On Escape,' in which he first expresses his critique of Heidegger's ontology.

In 1930, while still in Germany, Arendt was wed to Günter Stern, a Jewish thinker. In response to the rise in anti-Semitism, she began to participate in political discussions in Berlin. After ending up in jail for acting politically—a fact she was very proud of—she was forced to flee, which is how she ended up in Paris, where she began to work for both Zionist and other Jewish organizations. As with Levinas, she was known to travel in several academic circles and to participate in several soirées attended by other Jewish thinkers such as Walter Benjamin and Raymond Aron. Arendt's publications from this period (to which we will return in part II), published in 2007 as *The Jewish Writings*, all revolve around the question of Palestine, Jewish identity, politics and philosophy. Although both Arendt and Levinas were certainly far from naïve and understood that this increase in anti-Semitism was not simply a phase that would pass over Europe, neither was properly prepared for what would happen when the war broke out in 1939. Humanity, as Arendt often said, had not yet realized that anything really is possible, a reality that would perhaps have been better left undiscovered. By then a French citizen, Levinas was drafted into the army, serving as an interpreter, and spent the majority of the war as a Jewish POW in a labour camp in Germany. While all of his Lithuanian relatives, to whom he dedicated *Otherwise Than Being*, perished, his wife and daughter Simone, born in 1935, survived the war thanks to their many friends and to the Catholic nuns who hid them for most of the war.

In 1940 Arendt also spent time in a Nazi camp, a detention and transfer camp for 'enemy aliens' in Gurs, France (with her mother, who had managed to escape Germany just prior to the Anschluss—the annexation of Austria). As control of France was taken over by the pro-Nazi Vichy government, Arendt, along with her second husband, Heinrich Blücher, a Marxist, and her mother managed to flee Europe via Lisbon. They arrived in America in 1941 along with other fortunate refugees, fully aware of those, such as Walter Benjamin, who had not been so fortunate. Once in New York, Arendt found work writing for *Aufbau*, a German-language paper, where she continued advocating a Jewish army, support for the Zionist movement and for the need for Jews to respond politically to the Nazis. In addition, it was during this period that she began to reflect on totalitarianism. As soon as the war was over, she took a job with the Commission on European Jewish Cultural Reconstruction, which had as its mission to recover, gather and catalogue millions of artefacts and volumes of Judaica, most of which she could neither read nor properly appreciate. Levinas went back to work as soon as the war was over, and like Arendt he found it important to work for a Jewish organization, the Ecole Normale Israélite Orientale (ENIO), which allowed him to reinvigorate Jewish life, via education, after the war. In 1947 Arendt's and Levinas's intellectual paths intersected with the assistance of Jean Wahl's journal *Deucalion* (1947, no. 2), in which both published articles, at his request, outlining their critiques of Heidegger's notion of the self. While there is no evidence that Levinas read Arendt's article, entitled 'La philosophie de l'existence', she includes a comment about his article, 'L'Autre dans Proust', in a footnote to *Origins*: 'Compare the interesting remarks on this subject by E. Levinas' (OT 80). It is thus clear that at least Arendt was aware of the direction Levinas's thought was heading in the years after the war. While Arendt was busy travelling to Germany on behalf of Jewish organizations and gathering information for her book, Levinas made his critique of Heidegger public in the lectures now published as *Time and the Other* and in his 1947 *Existence and Existents*.

It was in the 1950s, a time when the world was desperately trying to make sense of the past decade, that both Levinas and Arendt were most prolific. In 1951, both Levinas and Arendt published works that established them as prominent scholars in the post-Shoah period. For Levinas, it was in the essay 'Is Ontology Fundamental?'[13] (analysed in chapter 4) that he formulated his response to Heidegger and to the Shoah in ethical terms. This essay, which forms the base of *Totality and Infinity*, was written while Levinas was founding the *Colloque des intellectuels juifs de langue française*, a temporal overlap that has consequences for both his Talmudic lectures (part of his so-called Jewish writings) and his philosophical essays. Arendt's response to this estrangement came in 1950 with the first draft of *Origins*, a draft that kept her editors occupied for over a year in order to 'Englishsize' it, and then several years later, in 1958 with her phenomenological analysis of labour, work and action in *The Human Condition*. It was also in 1951 that Arendt became an American citizen, ending eighteen years of statelessness, a condition she examined in *Origins*.

The 1960s, a controversial decade for the new state of Israel, was a period during which both Levinas and Arendt reflected on 'The Jewish Question'. In 1961 Arendt travelled to Jerusalem on behalf of the *New Yorker* to report on Eichmann's trial, a report that led her to be attacked by the Jewish community in America as well as the wider academic community of the New School for Social Research in New York, where she had recently been appointed as a professor. It is in response to her surprise both during the trial, and specifically Eichmann's references to Kant's categorical imperative, and to the harsh public reaction to her analysis, that Arendt dedicated the last decade of her life to questions of ethics and more philosophical pursuits, such as the life of the mind. Directly following the trial her book *On Revolution* (1963) was published, and then closely thereafter *Men in Dark Times* (1968), *Crisis of the Republic* (1972) and the first two parts of *The Life of the Mind*. It was also in the late 1960s that she lectured frequently on ethical topics and taught extensively on Kant and the faculty of judgement. Levinas also published many major writings, the most important of which were *Totality and Infinity* (1961) and *Difficult Freedom* (1963). The latter, along with his *Four Talmudic Readings* (1968), were published with a different publisher than his so-called philosophical writings.[14] In addition, he began to write on explicitly political topics such as the State of Israel and human rights.

It is also at the end of this decade, in 1970, after the Eichmann controversy, that Emmanuel Levinas and Hannah Arendt finally met. Both were awarded honorary doctorates by a Jesuit institute (Loyola University in Chicago), a school known for its synthesis of Catholicism and philosophy. Only in America did their lives cross paths. According to Simon Critchley, Levinas was taken aback by the enthusiasm with which Arendt sang the national anthem, an enthusiasm he may have interpreted to be overly political and thus, in his terms, unethical.[15] It is likely, had Levinas been more familiar with her writings in the last few years of her life, that he would have understood that Arendt's appreciation for the United States of America arose from the same experiences as his in France, which he often spoke of, an appreciation at having found a home in which to live, without constant threat, as both a Jew and a human being. It is also perhaps due to the fact that Arendt had made her home in New York and had written predominantly in English, and only rarely in German, that Levinas was unfamiliar with her ideas, which were not, at that time, translated in France. Likewise, Arendt never referred to Levinas, with the exception of the footnote in *Origins*, perhaps for the same reason or possibly due to her general unease with his religious ethics.

While Levinas would continue living and writing for another twenty-five years, by which time most of his books had been translated and were being discussed on both sides of the Atlantic, the same cannot be said for Arendt. After her husband's death in 1970, Arendt's own health rapidly deteriorated. In 1974, while delivering a series of Gifford Lectures, she suffered a near fatal heart attack. Yet rather than resting and recuperating, she quickly returned to teaching and writing, determined to finish *The Life of the Mind*. It thus came as no surprise that on Thursday, 4 December 1975, Hannah Arendt had a fatal heart attack in her living room where, sitting in her typewriter, was the title page of her 'Judging' manuscript. At the same time, Levinas was enjoying the wide success of his *Otherwise Than Being* (1974), and went on to publish *On Maurice Blanchot* (1975), *Proper Names* (1976), *From the Sacred to the Holy* (1977), *Beyond the Verse* (1982), *Of God Who Comes to Mind* (1982), *Outside the Subject* (1987), *In the Time of the Nations* (1988), *Entre Nous* (1991), *Unforeseen History* (1994), and *Alterity and Transcendence* (1995), to name but some of the most well known. What is also noteworthy is the number of interviews Levinas gave in these years, interviews that bring a great deal of clarity to his intensely complex essays. Levinas also received many honours in these last two decades, some of which were from German universities, to which he sent others to accept, never able to fully come to terms with the past. In the 1990s, struggling with illness, Levinas presented a few final Talmudic readings but for the most part was less prolific and passed away on Christmas Eve of 1995 in Paris.

PHILOSOPHICAL PARALLELS

What I aimed to illustrate by means of Arendt's and Levinas's life stories is that while they took divergent paths, several methodologies and concerns emerge that played a prominent role in both of their lives and, as I will demonstrate, in their writings. While there are many intriguing and interesting points of interaction to be explored in the dialogue between Arendt and Levinas, to do so systematically would be impossible in a single volume.[16] For this reason, I intend to focus only on the four aspects of their respective projects that are fundamental to the dialogue between alterity and plurality I seek to construct. First is the event that radically altered both of their lives and thinking—the Shoah. Their respective philosophical contributions are responses to the plethora of questions raised by the horrors of totalitarianism: how it happened, why it happened, how can it be prevented, and so forth. Second is their commitment to the phenomenological approach, albeit with different interpretations and importations from Husserl and Heidegger, respectively. Third, and closely related to the latter, both sought to understand what role the Western philosophical tradition—and especially the existential ontology of their teacher Martin Heidegger—played in preparing the ground for totalitarian thinking and government. And last, the most ambiguous of parallels, is their shared Judaic horizon. While the latter will only be developed in the final chapters, suffice it to say that the Judaic horizon is one that draws on a philosophical anthropology of hope, a relational approach and responsibility.

Reacting to the Shock of the Shoah

The Shoah is undoubtedly 'ground zero' for Arendt and Levinas, as well as many other thinkers, both Jewish and non-Jewish. As Adorno expressed it, art, the world and thought itself, seem barbaric after Auschwitz.[17] The reality in which they found themselves in 1945 raised so many questions for both Arendt and Levinas, there was so much to understand, or at least to try to make sense of. The Shoah, broadly construed, is the most important philosophical parallel. Both thinkers sought a means to reconcile the world with the horrors of the Shoah and, unlike so many others, refused to give up hope in humanity. Levinas stated that his life story was 'dominated by the presentiment and the memory of the Nazi horror' (DF 291). Arendt's response was *The Origins of Totalitarianism*, in which

> [s]he chose to study and understand the crucial political and moral issues of this age in the traditional manner of a theorist confronted with a deranged world. The Holocaust is one such significant event which occupied her erudite and probing attention. From this statement emerged a fundamental statement about man and politics.[18]

One of the main tasks of this book is to analyse the differences in their reactions to the Shoah. While both refuse purely theoretical responses, turning instead to the importance of praxis after Auschwitz, and specifically to the activity of human interactions, each understood these relations differently. Reconciliation, and change, was needed—and for this both found inspiration in existential phenomenology with its emphasis on concrete lived experience.

Given the importance the Shoah had in their lives, magnified by the fact of being born a Jew, regardless of whether one was a practicing Jew, crystallized the connection among their critiques of Heidegger, their phenomenological training and their commitment to *tikkum olam* (repairing the destroyed world). I am not suggesting that being Jewish meant the same thing to Levinas and Arendt, or that it defines their philosophy; nonetheless, the constellation of history and their identities as Jews (albeit as determined by the Nazis) has had a tangible impact on their respective oeuvres. As this parallel will continue to be discussed, it is not necessary to develop this further here, although it must not be underestimated. Arendt and Levinas, in their own ways, spent their lives trying to make sense, to understand and to prevent (another) 'Shoah'. This motivation was a means as well as an end, in that neither could be at home in a world where such horrors were possible.

What I hope to consider in my reading of Levinas and Arendt is first how, in light of Heidegger's betrayal and the Shoah, a Judaic horizon of meaning came to the fore that might otherwise not have arisen. While it is well known that Arendt first expressed an interest in the Judaic while living in exile in Paris among a Jewish intellectual community and had begun to learn about the Judaic from Benjamin prior to his suicide, it is less known that her library—in New York—was filled with annotated volumes on Judaism, and specifically on the difference between Jewish and Greek thought. Likewise, if one considers her writings between 1933 and 1945, now collected in *The Jewish Writings*, it is impossible to deny how historical events directed her research interests. The same is true for Levinas. While he was raised in a practicing Jewish household, he chose—prior to the war—to study philosophy and theology and thus not to engage in the Judaic. It was only in the postwar period, from 1945 to 1955, that he began to study—for days without rest. The Judaic world was opened up to him by his mysterious Talmudic master Chouchani.[19]

The Shoah also plays a role in their respective philosophical anthropologies, implicitly, and more explicitly, in respective pursuits of ethical and political responses. For both the Shoah was a painful reminder of the fragility of the human realm that was utterly shattered under totalitarianism. Yet both also realized that this fragility is part of the dignity of the human condition and that any attempt to reject this fragility affronts human dignity itself. In response to this they sought to rethink the world—without trying to refound it (which is a form of denying the fundamental fragility and contingency of human interactions), in a manner distinct from the traditional philosophical approach to thought, an approach both spent a great deal of time criticizing and connecting to the logic of totality and totalitarianism. This choice led both to embrace a new form of social or relational ontology (alterity and plurality respectively, neither of which is rooted in singularity or oneness) that is prior to epistemology. This priority expresses itself in Arendt's preference for *doxa*, or opinions, over truth, and in Levinas's ethics as first philosophy (thereby displacing both ontology and epistemology as first philosophy). As Taminiaux states: '[W]ithout their justifications being the same—plurality is not the face-to-face—Arendt and Levinas both denounce the pretension that *bios*, from the Greeks to Heidegger, can attain or accomplish, in solitude, an ultimate view of a totalising knowledge in the light beyond any exchange of words'.[20]

The Phenomenological Tradition

Given the emphasis in the Western philosophical tradition on the difference between ethics and politics, it is sometimes difficult to imagine a fruitful dialogue between thinkers such as Arendt and Levinas. Nonetheless, when read in light of their shared phenomenological roots and approaches, this dialogue is made possible and proves to be very fertile. The same can be said about attempting to think, or do philosophy, after the Shoah. 'The reality [of the Shoah] is more difficult to grasp; to do so, one needs to adopt a phenomenological approach that avoids the one sided standpoints of either the supposedly neutral outside observer or the participant in the process itself'.[21] What distinguishes phenomenology from traditional philosophy, implied in this quote, is its refusal to assume or engage with unobservable phenomena—as is the case with psychoanalysis, which was immensely popular at the turn of the twentieth century, choosing instead to focus on what is experienced by a subject—clearly drawing its inspiration from Kant's transcendental philosophy. 'Phenomenology investigates the intelligibility, significance, and appearance of the world. To engage in a reflective exploration of the structures and conditions of worldly significance and appearance differs from any direct metaphysical investigation of the real world'.[22] In this sense, 'phenomenology is a distinctively German response to the "crisis of metaphysics".'[23] After providing a brief and simplified definition of the phenomenological tradition, I will consider how Arendt and Levinas, in their own manners, engage with the phenomenological tradition, setting aside their specific engagement with Heidegger's ontological project for the next section.

Arendt and Levinas are both third-generation phenomenologists (circa 1950s), who according to Thompson and Embree's taxonomy address questions of ethics and politics, which were seen as lacking in the work of first- (Husserl, circa 1900) and second- (Heidegger, circa 1930) generation phenomenologists.[24] What distinguishes these two previous generations from each other, a distinction Levinas explores extensively in his pre-1950s writings, is that Husserl's approach, often called realistic or constitutive phenomenology, is focused in cognition, whereas Heidegger's focus is on lived experience (*erlebnis*), existential phenomenology or ontology, as it arises from *Dasein's existence* (being-with). Husserl, whose approach was defined by both Arendt and Levinas as too intellectual, sought to trace experience back to its intentional or constitutive roots in the subject, which led them to criticize the founder of phenomenology for failing to realize the other cannot be a product of the self's intentional consciousness, or what Levinas refers to in his dissertation as 'theoretical contemplation' (which comes very close to Arendt's criticism of the *vita contemplativa* in *The Human Condition*). Levinas's reading of Husserl is very much affected by Heidegger, who takes his leave from this purely cognitive approach, specifically in *Being and Time* (1927), by way of his project of fundamental ontology, in which he seeks to provide an account of human existence (*Dasein*'s existence) as it appears or is disclosed in the context of the world. 'The Heideggerian inspiration of Levinas' hermeneutic is obvious. . . . Husserl's preference for the object (*Gegenstand*), representation (*Vorstellung*), perception, evidence, adequacy, and theory expresses a specific orientation and a certain way of being . . . and which presupposes a genesis, a specific history, and a particular way of being in the world'.[25] However, even with Heidegger's focus on history and being in the world, according to Arendt and Levinas, he fails to recognize that the other cannot be understood or reduced to an object or product of *Dasein*'s existence. Both thinkers felt strongly that after the horrors of the Shoah, it was absolutely imperative that philosophy be rethought in such a manner that the other was not reduced to another self or object, to be instrumentalised by a system. 'The impetus behind this [third-generation] development was, of course, the necessity for those involved of responding to the challenge of Marxism and the emergence of the novel form of terror unleashed in the totalitarian regimes of Nazi Germany and Stalinist Russia'.[26] These events very much directed the focus of their phenomenological investigations towards the realm of politics, ethics and other social interactions, structures of oppression and exclusion, institutions, and in particular the question of intersubjectivity—first introduced to phenomenology by Husserl.

In this vein, Arendt and Levinas can both be read as third-generation existential phenomenologists focused on the question of intersubjectivity—specifically their respective foci on relational conceptions of alterity and plurality. Both thinkers are methodologically closer to Heidegger's existential approach, however thematically they reject his ontological project, and are thematically closer to Husserl's late analysis of intersubjectivity.[27] Levinas began his career, at the age of twenty-six, by translating Husserl's writings on intersubjectivity (into French), but only begins his own radical rethinking of the relationship between self and other in the 1940s. Arendt, who was also very much influenced by Karl Jasper's existentialism, provides a definition of the political created *between* people, in a space constituted by self-other relations, which she calls plurality. According to Arendt and Levinas, the phenomenological method has the ability to avoid the reduction of the other to the self, a reduction they see as fundamental to the philosophical tradition and Heidegger's ontological project. This is a view shared by other third-generation phenomenologists, 'the concrete transcendental subject grasps itself as Other in that it is "an other" for the Other, and introduces an absolutely original element into the problematic of this subject: the social. Here again phenomenology was led inevitably, by the very fact that it is not a metaphysics but a philosophy of the concrete'.[28]

However, while Arendt and Levinas are focused on rethinking intersubjectivity phenomenologically, the tradition of philosophy categorizes their approaches in terms of ethics and politics, respectively, a categorization that fails to appreciate their shared methods and thematic concerns. When viewed as phenomenological investigations of intersubjectivity that are reacting to the tradition of Western philosophy and Heidegger's ontological project, there is a clear rapprochement between Arendt's political and Levinas's ethical projects. From the perspective of postmodern philosophy, which takes the loss of metaphysical foundations as its starting point, both Levinas and Arendt explore '"the political", that is, the realm of human coexistence'.[29] Phenomenology is thus a fitting methodology with which to understand the self-other relation and avoid the reduction of the other to the self, a relation that constitutes the ground for Arendt's politics and Levinas's ethics.

Responding to Heidegger

Undoubtedly the most distinct parallel—biographical and intellectual—is the inspiration and education they received from Martin Heidegger (pre-1930) as well as the shock and disappointment at his behaviour that followed closely thereafter (post-1930). While there is a great deal of resonance in their writings with regard to the former, the latter is a major point of divergence. To forgive or not to forgive was the question that so many of Heidegger's disciples, and specifically his Jewish students, were forced to ask themselves in light of the horrors of the Shoah after the infamous rectoral address and his further links to Nazism. On a more personal level, both struggled throughout their lives with the question of how such a philosophical genius could have been so ethically and politically irresponsible. However important his lessons had been prior to 1930, the shock of his associating with Nazism led both to rethink the entire philosophical tradition and specifically Heidegger's ontological project. In an interview with François Poirié, Levinas said:

> went to see Husserl and I found Heidegger. Of course, I will never forget Heidegger's relation to Hitler. Even if this relation was only of a very short duration, it will be forever. But the works of Heidegger, the way in which he practiced phenomenology in *Being and Time*—I knew immediately that this was one of the greatest philosophers in history.[30]

In this vein, it is impossible to disentangle the Heideggerian parallel from that of the Shoah. This connection is quite explicit in the first major book each thinker published after the Shoah. For Arendt, in the *Origins of Totalitarianism*, the ontological project and its reduction of the other is related to totalitarianism's destruction of plurality and the dignity of the other. For Levinas, in *Totality and Infinity*, 'ontology is a totalizing enterprise. It is a philosophy of power characterized by a relentless movement of absorption and reduction';[31] it is the totality that prevents the ethical face-to-face relation. While Arendt later moderates her critique of Heidegger, it is evident that after the Shoah both felt it absolutely necessary to explicitly criticize and distance themselves from his ontological project. Had history and Heidegger been other than they were, Levinas might not have sought to establish that ethics precedes ontology, and Arendt might not have tried to assert plurality's priority over singularity for the sake of the political.

A concrete expression of Levinas's intellectual response is how he 'develops his ontology in deliberate contrast to the ontology of Heidegger'.[32] Cohen demonstrates this in 'Levinas: thinking least about death—contra Heidegger',[33] in which he demonstrates how Levinas rejects Heidegger's egocentric focus on the death of the self and turns instead to alterity and life by means of phenomenological analyses of fecundity and eros. Similarly, as developed by Jung, Arendt 'opposes Heidegger whose

Dasein is characterized by death or mortality, [whereas] Arendt defines the *initium* of action, which is the foundation of human capacity to create new realities, in terms of the facticity of birth or natality'.[34] The original reading of Augustine she presents in most of her writings, which focuses on hope, the new and natality, is an explicit response to Heidegger's understanding of *Dasein* as being-towards-death (*zum-Tode-sein*).[35] This shared rejection of the ontological focus on *Dasein*'s death as the origin of one's horizon is also the basis for their move away from the priority of the self, or *Dasein*, towards the other and intersubjectivity. In Heidegger's work the latter is addressed in terms of *mitsein* (being-with), and yet it is still understood as a possibility that arises from within the horizon of the self, of *Dasein*. Arendt's focus on natality, like Levinas's interest in fecundity, family and the feminine, is an expression of their prioritization of the other, a reworking of Heidegger's *mitsein*. 'Against a thought led by schemes of power and slavery [how Levinas defined Heideggerian ontology in 1949], Levinas looks for a way out . . . and points to the themes of createdness and sexuality'.[36] Unlike death, birth and sexuality are impossible without the other.

In contrast to their explicit rejection of the importance of death in Heidegger's ontology, Arendt and Levinas both maintain the importance of other Heideggerian concepts such as that of the world, and specifically of being-in-the-world (*in-der-welt-sein*). The latter, for Heidegger, replaces the Husserlian subject-object frame that is so central to the tradition after Descartes in order to emphasize *Dasein*'s (entanglement) in the world. Accordingly *Dasein* is always already in the world, not by conscious or intentional choice, but by being thrown or projected (*geworfen*) into it and defined by its limitations and possibilities (such as death). For Heidegger the world is thus not only an ontical term but also an ontological realm of possibilities. However, what is most important about the Heideggerian notion of the world for Arendt and Levinas is worldhood (*weltheit*), which is an existential and ontological notion, that can be best understood as the background or horizon upon which all things appear, and world disclosure (*erschlossenheit*), which is how things (including the other for Heidegger) become meaningful or appear to *Dasein*. Arendt relies heavily on the concept of world, worldliness and worldlessness in *The Human Condition* (explored in chapter 3). When she describes the modern world as worldless, this is not a factual claim about the nature of reality but an existential judgement from the perspective of experience, as the world that is lost refers to the reality created between people in the public realm. In his early work 'Levinas describes three levels of worldliness, finding beneath praxis and theory the more originary level of the self-sensing of embodied sensibility which he describes in terms of "enjoyment".'[37] While in his later work, the world is that which is outside the totality of the ego, in the space of externality, and in this sense is an openness to infinity.

Another shared Heideggerian concept is the focus on someone's (ontological) 'whoness' or personhood as opposed to someone's (ontic) 'whatness' (*quidditas*). For Heidegger the correct question to pose of *Dasein* is 'who' are you, rather than 'what' is *Dasein*. 'The "who" question "discloses" (to use Heidegger's term) the difference between *Dasein* and other beings'.[38] This emphasis on the *who* over the *what* of a person, which is focused on *Dasein* for Heidegger, on the self and other for Arendt, and on the other for Levinas, relates to the question central to this work concerning the constitution of the self. What is clear is that both Arendt and Levinas agree with Heidegger that the who has precedence over the what, but where both disagree is his focus on the who of the self at the cost of the who of the other. Both Arendt and Levinas explicitly react to the Heideggerian claim that 'being-with-others (*Miteinandersein*) is founded in a comprehension of Being in general and as such and that an authentic relationship with others presupposes a "letting be" (*Seinlassen*)'.[39] According to Arendt, the self can only answer the question 'who am I' by interacting with the other. Likewise, for Levinas, in his analysis of substitution or *hineni*,[40] the other constitutes the self's whoness. For both thinkers the 'who' is fundamentally a relational disclosure, as it is the other who singularizes the self as unique, irreplaceable and responsible.

Perhaps the most obvious, and thus most forgotten, inheritance from Heidegger—rooted in the phenomenological method—is the importance of space and time, or temporality. Space and time are so present in Arendt's and Levinas's writings and analyses of the self-other relation that it is impossible to do more than provide a few examples here (which will be followed by much more support in parts II and III). For Heidegger, space and time are 'existentials'—categories that make up the structure of *Dasein*'s existence. Other such existentials are care (*zorg*), anxiety, falleness, and so forth. 'This existential sense of space will be crucial to Arendt since, in contrast to physical space, our "being in" the *human* world depends to a great extent on the maintenance of *human* institutions such as publicness. . . . [Likewise] in human time the "present" is merely an incomplete, artificially detached slice of a whole movement that actually begins in the future',[41] an idea Arendt echoes in her essays collected in *Between Past and Future*. For Levinas time remains a fundamental existential, and yet he criticizes Heidegger's overcorrection of nonphenomenological notions of time, which puts too much emphasis on the temporalizing of history (*Geschichtlichkeit*). 'Levinas' solution is breathtaking in its originality: the irreducible alterity of time's dimensions is sustained precisely as the alterity of the face-to-face proximity'.[42] While this will be explained at length in chapter 5, briefly, Levinas explains that the past that gives meaning to the present (via history and memory) is never really present; it is only encountered when face-to-face with the other.

In addition to these shared Heideggerian heirlooms, there are many concepts and claims exclusively inherited by Arendt or Levinas. Many of these will be explored extensively in the chapters to come, but for now it is worth mentioning a few of the most significant. 'The stamp of Heideggerian thinking is especially noticeable in three elements of Arendt's work: the status of her elaborate system of distinctions and concepts, her approach to language, and her interpretation of action as self-revelation'.[43] The distinctions that structure *The Human Condition* are labour, work, action, the *vita activa* and *vita contemplativa*; and those that structure her investigation of *The Life of the Mind* are thinking, willing and judging. We will also be considering the importance of speech in relation to self-disclosure for Arendt's notion of the political, which has parallels to Levinas's position in *Totality and Infinity* with regard to language as a means to encounter the other without reducing the other to the same. Another critical Arendtian concept that was greatly inspired by Heidegger is her exploration of the phenomenon of loneliness. Loneliness is not a category for scientific analysis; it is an existential that arises when a human being is no longer 'in the world' because of a lack of relationality (or for now, self-other relations) and does not have a space in which to appear and be seen (to be glorified, in Heideggerian terms). The danger of course is that lonely denizens escape this painful experience of loneliness by joining the masses—or Heidegger's 'the they'—rather than turning to the political realm of plurality. For Arendt, it is by means of action—the concept central to her entire opus—that the self discloses itself and appears to others. In other words action brings together Heidegger's analysis of self-disclosure and Arendt's phenomenological commitment to the realm of appearances.[44]

Levinas, until the 1950s, remains much closer (than Arendt) in his approach and terminology to both Husserl and Heidegger; his project takes a much more radical divergence from that of Heidegger after the 1950s. For Heidegger the Other (*autrui*) does not disclose herself but is to be understood (or comprehended) against the horizon of Being, what Levinas will call the reduction of the other to the same or more polemically 'the murder of the other'. Nonetheless, Levinas remains much truer to the phenomenological method, which he claims is 'precisely the method by which we are going back to concrete man';[45] this is most evident from his analyses of dwelling, at-homeness, paternity, and so forth.

As we will see throughout this book, Arendt and Levinas retain certain of Heidegger's fundamental concepts as well as his phenomenological approach, yet nonetheless both reject the project of fundamental ontology (as is clear from their view on being-towards-death) by questioning the primacy he gives to *Dasein*. Furthermore, given that Heidegger saw his project as being a radical departure from the history of philosophy, which has its focus on ontical being (the factual being of positive science) and not on ontology (the phenomenal existence of Being as such), this questioning of Heidegger's project led them both to rethink its connection to the entire Western philosophical tradition. However, the aspects of the tradition they remain loyal to, for example to Kant, are remarkably similar;[46] this is most likely due to the fact that both criticize the tradition, and specifically ethics and politics, from the perspective of the phenomenological method. Well versed in the tradition—Arendt having studied at Berlin, Marburg, Freiburg and Heidelberg, Levinas at Strasbourg and Freiburg—both exhibited their creative licence with regard to their interpretation of the philosophical canon that grounds the tradition. Nonetheless, their originality comes at a price. They have—rightly so—been accused of intentionally misinterpreting the tradition, leading to controversial, polarizing, and hyperbolic oversimplifications. While I do not intend to apologize ad nauseam for this tendency, it would be remiss not to provide a few examples.

Let us begin by considering Arendt's reading of the tradition. First there is her problematic use of the term *philosophy*. With this term she categorizes all thinkers—rarely citing exceptions—from Parmenides to Heidegger as seeking singularity (whether in terms of the self, the same, the individual, *Dasein*) and as being averse to plurality. A second example of Arendt's lack of scholasticism is in her reading of Socrates and Plato—and specifically in *The Human Condition*. Seemingly Socrates can do no wrong, whereas Plato can do no right in her eyes. Arendt rarely even notes the fact that all we know of the former comes from the latter. Plato is depicted as a philosopher king whose obsession with singularity transforms him into a truth tyrant, which makes him solely responsible for turning the activity of the political into a contemplative activity—political philosophy. Nonetheless there are advantages to Arendt's peculiar reading of the tradition—take for example her highly original reading of Kant's third critique in relation to politics, which has been so influential for thinkers such as Ranciere and Butler. In this vein, it is perhaps possible to understand those sympathetic to Arendt—including myself—who acknowledge and then move beyond her lack of scholastic or historical subtlety.

This is equally true of those sympathetic to Levinas's highly reductive and critical reading of the Western philosophical tradition, which nonetheless provides an invaluable contribution, or alternative, to the tradition in terms of an ethics of alterity. He, like Arendt, all too often equates all of Western philosophy, with its roots in Athens, with ontology. What's more, he also seems to deem, although inconsistently, certain concepts as 'malicious'—such as totality, universality, and politics, and others as 'noble'—such as alterity, ethics, and responsibility. However, this does not prevent him from discovering potential in philosophers such as Plato, in terms of the Good, and Descartes's idea of infinity (both to be discussed in the section on *Totality and Infinity*). A question that has always puzzled me is why Levinas felt the term *ethics* could be rescued from the tradition, but *politics* could not? Likewise, until after the Eichmann trial, why could Arendt rescue the political but not ethics?

This perplexity is further reinforced by explicit parallels in their respective treatments of certain thinkers, such as their similar criticisms of the singularity or egocentric approach of Hobbes, which is the starting point for the tradition of political liberalism based on a vertical contract with a sovereign in response to a fear of other human subjects. While both thinkers are highly critical of the liberal state that takes for granted certain of Hobbes's views on autonomy, contracts, and so forth, they do not wish to do away with it because of its more recent philosophical emphasis on human dignity, liberty and equality. This philosophical liberalism is for both a potential springboard to a richer form of community rooted in heteronomy, responsibility and respect (as opposed to fear) for the other. They see the political as having more to offer than the rather minimalistic definition given to it by Hobbesian inspired liberalism. The liberal state is thus presupposed to be an absolute 'minimum', necessary but far from sufficient. As Muhlmann writes, 'Arendt insists upon that which goes beyond liberalism, but exactly that, beyond but not without liberalism as its basis'.[47]

Having acquired substantial backgrounds in classical philosophy, both Arendt and Levinas made the choice to follow Heidegger and adopt the language and method of phenomenology (to greater and lesser degrees) as well as several key Heideggerian concepts. Their shared methodological roots allow for the possibility of a dialogue between their distinct projects if approached from the perspective of phenomenology. It is too simple to assume that because Levinas, read superficially, opposes ethics to politics, and Arendt, read equally superficially, opposes politics to morality, that the two are quite obviously speaking incompatible languages. The language of both is that of phenomenology reinterpreted in light of Heidegger's actions prior to and during the Shoah. By taking a phenomenological approach, both are responding to the lacunae of Heideggerian phenomenology and focusing on the experiences of human beings in their alterity and plurality. In addition, both reject the basis of ontology in singularity by focusing on an intersubjective approach and asserting their continued faith in humanity in the aftermath of the Shoah. These similarities point to a rapprochement between Levinas's and Arendt's thought that while challenging is certainly worth considering.

A Judaic Inspiration

In order to avoid potential assumptions and misunderstandings, which are par for the course when one uses a term associated with religion in the context of a philosophical or political project, it is necessary to define the neologism *Judaic*. In using this term, I draw an analytically useful albeit artificial distinction between the Judaic and Judaism, a religion (as classified in the seventeenth century),[48] and being Jewish or Jewish(ness), a cultural heritage. While this distinction can only be theoretically or formally maintained, it is nonetheless an important one. The Judaic is the contemporary voice of an ancient tradition (oral and written) that inhabits the intellectually rich space between thinking and acting. As such, it is necessary to situate this tradition, which has always sought to relate what is particular to Judaism and being a Jew to the thoughts and activities of the rest of the world (which has given the geographic location of the diaspora, been predominantly influenced by Christianity, the Greeks, and their confluence in Rome). While inspired by the Torah or Hebrew Bible, it took on a life of its own only after the destruction of the Temple (approx. 135 CE). It is this tragic event that gave birth to a critical and hermeneutical Judaic tradition as guided by rabbis. While this rabbinic tradition is as rich as medieval philosophy, I believe that modernity, which occurred for the Jews somewhat later than for the rest of Europe,[49] brought with it yet another twist. This twist, which arose in the nineteenth century with emancipation, is evident from the fact that one can be Jewish without practicing Judaism. The term Jewish, that is, the experience of being Jewish, is the product of the modern possibility to no longer practice Judaism and yet still to be considered by others, as well as by oneself, to be a Jew.[50]

Given that Arendt found herself in this exact situation, which she explored in many of the essays collected by Feldman and Kohn (JW),[51] a situation that neither she nor her readers could properly understand,[52] it is important to understand that the 'theological' aspects of Judaism (a Christian term that does not properly apply here) took on a different form for the great majority of modern Jews of which both Arendt and Levinas are part. It is for this reason that a third term arises with modernity, which most often begins with Spinoza but must wait for Mendelssohn to find a warmer welcome. It is this tradition that can be traced via thinkers such as Hermann Cohen, as a representative of neo-Kantianism, and Franz Rosenzweig, a student of Hegel, which are important 'theological' and philosophical sources for thinkers writing after the Shoah. It is a tradition that is constantly struggling to find recognition in both the universities, as the centre of academic life, and the synagogues, as the centre of the Jewish community whether secular or not.

Although it would be useful if the Judaic could simply be categorized as theological or philosophical, it cannot. It is this refusal that serves as a reminder that the Judaic cannot simply be translated into the terms of contemporary—Christian or secular (post-Christian)—thought. As Bettina Bergo writes, 'It is precisely in these tensions, between the Jewish religious and philosophical traditions [read Judaic], *and* his phenomenological-existential thought, that Levinas' originality lies'.[53] Levinas—respected by both many prominent Jewish thinkers and Western philosophers—has made his home in the space between faith and philosophy. In his first-ever public remark at the Colloque des intellectuels juifs, Levinas, in his own terms, expressed this particular and peculiar aspect of the Judaic: 'Judaism [read Judaic] is not a *religion*. The word does not exist in Hebrew. It is much more than that. It is a way to understand [the human] being'.[54] It is in this nontheological and noncultural sense that I claim that both Arendt and Levinas are inspired by the Judaic and on this basis explore the Judaic in terms of a shared resonance in their writings.

To conclude, it is the intersection of the phenomenological approach, with its emphasis on meaning, experiences, and action and the need to respond to the Shoah, that I take as a basis for the engagement of Arendt and Levinas. It is my claim that because of Arendt's unique approach to the political from the perspective of plurality, her thought resonates remarkably well with the criteria of Levinas's ethics. Arendt's notion of the political is equally opposed to the reduction of the other that Levinas is reacting against and one that thinks of the political from the perspective of relationality as Levinas does the ethical. Furthermore, as I will show in my reading of Arendt, her notion of the political is based on an appreciation for the alterity that characterizes plurality as opposed to multiplicity: copies of the same. I conceive of a possible dialogue between the political and ethics because of how they are conceived by Arendt and Levinas. Furthermore, I claim that this dialogue takes places from within a common background, such as their shared phenomenological methodology as taught to them by Heidegger and their need to rethink the tradition, in light of the Shoah and as inspired by the Judaic.

NOTES

1. One of the reasons this promise remains significant today is the debate—primarily among Jews—with regard to its range of application. Does 'never again' mean never again against the Jews, or is it more universal, never again for any excluded and oppressed group? This debate is central to discussions of political Zionism and the State of Israel. While Arendt is very clear that she supports the more inclusive or universal interpretation of 'never again', with Levinas it seems that there is a shift in his later writings—and specifically his realization that the Palestinian is an other and has a face.

2. Jacques Derrida and Elisabeth Weber, *Questioning Judaism: Interviews by Elisabeth Weber*, 1st ed. (Stanford, Calif.: Stanford University Press, 2004), 81.

3. For an excellent analysis of this Arendtian tension, see Martine Leibovici, *Hannah Arendt* (Paris: Desclée de Brouwer, 2000), 142.

4. Elisabeth Young-Bruehl, *Hannah Arendt: For Love of the World*, 2nd ed. (New Haven, Conn.: Yale University Press, 2004), 11.

5. Now translated and published as *Love and Saint Augustine* (1996).

6. This choice, however, was not due to his recognition of the importance of Judaism but rather because of his lack of Greek.

7. This 1932 text is now available in *En découvrant l'existence avec Husserl et Heidegger* (1967).

8. Richard Wolin, *Heidegger's Children: Hannah Arendt, Karl Löwith, Hans Jonas, and Herbert Marcuse* (Princeton, N.J.: Princeton University Press, 2003).

9. Hannah Arendt, 'What Is Existential Philosophy?,' in *Essays in Understanding, 1930–1954: Formation, Exile, and Totalitarianism* (New York: Schocken, 2005), 163–187.

10. Jeffrey C. Isaac, 'Situating Hannah Arendt on Action and Politics', *Political Theory* 21, no. 3 (1 August 1993): 535.

11. A note with regard to my usage of gender-related language. While neither Arendt (although a 'she') nor Levinas used gender-inclusive language, I have decided to do so, with the exception of direct quotes. Not only was the political and ethical significance of this type of language less established when both were writing, neither Arendt nor Levinas wrote in her or his first (or second) languages. Rather than make excuses, I have decided to amend this oversight by altering my own use of language, which as both authors understand is the 'tool' human beings have to connect to each other.

12. Now translated and published in *Unforeseen History* (2004).

13. Published in *Emmanuel Levinas: Basic Philosophical Writings* (1996).

14. Anya Topolski, 'Listening to the Language of the Other', in *Radical Passivity: Rethinking Ethical Agency in Levinas*, ed. Benda Hofmeyr (Dordrecht, Netherlands: Springer Netherlands, 2009), 111–131.

15. Simon Critchley and Robert Bernasconi, eds., *The Cambridge Companion to Levinas* (Cambridge, England; New York: Cambridge University Press, 2002), xxvi.

16. A few other books in which their thought is brought together are Butler, *Parting Ways*; Taminiaux, *The Thracian Maid and the Professional Thinker*; Wolin, *Heidegger's Children*; Fleischacker, *Heidegger's Jewish Followers*; Botbol-Baum and Roviello, *Levinas et Arendt*; Mréjen, *La Figure De L'Homme*; and Poché, *Penser Avec Arendt et Levinas*.

17. Theodor W. Adorno, *Prisms* (Cambridge, Mass.: MIT Press, 1982).

18. Shiraz Dossa, 'Human Status and Politics: Hannah Arendt on the Holocaust', *Canadian Journal of Political Science/Revue Canadienne de Science Politique* 13, no. 2 (June 1980): 310.

19. Worth noting is that this turn to the Judaic, in the postwar period, by both Jewish and non-Jewish intellectuals was quite common, so much so that the Judaic became a trope in the 1950s and 1960s. This horizon, shared by other twentieth-century Jewish thinkers such as Edith Stein, Martin Buber, Jacques Derrida, Hans Jonas, Isaiah Berlin, Theodor Adorno, and Michael Walzer (to name but a fraction), helps to deepen our understanding of their respective projects by framing Arendt's and Levinas's writings in a broader conversation that converged around the Judaic in the years after the Shoah. There are several volumes dedicated to the post-Shoah engagement of Jewish thinkers in questions of ethics and politics. See, for example, Marc H. Ellis, *Encountering the Jewish Future: With Wiesel, Buber, Heschel, Arendt, Levinas* (Minneapolis, Minn.: Augsburg Fortress Publishers, 2010); Fleischacker, *Heidegger's Jewish Followers*.

20. Anne Kupiec and Etienne Tassin, *Critique de la politique autour de Miguel Abensour* (Paris: Sens & Tonka, 2006), 318.

21. Dick Howard, *The Specter of Democracy: What Marx and Marxists Haven't Understood and Why* (New York: Columbia University Press, 2013), 106.

22. Dan Zahavi, 'Phenomenology and Metaphysics', in *Metaphysics, Facticity, Interpretation*, ed. Dan Zahavi, Sara Heinämaa, and Hans Ruin, 17, Contributions to Phenomenology 49 (Dordrecht, Netherlands: Springer Netherlands, 2003), link.springer.com/chapter/10.1007/978-94-007-1011-5_1.

23. Lewis P. Hinchman and Sandra K. Hinchman, 'In Heidegger's Shadow: Hannah Arendt's Phenomenological Humanism', *Review of Politics* 46, no. 2 (April 1984): 186.

24. Kevin Thompson and Lester E. Embree, *Phenomenology of the Political* (Dordrecht, Netherlands: Springer Science & Business Media, 2000). An important exception to this taxonomy, as noted in the book, is the case of Edith Stein, a Jewish thinker who approaches the topic of the political phenomenologically directly in response to Husserl in the 1920s.

25. Adrian Peperzak, 'Phenomenology—Ontology—Metaphysics: Levinas' Perspective on Husserl and Heidegger', *Man and World* 16, no. 2 (1 June 1983): 116.

26. Thompson and Embree, *Phenomenology of the Political*, 3.

27. While I do not intend to consider other thinkers who could be brought into this dialogue, there are certainly others, such as Jean-Luc Nancy, who writes 'Being does not pre-exist its singular plural' (*Being Singular Plural* [Stanford, Calif.: Stanford University Press, 2000], 29), and whose work develops this same intuition in the form of a discussion of the human being as the singular plural. In some ways my project aims to bring Levinas and Arendt together in order to develop this notion of the human being as the 'alterity plurality' or 'particular plurality', if I try to adapt Nancy's terminology.

28. Jean-Francois Lyotard, *Phenomenology* (Albany: State University of New York Press, 1991), 75.

29. Gary Brent Madison, *The Politics of Postmodernity: Essays in Applied Hermeneutics* (Dordrecht, Netherlands: Springer Science & Business Media, 2001), ix.

30. Emmanuel Levinas, *Is It Righteous to Be? Interviews with Emmanuel Levinas*, 1st ed., edited by Jill Robbins (Stanford, Calif.: Stanford University Press, 2002), 32.

31. Zahavi, 'Phenomenology and Metaphysics', 4.

32. Bettina Bergo, 'Ontology, Transcendence, and Immanence in Emmanuel Levinas' Philosophy', *Research in Phenomenology* 35, no. 1 (2005): 2.

33. Richard A. Cohen, 'Levinas: Thinking Least about Death—contra Heidegger', in *Self and Other: Essays in Continental Philosophy of Religion*, ed. Eugene Thomas Long (Dordrecht, Netherlands: Springer Netherlands, 2007), 21–39, link.springer.com/chapter/10.1007/978-1-4020-5861-5_3.

34. Thompson and Embree, *Phenomenology of the Political*, 163.

35. Ann W. Astell, 'Mater-Natality: Augustine, Arendt, and Levinas', in *Logos of Phenomenology and Phenomenology of the Logos, Book Two*, ed. Anna-Teresa Tymieniecka, 374, Analecta Husserliana 89 (Dordrecht, Netherlands: Springer Netherlands, 2006), link.springer.com/chapter/10.1007/1-4020-3707-4_23.

36. Peperzak, 'Phenomenology—Ontology—Metaphysics', 123.

37. Sebastian Luft and Søren Overgaard, *The Routledge Companion to Phenomenology*, (New York: Taylor & Francis [Routledge], 2011), 76.

38. Hinchman and Hinchman, 'In Heidegger's Shadow', 190.

39. Peperzak, 'Phenomenology—Ontology—Metaphysics', 124.

40. The resonances between the question 'who am I' and Levinas's reference to '*hineni*'—'here I am'—are explored in Hilary Putnam, *Jewish Philosophy as a Guide to Life: Rosenzweig, Buber, Levinas, Wittgenstein* (Bloomington: Indiana University Press, 2008).

41. Hinchman and Hinchman, 'In Heidegger's Shadow', 192.

42. Luft and Overgaard, *Routledge Companion to Phenomenology*, 79.

43. Hinchman and Hinchman, 'In Heidegger's Shadow', 196.

44. Jacques Taminiaux, 'Bios Politikos and Bios Theoretikos in the Phenomenology of Hannah Arendt', *International Journal of Philosophical Studies* 4, no. 2 (1 September 1996): 215.

45. Emmanuel Levinas, *The Theory of Intuition in Husserl's Phenomenology* (Evanston, Ill.: Northwestern University Press, 1995), 73.

46. Samuel Moyn, 'Emmanuel Levinas's Talmudic Readings: Between Tradition and Invention', *Prooftexts* 23, no. 3 (2003): 12, doi:10.1353/ptx.2004.0007.

47. Kupiec and Tassin, *Critique de la politique autour de Miguel Abensour*, 320.

48. Tomoko Masuzawa, *The Invention of World Religions: Or, How European Universalism Was Preserved in the Language of Pluralism* (Chicago: University of Chicago Press, 2005).

49. For more see David G. Myers and David B. Ruderman, *The Jewish Past Revisited: Reflections on Modern Jewish Historians* (New Haven, Conn.: Yale University Press, 1998); and David B. Ruderman, *Jewish Thought and Scientific Discovery in Early Modern Europe* (Detroit: Wayne State University Press, 2001).

50. For an exceptional narrative illustration of this see G. A. Cohen, *If You're an Egalitarian, How Come You're So Rich?* (Cambridge, Mass.: Harvard University Press, 2009).

51. Hannah Arendt, *The Jew as Pariah: Jewish Identity and Politics in the Modern Age*, 1st Evergreen ed. (New York: Grove Press; distributed by Random House, 1978).

52. Richard J. Bernstein, *Hannah Arendt and the Jewish Question* (Cambridge, Mass.: MIT Press, 1996); Martine Leibovici, *Hannah Arendt, une Juive: Expérience, politique et histoire* (Paris: Desclée De Brouwer, 1998); Leibovici, *Hannah Arendt*; Martine Leibovici, *Hannah Arendt et la tradition juive: Le judaïsme à l'épreuve de la sécularisation* (Geneva: Labor et Fides, 2003); Leibovici, *Hannah Arendt*.

53. Benda Hofmeyr, *Radical Passivity: Rethinking Ethical Agency in Levinas* (Dordrecht, Netherlands: Springer Science & Business Media, 2009), 25.

54. 'Il faut quand meme partir des sources du judaisme. Le Judaism n'est pas une *religion*. Le mot n'existe pas en hebreu. Il est beaucoup plus que cela. Il est une comprehension de l'être. Le Juif a introduit dans l'histoire l'idee d'esperance. . . . L'ethique est une optique vers Dieu. . . . Le seule voie du respect envers Dieu est celle du respect envers le prochain' (Emmanuel Levinas, *Difficile liberté*, 4th ed. [Paris: Albin Michel, 1996], 15).

TWO

Divided by Disciplinary Confines?

Undoubtedly my claim that a dialogue is possible between the political and ethics by way of a post-Shoah Heideggerian-inspired phenomenological method will strike some as decidedly problematic. This is undoubtedly the case if I was aiming at a fusion or coherent reconciliation of their positions that would require the imposition of consensus where it does not exist. The irony of such an undertaking is that it would be precisely what Arendt and Levinas are reacting to, the reduction of difference to the same. Fortuitously, my claim is that it is the differences in their respective approaches that makes this confrontational dialogue promising. Nonetheless, I think it is necessary to consider why some (primarily non-Rawlsian political thinkers) consider any attempt to connect ethics with the political problematic. Is this presupposition based on an assumption about divisions between the academic disciplines of ethics and politics that arises from within the same philosophical tradition challenged by phenomenology, and in particular by Arendt and Levinas? As I will argue, Arendt's notion of the political cannot be understood from within the framework of political philosophy. Likewise, Levinas's ethics is also radically innovative. Having said all this, it important to acknowledge that there are some significant and insurmountable tensions between Arendt's and Levinas's thinking that cannot and need not be resolved for this dialogue to be possible. After briefly considering what I take to be the four most significant tensions, I turn to the question of disciplinary divisions and terminology to better understand how each thinker used these terms and how I will be using them in this volume.

INSURMOUNTABLE TENSIONS?

Undoubtedly the greatest challenge posed by this project is a linguistic one. Arendt and Levinas both develop highly idiosyncratic terminology, coin neologisms and engage in etymological exercises in order to recuperate terms hidden by the philosophical tradition. This project requires bringing two such vocabularies into dialogue. There is clearly a very good chance that something gets lost in translation. While purely semantically there is a great deal shared between Arendt and Levinas, most of which has its roots in German thought, phenomenology or Heidegger, the actual terms both thinkers use to refer to these concepts are not often shared. The most obvious example is the terminology that is most critical to this project. Arendt sees her contribution as political (although not philosophical) and often disparages ethics. Levinas, on the other hand, presents ethics as first philosophy and sees politics as nothing more than rhetorical swindling. There is, however, hope to be found in the fact that most of Arendt's and Levinas's readers recognize the idiosyncrasy of their respective lexicons. 'The Arendtian terminology appropriated to deal with ethics no longer fits into the usual way of addressing ethics, namely, in terms of what principles, universal or particular, define the good man, although the question of what values should guide our actions can hardly be avoided'.[1]

A similar shortcoming is visible with regard to Levinas. 'Thus, what Levinas calls politics refers to the traditional conception of ethics found in modernity. And in his view, the political—obscures the ethical as he describes it. Moreover, the ethical as he understands it makes the political possible'.[2] What Levinas is attacking when he refers to politics is not what Arendt means by politics. Arendtian politics is horizontal, plural and explicitly nonviolent. It has no connection to war or ontology. When Arendt criticizes political philosophy, from Plato to today, she means exactly what Levinas does when he attacks politics, a vertical, violent means of reducing and controlling people. This claim will of course need to be proven with a closer reading of both of their positions in the following chapters. Given the idiosyncrasies of their respective terminology, it will be fundamental to clearly define and distinguish certain shared referents (only in appellation).

From this point onward, I will have to ask my readers for patience and understanding with regard to the following distinctions. First, in order to facilitate a semantic dialogue and avoid a Babylonian perplexity, I will differentiate between *morality*, a term Arendt uses often in her engagement with Kant, and *ethics*, which we will use to refer to Levinas's project. I use the term ethics to refer to an ethics of alterity and in opposition to morality that arises from within singularity (as in Kant's Second Critique as argued by Arendt). In addition, I will use the term *political* to refer to a horizontal space and interaction, which arises from plurality, and in opposition to *politics*, which refers to conventional political philosophy rooted in ontology and the same. Last but not least, I will use the terms *religion* and *religious*, in full recognition of the fact that these terms are created with Christianity in mind (and as such pertain to faith, theological convictions and dogma, etc.),[3] in a manner that is inclusive of the Judaic. This accommodation is made in order to respect Levinas's position that 'Judaism is not a *religion*. The word does not exist in Hebrew. It is much more than that. It is a way to understand [the human] being'.[4] Without using the terms religion and religious, it would be very difficult to explore the relationship between the Judaic, ethics and the political. I hope that these distinctions will be of service to my readers. These terminological difficulties are, however, only the tip of the iceberg with regard to the greater issue of the relationship between ethics and the political, an iceberg that will be chipped away at in the next few chapters.

A second obstacle in the dialogue between Levinas and Arendt arises with regard to the metaphysics of presence and the notion of *appearing* (or *appearance*), a term clearly connected to the phenomenological approach and its rejection of the noumenal (that which cannot be experienced by the senses), the 'crisis of metaphysics' and Heidegger's notion of disclosure. For Arendt, it is by appearing in the public realm that one acts politically. Appearing, even if one is not seen but only heard, is central to her understanding of the political; it is the means by which we disclose ourselves and interact with others who are disclosing themselves. Nonetheless Arendt does not reduce human beings and their interactions to mere appearances. As she writes in *The Life of the Mind* (in relation to thinking), 'in contrast to the inorganic thereness of lifeless matter, living beings are not mere appearances. To be alive means to be possessed by an urge toward self-display which answers the fact of one's own appearingness. Living things make their appearance like actors on a stage set for them' (LF 21). The role of appearance is much more difficult to account for in Levinas's opus, especially given the shift that takes place after *Totality and Infinity* in response to Derrida's essay 'Violence and Metaphysics'. While on the one hand appearance has an important role in his ethics, in that the other appears like a revelation to the self (DF 17), making the face-to-face relation possible, on the other hand Levinas is very clear that the other cannot be understood in terms of her appearance, as the other expresses an exteriority and is infinite and cannot be reduced to comprehension or my consciousness. The face of the other breaks through its form; the form that demarcates a subject cannot contain it. In this vein, the other is not reducible to an appearance or a mere phenomenon—a position Arendt shares. In other words both thinkers hold ambiguous positions with regard to the metaphysics of presence. According to Derrida, who coins this term, the entire history of philosophy has prioritized the realm of appearance by developing a metaphysics that privileges presence. In his interpretation of Levinas, the emphasis placed on language as a means to escape the totality of ontology does not allow Levinas to evade this metaphysics of presence. The same could be said of Arendt, who stresses appearance in the form of speech—communication. Nonetheless, one could argue that their appreciation of the importance of the 'who' rather than the 'what', and the irreducibility of other, are expressions of their desire to critique this metaphysics of presence. In any case, this tension remains present in both of their writings.

A third tension is related to the question of ontology. How did Arendt and Levinas choose to deal with the ontological inheritance they received from their teacher and the philosophical tradition? Levinas explicitly seeks to go beyond ontology (although many challenge his success in this endeavour), and in his later writings clearly decentres the subject by claiming that the other constitutes the self. While he does not deconstruct or challenge the notion of the self or subject, he does destabilize it and recentre it, and in so doing clearly differentiates his own project from that of ontology. It is much harder to identify how Arendt navigates her own thinking in relation to the ontological project. While she begins, like Levinas, by distancing herself from philosophy by turning to the political (which she saw as opposed to philosophy), even in her more 'philosophical' writings (e.g., *The Human Condition, The Life of the Mind*), she relies heavily on many phenomenological and Heideggerian categories. In this vein, she more reworks the ontological project rather than rejecting it outright. Take for example her revision of Heidegger's prioritization of *Dasein* (being-there) over *mitsein* (being-with). Arendt rethinks *mitsein* in terms of plurality and privileges it over singularity. A similar revision rather than explicit rejection is to be found in her notion of the 'who' as an actor or agent in a web-of-relations rather than as an author. Whereas the former has a relational role to play, she is by no means in control or 'master' of her own story. There is no doubt that Arendt and Levinas are not 'on the same page' when it comes to the question of ontology and the subject. There are, however, certain parallels even within this difference. Both criticize Heidegger's *Dasein* and seek a form of intersubjectivity, but Levinas goes much further than Arendt in this regard. Rather than attempt to 'resolve' this difference, I will introduce my own frame, in the final chapter, in terms of post-foundational notion of relationality. Thus while Levinas and Arendt both use the language of intersubjectivity, I replace intersubjectivity with the term *relationality* in order to make clear that any subject is no longer central or complete.

With this brief list in mind, I maintain that notwithstanding these points (and other points of incongruity), it is worth engaging Arendt's political project rooted in plurality with Levinas's ethical project rooted in alterity. This engagement expresses a profound *amour mundi* and a desire to reconcile the world we inhabit, for better or worse, with the potential we, collectively, possess: *tikkun olam*.[5] Arendt's love of the world, her faith in humanity, her confidence in plurality, her hope in the political are limitless. Likewise, Levinas's commitment to the other in the form of responsibility or to the shared world in the form of justice is infinite. This is even more impressive given what they experienced during the Shoah. Yet as both thinkers were well aware, the world is extremely fragile. It is this fragility that makes the political realm as well as morality so vulnerable to domination, totality or terror. Her response to this fragility is, simply put, problematic. While she does call for its strengthening by means of promises, forgiveness, thinking without banisters, judgements and personal responsibility—all of which are valuable to her project—she seems blind to another potential, and as I will argue compatible, source of strength—one that is not found in the between of the *polis* but in the between of the self: the other. This is how Levinas's ethics of alterity can challenge and strengthen Arendt's political project.

WHAT IS THE POLITICAL?

The notion of the political I espouse is inspired by Arendt, who defines the political in phenomenological terms and as an explicit rejection of what Levinas refers to as politics and what she refers to as the tradition of political philosophy, which starts with Plato. In order to understand what she means by the political, it is first necessary to understand how a historically invested phenomenological notion of the political differs from other approaches. Furthermore, as Arendt develops her notion of the political in response to totalitarianism, the new political regime developed by the Nazis, the answer provided here to the question 'what is the political' is incomplete. It is also worth noting that one of the main reasons her account of totalitarianism has been so influential is its blending of historical and phenomenological approaches:

> Arendt's phenomenological method is a source of some of her valuable insights; it is also responsible for some of her weaknesses. . . . Thanks to it she focuses her attention on structures rather than formal features and analyses activities and experiences as integral wholes. Further, she pays close attention to the differences between activities and appreciates their distinctive character, thereby avoiding positivist reductionism. Again she does not analyse concepts in the abstract but locates them in their experiential contexts and uncovers the structures of underlying experiences.[6]

Arendt presents a significant part of humanity's story in the twentieth century from a human perspective rather than simply focusing on dates, numbers and places—although these 'facts' are of course not neglected. Thus while Arendt's reflection was motivated by concrete events which she sought to understand, such as totalitarianism, Eichmann's trial in Jerusalem and segregation in the United States, her reflection is certainly not limited to the facts of these events. Dick Howard also helps to clarify this distinction when he writes, 'the framework of meaning defined by the political is not itself the object of everyday politics'.[7] Her phenomenological account of totalitarianism focuses on the lived experience of people under a totalitarian regime. In the same manner her notion of the political is an expression of the lived experience of a political agent. Hwa Yol Jung, a phenomenologist interested in the political, captures this approach as follows:

> However attractive and precious the terms *self-reliance, rights, autonomy,* and *independence* may be, they are disconnected with affiliation, association and interdependence. Interdependence, that is, interdependence cum difference, cannot and must not be anathema to the human . . . condition of plurality.[8]

In his account he indicates the condition, or existential, that connects her account of totalitarianism to her notion of the political: plurality. The Nazis managed to almost completely destroy the human condition of plurality; it is thus necessary—if we wish to spare the world from such horror—to preserve plurality, which according to Arendt is only possible by means of the political. The political is thus a human activity, that has plurality as its condition, in which actors interact to create, shape and change the shared world (understood phenomenologically to be reality as we experience or live it). While this preliminary definition still needs to be developed, what is most important is to recognize phenomenological quality and its originality.

Less than a year after Arendt's death, Maurice Cranston described her as a political thinker 'altogether *hors catégorie*'[9] or as Shiraz Dossa explains, 'Hannah Arendt stands out among contemporary "classical" thinkers as one whose thinking constitutes political philosophy in the proper sense of the term',[10] a view shared and defended by Margaret Canovan. Yet it is precisely because of this unorthodox approach that Arendt's writings are famously difficult to classify or to compare with those of other thinkers. Given her critique of liberalism and her comments regarding the need for Jews to react politically, one might be tempted to label her as a communitarian. This being said, Arendt might feel most at home in classical republican theory, and yet even this categorization is problematic given her views on the separation of the political from any one conception of the good.[11] I thus approach her notion of the political as phenomenological, which also facilitates the dialogue with Levinas. This is also the approach taken by contemporary political philosophers who seek to rethink the political without the limitations imposed by the more hierarchical tradition of political philosophy.[12]

In order to further clarify Arendt's notion of the political, let us consider how she distinguishes it explicitly from the tradition of political philosophy. As Arendt is clearly following Heidegger in his attempt to destruct the metaphysical base that has dominated thought since Plato, it is important to appreciate that she is not trying to develop a systematic theory of politics or of providing a normative account of politics.[13] While certain principles for action and judgement arise from within the political, as developed in chapter 3, these are not to be understood as rules or universal norms. Her 'approach challenges models of the political based on ideal situations, thought experiments, or abstract theoretical approaches that are not prepared for the reality and non-theoretical nature of a crisis such as totalitarianism, models that are much more common in the Anglo-American tradition'.[14] While this approach makes it possible to interpret her project as both descriptive and prescriptive, leading some authors to read Arendt as a normative theorist and yet others to suggest that she is writing a meta-politics, I prefer to avoid forcing her into categories created by others. This choice is also an acknowledgement of her own rejection of such labels, as is the case with her refusal to identify herself as a philosopher. In this regard I find David Ingram's account of contemporary political philosophy to be of service in describing what Arendt understands to be central to the political:

> 'Political philosophy' is roughly cognate with thinking hard about the presuppositions underlying political order. These presuppositions include: the nature and justification of political rights and duties; the meaning and role of power—as distinct from violence—in maintaining political order; the metaphysical reality of political groups and their political relationships; the constitution of political identity and community; and the relationship of the political to the non-political, i.e., economic, social, cultural, and purely personal, aspects of human existence.[15]

While Arendt addresses, directly or indirectly, most of these presuppositions, her focus is clearly on the nature of political judgement and responsibility, the meaning and constitution of power, the relationship between identity and plurality revealed in action and between the political and the private.[16] This last point raises one of the greatest weaknesses, and sources of criticism, with regard to Arendt's notion of the political: its reliance on a separation between the private and public (discussed in the following chapter). In addition, Arendt's approach to the political focuses almost exclusively on the experience of acting politically rather than the institutions necessary to enable this type of action. While the two are without a doubt related, Arendt focuses on the horizontal relations between people in the public and their role for society at large, as this is what she believes was completely destroyed under totalitarianism. Institutional politics, according to Arendt, continued under the Nazis, although with a nonpolitical principle as its core. For this reason she focuses on the principles of the political rather than the institutions. This being said, her phenomenological approach to the political, developed in response to her analysis of totalitarianism, is still essential for an understanding of the political in nontotalitarian regimes (or non-explicit-totalitarian regimes). In this vein, her 'critique of totalitarianism can serve as an introduction to modern political philosophy insofar as the immanent critique points beyond itself toward an understanding of the political problems confronting a democratic society that cannot take for granted its own foundations'.[17] In other words, by understanding what happened during the Nazi regime, we gain invaluable insight into contemporary democratic politics. It is for this reason that I begin the following chapter with her analysis of totalitarianism.

WHAT IS ETHICS?

Like Arendt's notion of the political, Levinas's ethics is 'altogether *hors catégorie*'. It cannot be explained according to any of the categories normally applied to the field commonly referred to as ethics or moral philosophy. It is neither normative nor descriptive; it is neither applied ethics nor meta-ethics; and it does not fit the mould of any of the three traditional ethical theories: virtue ethics, consequentialism or deontology. As with Arendt, the best means to understand Levinas's unique notion of ethics is to connect it to the phenomenological tradition:

> Levinas's philosophy has been called ethics. If ethics means self-legislation and freedom (deontology), the calculation of happiness (utilitarianism), or the calculation of virtues (virtue ethics), then Levinas's philosophy is not an ethics. . . . It is an interpretative, phenomenological description of the rise and repetition of the face-to-face encounter, or of the intersubjective relation at its precognitive core.[18]

This quote, like Levinas's ethics, might at times seems deceptively simplistic—this could not be further from the truth. While I will here provide a preliminary 'working' definition of ethics, each of the claims calls for further attention—which occurs in chapter 5.

Levinas's ethics is an encounter with an other that occurs on a precognitive level. More often than not Levinas speaks of the ethical relation, which is an intersubjective relation between the self and other in which the other is not reduced to the self or the same. In light of the Shoah, Levinas tragically recognized that most human encounters are structured by such subject-object reductions, which he describes as violence and at times as murder. His ethics is an appeal to another type of human encounter that obeys the command 'thou shall not kill', and in which the other person is encountered as other and as such cannot be reduced to an object. When encountered as other, the self is overwhelmed and cannot totalize, interpret or comprehend the other. The self is transformed by this encounter—the self, or ego, is put into question. This ethical encounter, the focus of chapter 5, drives the self to open itself to another realm in which the other can be welcomed, responded to and elevated to its height. Reality, which for Levinas is the realm of the meaningful as the political is for Arendt, is made possible by the welcoming of the other. The self discovers itself as unique and irreplaceable in the ethical relation and is made responsible by this encounter. This 'process' is described by Levinas as an optics—a metaphor that will need to be investigated, as it appears repeatedly in both the so-called Jewish and so-called philosophical writings in the 1950s.

In his earlier writings he describes this ethical encounter by way of phenomenological analyses of different self-other relations in which the experience of the encounter in the form of the face-to-face is central. For Levinas, the face expresses an ethical demand, to which the self must respond. In his 1952 essay 'Ethics and Spirit' he writes: '[T]he fact that the vision of the face is not an *experience,* but a moving out of oneself, a contact with another being and not simply a sensation of self, is attested to by the "purely moral" character of this impossibility [of killing which is not real but moral]' (DF 10). As with the phrase 'ethics is an optics', the face (or face-to-face) is essential to both the so-called Jewish and so-called philosophical writings and is developed differently in each context. In *Totality and Infinity,* the face is first signification; it allows for the possibility of language in which the self and other can encounter each other without violence. In this vein, ethics founds language (at least in the early Levinas), a medium that is nonviolent.

Much like Arendt's phenomenological notion of plurality, Levinas sought to understand what totalitarianism, which he analysed philosophically in terms of totality, had destroyed—alterity[19]—and then set out to prevent its destruction by making ethics first philosophy. In this way his ethics can be, and often is, read as a powerful and inspiring reminder of how we should act in relation to the other, of our absolute responsibility for the other. There are moments in our lives when we heed the call of such an absolute ethics, such as when caring for our newborns. Their very lives depend completely and totally on our care and responsibility. Parents are often willing to do this for as long as possible, but at some point the weight of the responsibility is exhausting, physically and mentally. We are forced to care for ourselves and therefore devote a little less time and energy to the other. Levinas's ethics does not allow us to do so, as the call from the other is to take absolute responsibility for the other, an infinite responsibility. As I establish in chapter 5, this demand is too great for society and creates another form of violence. I argue that to save Levinas's inspiration, his ethics must be limited, a limit I create by means of a political framework.

A POLITICAL ETHICS

Is there a model of the political that allows for such an ethics? Such a model is certainly not easy to find, given that the schools of contemporary political theory tend to be divided into camps according to their defence of individuals (liberals), groups or multiplicities (communitarians) or citizens (republicans), and thus each potentially misses the locus of Levinas's intersubjective ethics. While this schematic depiction of political theory is clearly oversimplified, it helps to appreciate the reason why the political realm is rarely reflected upon from the position of relationality. This claim has been well argued by Fred Dallmayr, who has attempted to rethink the political on the basis of Heidegger's ontological project, with a particular emphasis on *mitsein*, in order to bring to light the often neglected intersubjective relations.[20] In order for Levinas's ethical appeal not to be violated by the political, we must seek an approach that also places alterity and intersubjectivity in the spotlight. What I seek to demonstrate in my analysis of Hannah Arendt's opus is that this is precisely what she does. For this reason, I claim that her notion of the political is a potential framework for a Levinasian ethics. In other words, while most political philosophers would argue that all forms of politics are antithetical and violently inhospitable to Levinas's ethics, I—inspired by Arendt—respectfully disagree.

While Levinas does move from ethics to the political, I do not follow his move to the realm of the third and justice. My interest lies in his project of developing an ethics as first philosophy. By moving from ethics to the political, Levinas is sketching an ethical politics—a politics limited by ethics—which I take to be quite different from my own project of a political ethics—an ethics limited by the political. An ethical politics fails to appreciate the fact that one cannot simply deduce a politics from an ethics—this is a failure to appreciate the importance of the political for human lives. However, it is worth noting that the distinction I draw between an ethical politics and a political ethics is an artificial one. What Drichel takes to be an ethical politics is in fact what I refer to as a political ethics. 'An *ethical* politics is therefore a politics without guarantees. While this might appear a very questionable "foundation" for any politics, it seems to me . . . this is the only politics worth having'.[21] When Drichel refers to a political space without guarantees as the only type worth having, he is expressing a fundamental aspect of post-foundationalism, its contingency, which is central to relationality as it will be developed in part IV.

The choice to develop a political ethics is also a means to differentiate my project from Levinas's. While I share his aim of realizing the promise *Never Again*, I do not share his method. Totalitarianism, a political regime that made the Shoah possible, arose from the destruction of the political. Arendt understood this, and she also understood that the political was not a sphere devoid of ethics. As Hans Jonas so correctly characterizes in his eulogy for her, 'thinking was her passion, and thinking with her was a moral activity. She was intensely moral, but completely unmoralistic'.[22] In other words, while Arendt did not offer her readers a set of moral rules (she saw this as the task of preachers), it would be absurd to deny that she was deeply concerned with ethics. Her readers have noted this same paradox: 'Arendt frequently laments the "monstrous immorality" of totalitarian domination because she sees the human condition in some ultimate sense as being distinctively moral in texture. Ironically, however, she refuses to see politics as primarily moral in intention or purpose'.[23]

While not all political models are hospitable to ethics, much less a Levinasian ethics, I am convinced an Arendtian-inspired political framework would be hospitable and strengthened by a Levinasian ethics. I do realize that by 'staging' this encounter, I reinterpret Levinas's project, from his perspective, within a different notion of the political than the one he operates within. Likewise, I appear to be doing Arendt injustice by blurring the distinction between the political and ethics. Yet as I will show in my reading of Arendt, she argues for this separation based on a notion of ethics captured by her claim that it is 'morality [as it] concerns the individual in his singularity' (RJ 97), which is equally anathema to Levinas. In my project, I will do Levinas injustice (although I argue that it is in fact just) by bringing him into an Arendtian political framework. Nonetheless, I am convinced, by Arendt, that what is in fact necessary is first and foremost to be found in the political. Yet in disagreement with Arendt, who had a very limited, philosophically defined understanding of ethics, I believe the political realm needs a more robust ethics to support its fragility and contingency.

NOTES

1. Bethania Assy and Agnes Heller, *Hannah Arendt—An Ethics of Personal Responsibility*, 1st ed. (Frankfurt am Main: Peter Lang International Academic Publishers, 2007), n328.

2. Claire Elise Katz, *Levinas, Judaism, and the Feminine: The Silent Footsteps of Rebecca* (Bloomington: Indiana University Press, 2003), 13.

3. Talal Asad, *Genealogies of Religion: Discipline and Reasons of Power in Christianity and Islam* (Baltimore, Md.: Johns Hopkins University Press, 1993); Talal Asad, *Formations of the Secular: Christianity, Islam, Modernity*, 1st ed. (Stanford, Calif.: Stanford University Press, 2003).

4. 'Il faut quand meme partir des sources du judaisme. Le Judaism n'est pas une *religion*. Le mot n'existe pas en hebreu. Il est beaucoup plus que cela. Il est une comprehension de l'être. Le Juif a introduit dans l'histoire l'idée d'esperance. . . . L'ethique est une optique vers Dieu . . . Le seule voie du respect envers Dieu est celle du respect envers le prochain' (Emmanuel Levinas, *Difficile liberté*, 4th ed. [Paris: Albin Michel, 1996], 15).

5. This is Hebrew for repair, mend or heal the world. It has its roots in the early rabbinic period (approx. 200 CE) and is defined as humanity's collective responsibility

to improve the world by means of good deeds or *mitzvahs*. The importance of this principle has remained constant through medieval and modern times.

6. Bhikhu C. Parekh, *Hannah Arendt and the Search for a New Political Philosophy* (New York: Macmillan, 1981), 182–183.

7. Dick Howard, *The Specter of Democracy: What Marx and Marxists Haven't Understood and Why* (New York: Columbia University Press, 2013), 131.

8. Kevin Thompson and Lester Embree, eds., *Phenomenology of the Political* (Dordrecht, Netherlands: Springer, 2000), 149.

9. Maurice Cranston, 'Notes & Topics: Hannah Arendt', *Encounter* (March 1976): 54–55, www.UNZ.org/Pub/Encounter-1976mar-00054 (accessed 7 November 2014).

10. Shiraz Dossa, 'Human Status and Politics: Hannah Arendt on the Holocaust', *Canadian Journal of Political Science/Revue Canadienne de Science Politique* 13, no. 2 (June 1980): 310.

11. As Schaap writes, 'whereas Arendt and the republican tradition view political life in terms of its horizontal dimension of freedom, Schmitt and the realist tradition emphasise the vertical dimension of necessity, rule and sovereignty. Consequently, republicans (such as Arendt, Walzer, Tully and Lefort) view political conflict as having a potentially world-disclosing or integrative function'. Andrew Schaap, 'Political Theory and the Agony of Politics', *Political Studies Review* 5, no. 1 (1 January 2007): 60, doi:10.1111/j.1478-9299.2007.00123.x.

12. For an example of this see Fred Dallmayr et al., *Border Crossings* (Lanham, Md.: Lexington Books, 1999); Fred Dallmayr, *Twilight of Subjectivity: Contributions to a Post-Individualist Theory of Politics* (Amherst: University of Massachusetts Press, 1981); Fred Dallmayr, *The Promise of Democracy: Political Agency and Transformation* (Albany; Bristol: State University of New York Press, 2011); Fred Dallmayr, *Being in the World: Dialogue and Cosmopolis* (Lexington: University Press of Kentucky, 2013); David Ingram, ed., *The Political*, 1st ed. (Malden, Mass.: Wiley-Blackwell, 2002); Thompson and Embree, *Phenomenology of the Political*.

13. For more on this see Arendt's rare discussion of her phenomenological methodology in 'Projektbeschreibung fur die Rockefeller Foundation, December, 1959', in Hannah Arendt and Ursula Ludz, *Was ist Politik? Fragmente aus dem Nachlaß* (München: Piper, 2005); Mordechai Gordon and Maxine Greene, *Hannah Arendt and Education: Renewing Our Common World* (Boulder, Colo.: Westview Press, 2002).

14. Ingram, *The Political*, 179.

15. Ibid., 1.

16. Parekh, *Hannah Arendt and the Search for a New Political Philosophy*; Margaret Canovan, *Hannah Arendt: A Reinterpretation of Her Political Thought* (Cambridge, England; New York: Cambridge University Press, 1994).

17. Howard, *The Specter of Democracy*, 99.

18. Bettina Bergo, 'Emmanuel Levinas', in *The Stanford Encyclopedia of Philosophy* (Fall 2014), 1, plato.stanford.edu/archives/fall2014/entries/levinas/. Or as Derrida writes: 'It is true that Ethics in Levinas's sense is an Ethics without law and without concept, which maintains its non-violent purity only before being determined as concepts and laws. This is not an objection: let us not forget that Levinas does not seek to propose . . . moral rules, does not seek to determine *a* morality, but rather the essence of the ethical relation in general . . . in question, then, is an Ethics of ethics . . . neither a determined ethics nor determined laws without negating and forgetting itself'. Jacques Derrida, *Writing and Difference* (Chicago: University of Chicago Press, 1978), 111.

19. For an interesting discussion of Levinas's particular approach to relationality, see Ivana Marková, 'Constitution of the Self: Intersubjectivity and Dialogicality', *Culture & Psychology* 9, no. 3 (1 September 2003): 249–259, doi:10.1177/1354067X030093006.

20. For more on this see Dallmayr, *Twilight of Subjectivity*. While I share many of Dallmayr criticisms, I cannot follow him in his project because of its Heideggerian roots, roots which even if they push the envelope of subjectivity towards the other always remain rooted in *Dasein* and thus in a notion of selfhood that verges on the

solipsistic. For evidence of this see Martin Heidegger, *Gesamtausgabe. 4 Abteilungen/ Überlegungen VII–XI* (Frankfurt am Main: Klostermann Vittorio GmbH, 2014), sec. 172, 198, 295, 322. Dallmayr is aware of this but does not seem to find it problematic for his project. This position is also supported by Robert Sokolowski, *Husserlian Meditations: How Words Present Things*, 1st ed. (Evanston, Ill.: Northwestern University Press, 1974). For a discussion of this see B. P. Dauenhauer, *Elements of Responsible Politics* (Dordrecht: Kluwer Academic Publishers, 1991). Adriaan T. Perperzak also addresses Heidegger's shortcomings in his article 'Intersubjectivity and Community', in Thompson and Embree, *Phenomenology of the Political*.

21. Simone Drichel, 'Of Political Bottom Lines and Last Ethical Frontiers: The Politics and Ethics of "the Other",' *Borderlands* 6, no. 2 (2007): 8.

22. Christian Wiese, *The Life and Thought of Hans Jonas: Jewish Dimensions* (Lebanon, N.H.: University Press of New England, 2007), 13.

23. Dossa, 'Human Status and Politics', 315.

II

On Hannah Arendt

The next two chapters are dedicated to the work of Hannah Arendt; chapter 3 aims to elaborate her notion of the political, whereas chapter 4 is focused on her less-well-known position on ethics. Potential engagements with Levinas's thought will appear in these chapters as endnotes and tangents, as a proper dialogue first requires that we provide the same close attention to Levinas's opus (part III). In the following chapter I chronicle Arendt's early intellectual journey in order to better appreciate how she came to her unique notion of the political and specifically the significance of plurality for the political. This begins with her analysis of the phenomenon of totalitarianism, which she establishes as a new type of political regime that destroys human plurality. I also explore the connections she draws between the horrors of the Shoah and her notion of *amor mundi* rooted in classical, phenomenological and theological studies. An example of this is the Heideggerian and phenomenological term 'world', which first appears in her thesis on Augustine,[1] then reappears in *The Origins of Totalitarianism*, and which she reinvests with political meaning in *The Human Condition*. I will not focus on the basic but highly problematic distinction between the private and public realm, on the one hand, and labour, work and action, on the other hand, as neither is essential to understanding the meaning of plurality for Arendt. Instead, I focus on her description of the political as the realm in which particularity and plurality paradoxically meet in a space of interaction—a meeting Arendt refers to as *action*. 'Action, the only activity that goes on directly between men without the intermediary of things or matter, corresponds to the human condition of plurality, to the fact that *men, not Man,* live on the earth and inhabit the world' (HC 7). With this quotation as a guide, I engage in a three-part analysis of the political. First, I consider the political in terms of action in a public space of equality and distinction; second, I turn to its worldly character to be found in freedom; and third, I consider her notion of power, one that challenges and redefines the vast majority of contemporary uses of power. In addition to considering this encounter in the form of action, I look at her reflection on the life of the mind, often considered as a solitary endeavour but to which 'Arendt ultimately ascribes a communal and pluralistic dimension'.[2]

In the fourth chapter I turn to a more contested aspect of Arendt's work. I argue that an unsystematized non-normative political ethics of plurality can be discerned from her writings, a position that runs contrary to the common assumption that Arendt was averse to all ethics. While I do not find her 'ethics' to be adequately developed, her clear attempt to engage with ethics after the Eichmann trial is evidence that there is space for a particular kind of ethics within the political. We can thus use her discussions of morality and ethics to determine what precisely Arendt is averse to with regard to morality, and why (and to argue that this is precisely the type of morality that Levinas is averse to). In addition, I consider two types of actions that are ethical for Arendt but which are also politically essential, both of which also have an important place in Levinas's opus: promises and forgiveness. According to her analysis, without these two human faculties, human beings would not dare act. Promises and forgiveness allow for judgement within the fragile and precarious human realm. Second, I consider the *vita contemplativa* and specifically the faculties of thinking and judging, both of which Arendt re-grounds in plurality. I also argue that the *vita contemplativa* remains incomplete without responsibility, which I argue is a bridge to the *vita activa* in her work. It is my contention that by considering her rethinking of the *vita contemplativa*, specifically in terms of thinking and judging, in relation to a political responsibility characterized by particularity and plurality, the basis of Arendt's unwritten praxis of political ethics can be outlined. In the final pages of that chapter, after having shown where and how Arendt does make space for ethics in the *polis*, I consider why Arendt's minimal political ethics is unsatisfactory with regard to today's political landscape.

NOTES

1. Because Arendt's thesis on Augustine was not published until much later in her career, many of her readers have overlooked its importance to her mature work. With regard to the political, the most interesting parts concern her critique of Augustine's expectation that God can answer the question 'who am I?' (25); her Levinasian discussion of neighbourly love (42); the importance of the notion of the world (66–67, 100); and original sin (108).

2. Bethania Assy and Agnes Heller, *Hannah Arendt—An Ethics of Personal Responsibility*, 1st ed. (Frankfurt am Main: Peter Lang International Academic Publishers, 2007), 136.

THREE

On the Political

From Ashes to Hope

While history provides no 'solutions' for present-day problems, it can provide contemporary thinkers with a better understanding of the connections between totalitarianism and the political. In this vein, we can perhaps glean some insight from the dark times of Arendt's analyses to brighten our current dark days, demarcated—if media headlines are any indication of reality—by economic, political and ethical crises. Perhaps the most arresting parallels between the problems of the 1930s and the first decade of the twenty-first century, many of which Arendt predicted would only continue to trouble humanity, are first, the dominance of technocrats, and specifically economists, in political affairs; second, the increasing number of refugees in Europe and the extension of the refugee crisis—which is both ethical and political—beyond the borders of Europe; and third, the mounting alienation from the public sphere and its relation to the rising rates of loneliness, often expressed as lack of interest in all things political. According to Arendt, the trace of totalitarianism is still present in our modern democracies—primarily in the rise of the social (which she sees as the private and intimate realms taking over the public realm), an aspect of her work well developed by Claude Lefort, who writes, 'the project of totalitarianism . . . helps to shed light on democracy and urges us to investigate anew the religious and the political'.[1]

For this reason, among others listed in the introductory pages, I turn to the writings of Hannah Arendt, who dedicated herself to rescuing the political from the hands of bureaucrats and bankers and returning it to the people by understanding (and preventing) totalitarianism. 'Understanding, while it cannot be expected to provide results which are specifically helpful or inspiring in the fight against totalitarianism, must accompany this fight if it is to be more than a mere fight for survival' (EU 310). For her, this 'more than survival' is what is possible in the experience of the political that we share with others. By focusing on political action and agency, freedom and power—all of which were eliminated under the Nazi regime—Arendt tries to keep alive what she believes makes the human condition meaningful: human interaction. In order to fully grasp the connection between totalitarianism and the political, and specifically the originality and importance of Arendt's notion of plurality as a new principle for the political, we must begin with her book *The Origins of Totalitarianism*. For this reason, the structure of this chapter moves from a concrete consideration of Arendt's analysis of totalitarianism to her development of the meaning of the political in terms of plurality.

TOTALITARIANISM: THE LOSS OF THE HUMAN WORLD

Totalitarianism has 'exploded our traditional categories of political thought (totalitarian domination is unlike all forms of tyranny and despotism we know of) and the standards of our moral judgement' (EU 405). While totalitarianism—a term coined by Mussolini in 1926—has been studied by many authors, Arendt's *Origins* is considered to set the standard, as it defines what demarcates this new political regime from all others and specifically from tyrannical regimes, such as dictatorships or authoritarian regimes. Albeit oversimplified, totalitarianism is unique in that it not only dominates the public sphere; it also rules the private sphere, that is, the family, the house, and other such spaces of privacy and intimacy. It does so by means of organized violence and terror according to ideological laws. Furthermore, Arendt does not try to understand totalitarianism as a political anomaly but tries to understand it both experientially and in relation to other forms of politics. Seeking to understand totalitarianism and to revitalize the political is much more than an academic endeavour for Arendt, it is a personal search for the meaning of human existence. 'If we want to be at home on this earth, even at the price of being at home in this century, we must try to take part in the interminable dialogue with the essence of totalitarianism' (EU 323). Her account of the Shoah, a central part of the Nazi totalitarian regime, 'contains, *inter linea,* Hannah Arendt's political story'[2] and the story of the loss of the shared world.

Driven by an uneasy need to grapple with the horrors of the Shoah, which she does in part three of her 1951 analysis of totalitarianism, she develops a notion of the political in which human beings, by way of the activity of action, can discover and create meaning. It is important to maintain the distinction Arendt develops between the human condition and human nature or essence. In this vein she writes: '[T]o avoid misunderstanding: the human condition is not the same as human nature, and the sum total of human activities and capabilities which correspond to the human condition does not constitute anything like human nature . . . if we have a nature or essence, then surely only a god could know and define it, and the first prerequisite would be that he be able to speak about a "who" as though it were a "what"' (HC 10).[3] While Arendt constantly revised and sharpened her understanding of the political, her approach always remained rooted in the phenomenological tradition (which is partially why it is so original). The political is the disclosure of the world that lies between us; it exists intersubjectively. 'Only when men and women are equally free to interact with each other can an intersubjective reality be constituted from the plurality of perspectives that each individual brings to bear on the world that they share in common'.[4] For Arendt, the political is intersubjective both in its constitution of subjective interactions and its standard of judgement. In this vein, the political is a realm that brings together human agents and helps create bonds between them. In the final chapters, I will take this intersubjective orientation to the political in Arendt and reframe it in terms of relationality, in which there is a no clear subject-object structure, and as such it escapes the dangers of Heideggerian ontology.

While Hannah Arendt's *The Origins of Totalitarianism* merits a prolonged analysis,[5] even more so half a century after its publication, when public opinion imagines it is a thing of the past that can, and will, never repeat itself,[6] I focus on how the experience of totalitarianism, which in phenomenological terms is equivalent to the loss of the world, influences her conception of the political as an activity that can (re)-found and preserve the fragile human world, a fragility exposed by the Nazi regime. The basis of this fragility is its 'dependence' on the intersubjective bond between people, a bond that is fundamentally political for Arendt (and thus cannot be substituted for by a social or a theological bond).[7] In this vein, this bond is central to my reading of her analysis of totalitarianism. Additionally, I focus on the principles she uncovers (rather than the historical aspects of totalitarianism) by focusing on the final chapter of *Origins*, which serves as its conclusion with regard to the philosophical and political aspects of her inquiry. Connected to this inquiry is her political reference to the world,[8] a term that remains central to her project from her study of action to the life of the mind and helps shed light on her phenomenological exposition of worldlessness or world-alienation, and loneliness.

Totalitarianism: From Common Sense to Ideology

While the adage 'to wear one's heart on one's sleeve' generally refers to clothing, it is fundamentally true with regard to the sleeve of Arendt's *Origins of Totalitarianism*. For all its flaws, which are primarily historical (much of the information we now have about the Nazi regime was not accessible in 1945–1948), this book is one of the earliest and remains one of the most important attempts to understand the nature and essence of totalitarianism. It intertwines an analysis of nineteenth-century anti-Semitism (as distinct from pre-nineteenth-century anti-Judaism), European imperialism, the rise of totalitarianism, and the destruction of the Jewish people (as well as many other groups deemed racially inferior). *Inter linea* it also offers a phenomenological account of these different experiences of dehumanization, which is what makes it unique. Given that Arendt seeks to understand the relationship among anti-Semitism, imperialism and totalitarianism, many of the conclusions she draws are presented in the final part. Nonetheless, a brief introduction to each part is necessary, not only to understand her conclusions, but more important, to shed light on the topics that shape her future political project.

While Arendt is clear that anti-Semitism and imperialism are not the 'causes' (a term to be reserved for nonhuman interactions that abide by scientific laws) of totalitarianism, she explores both in order to better understand its origins, elements, sources or precedents:

> The book, therefore, does not really deal with the 'origins' of totalitarianism—as its title unfortunately claims—but gives a historical account of the elements which crystallized into totalitarianism; this account is followed by an analysis of the elemental structure of totalitarian movement and domination itself. (EU 403)

The first chapter, aptly titled 'Antisemitism as an Outrage to Common Sense', has a twofold purpose. Factually, or historically, it seeks to describe the process, which began with the emancipation by Napoleon of Europe's Jewish population and eventually led to the rise of anti-Semitism in the nineteenth century. Second, by focusing on common sense—a philosophical term often used by thinkers such as Kant—she tries to understand how through society's rejection of 'the Jews' common sense itself began to degenerate. For Arendt, the history of anti-Semitism is also the history of the failed attempt to embrace the plurality that demarcates humanity. In part two of *Origins*, this same failure to embrace the other and plurality extends beyond the border of any particular nation in the economically driven practise of imperialism. In part three of *Origins*, Arendt tries to understand totalitarianism—both as a new political regime and as a form of governance that disregards common sense, ethics and most tragically the fundamental dignity of every individual. Through her analysis of the Nazis' (and secondarily Stalin's[9]) institutions, organizations, 'laws of movement' and their use of force, fear, terror and propaganda to transform distinct classes of people into isolated, alienated and lonely masses (all the while maintaining some control over them), Arendt seeks to understand how totalitarianism creates an alternative 'reality' in which all previous laws, ethics and common sense itself are seemingly meaningless. By analysing how human beings destroyed reality and the world, Arendt also understood that the world and reality can also be (re)created by human beings, even after the horrors of the Shoah. To be able to begin to be at home in the world again, it was therefore necessary to engage in political action, the only real means to create a space for humanity to appear together and to keep loneliness at bay.

Turning to the final chapter of *Origins*, 'A Novel Form of Government', Arendt identifies two fundamental aspects of totalitarianism: ideology and terror. 'Only in the hands of the new type of totalitarian governments do ideologies become the driving motor of political action' (EU 349). In other words, while ideology has always played a fundamental role in politics, totalitarianism is distinct in that it is driven by ideology at the cost of all other factors, such as economic, military, efficiency and so forth. Under totalitarianism, ideology replaces the law. However, unlike positive law, which introduces stability to the political, totalitarian, ideologically based laws of movement intentionally destabilize the political realm by introducing more uncertainty, fear and unpredictability. 'In these ideologies, the term "law" itself changed its meaning: from expressing the framework of stability within which human actions and motions can take place, it became the expression of the motion itself' (OT 464). Arendt likened an ideology to the scripting of a story (or performance) for humanity to enact. Ideologies turned individuals into a means to the ends predefined by a scripted story. She identified an analogous danger with regard to political philosophy that approached the political from the perspective of an epistemic theory rather than based on experience and praxis:[10]

> An ideology differs from a simple opinion in that it claims to possess either the key to history, or the solution for all the 'riddles of the universe,' or the intimate knowledge of the hidden universal laws which are suppose to rule nature or man. Few ideologies have won enough prominence to survive . . . only two have come out on top and essentially defeated all others: the ideology which interprets history as an economic struggle of classes [Stalinism], and the other that interprets history as a natural fight of races [Nazism]. (OT 159)

In the case of the Nazis, the ideology that inspired its law of movement was a racial one, the 'Law of Nature'. The distortion of Darwinism by the Nazis led to the creation of death camps, whose sole purpose was to cleanse the earth of those deemed unfit for survival and who prevented the flourishing of the superior Aryan race. The script thus required the elimination of Jews as well as any other individuals or groups that prevented this Aryan flourishing. In the case of Stalinism, the ideology that underpinned its particular law of movement, the 'Law of History', was loosely based on Marxism and called for the creation of a workers' class by eliminating all other forms of social difference. 'Totalitarian rule is "lawless" insofar as it defies positive law; yet it is not arbitrary insofar as it obeys with strict logic and executes with precise compulsion the laws of History or Nature' (EU 339–340).

By way of propaganda and terror, these ideologies silenced all other opinions or perspectives. Neither could tolerate any form of alterity or plurality. They were so successful that many people believed in the absolute truth claims of their respective ideologies, to such an extent that even those falsely arrested or persecuted seemed to accept their guilt. Just as the commonsense-based distinction between innocence and guilt seemed to evaporate, so did any sense of a shared 'reality' that supports this distinction. The latter, for Arendt, was a phenomenological claim, in that 'reality' is created between people and plays a critical role in stabilizing the public realm within which political acts appear. According to Halberstam, Arendt's 'approach to the idea of totalitarianism takes a phenomenological perspective by placing at the centre of its concern the way in which the person stands in a meaningful relation to the world as it appears to him or her in everyday experience'.[11]

Totalitarianism: The Total Manipulation of Reality

In her study of totalitarianism, Arendt investigated how the law plays a fundamental role in stabilizing and maintaining political spaces. Totalitarian regimes intentionally set out to destroy all forms of positive law, upon which the legitimacy of the political is established. 'It is the monstrous, yet seemingly unanswerable claim of totalitarian rule that, far from being 'lawless', it goes straight to the sources of authority from which all positive laws—based on "natural law", or on customs and tradition, or on the historical event of divine revelation—receive their ultimate legitimation' (EU 340). Her realization led to the following paradoxical conclusion regarding the role of the law in relation to the political (developed in the *Human Condition*). While the law is absolutely necessary for the support and stabilization of the *polis*, it is not political in itself (HC 194). 'The laws protect and make possible its political existence, are of such great importance to the stability of human affairs precisely because no such limiting and protecting principles rise out of the activities going on in the realm of human affairs itself' (HC 191). Thus, while laws are fundamental supporting structures, they are not per se political. This is also the ground for her claim (echoed by Levinas) that liberalism, a form of government based on the law, is not a sufficient guarantee for a thriving *polis*.[12] This is tragically the lesson she draws from totalitarianism: the positive laws, mores and traditions were not able to withstand the ideologically based 'laws of movement'. The elimination of all forms of positive law was, according to Arendt's phenomenological account of totalitarianism, *the first step* in the destruction of the political.

The second step, brought about through the use of fear, leads to the destruction of the shared bonds between isolated individuals:

> Fear is always connected with isolation—which can be either its result or its origin—and the concomitant experiences of impotence and helplessness. . . . Fear is the principle of human movements in this desert of neighborlessness and loneliness; as such, however, it is still a principle which guides the action of individual men, who therefore retain a minimal, fearful contact with other men. The desert in which these individual, fearfully atomized men move retains an image, though a distorted one, of that space which human freedom needs. (EU 344)

By breaking the bonds between people, totalitarianism succeeded in destroying the sense of solidarity that is the basis of the social bond. For Arendt, totalitarianism 'proved' what Nietzsche claimed: morality is neither universal nor absolute; there is no objective truth upon which to create standards or rules, such as Kant's appeal to Reason in the categorical imperative. The goal of this second step of totalitarianism was precisely to destroy this horizontal bond. Without a shared space to come together and experience the 'reality check' offered by others, people were overwhelmed by fear and terror. What increased these latter feelings was that individuals, having lost touch with other individuals, had no ability to verify what was real and what was the product of propaganda. In this manner, totalitarian regimes manage to reduce the plurality of society to isolated and fearful individuals. Furthermore, by denying the difference between reality and ideology, these solitary persons lose their ability to make judgements of any sort. 'Given the chaotic quality of life for members of the mass who enjoy no worldly ties with one another, totalitarian propaganda thrives on the escape it provides from reality into fiction, from coincidence into consistency'.[13] For Arendt the destruction of the shared bond that exists between people is most evident in the concentration camps, where one was forced to murder another human being in order to save oneself. Thus, in addition to eliminating the legal difference between innocence and guilt, totalitarianism managed to erase the horizontal 'moral' bonds that exist between individuals.

The third and final step taken by totalitarian regimes was the destruction of individuality, leading to what was referred to by fellow inmates in the camps as the *Muselmann*—a lifeless yet living corpse.[14] Once the space between people that is created by legal and moral bonds was abolished, the Nazis were able to do what was previously deemed the impossible—destroy the human person. 'The killing of man's individuality, of the uniqueness . . . creates a horror that vastly overshadows the outrage of the juridical-political person and the despair of the moral person' (OT 454). Already isolated from other human beings, every person—fearing for her bare biological survival—is driven to do whatever it takes to save herself. 'Totalitarian terror achieved its most terrible triumph when it succeeded in cutting the moral person off from the individualist escape and in making the decisions of conscience absolutely questionable and equivocal . . . the alternative is no longer between good and evil but between murder and murder' (OT 452). Human life, at this last stage, is reduced to an animalistic desire to live. 'The experience of the concentration camps does show that human beings can be transformed into specimens of the human animal' (OT 455). Levinas also notes how Jews were not seen as humans by the guards of the POW camp (in which he was a prisoner) and that, oddly enough, it was actually their dogs who were 'the last Kantians in Nazi Germany', as they still recognized his humanity (DF 151–153). Both Levinas and Arendt understood there was no longer a sense of reality, of community or of individuality, and as a result, people no longer felt or acted like human beings.

The totalitarian regimes forced 'the fictitious enemy' it had created to prove their ideological claim that Jews were not human. This transformation also served propaganda purposes, in that the Nazis had claimed that Jews were not humans but closer to animals or insects. By destroying legal and moral bonds and any sense of self, the Nazis proved that their claims were 'real'. This ideological claim and the 'onion' organization of totalitarian societies allowed the murderers to commit atrocities without a sense of responsibility. 'The onion structure makes the system organisationally shock-proof against the factuality of the real world' (BPF 100). As those in each layer of the onion acted according to the leader's will, they negated their own identity and identified with that of the centre:

> Nazi propaganda was ingenious enough to transform antisemitism into a principle of self-definition, and thus to eliminate it from the fluctuations of mere opinion. This gave the masses of atomised, undefinable, unstable and futile individuals a means of self-definition and identification which not only restored some of the self-respect they had formerly derived from their function in society, but also created a kind of spurious stability which made them better candidates for an organisation. (OT 356)

Overwhelmed by terror and propaganda, the individual chose to become superfluous rather than risk death, which was precisely what the Nazis intended. 'The triumph of the SS demands that the tortured victim allow himself to be led to the noose without protesting, that he renounce and abandon himself to the point of ceasing to affirm his identity' (OT 455). The destruction of one's identity, the particularity of each and every human being, is the final step in the totalitarian transformation of reality. By destroying the bonds between people, not only in the public spaces but also within private homes, the Nazis made even having an opinion life threatening. The flipside, with regard to the political, is that speaking, expressing one's thoughts, is clearly a form of political action that—particularly in dark times—carries with it consequences. Even in the private sphere, dissent—in any form—is unacceptable. While in our current political climate the private sphere still seems 'safe', public dissent is increasingly becoming punishable, whether by the mass arrest of nonviolent protesters or in the more racial case if others identify one as a Muslim.[15]

Loneliness: Totalitarianism's Contemporary Trace

That Arendt's analysis of totalitarianism is still germane in contemporary 'democratic' societies is due to a great extent, due to her phenomenological analysis of the human experience of loneliness (OT 474–478). In her assessment, 'the distinctive experience of modern mass societies is loneliness, and that modern totalitarian parties could only recruit so many members in a society of lonely people'.[16] While totalitarianism and the power of political parties are waning, modern democratic governments (often driven by economic priorities and technocrats) have also grasped that ruling large-scale populations, such as those organized into states, is much 'easier' when society is composed of 'lonely', atomized individuals. Tragically for true believers in democracy and providentially for those who wish to rule without opposition, the experiences of world and self-alienation, superfluousness and rootlessness are sadly not limited to the totalitarian times Arendt analysed. 'Radical alienation from the world and radical alienation from oneself go hand in hand',[17] and both are discernible in today's highly individualized, neo-liberal societies, as was expressed by those who defined themselves as the 99 percent in the recent Occupy movement protests.[18]

While Arendt's analysis focuses on marginalized groups in which loneliness is widespread because their members have been excluded from the shared world, the effects of loneliness are not limited to the marginal; all of society suffers. With reference to Socrates she wrote that 'as citizens, we must prevent wrong doing because the world in which we all live, wrong doer, wrong-sufferer, and spectator, is at stake; the City has been wronged' (LM 182). Arendt clearly understood that the suffering of the marginalized was politically significant. The horrors of the Shoah, the tragedies inflicted on Jews, Romas, homosexuals and so many other persecuted groups, damaged the world and not just the victims. According to Arendt, only when the most persecuted and alienated among people, humanity's 'weakest link', is included, accepted and respected—and experiences this feeling—is the world suitable for humanity to inhabit. (Levinas also repeatedly makes this claim by identifying the Jews as the trope of the oppressed, which has an essentialist ring to it. This is clearly not the case for Arendt, who was able to see that in 1948 when the State of Israel was created it was not the Jews but Arabs who were being excluded and made into refugees.) It is worth emphasizing that a phenomenon such as loneliness is not measurable or objective enough to be of interest to most social scientists; one cannot quantify or poll loneliness. Only a phenomenological account of the political can understand the political meaning of loneliness. Loneliness is produced by the loss of bonds—legal, moral, and so forth—with other human beings as well as with the world of work, which provides some stability. 'Many denizens of mass society undoubtedly lack the learning or personal experience to compare their current state with any previous one that would have been unqualifiedly different. Hence they would not describe their own situation as lonely'.[19] By analysing totalitarianism in phenomenological terms, Arendt offers us a tool with which to better understand similar phenomena today, phenomena that manifest themselves in terms of a democratic deficit, the rise of extreme right parties (who offer false substitutes for these lost bonds to other human beings) and the persecution of minorities such as Muslims living in Europe (OT 476 and LM 19).

While the first two steps (political-legal and moral) of totalitarianism's destruction of reality are taken to create isolated and atomized individuals within a public space, loneliness is the goal of the third and final step. 'The collapse of the groundwork of the world at the same time as the radical attack on the human bond that accompanies it, the withdrawal of other human beings beyond the reach of human communication, lead to the individual's inner collapse'.[20] This reduction of all bonds created within the public realm, through terror and propaganda, is not yet distinctive of totalitarianism, as it repeats the age-old strategy of tyrannical leaders: *divide et impera*. It is the next step that is unique to totalitarianism: the bonds between people that exist in the private realm are destroyed. 'What we call isolation in the political sphere, is called loneliness in the sphere of social intercourse' (OT 474). Tyrannical governments that still wish to be profitable do not attempt to destroy these spaces, which are necessary for work. The desire to reduce the individual to a state of loneliness, 'to the experience of not belonging to the world at all, which is among the most radical and desperate experiences of man' (OT 475), is essential for totalitarianism, because it is only in this latter state that human beings can be totally dominated, controlled and eliminated. Sadly, now that the world—and especially those who desire to rule rather than share the world—realize that it is possible to radically dehumanize and destroy the human person, this possibility can never be fully erased. In this vein, there will always be leaders and groups who desire such domination and are willing to do anything to have it.

The result of these three steps is the loss of the world, spatially and experientially. The Nazis succeeded in creating 'a system in which men are superfluous' (OT 457). They succeeded in doing the impossible, making the human inhuman, by means of total domination. 'Total power can be achieved and safeguarded only in a world of conditioned reflexes, of marionettes without the slightest traces of spontaneity. Precisely because man's resources are so great, he can be fully dominated only when he becomes a specimen of the animal-species man' (OT 457). According to Arendt's analysis, the pace with which the Nazis achieved this would not have been possible had it not been for the dehumanization that had already occurred by way of anti-Semitism and imperialism. The term anti-Semitism is now specifically used to refer to the racial hatred of Jews, yet in the nineteenth century it was used with reference to those defined as Semitic people (Jews and Arabs/Muslims),[21] yet it is debatable whether Islamophobia is the return of this original nineteenth-century anti-Semitism.[22] While there is a great deal of literature on who the current victims are of political exclusion, such as the Romas in Europe or African Americans in the United States, there is no doubt that what Arendt describes as racism and Levinas refers to as 'the same hatred of the other man' is still present in our 'democratic' societies. He also emphasized that what ended in Auschwitz began much earlier, in a seemingly unproblematic allergic reaction to alterity:

> The crime of extermination begins before murders take place, that oppression and economic uprooting already indicate its beginnings, that the laws of Nuremberg already contain the seeds of the horrors of the extermination camps and the 'final solution'. (NTR 27)

Likewise, while imperialism as Arendt analyses it is a specific historical phenomenon of the late nineteenth and early twentieth centuries, today's global economic crisis and the rise of neo-liberalism should provide evidence that the drive for economic profit—at any cost—is not a phenomenon limited to imperialism. Anti-Semitism and imperialism set the stage for massive experiences of uprootedness and superfluousness, both phenomena Arendt identified as fundamental to loneliness. 'To be uprooted means to have no place in the world, recognized and guaranteed by others; to be superfluous means not to belong to the world at all' (OT 475). Both Arendt and Levinas focus on the phenomenological experience of uprootedness, of being torn from the world and from one's relations to the other—it is this uprootedness that must continue to be combated today. The lesson we must draw from *Origins* is that its protean origins—the hatred of the same man and an unchecked drive for economic profit—are still present in our democratic regimes (as are loneliness, ideologies, refugees and propaganda).

While roots are often visualized as vertical, connecting a tree or flower to the soil, a metaphor that Heidegger often used, Arendt's analysis of the increasing experience of uprootedness leads her to search for another type of root or bond that is an (intersubjective) bond between people, which forms what she refers to as the web-of-relations. In this vein, she helps us rethink roots in horizontal rather than vertical terms. She concludes that once people have been uprooted, the only bonds connecting them to reality are these horizontal roots to others. As such, totalitarianism sought to destroy these as well in its pursuit of total domination. 'Not only are uprooted people who have lost a stable human world easy victims for terror, but loss of the world also damages people's hold on reality'.[23] According to Arendt, it is thus through the total loss of reality that the world created and shared between people disappears and with it the possibility of appearing to others as unique human beings.[24] 'Loss of the world that gathers and separates us, although not necessarily permanent, represents at least a temporary loss of the capacity to be specifically human'.[25] Writing from within the phenomenological tradition, which rejects the notion of an essence, which can never appear, Arendt does not believe there is either a nature or essence to being human. Analysing loneliness in terms of a dehumanizing experience is an existential rather than scientific or factual assessment. 'Total domination, which strives to organize the infinite plurality and differentiation of human beings as if all of humanity were just one individual, is possible only if each and every person can be reduced to a never-changing identity of reactions, so that each of these bundles of reactions can be exchanged at random for any other' (OT 438). Totalitarian loneliness is inhuman in a twofold sense. First, it denies the fact of plurality, and second, it aims to reduce human being to a 'bundle of reactions', thereby denying any form of human subjectivity.

Totalitarianism purposefully seeks to create the conditions in which loneliness flourishes; it aims to create individuals engulfed by loneliness:

> Luther (whose experiences in the phenomena of solitude and loneliness probably were second to no one's and who dared to say that 'there must be a God because man needs one being whom he can trust') in a little-known remark on the Bible text 'it is not good that man should be alone': A lonely man, says Luther, 'always deduces one thing from the other and thinks everything to the worst'. (OT 477)

While totalitarianism achieves total control by making loneliness prevalent, the possibility to speak and share with others has been destroyed by means of terror. As such the only hope of repairing the world has also been destroyed. A lonely person has lost the ability to turn to the other for help, which is necessary in order to reconnect to the world—this is the destruction of plurality. This experience leads people to cling to movements and to ideological logicality as a substitute for the loss of the world and reality:

> It is only because we have common sense, that is only because not man, but men in the plural inhabit the earth that we can trust our immediate sensual experience [differentiate between reality and ideology]. Yet, we only have to remind ourselves that one day we shall have to leave this common world which will go on as before and for whose continuity we are superfluous in order to realise loneliness. (OT 476)

Loneliness is the experience of being disconnected from ourselves, others and the world. And yet such reflective loneliness differs from the loneliness created by totalitarianism, in that the former is not externally imposed through terror, nor does it occur simultaneously with the loneliness of everyone else. Nontotalitarian loneliness is intensely difficult to bear (as anyone who has ever suffered from loss or depression can attest to) partially because one feels that no one else can possibly understand the pain one feels. While this might in fact be true, this does not mean that connecting to others, sharing and speaking, won't help—most likely it is the only thing that will help, by enabling one to reconnect to the world. Stories of individual suicide, often referred to as a means to escape reality or the world, are evidence of this suffering. By contrast, stories of mass suicide are sometimes construed as inspiring or heroic, such as during the siege of Masada[26] or during the Warsaw Ghetto Uprising, as they are communal actions in which people refuse to succumb to loneliness by acting collectively.

Although Arendt wrote *The Origins of Totalitarianism* after the war, she had already come to this conclusion in January 1943 after learning of the truth of the existence of the death camps:

> we should start telling the truth that we are nothing but Jews, it would mean that we expose ourselves to the fate of the human beings who, unprotected by any specific law or political convention, are nothing but human beings. I can hardly imagine an attitude more dangerous, since we actually live in a world in which human beings as such have ceased to exist. (JW 273)

Nonetheless, it was only when she concluded *Origins* that she came to see the connection between totalitarianism and the shared world in which we can act politically—a connection most visible in her writings on loneliness. 'Totalitarianism is rooted in and reinforces two critical developments: the attack on plurality and the increasing pervasiveness of atomism and loneliness'.[27] By destroying individuality, and as such the possibility of plurality, totalitarianism destroys the world.

In her account of uprootedness, superfluousness and loneliness, Arendt describes the experience of being in the world and feeling replaceable, unnecessary, a number or 'what' rather than a 'who'.[28] When the shared world is destroyed, so is the possibility of being a 'who', which only further amplifies the feeling of being uprooted and superfluous. This is what Arendt referred to as worldlessness or world-alienation. She declared 'world alienation, and not self-alienation, as Marx thought, [is] the hallmark of the modern age' (HC 254). 'For Arendt totalitarianism was the ultimate, though never inevitable, outcome of the modern phenomena of worldlessness'.[29]

Every subsequent attack on individuality and plurality, whether under the cloak of totalitarianism or in a free 'democratic' society, contributes to loneliness, uprootedness and superfluousness, thereby further weakening the world. This is the fragility of the world Arendt was confronted by in her analysis of totalitarianism. 'To be able to appear and act in our human plurality we need the frame, the limits and the setting provided by the human world of civilization, and that world is very fragile'.[30] This is precisely what totalitarianism, in its eradication of human plurality, proved. This also led her to better appreciate the importance of plurality. That it was possible to destroy the world by eliminating plurality provides hope that it is possible to recover the world through plurality. This is the most important conclusion Arendt drew from her analysis of totalitarianism with regard to the political: totalitarianism is the loss of the political, the loss of the shared world, by means of the destruction of plurality. It is for this reason that Arendt's concept of the political takes plurality as its principle.

THE POLITICAL: CREATING A WORLD TOGETHER

In order to combat the phenomena of loneliness and worldlessness, it is clear that the political realm must speak to those struggling with rootlessness and uprootedness. Arendt's phenomenological reconceptualization of the political centres on the space in which humans interact. These empowering and agonistic interactions make it possible for actors, or agents, to take responsibility for the shared world, which enables one to better understand the world as well as the collective power to change the world, for better or worse:

> Only when we come to feel ourselves part and parcel of a world in which we, like everybody else . . . only when we recognise the human background against which recent events have taken place, knowing that what was done was done by men and therefore can and must be prevented by men—only then will we be able to rid the world of its nightmarish quality. (JW 384–385)

The final paragraphs of 'On the Nature of Totalitarianism', published in 1954, could have been the first pages of *The Human Condition*. Both texts focus on the *political* importance of remaining connected to others. It is her claim that intersubjectivity and human relations are fundamental to an understanding of the political that is unusual in comparison to other political thinkers. The experience of reality, of the 'given world depends, in the last analysis, upon the fact that not one man but men in the plural inhabit the earth' (EU 360/HC 9). In this vein she refuses to categorize her writings as philosophical, as she does not begin from the individual in her singularity, but instead takes the world that arises from plurality as her starting point for describing the political. According to her, most philosophers overlook the 'primary relationships between men and the realm they constitute, springing simply from the fact of human plurality' (EU 360). She concludes that in order to recover the world, we must think from the perspective of plurality, a perspective she sees as depreciated by the philosophical canon, and specifically by political philosophers. 'The only answer to the contemporary predicament lay, in her view, in affirming and putting our faith in the aspect of the human condition that totalitarianism had denied: human plurality',[31] which is exactly what she does in *The Human Condition*.

One of the most astonishing aspects of Arendt's academic career is that she managed to publish not one but two masterpieces within a decade—both in her third language (German and French being her first and second languages, respectively).[32] While traces of her insights into the *vita activa*, where plurality takes central stage, are already present in *Origins of Totalitarianism* (as well as other essays from the 1950s), it was not until the 1958 publication of *The Human Condition* that Arendt's focus turned to the meaning of the political. As was her previous publication, it was received with great praise, although, as was the case for *Origins*, it was often misunderstood because of her phenomenological approach. In what follows I intend to address these oversights by focusing on the productive tension between plurality and particularity at the basis of her notion of the political. She begins the chapter on action in *The Human Condition* with the following: 'Human plurality, the basic condition of both action and speech, has the twofold character of equality and distinction' (HC 175). In this vein, the question 'who am I', while seemingly singular, and thus by Arendt's definition antipolitical, is in fact the political question par excellence of the *vita activa*. This paradoxical position makes clear the significance of the particular for Arendt's principle of plurality. With this paradox as a guide, I engage in a three-part analysis of the political. First, I consider the political in terms of action in a public space of equality and distinction; second, I turn to its worldly character to be found in freedom; and third, I consider her notion of power, one that challenges and redefines the vast majority of contemporary uses of power.

Action: Between Equality and Distinction

'The political realm rises directly out of acting together, the "sharing of words and deeds". Thus action not only has the most intimate relationship to the public part of the world common to us all, but is the one activity which constitutes it' (HC 198). Action, unlike the activity of labour, which is rooted in necessity or that of work, which is structured by way of a means-ends relationship, cannot be performed in isolation (HC 188).[33] While she distinguishes action from both labour and work, it is not the case that she does not appreciate these activities as essential to the human condition. In her analysis, labour guarantees the survival (of the biological self and species), whereas work guarantees a physical permanence to the world. She is also explicitly critical of Marx for failing to properly appreciate the difference between labour and work and most important for failing to recognize the danger of defining the political in terms of fabrication. Given her conclusion in *Origins* that it is only by means of the preservation of plurality that there is promise for the human world, her focus lies on action that creates a space for human interaction and flourishing. Words and deeds, which together constitute action, can only be actualized in the presence of others; action thus requires plurality and cannot occur either in the private ream or in isolation from others. It is, as it were, a second birth into the world where beings become unique, irreplaceable human beings. 'With word and deed we insert ourselves into the human world, and this insertion is like a second birth. . . . This insertion is not forced upon us by necessity, like labour, and it is not prompted by utility, like work' (HC 176).[34] While our biological birth introduces us to a world of necessity defined by biology and production, and work preserves the physical world into which we are born, our second birth—into the human realm of interaction—is rooted in freedom and plurality (HC 9). 'If action as beginning corresponds to the fact of birth, if it is the actualization of the human condition of natality, then speech corresponds to the fact of distinctness and is the actualization of the human condition of plurality, that is, of living as a distinct and unique being among equals' (HC 178).

While Arendt stresses the need for distinction in the political, distinction entails the institution of an artificial political equality. The plurality of the political is a principle that opposes any conception of inherent or 'natural' equality. To presuppose equality is to deny our differences, which is the basis of the plurality fundamental to the shared world. This rejection of an essential equality by no means implies that one should be treated as lesser or without respect. On the contrary, one of the 'requirements' of engaging with others in the public sphere is that one treats all others, and not just those with whom one agrees, as equals, although in reality, and beyond the *polis*, there is no such equality.[35] 'The equality attending the public realm is necessarily an equality of unequals who stand in need of being "equalized" in certain respects and for specific purposes. As such the equalizing factor arises not from human "nature" but from outside' (HC 215).

Much like her focus on the two types of birth in her discussion of natality and Augustine,[36] Arendt opposes the political to the experience of death with regard to equality, an implicit critique of Heidegger (also repeated in HC 9):

> Political equality, therefore, is the very opposite of our equality before death, which as the common fate of all men arise out of the human condition, or of equality before God, at least in the Christian interpretation. . . . In these instances, no equalizer is needed because sameness prevails anyhow; by the same token, however, the actual experience of this sameness, the experience of life and death, occurs not only in isolation but in utter loneliness. (HC 215)

In political terms, there is no sameness, only difference. As this question of difference clearly touches on the notion of alterity, central to Levinas's ethics, I will return to it both in the following section on freedom and in part III. While birth and death are experiences that all human beings undergo, they do not make us equals. Arendt is quite clear that we must recognize our inequality and celebrate our differences—hence her foundation of politics on plurality—and institute an artificial equality in the political realm for the sake of the world. The space in which we co-create the shared world is a realm of difference and distinction, and as a result it requires an artificial equalization. This is necessary to create a place and space where we appear to each other as a 'who' and not as a 'what'. What we are and do is relevant for the activities of labour and work, whereas the who can shine by acting with others:

> This disclosure of 'who' in contradistinction to 'what' somebody is—his qualities, gifts, talents, and shortcomings, which he may display or hide—is implicit in everything he says and does. . . . It is more likely that the 'who,' which appears so clearly and unmistakably to others, remains hidden from the person himself. (HC 179)

For Arendt the political is about the disclosure of the 'who'. This 'who' is an actor or agent and is utterly unique and irreplaceable. The who is however not to be understood as an author, as the latter implies control over the end product. Those who interpret Arendt's work to be in line with Habermas assume that she is a thinker of consensus, or that 'acting in concert' is conflict-free and congruous and thereby fail to appreciate the agonism that arises from her focus on the 'who'. Action requires stepping outside of the comfortable and sheltered space of the private realm in which one's ideas and opinions are not confronted and challenged. She stresses that action requires courage, as the political realm is full of disagreement, debate and strife. 'The public realm itself, the *polis* was permeated by a fiercely agonal spirit, where everybody had constantly to distinguish himself from others . . . the public realm was, in other words, reserved for individuality; it was the only place where men could show who they really and inexchangeably were' (HC 41).

Arendt's emphasis on distinction arises from her analysis of totalitarianism. It is only by means of agonism, which forces one to distinguish oneself and one's opinions, that action counteracts the dangers of superfluousness and loneliness. If we were all the same or had all the same opinions and perspectives, we might indeed be redundant. In an allusion to the Bible she writes: 'Nobody is ever the same as anyone else who ever lived, lives or will live' (HC 8). Political agonism confronts anonymity and is thus fundamental to the political. Action requires initiative in that people must choose to appear and disclose 'who they are' under the scrutiny of others. For Arendt, the political experience of action offers each person the chance to appear as a particular individual in a shared public space and to distinguish herself through word and deed. Appearing is about expressing who one is to others; it is not enough to simply be physically present. 'It is the function of the public realm to throw light on the affairs of men by providing a space of appearances in which they can show in deed or word, for better and worse, who they are and what they can do' (MDT viii).

In addition to the prominence of word and deeds for action, Arendt also introduces a spatial and temporal dimension, part and parcel of her phenomenological approach. The spatial and temporal (between past and future) dimensions of political action are related to the analysis of the law in *Origins*. Arendt reinterprets the *polis* in terms of a space that is created between individuals, a space bounded and supported by the law, which is symbolized by the walls of the city. While laws are fundamental to the city, Arendt is adamant that they are not political, as they have the fundamentally nonpolitical role of acting as stabilizers (to counterbalance the unpredictability and spontaneity of life in the *polis*). In a lecture she stated: 'laws gave stability to a community composed of mortals, and therefore continually endangered in its continuity by new men born into it. The stability of the laws corresponds to the constant motion of all human affairs.'[37] This space is a common space open to those prepared to participate. What is common is the space and not the contents of this space, which is one of dissensus. It is here, by means of communication, that reality is affirmed by means of manifold distinct and diverse perspectives from which people (as opposed to things) can be seen and heard by others.

The meaning of this space is also related to the idea of the world, rooted in Heidegger's phenomenology, so prominent in *Origins*. Arendt seeks to restore the political in response to the world-alienating experiences of modernity. She, as well as so many other members of excluded groups, understood what it meant to be deprived of the right to appear, to count for something (as opposed to being counted), and to discover 'who one is'. While she was excluded because she was Jewish, her claim is not limited to Jews but rather is a demand that all people excluded from the *polis* be allowed to appear. In this sense she has a very Judaic notion of justice, as does Levinas, rooted in a longing for the inclusion of all those who are excluded, oppressed and marginalized. But for Arendt, justice is both political and phenomenological. 'The existential significance that she granted to the space of appearance was such that, "to be deprived of it means to be deprived of reality, which, humanly and politically speaking, is the same as appearance".'[38] As developed in the first chapter, her concept of the world, of a nonphysical space created by political action, is a phenomenological one based on her reinterpretation of Husserl's natural standpoint and Heidegger's world, albeit in political terms.[39] For Arendt, the world is relationally constituted. It is on this basis that she prioritizes Heidegger's *mitsein* over Heidegger's primacy of

Dasein, a strategy Levinas also follows by prioritizing an ethics of alterity over ontology. It is thus in terms of their shared priority for human relationships that are world creating that their thought beckons to be brought into dialogue.

Freedom—External and Worldly

In order to further explore Arendt's conception of political action, I will now consider its raison d'être, freedom. Arendt's particular and unorthodox understanding of freedom challenges both philosophical and Christian notions of freedom. According to her analysis, something fundamental to the political realm is lost when freedom and free will, a Christian-inspired notion of freedom, are used interchangeably. In *On Revolution* she reflects on the terror that followed the declaration of the French Republic, describing it as the process by which freedom—an external and worldly 'possession'—became internalized, in line with philosophical and theological freedom, thereby losing its political significance. Arendt's notion of freedom, which she suggests has been buried by the history of philosophy, must be distinguished from a notion of freedom connected to the will. Once this distinction is made, it is possible to grasp Arendt's positive alternative: political freedom rooted in plurality. In her well-known essay 'What is Freedom?' (BPF 1963), Arendt concentrates on the tension between political freedom and the Christian notion of the will (which she further develops in the second part of *The Life of the Mind* from 1978). Arendt mulls over the meaning of freedom and the faculty of the will throughout the history of philosophy (rather than thematically, as she does with regard to thinking and judging). She is searching for the stage at which the Greek notion of political freedom was internalized by way of the free will, paving the path for a re-interstation of freedom as rooted in singularity.

According to Arendt, who is by no means a fair reader of Plato, the tale of political freedom's fall from grace begins with Plato's desire to right the wrong of the Athenians' condemnation of Socrates. Plato refuses to accept the fact that *doxa*, the opinions of the *hoi polloi* that form the *demos*, trumped what he defined as the *good* (even when Socrates disagreed). He concluded that the people could not be trusted to rule themselves and needed to be controlled; as such politics came to be defined in terms of the relationship between the ruler and the ruled, a deeply hierarchical institution. Plato's rejection of plurality led to the association of the political realm with security and certainty, both of which oppose the spontaneity and unpredictability of the realm of human affairs (LM 198). Arendt thus concludes that while Plato may have planted these seeds, they found truly fertile soil in Christianity by way of Augustine.

Having written her dissertation on Augustine, it is no surprise that Arendt returns to his thought in her examination of freedom. As one of the first Christian philosophers, writing at a time when slavery was commonplace, he found it essential to reconsider the meaning of freedom in order to make it more inclusive and universal. However, rather than protesting the lucrative institution of slavery, he redefined freedom in order to prevent slaves from protesting by making free will of higher importance than an external freedom. Mirroring Plato's prioritization of freedom as necessary in order to pursue the *vita contemplativa,* the good life, Christianity reinterpreted this inner freedom in the form of the will. One was always free to choose good over evil, to turn towards God even when bounded by chains and prevented from engaging with others. Such inner security provided a sense of peace to those whose lives were rarely under their own control. Victory over the infidels was the domain of the ruler. The people were taught to seek victory over their inner, sinful, fallen selves, the 'conflict within myself, the inner strife between what I would and what I do, whose murderous dialectics disclosed first to Paul and then to Augustine the equivocalities and impotence of the human heart' (BPF 157). The theological journey of freedom, from Plato to Augustine via Paul, is the locus of freedom's transformation from an external, worldly, plural action to an internal and personal struggle, the singularizing principle of the Will, the *principium individuationis* (LM 121).[40]

Unwittingly engaging with Levinas, Arendt explores the will in the *Life of the Mind* in terms of the history of philosophy in order to demonstrate its apolitical nature (LM 195–216). She makes a sharp distinction between plurality and alterity, which would seemingly deny space for Levinasian ethics in the political (HC 176). And yet upon closer examination, the contrary is evident. Plurality for Arendt is rooted in a relationship to other, different selves. By contrast, she uses alterity according to its medieval formulation *alteritas* to refer to a relationship rooted in sameness (rather than difference). This medieval definition of alterity clearly opposes Levinas's notion of alterity (to be explored in depth in chapter 5). Thus while Arendt claims plurality is opposed to *alteritas,* this term does not mean what it does for Levinas. Her definition of plurality is closer to Levinas's notion of alterity, as both are based in a relation to another external to the self in which difference is essential.

Sadly, according to Arendt, the end of the 'Dark Ages' in which Christian theology ruled supreme did not bring about the end of this reduced sense of freedom. 'Even Montesquieu, though he had not only a different but a much higher opinion of the essence of politics than Hobbes or Spinoza, could still occasionally equate political freedom with security' (BPF 150). Hobbes wished to reduce politics to a contract in order to ensure that society could be controlled rather than promote spontaneity and freedom.[41] While Montesquieu at times fell into this trap, he was certainly less interested in approaching the political in terms of the model of the sciences. He was 'the greatest representative of this political secularism [which arose from the separation of church and state] . . . deeply aware of the inadequacy of the Christian and the philosopher's concept of freedom for political purposes. In order to get rid of it, he expressly distinguished between philosophical and political freedom' (BPF 161). Montesquieu

> maintained that power and freedom belonged together; that conceptually speaking, political freedom did not reside in the I-will but in the I-can, and that therefore the political realm must be construed and constituted in a way in which power and freedom would be combined. . . . [L]iberty was 'a natural Power of doing or not doing whatever we have a Mind'. (OR 150)

Yet Montesquieu's notion of political freedom lacked a connection to publicity. It is Machiavelli who, according to Arendt, is to be credited for reinvigorating this aspect of freedom in his concept of virtue.[42] He reminds us of the performative and public aspects of politics, of freedom as virtuosity (LM 200). It is only in this public and performative manner that action can be transformed into stories, to be shared with others in the future. In sharp contrast to Machiavelli, the apolitical freedom of the philosophers promoted by Jean-Jacques Rousseau, 'the most consistent representative of the theory of sovereignty, which he derived directly from the will' (BPF 163), reduces plurality to that of a singular undivided will. It is this identification of freedom with the will, and finally with absolute sovereignty, that Arendt sees as Plato's final victory over the *polis*.

What concerns Arendt most is that the critical link between freedom and judgement is lost during this transformation. By emphasizing believing over doing, intentions over actions, the only possible judge is God. Other people, with whom we speak and interact in the public sphere, can no longer judge. Without judgement, political action, which is always collective, becomes impossible, in her view. The priority of the will for freedom means that singularity, and personal decisions, take priority over collective debate, putting plurality itself in jeopardy. Willing is a solitary endeavour. Freedom rooted in action, by contrast, requires plurality. 'We first become aware of freedom or its opposite in our intercourse with others, not in our intercourse with ourselves' (BPF 148). Arendt thus sets out to rescue freedom from the confines of the will and Christian theology. In order to rediscover the political meaning of freedom, 'Arendt emphasizes the difficulty we have in thinking of freedom as a worldly phenomenon, one manifest in plural action. The problem (to oversimplify) is that our tradition extends and perpetuates the Greek philosophical and early Christian prejudices against such freedom.'[43]

Compelled by the horrors of totalitarianism, Arendt endeavours to rescue political freedom and to re-establish its fundamental connection to action, plurality and the world. She does so by arguing for freedom as (1) intersubjective, (2) contrary to domination and (3) world-oriented. Freedom does not exist in the singular, I am not free, only we are free; freedom is an intersubjective phenomenon. Freedom is experienced in the domain of plurality and is not the handmaiden of autonomy; it is its antithesis (HC 234). Both Arendt and Levinas reject the claim that the subject is, or ought to be, autonomous. Political freedom thus finds its meaning in human relations and not in the self (HC 254). An individual is not free, as freedom does not belong to a subject, to a singular self. Political freedom is intersubjective and worldly. This radical position is only fully developed in *The Life of the Mind*. 'Freedom is conceived not as an inner human disposition but as a character of human existence in the world' (LM 3, 135–141). Freedom's 'place of origin is never inside man, whatever that inside may be, nor is it in his will, or thinking, or his feelings; it is rather in the space between human beings' (PP 170). Plurality, which is the condition for the creation of a human world, is thus an essential prerequisite for the space within which freedom can be experienced; without the participation of other human beings interaction is not possible, as there is neither a between, an 'inter', nor a stage for actors.

A second fundamental aspect of freedom is that to be free to enter the public realms, in addition to being free from necessity, one must also be free from domination—neither giving nor taking orders from another. Neither the slave nor the slave-owner can enter the political space of freedom, as inequality is antithetical to freedom. 'Politics is therefore centred around freedom, whereby freedom is understood negatively as not being ruled or ruling, and positively as a space which can be created only by men and in which each man moves among his peers. Without those who are my equals, there is no freedom' (PP 117). Arendt's claim is not an attempt to rewrite the history of the political, or to argue for the validity of universal equality. According to Arendt, this latter concept 'within the tradition of political thought means nothing other than no man is free' (PP 78). Freedom requires distinction, which is only visible upon a background of equality; thus any attempt to deny our differences is a denial of freedom. 'Politics deals with the coexistence and association of *different* men' (PP 93). For Arendt, while we are all equally *human* beings, it is only by acting—through word and deed—that we manifest this (e)quality. There is no innate natural equality between individuals; it is only by entering the public realm that we can 'level the playing ground'. This artificial equality is the basis from which we can distinguish ourselves so that we can turn to others and ask 'who am I?' Equality is thus the price of entry into the public realm, and alterity, in a Levinasian sense, its currency.

In addition to freedom from necessity and oppression, Arendt designates a third condition, freedom as world-oriented. This is the reason that liberation is not to be equated with freedom; it is but the first step towards political freedom.[44] 'This freedom [of the ancients] clearly was preceded by liberation: in order to be free, man must have liberated himself from the necessities of life. But the status of freedom did not follow automatically upon the act of liberation' (BPF 148). In addition to being free from oppression, freedom needs a direction—that of the world. It is for this reason that Arendt states: 'Courage is indispensable because in politics not life but the world is at stake' (BPF 156). While Arendt does not classify her own understanding of freedom as positive, her critique of negative freedom as well as her affirmation of the worldly orientation of political freedom certainly shows certain affinities to this position.[45] Her criticism of the 'liberal credo, "the less politics the more freedom"' (BPF 149), exemplifies this. Likewise, she refuses the reduction of the political to either law or governance. 'It has become almost axiomatic even in political theory to understand by political freedom not a political phenomenon, but on the contrary, the more or less free range of non-political activities which a given body politic will permit and guarantee to those who constitute it' (OR 30). Another reason that freedom is world-oriented is that 'unlike the spaces which are the work of our hands, [freedom] does not survive the actuality of the movements that brought it into being . . . wherever people gather together, it is potentially there, but only potentially, not necessarily and not forever' (HC 199). Freedom has no permanence; it is not a product of work. Freedom, like action, is a worldly phenomenon that is as fragile as all human experiences rooted in plurality. Freedom relies on intersubjective interactions, on the potential for people to appear and act, on the promise of the political to transform the world.[46]

Reconceptualizing Power in Terms of Empowerment

But what does freedom, worldly and external, create? What comes from interacting in a space of equality and distinction? It is power, albeit reconceptualized phenomenologically as empowerment, that completes Arendt's political trinity. She reconfigures canonical notions of power, which tend to be vertical concepts relating ruler and ruled, by focusing on how power changes those who experience it as well as how it has the potential to transform the shared world. Not surprisingly, her distinct interpretation of power makes engagement with other political theorists quite complex, as is often misunderstood. The advantage it offers is a completely different analytic lens from which to examine the political. 'For we all in some sense take politics to be about power, domination, pursuit of interests, and the struggle to prevail over others. The purpose of this inquiry [Arendt's] is to suggest a very different basis for delimiting the bounds of the political'.[47] In addition, her notion of power is ideal for the bottom-up horizontal political movements that have appeared across the globe in the past few years (e.g., the Occupy movement, Indigniados, Tahir Square, Gezi Park, 2013 Brazil bus protests), as it challenges the verticality and singularity of politics today.[48]

Let us begin with the clearest definition Arendt offers of power:

> *Power* corresponds to the human ability not just to act but to act in concert. Power is never the property of an individual; it belongs to a group and remains in existence only so long as the group keep together. When we say of somebody that he is 'in power' we actually refer to his being empowered by a certain number of people to act in their name. The moment the group, from which the power originated to begin with (*potestas in populo,* without a people or group there is no power), disappears; 'his power' also vanishes. (CR 143)

Power in an Arendtian sense is directly opposed to the type of 'power' that totalitarianism sought. She refers to the latter in terms of strength, force and violence. Strength, for Arendt, is always connected to singularity, as an individual can possess it. By contrast, force, often confused with violence, is a physical descriptor and can be applied to nature. Violence is unique for Arendt because of its specifically instrumental character. 'Phenomenologically, it is close to strength, since the implements of violence, like all other tools, are designed and used for the purpose of multiplying natural strength until, in the last stage of their development, they can substitute for it' (CR 145).[49] Domination, which she radically disconnects from power, comes at a great cost—'the eradication of human plurality'[50]—and relies on strength, violence and terror. Arendt's position is that there is no greater power than that created by means of collective actions. While there is no doubt that the destruction created by means of violence, strength and terror is immense, Arendt defends the position that even at its zenith, Nazi totalitarianism was unable to completely annihilate all plurality. As such, the potential power of plurality, which is at the source of revolutions and social movements such as those led by Gandhi, Solidarnosc, the civil rights movement in the United States, the student movements in 1968 and so forth can never be fully extinguished. Moreover, the power of plurality has much greater permanence in the world—it brings about lasting change by transforming both people and the world. This is in stark contrast to totalitarianism, which is always a threat to itself. While Arendt does not doubt that new forms of totalitarianism will arise after the demise of Nazism and Stalinism, these too will certainly be self-destructive and cannot last for too long (although she does not underestimate the harm they can do in a short time span) because of their reliance on violence and terror and the need to constantly stay in motion.

Power is a collective endeavour that creates and sustains the world. 'Power is what keeps the human realm, the potential space of appearance, between acting and speaking men, in existence . . . power springs up between men' (HC 200). Empowerment is what we experience by means of action. This experience is an end in itself. Nonetheless, there are other potential 'by-products' such as a transformation of the political or a contingent and temporary empowering 'we' formation. Nonetheless, the political must remain a noninstrumental realm to preserve its principle of plurality. This principle is exemplified by its unpredictability and spontaneity, both of which are rooted in its intersubjective nature. Power experienced from within the political is, like the political, an intersubjective phenomenon that arises from within plurality. No individual alone has power. It 'springs up between people'; power thus has a form of horizontal transcendence, rooted in plurality, from within the political.

While power is rooted in plurality, it does not exist without particularity; every actor is a distinct and irreplaceable human being. By participating in the *polis*, one discovers—by learning from the other—who one is and—at the same time—helping to create a shared world. In this manner, Arendt broadens the 'definition' of political action beyond its often-impoverished association with elections and the ballot box. Her approach is refreshing and empowering, as it reminds us that governments have no real political power. Power, as most political thinkers use it, is entirely vertical. Arendt's notion of political power is horizontal and spontaneously infectious—its spreads itself without resorting to violence or terror. 'Human power corresponds to the condition of plurality . . . for the same reason, power can be divided without decreasing it, and the interplay of powers with their checks and balances is even liable to generate more power' (HC 201). Power increases with participation; it flourishes in plurality, thereby always acting as a challenge to totalitarianism. Her notion of power inspires political critique, disobedience, resistance and revolution. Power is what has been the driving source of all great political changes and revolutions, a view shared by many anarchist political thinkers. While this may not be what any government, democratic or not, would seek, as it is potentially destabilizing and certainly unpredictable, Arendt is much more interested in the political as it speaks to people, and less in the institutions that attempt to control and regulate people. While she is aware that her notion of power is potentially destabilizing and keeps a door open to forms of government such as totalitarianism, it is the same door that must be kept open to remind both the people and their representatives not to forget who holds the power, and equally, who is responsible for the world—this is the fundamental risk of the political realm.

In addition to power's self-sustaining capacity and ability to bring about change in reality, power also plays a fundamental role in providing the political with a sense of security that it lacks, especially when contrasted with the cyclical continuity of labour or the physical products of work. 'What keeps people together after the fleeting moment of action has passed (what we today call "organization") and what, at the same time, they keep alive through remaining together is power' (HC 201). It is my contention, to be developed in the following chapter, that power stabilizes and humanizes the world, and in this vein it is an implicit political ethics.[51] With regard to power's implicit ethics, Arendt makes clear that one's actions cannot be violent, nor can one's words have the intent to be harmful. Rather, one's words and deeds must be oriented towards understanding and repairing the shared world. While this by no means implies that political action is not painful or confronting, it is important that this agonism be oriented towards the world and not intended to simply harm an individual. 'Power is actualized only where word and deed have not parted company, where words are not empty and deeds not brutal, where words are not used to veil intentions but to disclose realities, and deeds are not used to violate and destroy but to establish relations and create new realities' (HC 200).

PLURALITY: A NEW PRINCIPLE FOR THE POLITICAL

In the preface to *Origins*, Arendt writes: 'Human dignity needs a new guarantee which can be found only in a new political principle, in a new law on earth, whose validity this time must comprehend the whole of humanity' (OT ix). While she uses the terms *principle* and *law* interchangeably, the former does have a rather specific and distinct meaning in her writings. In her 1953 lecture, 'The Great Tradition', Arendt provides the following definition of a principle. Principles 'are not the same as psychological motives. They are rather the criteria according to which all public actions are judged and which articulate the whole of political life'.[52] A principle is the criteria by which the political actions can be judged and which help us to understand what is political. Laws, she reminds us in this same lecture, are not political, because a lawmaker is not necessarily a member of the community; she can be called in from the outside, as in the case of Rousseau's lawgiver.[53] Arendt takes this rather particular notion of principle from Montesquieu, who associated a particular principle with each distinct type of government (e.g., republican, monarchic).[54] According to Montesquieu, a principle is that which leads to action, what brings about or motivates the political in Arendtian terms.

So what would it mean for plurality to be this principle, and how can a principle also 'function' as a guarantee in a realm in which there are no certainties? It is my contention that Arendt does not define plurality as a principle in the way of classical foundationalism. Plurality is a post-foundational ground, a contingent but temporarily necessary foundation, a term that will be developed in the following chapter.[55] However, we have now prepared the ground to answer the first of these questions: What is plurality? Plurality, Arendt repeatedly states, is a paradox. It is the paradox of equality and distinction that characterizes the public sphere and the human condition. The activity of speech makes this clear in that we would not need to communicate with others if were all identical, we are in this sense all distinct; likewise, speech would not help us if we were not in some manner able to communicate, and in at least this sense equals. It is the paradoxical double-sidedness of speech that makes it so central to her notion of the political. Without speech and the possibility of (mis)communication, we are also much more exposed to the dangers of world-alienation and feeling as if we do not belong in the world and are in some sense superfluous. By way of speech and interactions we form a community; we become part of a polity and make ourselves at home in the world.

Having discussed Arendt's notion of political equality above, let us now consider her notion of particularity, or uniqueness, a notion that brings her into dialogue with Levinas. 'Human distinctness is not the same as otherness—the curious quality of *alteritas* possessed by everything that is and therefore, in medieval philosophy, one of the four basic, universal characteristics of Being, transcending every particular quality' (HC 176). Arendt differentiates between distinctness and otherness (and repeats this position in her final publication; LM 200–211). Distinction is what she takes to be fundamental to plurality and the political. Let us first clarify the meaning of otherness in order to better grasp what distinctness is. Otherness, which Arendt connects to the medieval notion of *alteritas*, is possessed by everything; it is a universal characteristic of Being and in this sense is shared by all beings. In other words, when Arendt uses the terms otherness or *alteritas*, she is not speaking phenomenologically but more criticizing the medieval position that there is some essence shared by all human beings.

As we will examine in chapter 5, this is precisely the opposite of Levinas's meaning of the term alterity. Levinas does not use this medieval notion of alterity, but rather as he acknowledges, he explicitly adapts the Platonic notion of *alteritas* by making its contents that of the other person. Alterity, in Levinas's sense, is thus much closer to what Arendt means by distinctness, which is fundamental to plurality. Levinas also uses the term unicity as a synonym for alterity, by which he means the irreducibility of the human being to any totality. The term unicity comes very close to Arendt's notion of distinctness:

> Only man can express this distinction and distinguish himself, and only he can communicate himself and not merely something—thirst or hunger, affection or hostility or fear. In man, otherness, which he shares with everything alive, becomes uniqueness, and human plurality is the paradoxical plurality of unique beings. (HC 176)

All things living can express something, their *quidittas*, but only human beings can express their particularity (what Levinas refers to as *haecceity*), their 'who'-ness, uniqueness or distinctness. The fact that we are all unique is what we share—is paradoxically our *alteritas* or otherness—with all other beings. No other beings are absolutely distinct and unique the way human beings are, or in Levinasian terms absolutely other.

Arendt here states that alterity (in Levinas's sense) is the paradox of plurality. This singular otherness, when interacting with others, is our uniqueness. In other words, plurality can be defined as the paradox of equality, that is otherness or *alteritas*, and particularity, that is distinction or alterity in Levinas's sense. Plurality, the principle of the political, is paradoxical in that it reaffirms the basic fact that we are all distinct humans and yet at the same time we are all beings—part of the 'same species'. Arendt, in order to escape the biologism of the latter phrase, often refers to the latter in terms of 'sheer human togetherness'. 'The revelatory quality of speech and action comes to the fore where people are *with* others and neither for nor against them—that is, sheer human togetherness' (HC 180).[56] However, this sheer human togetherness should not be confused with the notion of multiplicity, which for Arendt is the total erasure of plurality and particularity that totalitarianism strives to enforce. Togetherness is a phenomenological term that expresses what is created by the reality of dialogue, exchanging opinions and opposing perspectives. It arises by the sharing of interests, interests being defined by Arendt as '*inter-est*, which lies between people and therefore can relate and bind them together' (HC 182).

In contrast to this sheer human togetherness is Levinas's alterity or absolute otherness. While for Levinas the face-to-face encounter is an encounter with alterity, according to Arendt, it is by means of action that we become aware of this distinctness. Action reveals our particularity to ourselves and to others (without whom it would not be possible), as does its pre-political prefiguration, our first birth in the form of natality. Arendt notes 'the curious fact that both the Greek and the Latin language possess two verbs to designate what we uniformly call "to act"' (BPF 165); the first (in both languages) means to begin, initiate, to lead or rule, whereas the second implies the continuation of this process, carrying it through and supporting. Searching for the trace of these distinct notions of action in the history of philosophy, Arendt notes that Augustine—in his only *political* treatise, *De Civitate Dei*—refers to freedom as beginning in the guise of the miracle of natality. Not only does Arendt embrace this aspect of Augustine's theory, she cites it in every one of her major works. 'In the birth of each man this initial beginning is reaffirmed, because in each instance something new comes into an already existing world. . . . Because he *is* a beginning, man can begin; to be human and to be free are one and the same. God created man in order to introduce into the world the faculty of beginning: freedom' (BPF 167). While in the *Human Condition* Arendt differentiates birth or natality from action, as two distinct beginnings, the former ontological and the latter political, she continues to refer not only to Augustine but also to God and the miraculous nature of natality and action. 'Our whole existence rests, after all, on a chain of miracles' (BPF 169). Every human being is unique, is a miracle, as is every political action. This is also the reason spontaneity and uncertainty are a reality in the political.

Arendt's understanding of particularity in terms of miracles can also be understood by putting it back into the context of her response to totalitarianism. By emphasizing particularity, she challenges the superfluousness central to self- and world-alienation. This emphasis is also what puts her notion of the political into tension with conventional politics. 'Philosophers have been uncomfortable with the sheer contingency involved in the activity of the will [not in the sense of the *principium individuationis*], finding a belief in necessity much more congenial. Once again, thinking and doing, philosophy and politics seem to be at odds'.[57] Arendt, it should now be clear, chose the political over the philosophical, recognizing philosophy's tendency to reduce thinking to singularity, a reduction reproduced in reality by way of the terror and ideology of the Nazis. Her response is thus to redefine the political in terms of plurality, the paradox of equality and distinction, a redefinition that should by no means be underestimated in terms of its originality or importance, both then and now.

NOTES

1. Claude Lefort, *Democracy and Political Theory*, trans. David Macey, 1st ed. (Cambridge, England: Polity, 1991), 224. See also Claude Lefort, *The Political Forms of Modern Society: Bureaucracy, Democracy, Totalitarianism*, ed. David Thompson, 1st MIT Press ed. (Cambridge, Mass.: MIT Press, 1986); Claude Lefort, 'Thinking with and against Hannah Arendt', *Social Research* 69, no. 2 (1 July 2002): 447–459.

2. Elisabeth Young-Bruehl, *Hannah Arendt: For Love of the World*, 2nd ed. (New Haven, Conn.: Yale University Press, 2004), 113.

3. 'The term "condition" here carries a critique of speculative or metaphysical theories of "human nature" in a double sense: it refers to the fact that there is no such thing as a universal essence of the human. . . . [I]t also refers to the 'alienating' character of the relationship between two kinds of conditions . . . the natural (birth) and the political (public realm)'. Etienne Balibar, '(De)Constructing the Human as Human Institution: A Reflection on the Coherence of Hannah Arendt's Practical Philosophy', *Social Research: An International Quarterly* 74, no. 3 (2007): 728.

4. Andrew Schaap, 'Political Theory and the Agony of Politics', *Political Studies Review* 5, no. 1 (1 January 2007): 66.

5. See, for example, Antonia Grunenberg, 'Totalitarian Lies and Post-Totalitarian Guilt: The Question of Ethics in Democratic Politics', *Social Research* 69, no. 2 (1 July 2002): 359–379; Bernard Crick, 'On Rereading "The Origins of Totalitarianism",' *Social Research* 44, no. 1 (1 April 1977): 106–126; Margaret Canovan, 'Arendt's Theory of Totalitarianism: A Reassessment', in *The Cambridge Companion to Hannah Arendt*, ed. Dana Villa (Cambridge, England: Cambridge University Press, 2000); Jerome Kohn, 'Arendt's Concept and Description of Totalitarianism', *Social Research* 69, no. 2 (1 July 2002): 621–656; and the following essays (all collected in Gareth Williams, ed., *Hannah Arendt*, 1st ed. [New York: Routledge, 2006]: Richard Bernstein's 'The Origins of Totalitarianism: Not History but Politics', Jacques Taminiaux's 'The Philosophical Stakes in Arendt's Genealogy of Totalitarianism', Claude Lefort's 'Thinking With and Against Hannah Arendt', Andrew Arato's 'Dictatorships Before and Beyond Totalitarianism',

Elizabeth Young-Bruehl's 'On the Origins of a New Totalitarianism', and Roy Tsao's 'The Evolution and Structure of Arendt's Theory of Totalitarianism'.

6. It is worth remembering that part of the lesson to be learned from the Shoah is that no one, whether in Nazi Germany, occupied Europe or abroad, believed that such atrocities could occur in such a 'civilized place'. Claims like 'it could never happen here' or 'it could never happen again' should always be considered in this context.

7. It is precisely this insight that inspired both Jürgen Habermas and Claude Lefort's own political reflections on democracy.

8. Although I will always use the term 'world' in Arendt's sense, its roots are clearly Heideggerian. According to Martin Heidegger, *Being and Time*, trans. John Macquuarrie and Edward Robinson (Malden, Mass: Blackwell, 1962), 63, Arendt's use refers to both the third and fourth definition presented by Heidegger. Thus, for Arendt, 'world' signifies both *'wherein' Dasein* 'lives' (ontic *existentiell*) as well as the concept of *worldhood* (ontological-existential).

9. As many of Arendt's readers, such as Claude Lefort, point out, this is one of the weaknesses of her analysis of totalitarianism; that is, its focus on Nazism and lack of appreciation of the distinction between Marxism and racism as 'philosophical' foundations for totalitarianism.

10. It is her prioritization of praxis that has led some philosophers to define her as a neo-Aristotelian, a reading that puts her work closely in line with that of Jürgen Habermas. This is a reading I would problematize, prefering to read Arendt with a focus on the agonistic and performative rather than on the rational exchange of speech. For more on these two different ways of interpreting Arendt, see Dana Villa, *Arendt and Heidegger: The Fate of the Political* (Princeton, N.J.: Princeton University Press, 1995), 49.

11. Steven E. Aschheim, ed., *Hannah Arendt in Jerusalem* (Berkeley: University of California Press, 2001), 7.

12. Although Arendt rarely speaks of civil society and institutions, focusing instead on the political, it is clear that in the destruction of the legal and moral bonds between people, civil society is also fundamentally destabilized and eventually destroyed. Thus in this sense, civil society also plays a fundamental role in upholding reality.

13. Phillip Hansen, *Hannah Arendt: Politics, History and Citizenship* (Stanford, Calif.: Stanford University Press, 1993), 144.

14. Agamben very much builds his theory of bio-politics upon this figure and accounts of the Muselmann. For more see Giorgio Agamben, *Remnants of Auschwitz: The Witness and the Archive* (New York: Zone Books, 2000).

15. Arun Kundnani, *The Muslims Are Coming! Islamophobia, Extremism, and the Domestic War on Terror* (London; New York: Verso, 2014).

16. Lewis P. Hinchman and Sandra K. Hinchman, 'In Heidegger's Shadow: Hannah Arendt's Phenomenological Humanism', *Review of Politics* 46, no. 2 (April 1984): 198.

17. Anne-Marie Roviello and Catherine Temerson, 'The Hidden Violence of Totalitarianism: The Loss of the Groundwork of the World', *Social Research: An International Quarterly* 74, no. 3 (2007): 924.

18. There are several interesting nonacademic articles written by protestors, or those observing them, about this phenomenon; see capitalismisover.com/category/the-99/.

19. Hinchman and Hinchman, 'In Heidegger's Shadow', 198.

20. Roviello and Temerson, 'The Hidden Violence of Totalitarianism', 924.

21. Gil Anidjar, *Semites: Race, Religion, Literature* (Stanford, Calif.: Stanford University Press, 2007); Bernard Lewis, *Semites and Anti-Semites: An Inquiry into Conflict and Prejudice* (New York: W. W. Norton & Company, 1999).

22. Kundnani, *The Muslims Are Coming!*

23. Margaret Canovan, *Hannah Arendt: A Reinterpretation of Her Political Thought* (Cambridge, England; New York: Cambridge University Press, 1994), 29.

24. For a discussion of reality and world-alienation as central to the modern age in Arendt, see chapter 2 in Kimberley Curtis, *Our Sense of the Real: Aesthetic Experience and*

Arendtian Politics, 1st ed. (Ithaca, N.Y.: Cornell University Press, 1999); and chapters 6–7 in Michael Halberstam, *Totalitarianism and the Modern Conception of Politics* (New Haven, Conn.: Yale University Press, 2000).

25. Curtis, *Our Sense of the Real*, 83.

26. Masada is an ancient fortress in Israel built in approx. 35 BCE. At the end of the Jewish-Roman war (approx. 70 CE), 960 Jewish rebels and their families committed mass suicide rather than be captured when under siege.

27. Hansen, *Hannah Arendt*, 133.

28. A frequent albeit microcosmic example of this phenomenon is encountered in the weeks prior to most elections. A common frustration expressed by potential voters is 'what difference will my vote make?' or 'why bother?'.

29. Richard H. King, 'Endings and Beginnings: Politics in Arendt's Early Thought', *Political Theory* 12, no. 2 (1 May 1984): 248.

30. Canovan, *Hannah Arendt*, 34.

31. Ibid., 35.

32. Interestingly, Levinas also published the vast majority of his writings in his third (or fourth) language, Yiddish, Russian, and Hebrew being, in his case, his other mother tongues. Raoul Mortley, *French Philosophers in Conversation: Levinas, Schneider, Serres, Irigaray, Le Doeuff, Derrida* (London; New York: Routledge, 1991), 12.

33. Given the potential for isolation to become loneliness, Arendt adhered to her distinction between work and action even while acknowledging the interactive and creative aspects of work. This is most evident in her unedited and unapproved, posthumously published texts on Marx, now published as *The Promise of Politics* (2005).

34. For an interesting discussion on the role of natality in Arendt's work, see Hauke Brunkhorst's 'Equality and Elitism in Arendt' in Villa, *Cambridge Companion to Hannah Arendt*.

35. Parekh also helps to clarify this point when she writes: 'Political equality cannot be granted by law but must be attained by each citizen for himself and can only exist in the course of a public interaction with other citizens. . . . The law grants civil not political equality'. Bhikhu C. Parekh, *Hannah Arendt and the Search for a New Political Philosophy* (New York: Macmillan, 1981),17.

36. Hannah Arendt, *Love and Saint Augustine*, ed. Joanna Vecchiarelli Scott and Judith Chelius Stark, 1st ed. (Chicago: University Of Chicago Press, 1998).

37. Hannah Arendt, 'The Great Tradition: I, Law and Power', *Social Research: An International Quarterly* 74, no. 3 (2007): 716.

38. Mary Dietz in Villa, *Cambridge Companion to Hannah Arendt*, 101. See also HC 199.

39. For a thorough discussion of this connection see Halberstam, *Totalitarianism and the Modern Conception of Politics*.

40. Unfortunately, while she recognizes the difference between Judaism and Christianity—'the Old Law said: thou shalt *do*; the New Law says: thou shalt *will*' (LM 68)—she fails to appreciate its significance in relation to her project. Not only does Arendt seem to implicitly assume the validity of Christian supersessionism in her use of the past tense to refer to the Hebrew Law, she also fails to note that the Judaic tradition did not follow Christianity in making this inward turn. While both traditions share many concepts, the role of the creation of a faculty of willing is not one of them. Judaism remains action oriented, with intentions playing a secondary role. This is clear from the fact that it is more important to act as if one believes in God and thus according to the law than it is to actually believe in God. Furthermore, because of this orientation towards actions, Judaism does not 'privatize' judgement. The faculty of judgement remains the responsibility of every person. A similar oversight appears with regard to the faculty of memory, which Arendt argues is forgotten after Augustine (LM 117). Once again, had Arendt been more familiar with the Judaic, she would have made this connection to the weekly Jewish holiday, Shabbat, on which two candles are lit, each symbolizing one of the commandments 'observe (*Shamor et yom*

ha-Shabbat l'kad'sho)—Deuteronomy 5:12 and remember (*Zakhor et yom ha-Shabbat l'kad'sho*)—Exodus 20:8'.

41. It is interesting to note that both Arendt and Levinas always have Hobbes in the back of their minds when criticizing politics. This is equally true for his understanding of human nature in the state of nature. Both thinkers refuse Hobbes's very negative philosophical anthropology, encapsulated in his catchphrase 'the life of man, solitary, poor, nasty, brutish and short' even after witnessing the Nazis' ability to replicate it during the Shoah.

42. See Jerome Kohn's article on freedom in Villa, *Cambridge Companion to Hannah Arendt*, regarding Machiavelli, whose love for the world was greater than his love for God but was perhaps still ethical in that the world is God's kingdom for humankind.

43. Villa, *Arendt and Heidegger*, 117.

44. George Kateb, 'Existential Values in Arendt's Treatment of Evil and Morality', *Social Research: An International Quarterly* 74, no. 3 (2007): 145–146; Hansen, *Hannah Arendt*.

45. As such, we will use this term, although cautiously, aware of the fact that this label is potentially constricting. The same situation applies to the notion of freedom in Levinas and that of the Judaic, both of which espouse several aspects of positive freedom.

46. In an interview she explains that she bases her notion of the political on trust, even if trust is a difficult notion to formulate; it nonetheless remains fundamental to human relations. 'Hannah Arendt "Zur Person": An Interview from 1964 with Günter Gaus', plus.google.com/+aliasinkhorn/posts/UJ6UBkutcRU.

47. Ronald Beiner, *Political Judgement* (Chicago; London: University of Chicago Press, 1984), xiv.

48. Her notion of power is explored in HC, CR, and OR. An excellent secondary source is Villa, *Cambridge Companion to Hannah Arendt*.

49. Arendt follows this citation with a rare but fundamental methodological clarification with regard to her use, often criticized, of categories. 'It is perhaps not superfluous to add that these distinctions, though by no means arbitrary, hardly ever correspond to watertight compartments in the real world, from which nevertheless they are drawn' (CR 145). The same can surely be said with regard to her distinctions among labour, work and action; private and public; social and political; *vita activa* and *contemplativa*, and so forth.

50. Canovan, *Hannah Arendt*, 27.

51. As I intend to argue, this type of political ethics is implicit throughout her political project. It is a type of ethics that is not external to the political but arises from within plurality and is thus bounded by the political. This is also the reason Arendt argues for political response/responsibility rather than an ethical response that lacks a space in which to be actualized. The difficulty with her political ethics is that it lacks the certainty or guarantees we often seek from ethics and requires that there be a space for political action, a space that is greatly endangered today as it was at the time she wrote. In addition to the power of promises and forgiveness, rooted in plurality, Arendt's concepts of judgement and responsibility form the basis of her political ethics.

52. Arendt, 'The Great Tradition', 724. Williams adds that a principle 'exists only in the world, the space between persons, but then as nothing other than an abstraction, a universal *except by virtue of the actual actions* which appear to others'. Gareth Williams, ed., *Hannah Arendt*, 1st ed. (New York: Routledge, 2006), 943. This analysis by Williams comes very close to Marchart's notion of the post-foundational, as it recognizes that all aspects of the political are contingent and yet nonetheless have a certain 'generality' (a better term than Williams's reference to universality). While some readers overlook this explicit goal in *Origins*, I take it to be the link in her analysis of totalitarianism and *The Human Condition*, between the total extermination of plurality and its revival in the form of the political. Plurality, strengthened by an ethics of

alterity (which together constitute relationality), I will argue, is the new political principle that can help guarantee human dignity.

53. Arendt, 'The Great Tradition', 717.

54. In the third book of *De l'esprit des lois,* Montesquieu identifies the principles of each of the three types of government: republican (democratic or aristocratic), monarchic and despotic. Just as each type has a particular nature based on the source of its sovereignty (the people, the prince via laws or the despot, respectively), each also has a principle. Montesquieu makes a point of emphasizing the importance of the distinction between the nature and principle of each type of government. While the nature makes the government what it is (its particular structure), the principle is 'ce qui le fait agir . . . les passions humaines qui le font mouvoir'. [Charles de] Montesquieu, *Montesquieu: The Spirit of the Laws,* Cambridge Texts in the History of Political Thought (Cambridge, England: Cambridge University Press, 1989).

55. What characterizes a post-foundational approach is the recognition of its own contingency as well as of the human need for such a partial ground as a form of 'security blanket'. For more see Oliver Marchart, *Post-Foundational Political Thought: Political Difference in Nancy, Lefort, Badiou and Laclau* (Edinburgh, Scotland: Edinburgh University Press, 2007).

56. It is worth remarking that this quote is often misunderstood to mean that plurality denies particularity. Plurality is the paradox of particularity.

57. Canovan, *Hannah Arendt,* 271.

FOUR

An Ethics from Within the Political

In 1961 Arendt was hired by the *New Yorker* to write a series of articles on Adolf Eichmann's trial, which was of great interest to their significant Jewish readership. Her report, subtitled 'A Report on the Banality of Evil', was to become, and remains, the most controversial work she published.[1] In addition, Arendt found herself in intellectual commotion—she could not come to terms with Eichmann's usage of Kant to justify his crimes. It was both the trial and the controversy her articles caused that led to a shift in her intellectual interests. In her lecture 'Thinking and Moral Considerations', she states:

> Some years ago, reporting the trial of Eichmann in Jerusalem, I spoke of 'the banality of evil' and meant with this no theory or doctrine but something quite factual, the phenomenon of evil deeds, committed on a gigantic scale, which could not be traced to any particularity of wickedness, pathology, or ideological conviction in the doer. . . . However monstrous the deeds were, the doer was neither monstrous nor demonic, and the only specific characteristic one could detect in his past as well as in his behaviour during the trial and the preceding police examination was something entirely negative: it was not stupidity but a curious, quite authentic inability to think. (RJ 159)[2]

Eventually she concluded: 'Morally and politically speaking, this indifference though common enough, is the greatest danger. . . . Therein lies the horror and, at the same time, the banality of evil' (RJ 146). In other words, Arendt began to understand how loneliness and worldlessness, dangers under democratic as well as totalitarian regimes, can lead to indifference, which is both ethically and politically perilous. Until Eichmann's trial she had focused on the latter; it was now time to start to consider the former. Is it the case that there is simply no space for ethics in Arendt's account of the political? Or rather, as I will argue, did Arendt begin to rethink the relationship between the political and ethics after the Eichmann trial? What does Arendt mean by the term morally here? What role does such an ethics play in her notion of the political? After considering these questions, I turn to Arendt's account of promises and forgiveness, which she refers to as ethically necessary aspects of the political, and in which there are clear parallels to Levinas. I then move beyond promises and forgiveness in order to develop an Arendtian-inspired political ethics. It is my contention that by considering her rethinking of the *vita comtemplativa* in relation to a political responsibility, the basis of Arendt's unwritten praxis of political ethics can be outlined. The question I must then consider is whether this reconstruction of an Arendtian-inspired political ethics is sufficient. Is there a need to go beyond Arendt to strengthen the ethical voice that arises from between the walls of the *polis*? While there is clearly an ethical preoccupation in Arendt's thought,[3] I conclude that Arendt's political ethics is lacking—a lack that I suspect (but cannot prove) might have been addressed in her unfinished volume on judgement.

THE CRITERION FOR AN ARENDTIAN ETHICS

The following quote expresses a widely accepted position:

> One of the most difficult aspects of Arendt's political theory is her insistence that the ethical be removed from the political. Perhaps George Kateb best expresses the difficulty when he asks, 'How could the author of the *Origins of Totalitarianism* seek in her later writings to purge politics of love, goodness, conscience, compassion and pity?'[4]

Is Kateb, a prominent scholar, justified in his assessment of Arendt's later writings? Is Peg Birmingham, who has written the standard work on Arendt and human rights, right to conclude that she removes ethics from the political? And if so, is this inescapably problematic: What do both of these scholars believe ethics offers the political what it cannot discover within itself? In order to answer these questions, let us first consider Arendt's position on morality. She is highly critical of all attempts by political philosophers, following Plato's lead, to reduce politics to a controlling relationship between ruler and ruled; is the same true with regard to how the canon defines morality? While she does not spend sufficient time considering the contributions of canonical thinkers such as Aristotle, Aquinas, Mill and Hume, she argues that they commit the same basic fundamental error that Plato, Kant and Heidegger made—an error that makes clear why she wants to remove morality from the political.

Given her explicit distress over Eichmann's reference to the categorical imperative, it is not surprising that she returns to Kant. According to

Arendt, 'the inhumanity of Kant's moral philosophy is undeniable' (MDT 27); Kant's second critique, which for many is the pinnacle of the philosophic tradition from Plato to Heidegger, has rarely been described with such disdain (Nietzsche seems to be the only notable exception). While we must examine Arendt's justification for this claim, we can already conclude that if Arendt deems Kant's morality inhumane, it is comprehensible that she would want to completely distance morality from the political. So what, according to Arendt, makes Kant's morality inhumane? What point is Arendt trying to make with such an outrageously strong claim about one of the most important moral philosopher in the Western canon?

The above claim arises in her essay on Lessing in the 1968 collection of essays *Men in Dark Times*, written after the Eichmann trial. In it she states that Kant's morality 'introduces [an absoluteness] in to the interhuman realm—which by its nature consists of relationships—something that runs counter to its fundamental relativity' (MDT 27). For Arendt, as argued in the *Human Condition*, the interhuman realm is one rooted in relationships in which no absoluteness or absolute truth is possible or desirable. Her key insight into the fundamental interdependence of human interactions and its absolute incompatibility with this type of totalizing logic or truth clearly echoes the conclusions she draws from *Origins*. She reaffirms the danger of such absoluteness in the interhuman or public realm in this essay and goes further by rejecting all forms of foundationalism. Arendt reiterates that absolute guarantees, such as those promised by ideologies, and total certainty are not possible in the realm of human interactions without destroying these spaces. It is this rejection of absolutes that justifies my classification of her project as post-foundational.[5] Foundationalism is an appeal to truth as absoluteness that refuses to be undermined and that aims to silence *doxa*, thereby preventing the plurality of the human realm from emerging and it has no place in the political realm for Arendt. 'The most interesting aspect of Arendt's reinterpretation of contingency [the basis of the post-foundational], however, is the elucidation of contingency as condition of the phenomenon of the new, elaborated in relation to human existence, to history, and to freedom'.[6] Freedom, as presented in *The Human Condition*, is world-oriented and arises in the interhuman realm, and as she makes clear it is opposed to necessity; 'everything that appears to human eyes, everything that occurs to the human mind, everything that happens to mortal for better or worse is "contingent", including their own existence' (LM 60).

Arendt's advocacy of contingency, and rejection of absoluteness, in the political realm is both what makes her a post-foundational thinker and justifies her harsh criticism of Kant's moral philosophy. By justifying absoluteness (by way of the categorical imperative) in the realm of human interactions and relationships, Kant's morality is inhuman. It denies the fundamental plurality, contingency and freedom of human interactions and as such is unwelcome in the *polis*. In other words, Arendt interprets Kant's practical philosophy, an interpretation that many Kant scholars would indisputably challenge, as a form of Truth or 'expertise', neither of which promotes plurality. She makes an analogous claim in her 1967 essay 'Truth and Politics' (originally published in the *New Yorker*), which is highly relevant in today's technocracy-led democracies, as exemplified by the EU or the nondemocratic Monti government in Italy. She argues that truth, most often as presented by scientists or economists, enters the public realm by way of experts who justify ignoring the people's voice, which they claim is ignorant and incapable of making political judgements. According to Arendt this is precisely Plato's justification, one repeated by many canonical philosophers and one that reappears in Kant's Second Critique. This new form of governance or rule by technocrats is precisely what Arendt defines as antipolitical and undemocratic and which she rejects as inhuman and potentially totalitarian. In this vein, Arendt regards Kant's moral philosophy as yet another attempt to control or regulate the human realm by introducing certainty, laws and universality. While Arendt agrees with the tradition from Plato to Heidegger that the human realm is characterized by its fragility, she—like Levinas—does not follow the tradition in its response to this fragility. She does not try to escape it but embraces it as human. This however does not mean that Arendt, or Levinas, rejects stabilizing elements which might be supportive, but only if they do not come at the cost of what makes the human realm *human*—its freedom. It is the sacrifice of freedom in the name of certainty that makes morality, whether Platonic or Kantian, problematic and essentially inhuman for Arendt. It is also for this reason that she seeks to separate morality from the political.

While we can conclude, with Birmingham, that Arendt insists that morality, such as that espoused by Plato and Kant, be removed from the political, it is still not clear that Kateb's conclusion is justified or that all ethics, such as Levinas's, are equally rejected. Did Arendt ever take the time to properly assess different ethical approaches? In all likelihood, Arendt had a very limited appreciation of alternative types of ethics. While she was at least superficially familiar with Levinas's opus (given that she refers to him in a footnote in *Origins*), she does not seem to appreciate how radically he transformed the realm of ethics. On the contrary, she rather thoughtlessly accepts what she takes to be the standard philosophical definition of morality, that 'first, there is a distinction between right and wrong, and that it is, an absolute distinction . . . ; and that, second, every sane human being is able to make this distinction' (RJ 75). While it is clear from her criticism of Plato, Kant and Heidegger that Arendt has no interest in such foundational moral claims, she fails to recognize that not all forms of ethics accept the above definition.

In this same lecture, 'Some Questions of Moral Philosophy', given just after the Eichmann trial, Arendt also accuses the tradition of moral philosophy of the same violation as the tradition of political philosophy and, most problematically, Heideggerian ontology, which is that it sets as its 'standard the Self and hence the intercourse of man with himself' (RJ 76). In her interpretation, morality is rooted in singularity rather than in plurality, as it should be, given that it is based on human relationships and interactions. As we have clearly seen in the previous chapter, the political is a space of plurality and not of singularity. Any ethics that could be hospitable to (or hosted by) the political in Arendtian terms would need to embrace this plurality rather than seek to reduce it to singularity. Thus, it is now clear that the reason that morality is antipolitical for Arendt is that for her 'morality concerns the individual in his singularity' (RJ 97), a singularity that is hostile to plurality, the principle of the political.

While Arendt certainly closes the door to morality within the *polis*, I argue that she does not do the same for an ethics that is nonsingular and nonfoundational. Arendt does fail to realize that not all forms of ethics are by definition rooted in singularity and absoluteness. Thus while she does not sufficiently consider the possibility of such an ethics, she does not close the door to ethics in the *polis*. On the contrary, there is evidence, in the *Human Condition*, of ethical faculties that are not hostile to the political, but on the contrary, are fundamental to it. Rather than view these examples as exceptions (which enables one to maintain a consistent reading of Arendt as rejecting all ethics in the political), I see them as an invitation to think—with and beyond Arendt—about the need for an ethics of the *polis*.

Arendt's Ethical Faculties: Forgiveness and Promising

Forgiveness and promising are introduced as two human 'faculties' rooted in plurality that support and strengthen the political. 'Since these faculties [forgiving and promising] correspond so closely to the human condition of plurality, their role in politics establishes a diametrically different set of guiding principles from the "moral" standards inherent in the Platonic notion of rule' (HC 237). They are presented as having a political role and yet not explicitly described as political. In addition, Arendt feels it necessary to immediately clarify that they are not rooted in a Platonic standard. It is worth noting that she puts 'moral' in quotes, thereby acknowledging that there might be an alternative to such morality. It is this alternative that we seek to uncover by way of her account of these two faculties. Let us first consider what promising and forgiveness are before trying to understand the nature of their contribution to the political. What we can gather from her negative reference to Plato is that forgiveness and promising are not guided by the 'moral' standard inherent in Plato's notion of rule. Based on her analysis of Plato in *The Human Condition*, rulership is vertically imposed (possibly by fear) and has absolute control as its goal, which can only be guaranteed by doing violence to plurality, most often by reducing it to singularity (producing multiplicity or conformity). So what non-'moral' standard or principle guides promising and forgiveness and in so doing preserves plurality? What non-'moral' political role do these two faculties play, and how?

In *On Revolution,* published five years after *The Human Condition,* Arendt elaborates on the faculty of promising:

> Binding and promising, combining and covenanting are the means by which power is kept in existence; where and when men succeed in keeping intact the power which sprang up between them . . . they are already in the process of foundation, of constituting. The grammar of action: that action is the only human faculty that demands a plurality of men; and the syntax of power: that power is the only human attribute which applies solely to the worldly in-between space by which men are mutually related, combine in the act of foundation by virtue of the making and the keeping of promises, which in the realm of politics, may well be the highest human faculty. (OR 175)

Promising is here described as a means of introducing some stability, albeit without any absolute guarantees, to the political realm. It helps to keep power 'alive', to sustain a space of action, for longer than a moment. The faculty of promising enables the change that arises during revolutionary moments (which are always temporary and transitory) to develop into a foundational or constitutional mode—potentially creating a bridge to the legal realm that also stabilizes and enables the space of the political. Action and power mutually reinforce each other by way of promising. In this manner, the human ability to make promises helps to support the unpredictability of plurality by strengthening the fragile web-of-relations that characterizes the human realm. Arendt surprisingly, especially for those who deny the importance of her Jewish heritage for her political project, tells the following *midrashic* story in order to exemplify the power of promises:

> Abraham, the man from Ur, whose whole story, as the Bible tells it, shows such a passionate drive toward making covenants that it is as though he departed from his country for no other reason than to try out the power of mutual promise in the wilderness of the world, until eventually God himself agreed to make a Covenant with him. (HC 243)

As this *midrash* illustrates, mutual promises can, in the form of covenants, also act as public expressions of trust in each other, thereby strengthening the fragile web-of-relations that sustains the political realm.

Through agreements, covenants and compacts (as opposed to contracts), humans make public promises to each other to offer trust to those in the public realm. Explicitly referencing Hobbes, Arendt criticizes the model of contracts with regard to the political as yet another Platonic, vertically structured, control-oriented mode of politics that destroys the plurality that is the condition of the political. According to Arendt,

Hobbes's philosophical anthropology, upon which he justifies his political philosophy, is inhuman. 'A being without reason, without the capacity for truth, and without free will—that is, without the capacity for responsibility—man is essentially a function of . . . his price . . . for the use of his power [in a non-Arendtian sense]' (OT 139). Hobbes's solitary, isolated, fearful and private subject is, according to Arendt, incapable of forming the types of relationships necessary for political action. It is this philosophical anthropology that both Arendt and Levinas explicitly reject, claiming that Hobbes has introduced it into the liberal tradition. For this reason, she critiques popular notions of sovereignty (as does Strauss, another Jewish political thinker[7]), which she interprets as forced agreements rather than promises, based on singularity rather than plurality, and hence as nonpolitical. This is the essential distinction she identifies between contracts and covenants, and her reason for preferring the latter is that they allow for a horizontal form of promising that sustains rather than destroys plurality. Hobbes's social contract 'gives birth to a state that asks for absolute obedience, depriving all his subjects of political, or (for Arendt) participation rights. This leads to Arendt's understanding of sovereignty as domination. According to Arendt, Hobbes's *Leviathan* not only gives rise to power politics, but also to totalitarianism'.[8] In this vein, contracts are rooted in domination and have no place in the *polis*, whereas covenants and compacts (which Arendt discusses at length in *On Revolution*) are rooted directly in intersubjective relations. The preference for compacts and covenants is also affirmed by Levinas.[9]

Covenants and promising both also offer an element of publicity that is critical for the political, in that it helps establish reality for all those present in the public realm, whether as actors or spectators. One only has to recall Arendt's account of totalitarianism to appreciate how in dark times it is difficult to know what is 'real'. Even in better times, due to the nature of action, whose ends are unknowable, the world can often appear extremely unstable and intimidating. Promises, which are a response to the unpredictability of action, provide the world with stability and hope. Their ability to introduce some stability is clearly connected, for Arendt, to temporality, as promises help to support the world by giving hope for the future. To summarize, promises, which can take the form of covenants, symbolically extend political action and power, which can only appear in the present, into the future.

Forgiveness, in terms of temporality, complements promising in that it connects the present to the past. In this manner, promising and forgiveness frame action that occurs between past and future. Forgiveness allows for the actor's actions, which are irreversible, to be transcended—it allows for action to continue in the future even after the world has been harmed by a past wrongdoing. Arendt reminds us that 'trespassing is an everyday occurrence which is in the very nature of action's constant establishment of new relationships within a web of relations, and it needs forgiving . . . releasing men from what they have done unknowingly' (HC 240). In relation to totalitarianism, where the 'trespassing' was more horrific than anything human beings had previously conceived was possible, forgiveness (which does not mean forgetting, hence the phrase *Never Again*) allowed for steps to be taken towards reconciling ourselves to a world in which such horrors took place by engaging in action and thus beginning once again to mend the world. What is clear from Arendt's definition of forgiveness is that it is not 'easy' or 'cheap' forgiveness; it requires that an actor take responsibility. In this vein, forgiveness is not something simply granted or guaranteed; it must be earned by means of action in the form of a response from the wrongdoer(s). This aspect of Arendtian forgiveness comes very close to both Levinas and the Judaic tradition of *teshuvah* (which she explicitly refers to in JW 42 and which will be developed in part III).

Given that no one would take the risk of acting if there were no space to be forgiven for failed actions, forgiveness is absolutely indispensable in a world that is constantly changing and needs actors who are willing to make mistakes. Only through forgiveness can this world marked by uncertainty be made a little more human. 'But the fact that the same *who*, revealed in action and speech, remains also the subject of forgiving is the deepest reason why nobody can forgive himself; here, as in action and speech generally, we are dependant upon others, to whom we appear in a distinctness which we ourselves are unable to perceive' (HC 243). By forgiving others, we remind ourselves of the shared world and the value we place on this fragile web in which we all depend upon each other. In this vein, forgiveness and promises are nonpolitical faculties that support plurality and the political by strengthening the fragility of the web-of-relations that constitutes the world. Much like Kant's 'absoluteness', they 'stabilize' human interactions, yet unlike Kant's moral philosophy, they do not sacrifice plurality and freedom but rather support it. These faculties 'arise directly out of the will to live together with others in the mode of acting and speaking, and thus . . . they are like control mechanisms built into the very faculty to start new and unending processes' (HC 246). While they are non-'moral', these faculties have a political role similar to that of Kantian morality. For this reason I take the liberty of defining them as examples of Arendtian ethics that demonstrate her openness to an alternative ethics rooted in plurality. In this way, we can conclude that an ethics that arises directly from plurality is not opposed to the political, as it strengthens, rather than destroys, the fragile human realm by bridging the present political space with a past, which cannot be overcome without forgiveness for its mistakes, and a future, which is filled with promises that promote trust and inspire hope.

Based on this conclusion, I claim that we must begin to correct the common misrepresentation of the political, as defined by Arendt, as hostile to ethics. Her hostility is limited to traditional morality that is absolute, foundationalist and rooted in singularity. This definition by no means covers the entire spectrum of ethics. Furthermore, as is evident from her account of promises and forgiveness, Arendt believed that such faculties were politically significant, as they help fortify the fragility of the political realm. While it is unfortunate that she did not further explore these examples, or provide others, this by no means prevents us from using the above analysis to establish the threefold criterion for an ethics compatible with Arendt's vision of the political. First, such an ethics must embrace a post-foundational and intersubjective approach. Second, such an ethics must be rooted in, and strengthen, plurality. Third, it must serve to reinforce, from within (rather than threaten) the political by bolstering the public realm as well as the bonds of political solidarity created by power. Examining her opus with this criterion in mind, I would now like to consider what I take to be her attempt to develop a political ethics in terms of the *vita contemplativa*, a project she never completed due to her untimely death.

RETHINKING THE *VITA CONTEMPLATIVA* IN POLITICAL AND ETHICAL TERMS

In the period following Eichmann's trial, Arendt not only began to reread Kant, she also returned to a topic first developed in the *Human Condition* vis-à-vis the relationship between the *vita activa* and the *vita contemplativa*. One of the problematic aspects of Arendt's work, most apparent in her early writings, is her overly polemical account of the conflict between politics and philosophy, which stems from an overly simplistic reduction of the *vita contemplativa*. She writes as if all philosophers blindly follow Plato in his fear and disdain of action, an activity characterized by *doxa* in which the *hoi polloi* are empowered. Aristotle, whom at times she praises for his emphasis on praxis,[10] is also seen as 'being clearly guided by the ideal of contemplation (*theoria*)' (HC 14) and maintaining the 'old argument against the *sophoi*, wise men, which recurs in Aristotle as well as Plato, that they do not know what is good for themselves' (PhP 75) and of reducing the political to the logic of work with its means-ends instrumental relationship.[11] By ignoring important differences between canonical figures such as Plato and Aristotle, Arendt concludes that the *vita contemplativa* is a form of intellectual abstraction sanctioned by the ideal of life in the ivory tower and in this sense permits philosophers to withdraw both physically and intellectually from all earthly activities in order to contemplate *theoria in isolation*. While she is clearly biased, Heidegger's failure to act further justifies her suspicion that philosophical contemplation can serve as an excuse to avoid thinking or taking responsibility for the common world. It is this antipolitical aspect of certain canonical figures in philosophy that led Arendt to draw an overly divisive opposition between the *vita activa* (which includes the activities of labour, work and action) and the *vita contemplativa*. It was only after the Eichmann controversy, when she began to consider the banality of evil in terms of unintentional evil or thoughtlessness, that she began to question her own hasty assessment of the *vita contemplativa*. Primarily in the unfinished *Life of the Mind*, she discovers a new politically significant appreciation for the activities of thinking, willing and judging. In essence, Arendt sought to rethink these faculties, conventionally considered by philosophy to be rooted in singularity, in terms of plurality. It is my contention that in so doing, Arendt aimed to overcome what she had previously deemed to be a conflict between philosophy and the political and to create a space for ethics in the political.

The Socratic Inspired Model of Thinking

Following upon conclusions drawn in *Eichmann in Jerusalem*, the starting point of *The Life of the Mind* begins with the claim 'it was not stupidity but *thoughtlessness*' (4). This tripartite exploration of the *vita contemplativa* is the beginning of Arendt's venture into *political* thinking. In this vein it is neither a turn away from the *vita activa* nor a further rejection of the *vita contemplativa*. Inspired by Socrates and Kant's Third Critique, Arendt sought to understand thinking's *political* role, an investigation that forced her to confront many of the ethical questions she had avoided prior to Eichmann's trial. Hearing him justify his horrific actions, Arendt asked herself: 'Is evil-doing, not just the sins of omission but the sins of commission, possible in the absence of not merely "base motives" (as the law calls it) but of any motives at all?' (RJ 160). It was this question of action, related to thinking and motivation (and thus to the will), that led her to write *The Life of the Mind*. Sadly, the third volume, on judging, was never completed, leaving the fundamental question, 'Is our ability to judge, to tell right from wrong, beautiful or ugly, dependent upon our faculty of thought?' (RJ 160) unanswered (with the exception of the Kant lectures she taught on this topic).

A remarkable example of Arendt's rethinking of the *vita contemplativa* is her return, twenty-five years after writing *Origins*, to the phenomenological analysis of loneliness, in which she reconsiders its relationship to thinking (and by way of plurality, to the political):

> The mind can be said to have a life [the sign of living is being in the company of men] of its own only to the extent that it actualises this intercourse in which, existentially speaking, plurality is reduced to the duality already implied in the fact and word 'consciousness'. . . . I call this existential state in which I keep myself company 'solitude' to distinguish it from 'loneliness', where I am also alone but now deserted not only by human company but also by the possible company of my-

> self. . . . Mental activities themselves all testify by their *reflexive* nature to a *duality* inherent in consciousness. (LM 74)

Thinking is a process done in solitude, a term she differentiates from loneliness as it retains a fundamental aspect of plurality—the duality of consciousness. In this vein of thinking, an internal discourse (or intercourse), is the faculty by which the self 'internalizes' the plurality of the political realm—albeit in the reduced form of a duality. It is thus distinguished from contemplation, which is connected neither to the world nor to plurality and occurs in the ivory tower. From singularity and abstraction to duality and reflexivity, in the company of other humans, Arendt's model of thinking does not lose touch with the plurality of the human realm. In this vein, political thinking, like acting, is a difficult and dangerous activity that calls for courage. 'The quest for meaning, which relentlessly dissolves and examines anew all accepted doctrines and rules, can at any moment turn against itself. . . . [Thus] there are no dangerous thoughts; thinking itself is dangerous' (LM 176). Thinking is fundamentally anti-dogmatic, challenging all foundational claims, whether theological, moral or about politics, and as such it provides no certainties. However, since the rise of totalitarianism, the alternative is even less promising:

> Non-thinking, which seems so recommendable a state for political and moral affairs, also has its perils. By shielding people from the dangers of examination, it teaches them to hold fast to whatever the prescribed rules of conduct may be at a given time in a given society. (LM 177)

Holding fast to prescribed rules, precisely what Arendt claims Eichmann did, can lead to horrors such as the Shoah and thus must be avoided. 'This century has offered us some experience in such matters: How easy it was for the totalitarian rulers to reverse the basic commandments of Western morality—"Thou shall not kill" in the case of Hitler's Germany' (RJ 178/LM 177). Levinas also was disturbed by how easily so many European, often highly educated, citizens seemingly overnight denied what had always been a moral commandment, 'thou shall not kill', and takes this reversal as a starting point for thinking about ethics after the Shoah. Given that such prescriptive norms and values, repeated in cliché-like form by Eichmann throughout his trial, failed to prevent genocide, Arendt begins to question what political value they possibly have.

The same uncertainty and contingency Arendt emphasized in her early works concerning the *vita activa* now applies to her political reading of the *vita contemplativa*. It is precisely for this reason that Arendt seeks a new type of thinking, one that is fundamental for the political, a 'thinking without banisters'. This type of thinking embraces the post-foundational. It is contingently grounded in a form of horizontal intersubjectivity. In addition, it is—like action—a process that is never complete. 'The business of thinking is like the veil of Penelope: it undoes every morning what it had finished the night before' (RJ 166). Arendt therefore calls for a thinking without banisters, the banisters being prescribed rules, norms and mores. It does not provide any political guarantees, but does provide hope that people will not simply blindly follow others, entirely ignoring their own consciousness or the conversations they have had with others in the *polis*. What is essential, and assumed by Arendt, is that this consciousness has been nourished by conversations characterized by agonism and plurality. This in our modern democracies is by no means a given. Today's *polis* may not tolerate a Socrates-like denizen who helps enrich the minds of others.

Like forgiveness and promising, 'thinking without banisters' is politically significant and yet not political itself, as it happens outside the space of action. In this vein, thinking without banisters is a type of Arendtian ethics inspired by Socrates, an alternative to philosophical abstraction. As such we must ask who, according to Arendt, Socrates was?

> He knows how to arouse the citizens who, without him, will 'sleep on undisturbed for the rest of their lives.' . . . And what does he arouse them to? To thinking, to examining matter, an activity without which life, according to him, was not only not worth much but was not fully alive. . . . Socrates is a midwife . . . he purged people of . . . those unexamined prejudgments which prevent thinking. (RJ 174)

Socrates's unsolicited conduct towards his fellow citizens forced them to question themselves, to form considered opinions rather than accept unreflected-upon prejudices. In so doing he empowered them to come together and create a space of worldly freedom, within and around themselves, for thinking and judgement. He constantly sought to help them discover themselves and their full potential, as well as their world and its potential to be inspiring and meaningful. While this agonistic disruption was often unappreciated, and eventually led to his death, Socrates was convinced that a life without thinking was not worth living.

It is for this reason that, according to Arendt, Socrates played such a fundamental role in the Athenian *polis*. His questions, while pestering, pushed others to ask themselves questions, which allowed them to learn to 'think without banisters'. For Arendt, Socrates is exemplary not because of the content of his political claims but because of his conviction, which he acted upon, that within each one of us there is a citizen of the world waiting to be born. Socrates's ideal, like Arendt's, was 'to work himself out of a job',[12] as this would have signified that people had learned to think (necessary if they are to judge and/or act) for themselves. It is precisely for this reason that Arendt refers to Socrates as a midwife:

> He wanted to help others give birth to what they themselves thought anyhow. . . . Every man has his own *doxa*, his own opening to the world. . . . Socrates did not want to educate the citizens so much as he wanted to improve their *doxai*, which constituted the political life in

> which he took part. To Socrates, maieutics was a political activity, a give-and-take, fundamentally on a basis of strict equality. (PP 15)

Arendt shares Socrates's vision that by engaging others, often agonistically and provocatively, one's consciousness or inner dialogue is awoken. In this vein, the parallel to childbirth, and to the notion of natality, can be further developed. This awakening is miraculous, but it is also painful, messy, dangerous and risky. There is no guarantee with regard to what types of thoughts are awakened; they are just as likely to be racist as inclusive. In other words, thinking is not the same as learning—there is no predetermined educational agenda—it is simply a process of shaking people to such an extent that they can no longer cling to dogma and hoping that they might begin to engage with a plurality of agonistic views before making judgements. Trusting in this process therefore requires an immense trust in the potential of human beings (in the plural). Arendt, even after the Shoah, continues to believe that all human beings, if shaken by others, are capable of thinking without banisters:

> Thinking in its noncognitive, nonspecialized sense as a natural need of human life, the actualization of the difference given in consciousness, is not a prerogative of the few but an ever-present faculty of everybody; by the same token, inability to think is not the 'prerogative' of those many who lack brain power but the ever-present possibility for everybody. (RJ 187)

It is the latter danger that everyone shares with Eichmann, the possibility to choose not to think—to exclude the plurality of the world from one's mind. While every individual has the ability to think, the choice to think without banisters is not always an easy one to make. It is sometimes easier to silence or stifle the voice of the other, of plurality, within the mind. Nonetheless, one always remains—at some level—aware that one has silenced a part of oneself. 'A life without thinking is quite possible; it then fails to develop its own essence—it is not merely meaningless; it is never fully alive. Unthinking men are like sleepwalkers' (LM 191). A sleepwalker cannot know that she is asleep unless she has experienced being awake, an experience that Socrates and Arendt are convinced she will always want to repeat.

Significantly, Arendt's notion of thinking without banisters contains an ethical imperative, one that I will, in the following chapter, also show is present in Levinas's thought when he demands that the ego constantly be challenged and put into question (DF 17). Political thinking requires one to recognize the significance of plurality within the world and within oneself. While plurality cannot be actualized in one's mind, it can be 'represented'. Thinking has political potential if oriented by plurality and the world. This is in fact a reversal of the paradox of the political. Rather than being particularity within plurality, thinking is plurality within the particularity of the self. It is also in this sense relational. Thinking can have the plurality of the public *represented* within the mind and thereby connects the self to the world within the life of the mind. 'All thinking, strictly speaking, is done in solitude and is a dialogue between me and myself; but this dialogue of the two-in-one does not lose contact with the world of my fellow-men because they are represented in the self with whom I lead the dialogue of thought' (OT 476). Inherent in the reduced plurality of thinking's duality is a *representative* plurality.

This two-in-one, which she associates with Socrates and develops in *The Life of the Mind*, is the means by which plurality—albeit in a limited form—is part of the *vita contemplativa*. To be clear, the represented plurality of thinking is no substitute for the plurality of action; it lacks the spontaneity and unpredictability that characterizes the *polis*. Yet 'when the plurality of human beings is no longer *represented* in the dialogue of thought, dialogue ceases',[13] which makes *represented* plurality essential for the political. The difference between 'thinking without banisters' and what Eichmann did is to be found in the role plurality plays. It is in this sense that representing plurality by way of two-in-one is an ethical principle. Eichmann was not stupid but simply thoughtless; he refused to consider a plurality of perspectives. It is such thoughtlessness that Arendt associates with the dangers of political indifference and which continues to confront contemporary democracies, a thoughtlessness greatly assisted by the reductive spectrum of reality we are permitted to know by way of the media. To combat this we must seek both in our action and in our thinking to create a space for plurality. It is the mental creation of such a space and the continuous dismissal of dogma from it that makes thinking more 'ethical' by embracing the post-foundational, refusing singularity and helping to strengthen the political.

In addition to the political importance of such ethical thinking, Arendt also finds inspiration in Socrates's statement in the *Gorgias* that '"it is better to be wronged than to do wrong"' (RJ 181/LM 181). This is a rare moment when Arendt explicitly endorses an ethical position. In addition, it is one central to Levinas's ethics of alterity. Levinas, as we will see, consistently emphasizes that what an ethics of alterity commands is that the other has priority over the self, and a concrete manifestation of this ethics is that it is better to allow oneself to be harmed than to harm or murder another (UH 117). Arendt justifies this claim in political terms by reminding us that the political realm is world-oriented and that any wrong done in the public realm, including harm done to another human being with whom we share this world, harms the world. This harm, regardless of who has committed it, destroys the shared world, which is what the political seeks to maintain. She calls all people, actors and spectators, to actively prevent any wrongdoings for the sake of the shared world (LM 182). By taking on a perspective rooted in the plurality of the shared world rather than an individual perspective, the claim 'it is better to be wronged than to do wrong' is political rather than moral, as it arises from within the *polis*, that is, from plurality. Arendt recognizes this explicitly when she writes, 'a purely moral proposition actually arose out of the thinking experience as such' (LM 183), but is quick to warn us that we must be careful not to instrumentalize thinking (or the political). Ethics is, and must remain, a *by-product* of thinking. If one were to try to 'use' thinking in order to found ethics, it would require the instrumentalization of the plurality that inspires it:

> This, then, is the problem: our ability and need to think make it possible for us to prepare for moral action and yet give us no positive guidance on what to do. But that does not mean that thinking changes nothing. It actualises and develops certain basic human abilities—it has, not results-as-products, but effects. What, then, are the effects of thinking? From the perspective of the person, the particular 'who' that thinks, the 'who' that lies at the heart off all human being, the effect is far from negative. Thinking opens us to the unmediated experience of the subject. And that, the experience of being human in the essential mystery of the unknowable subject-self, is in itself moral.[14]

Thinking without banisters, by requiring the presence of plurality, helps to strengthen plurality in one's mind—it is a virtuous circle. Equally virtuous is the fact that this represented plurality prevents the petrification of dogma, or banisters, which lead to thoughtlessness and political indifference. Thinking, ideally, takes us out of ourselves and into dialogue with others, who not only make us question ourselves but who force us to question each other. This, however, requires that we confront ourselves with others who have different perspectives, with real plurality rather than an empty multiplicity (which is sadly what tends to happen in our contemporary democracies).

The Kantian-Inspired Model of Judgement

There is little doubt among Arendt scholars that her analysis of the faculty of judgement would have been the apex of her political thought. What I would add is that this also would have bridged her political and ethical writings and thus makes her political ethics explicit. What Arendt indicates in her incomplete writings on judgements is that they make the world more hospitable by enabling people to be at home in the world, thereby combating superfluousness and indifference. The importance of judging was already clear from her writings on totalitarianism. In 1954 she wrote, 'the originality of totalitarianism is horrible, not because some new "idea" came into the world, but because its very actions constitute a break with all our traditions; they have clearly exploded our categories of political thought and our standards for moral judgement' (EU 309–310). Judgements promote particularity without denying the importance of community. While actions can never be reversed, which is why forgiveness is so essential to the political, judgements allow people to determine the meaning of both affirming and damaging actions, thereby deciding an event's meaning in humanity's story. Judgements are a means to balance the fact that 'the political does not encompass the whole of man's and the world's existence. It is limited by those things which men cannot change at will' (BPF 263–264). Without denying the agonism of the political realm or the courage it takes to appear and act politically, it is important to acknowledge that action is also what humanizes the world. It is never easy to accept that we are powerless to change reality, which is why the political is so vital to humanity—it provides us with a realm in which we can create reality together and more important, reconcile ourselves to what we cannot change by way of a story. This is what the faculty of judgement enables. Thus, although 'it is not possible to be reconciled to Auschwitz. In judging it, however, making it exemplarily valid for what should never have happened, it is possible to be reconciled to the world in which it did happen'.[15] Judgement helps us to be at home in a world that is increasingly inhospitable. In order to better understand this process, let us return to the courtrooms of Jerusalem, in which Arendt began to reflect upon the political importance of judging.

Arendt was intrigued by the fact that the court's legal judgement did not (and could not) offer Eichmann's victims what they sought—a sense of peace and reconciliation with regard to the horrors of the Shoah. Although symbolically Eichmann was on trial for his part in the suffering of European Jewry, she was adamant that the law can only judge particular deeds and present its judgement regarding the breach of a particular set of laws. While Arendt was impressed by the judges' continual clarification of this fact, she nevertheless understood the needs of the audience, most of whom were survivors, to feel at home in the world after their experiences. What was apparent was that the law, while the appropriate framework to try a particular individual such as Eichmann for particular crimes, could not replace the need for some form of public judgement. A legal trial could only offer the world a chance to hear the facts, their manifold and contradictory interpretations (EJ 12), most of which were communicated by means of victim's stories that could not be endured in private (EJ 8).[16]

The trial led Arendt to rethink the meaning of the political in terms of the orientation of one's thinking and actions. While the law could only judge a particular individual for a particular crime, what needed to be addressed and judged concerned humanity itself; it thus called for a worldly perspective. She came to this conclusion when considering the hotly debated question regarding Eichmann: Was he an inhuman monster or was he human, and if so how could he have committed such atrocities? Many of Arendt's readers refused to understand her conclusion that while Eichmann's crimes were horrific his intentions were banal; he was no monster or psychopath, he simply refused to think or judge:

> Those few who were still able to tell right from wrong went really only by their own judgments, and did so freely; there were no rules to be abided by, under which the particular cases with which they were confronted could be subsumed. They had to decide each instance as it arose, because no rules existed for the unprecedented. (EJ 295)

While Arendt's reference here to 'the unprecedented' clearly refers to the Shoah, it is important to clarify that all political action—for better or worse—is unprecedented and as such her conclusion is by no means limited to this event.

In her writings on Eichmann, Arendt has no qualms about the fact that the question of judgement, which she later defines as the political faculty par excellence, is central to ethics. This claim comes in the final pages of *Eichmann in Jerusalem*, where Arendt explores the significance of his crimes, as exemplary of crimes against humanity. Accordingly she states that this is 'the central moral questions of all time, namely upon the nature and function of judgement' (EJ 294). In addition, she clarifies that justice, a term central to Levinas that is much less prominent in Arendt's opus, is a matter of judgement (EJ 296) and that it must always be distinguished from mercy.[17] While I cannot assume that Arendt was familiar with Hebrew, although there is evidence of her interest in the language based on her personal library, it is worth noting that in Hebrew the terms justice and judgement are closely related and sharply distinguished from mercy. What Arendt does say explicitly is that she is concerned that public opinion, greatly influenced by Christianity, often substitutes judgement for mercy, with reference to Luke 6:37, which tells followers not to judge another for fear of being judged. This is yet another means by which Arendt supports her claim that Christianity brought about the depoliticization of the world, a claim that arose previously in her discussion of the will and political freedom. While she does not contrast Christianity to the Judaic, her concern is specifically Christian in that the process of Judaic forgiveness, *teshuvah*, requires both judgement and taking responsibility.

In order to reflect upon the nature of judging, Arendt turns to the same thinker Eichmann has the audacity to cite in his defence—Immanuel Kant. However, she does not find answers in his moral philosophy. 'Since Kant did not write his political philosophy [according to Arendt's definition of the political], the best way to find out what he thought about this matter is to turn to his "Critique of Aesthetic Judgement"' (KL 61). In contrast to Kant's *Critique of Pure Reason* and *Critique of Practical Reason*, aesthetics is a realm in which heteronomy and particularity (KL 26) are present, and as such 'the validity of these judgments never has the validity of cognitive or scientific propositions' (KL 72), which is destructive of plurality. The point she is making by focusing on the Third Critique is that the political realm, like the realm of aesthetics, requires a unique standard for judging. In this vein, she identifies reflective judgements (used to judge beauty in Kant) as political because they '"derive" the rule from the particular [rather than] subsume the particular under a general rule' (KL 83). Reflective judgements create a bridge from the particular to the general, which is politically significant given that actions, and judgements, are always unique events. 'A reflective judgement is made when a jury pronounces what is just in a case though no juror knows what justice itself is. Justice develops through cases as taste develops through a study of exemplary models'.[18]

What Arendt intended to do was to rethink judgement, the third faculty of the life of the mind (as she had done with thinking and willing), in terms of plurality. Based on her lectures on Kant, judging was a two-step process. The first step is a preparatory imaginative one and is followed by a reflective one. By way of these steps Arendt claims that plurality is introduced into the act of judging. Through the use of our faculty of imagination one can enlarge one's mentality, thereby including others in our reflection, an inclusion that creates bonds between people and also provides our judgements with validity beyond the singularity of our own mental activity. The use of one's imagination also allows for the standard of judgement to move from purely subjective towards a more intersubjective perspective. We have the ability to make present to our imagination what is absent by creating a mental place for plurality within the self (which is a duality or two-in-one). This confers judgement with both political and ethical validity (KL 66). Without these distinct perspectives, which the faculty of imagination represents to us after they are no longer present, our world-orientation is reduced to a self-orientation:

> the individual has lost his specific place and become totally 'coordinated' to all others, he has lost his unique perspective on the whole [and] with the loss of these specific and unique and multiple perspectives, the world that arises among them, the world we share in common, disappears.[19]

It is also by means of these representations that the condition of impartiality that strengthens the validity of judgements is fulfilled (KL 66). While there is no objective perspective, the differences between subjective perspectives, like that between different opinions, are exposed to publicity and external challenges and those shielded from the world. The former, intersubjective perspectives, allow for agonism, which opens up the purely subjective view of the self to the views of others (the second step of judgement). In this way, reflective judgements require that we train our imaginations to go visiting, to be open to other interpretations, to be open to plurality. Moreover, Arendt emphasizes that the more we go visiting, ideally to places that are strikingly different than our place of origin, the more 'world' validity our judgements have. Whether or not this imaginative journey alters our opinion is secondary to the fact that this process strengthens the validity of our judgements, moving from the singular towards the general. In addition, the more we are confronted with opposing views, the better our ability to personally and publicly defend our perspective and judgement. In this vein, Arendt seems to consider the importance of Levinasian alterity with regard to judging, because 'in judging these affects we can scarcely help raising the question of selflessness, or rather the question of openness to others, which in fact is the precondition for "humanity" in every sense of that word' (MDT 15).

The implications of this worldly perspective, inspired by Kant's 'enlarged mentality', are that the validity of judgements is determined intersubjectively and does not strive towards universality. Rather than invalidate these judgements for their lack of universality, Arendt reminds us that our plurality and humanity is in fact our greatest strength, as it, unlike universality, comes into existence between people. It has a horizontal transcendence, which arises from the web-of-relations created in the interhuman realm. The validity of judgements is also strengthened by means of publicity, by appearing in the public realm. Given that publicity requires plurality and that spectators only exist in the plural (KL 63), the 'making public' of these mental faculties takes them from the realm of singularity and brings them into the world of the citizens, exposing our judgements to the questioning, examination and challenges of others, which only strengthens them and the shared world. In line with her distinction between truth and opinion, Arendt believes that the latter is best formed in the company of others who challenge our views by requiring that we provide a justification. While critical thinking can be done in isolation, its depth and validity increase exponentially with every critique. The criterion of publicity for the reflective process within political judgements compels, without forcing, the individual to give an account for her position and thereby take responsibility for it. As are actors, spectators—or world participants—are responsible for their judgements. Thus, one enters the public realm—either by acting or judging—and in both cases one becomes part of humanity's (hi)story (KL 41) in that '[the spectators] reaction to the event proves 'the moral character' of mankind' (KL 46).

In disagreement with Kant, Arendt claims that judgements between right and wrong, ethical judgements, are 'grounded', I would add postfoundationally, in a shared interhuman sixth sense (KL 65). It is important to note that Arendt does not call this sense 'objective', but 'nonsubjective', meaning it is not unique to a particular subject. Her terminology implies that the sixth sense arises and exists only between people (like power):

> Judgment . . . always reflects upon others and . . . takes their possible judgments into account. This is necessary because I am human and

> cannot live outside the company of men. I judge as a member of this community and not as a member of a supersensible world. (KL 67)

It is thus neither completely objective nor entirely subjective—it has a status of intersubjective or relational validity—the standard Arendt argues is most appropriate for the political realm. All individuals share reality and this sixth sense, as both require plurality and publicity as their conditions. This latter condition, that of publicity, is significant for yet another reason: it is what allows us to distinguish ourselves as human beings, our ability to speak and communicate. Through 'words and deeds' we persuade and convince others in order to help each other understand our perspective; 'similarly, one can never compel anyone to agree with one's judgments . . . one can only "woo" or "court" agreement of everyone else' (KL 72). Unlike under totalitarian rule, we cannot claim authority based on the Truth or the Law; all 'authority' is intersubjective and arises from within the between. It is also for this reason that our authority is not absolute or universal but particular and limited, that is, in Marchart's terminology, post-foundational.[20] By exercising our ability to publicly communicate, we appeal to others and in so doing reaffirm bonds that manifest the solidarity that defines both the *vita activa* and *contemplativa*.

Arendt's analysis of judging, although incomplete, does provide enough insight to make clear that judgement, like thinking, is fundamental to the political. Judgement, in addition to arising from and sustaining plurality, embraces the post-foundational ground of an intersubjective standard. In so doing judgement has an ethical role, as it strengthens the *polis* by helping to make the world more hospitable, creates a space for plurality in the mind by means of the imagination and demands the publicity and agonism provided by plurality. Arendt herself, in her posthumously published writings, recognizes this very ethical aspect of judging:

> The loss of standards, which does indeed define the modern world in its facticity and cannot be reversed by any sort of return to the good old days or by some arbitrary promulgation of new standards and values, is therefore a catastrophe in the moral world only if one assumes that people are actually incapable of judging things per se, that their faculty of judgement is inadequate for making original judgements. (PP 104)

RESPONSIBILITY: BRIDGING THE *VITA ACTIVA* AND *VITA CONTEMPLATIVA*

While Arendt does not confer a specific structural role on responsibility in her rethinking of the human condition, it is my contention that, when understood as more than a mental state, responsibility bridges the *vita activa* (labour, work and action) and the *vita contemplativa*. Reinterpreting thinking, willing (externalized in freedom) and judging in terms of plurality develops the political significance of the *vita contemplativa*, by making their standard an intersubjective one. Responsibility connects the *vita activa*, and specifically the human condition of action, the space of actualized plurality, to the *vita contemplativa*, the space of imagined or represented plurality. Responsibility therefore has the potential to bridge the gap between thought and action. While there are no guarantees that one's thinking or judgements will lead one to act, or that if one acts one will not harm the world, nonetheless both are preconditions for world-oriented political action. However, responsibility is by no means an unequivocal signifier, and certainly as with all terms Arendt uses, she gives it her own unique meaning.[21] As such, we must consider what Arendt meant by responsibility, and specifically what she meant by political responsibility (which she distinguishes from personal responsibility, and is most often defined as moral responsibility). As with all interhuman activities, Arendt's notion of responsibility must seek a political guarantee that is post-foundational and intersubjective. However, what makes responsibility different is that it calls for a response, in the form of action. Furthermore, what characterizes political responsibility is its worldly orientation. Responsibility for the world not only arises from an orientation rooted in plurality, it is also motivated by the principle of plurality.

Her first essay focused on responsibility, written in 1945, is 'Organised Guilt and Universal Responsibility'. In it she contemplates how the vast majority of German citizens were made to feel responsible for the Shoah by the Allies' post-victory de-Nazification 're-education' campaign. While clearly many people were responsible, Arendt was very uncomfortable with such forms of blanket responsibility. According to her such attempts at universalizing responsibility[22] make it meaningless, because they erase plurality and particularity, both in terms of thinking and acting, reducing them to the same or a form of multiplicity (which is precisely what Levinas claims ontology does to both the other and the third). She draws a parallel to the Nazis' denial of any distinction between innocence and guilt, the first step in the destruction of plurality. By making all Germans responsible, the Allies denied this fundamental plurality (EU 121). Much like thinking and judging, in which two people can both have the same thought or judgement, two people can both be responsible, but this does not mean that their responsibility is equivalent or additive. This logic of equivalence leads to multiplicity (*otherness* or *alteritas* rather than alterity in Levinas's sense), many identical copies of the same rather than plurality. Plurality requires that particularity and differences be recognized and respected. Judgements and responsibility cannot be conceived of in terms of multiplicity, as they arise from distinct unique and noninterchangeable persons. This position, first mentioned in the 1950s, becomes more explicit in her *Kant Lectures*, in that she reinterprets it in terms of Kant's distinction between universal and general (*alleg-*

meine) judgements.[23] In other later writings, she uses the term *collective* responsibility as a synonym for political or plurality. The term collective is political in that it only applies to groups, organizations, institutions, government and nations and so forth. Yet one cannot forget that for Arendt a collective is always a plurality of particulars—in other words, every individual in a collective is distinct.

A further distinction Arendt draws is between political and legal responsibility. The latter is only relevant to crimes previously circumscribed by the juridical system (RJ 21). Legal responsibility is neither personal nor political responsibility. While legal judgements are public and as such can be politicized, it is important to recognize that the courtroom is public but not political; a legal judgement is not equivalent to a political judgement; its standard is the law, which may be influenced by plurality but does not arise from plurality.[24] What interested Arendt most with regard to legal judgements was how Eichmann's judges referred to the notion of conscience that lies within an individual and 'ought' to guide his, and others', actions even in dark times. In Arendt's view, those who acted responsibly during the Shoah did not accept the laws and mores of the Nazis but rather, they thought, judged and acted from the position of people responsible for the world (often supported by their religious convictions) (RJ 45). She was greatly bothered by the fact that the Shoah was proof of how few people heard the voice of their conscience or simply silenced it. That this was, and remains, possible is precisely why she argues for the political realm being reconceptualized in terms of a space of appearance in which we subject our conscience to the public and political test of plurality. Arendt also felt that legal responsibility was limited in a way that political responsibility was not, in that it cannot judge an individual for a sin of omission (RJ 21). While this is both its strength and its weakness, it is clearly not the case for the public realm, in which both types of crimes must be judged to make the shared world more hospitable.

The question of responsibility when there is no political realm, as is the case under a totalitarian regime, is of particular interest today as our public spaces are greatly under threat (especially if one aims to express dissent).[25] According to Arendt, in dark times, 'only those who withdrew from public life altogether, who refused political responsibility [to support the government] of any sort, could avoid becoming implicated in crimes, that is could avoid legal and moral responsibility' (RJ 34). What this means is that in a situation in which the public realm has completely disappeared, the only way to be political is by refusing to participate—which under these conditions requires great courage. Arendt does provide a historical example of this in the 1955 German edition of *Origins*:

> The gas chambers of the Third Reich and the concentration camps in the Soviet Union have disrupted the continuity of occidental history

> because in reality nobody can assume responsibility for them. At the same time they pose a threat to the solidarity among people which is a prerequisite for our taking the risk to access and judge the actions of others.[26]

The enormity of the crimes is such that no one can assume responsibility, which makes any form of political responsibility impossible. Under such conditions, when collective political responsibility is no longer possible, personal responsibility can become political, as individuals can take responsibility for the shared world by refusing to participate in its destruction. While this form of personal responsibility under dictatorships is to be applauded, it remains fundamentally problematic for Arendt because personal responsibility, unlike political responsibility, does not strengthen the *polis* by creating 'solidarity'. In this sense, political responsibility is comparable to promises and forgiveness, as it helps strengthen the fragile bonds that support the human realm.

In the essay 'Truth and Politics', Arendt provides an interesting example of the intersection between judgement and responsibility. In her analysis of propaganda, or political lies, she states that lying can destroy the fabric or reality by eroding the *sensus communis* (257). In these situations, simply countering these lies is a form of action that helps to strengthen the human realm. By judging propaganda to be factually untrue and by publicly pronouncing one's judgement, one is both an actor and a spectator. In this way we are each, individually, responsible for contributing to the creation of the shared world, and by denying this responsibility we deny the world. Through our judgements we become participants in the public world, helping to affirm—whether by agreeing or disagreeing with—the plurality of perspectives presented by the community. In this way we both teach and learn from others, thereby recognizing our connection to others, the basis of our humanity.

According to Arendt, 'what is finally left of our sense of international solidarity [after the Shoah]; and it has not yet found an adequate political expression' (EU 131), is an elemental shame.[27] What is striking about this claim is that shame is interpreted here as being potentially political significant. Shame is symbolic of this lost solidarity and thus, if it appears in public, it is a reminder of what was destroyed. Shame, in its personal manifestation, is a residual feeling rooted in responsibility for others, and in this sense is directed towards others, towards the world. Shame is an affective trace of a sense of collective or political responsibility, of our 'solidarity' with others, of our shared humanity. More importantly, it further demonstrates that responsibility cannot be founded on the same basis as a philosophy of rights—that of the singular subject.[28] While a philosophy of rights remains valid when there is but a single soul on the planet, responsibility (and shame) is inconceivable without others, without plurality. For this reason it can be conceived of in terms of a world without plurality that both Arendt and Levinas are highly critical of rights discourse:[29]

> The hands of God are closed. The rationality of nature, the self-evidence of reason and the progress of history have given way to the death camps and holes of oblivion, leaving us facing nothing but ourselves. For Arendt, humanity itself must guarantee the right to have rights, or the right of every individual to belong to humanity. . . . Arendt refuses simply to abandon the idea of humanity. Indeed, she argues that such abandonment is impossible insofar as the idea of humanity 'which for all preceding generations was no more than a concept to an ideal, has become something of an urgent reality'.[30]

Fundamental to Arendt's notion of political responsibility is the emphasis on inclusion, 'excluding no people'—this is what she means when she refers to the term humanity. 'In political terms the idea of humanity, excluding no people and assigning a monopoly of guilt to no one, is the only guarantee [that one group will not try to exterminate another]' (EU 131).

By introducing plurality into the *vita contemplativa*, Arendt makes an appeal to the idea of humanity and as such to the inclusion of all others, coming very close to ideas that are central to Levinas's ethics:

> For our purposes, however, it is important that humanity manifests itself in such brotherhood most frequently in 'dark times'. This kind of humanity actually becomes inevitable when the times become so extremely dark for certain groups of people that it is no longer up to them, their insight or choice, to withdraw from the world. (MDT 13)

Arendt's desire to recover the political is precisely to prevent situations—such as during the Shoah—when a group of people are forced, because of what (not who) they are, out of the shared world. This exclusion of 'others' leads to their radical worldlessness and destroys the shared world for all people:

> Humanity in the form of fraternity invariably appears historically among persecuted people and enslaved groups. . . . This kind of humanity is the great privilege of pariah peoples; it is the advantage that the pariahs of this world always and in all circumstances can have over others. The privilege is dearly bought; it is often accompanied by so radical a loss of the world, so fearful an atrophy of all organs with which we respond to it—starting with the common sense with which we orient ourselves in a world common to ourselves and others. (MDT 13)

What Arendt comes to understand in her later writings is that the worldlessness, first analysed in *Origins*, can only be combatted when the *vita activa* is not disconnected from the *vita contemplativa*, a connection made by responsibility. 'We humanize what is going on in the world and in ourselves only by speaking of it, and in the course of speaking of it we learn to be human' (MDT 25). To take responsibility for the world, to engage with the world is what Arendt defines as humanizing ourselves and the world. This taking of responsibility is something we do as individuals, and yet as it affects the shared world it is political. Recognizing that we each have a unique contribution to offer the world and allowing this to inspire action is to take responsibility.

However, inasmuch as political responsibility is collective, it is 'everybody's business' (RJ 35), that is every individual body's responsibility. One cannot simply assume that someone else will take responsibility; each one of us is called to act upon our judgements. While not everyone can be a saint or hero, this does not make everyone any less responsible, as *everything* we do (or don't do) affects the shared world.[31] If one considers the implications, heavy as they are, of this claim, it becomes clear that Arendt's notion of responsibility is almost as demanding as that of Levinas (to be explored in the following chapter). Arendt—like Levinas—acknowledges that we are never 'free' from responsibility. While Arendt limits political responsibility to the public realm, it nonetheless remains a heavy burden, in that we are responsible for repairing the world even if we were not part of it when the harm was done.

Another interesting similarity between Arendt and Levinas with regard to responsibility is how it is often to be found in small acts of kindness that every one of us can choose to perform every day. Based on the experience of the Shoah, in which so many denied taking any responsibility, Arendt and Levinas try to conceive of responsibility in such a way that the common excuse, 'it's just too much for one person to make a difference', is not an acceptable response. According to Arendt, each and every act of responsibility strengthens the fragile web-of-relations that supports the world and is thus important. Every little deed counts. This makes responsibility much more difficult to evade. They reject the justification for denying responsibility because it is too great a burden. This makes sense, as neither views life as easy, or made only for one's enjoyment; life—especially in terms of the interhuman realm—is demanding (or difficult, for Levinas). Even those expelled from the shared world, as Jews were during the Shoah, are not excused from acting responsibly. Refusing to take responsibility is also a means to deny one's agency. She makes this point with reference to the *Judernat*'s responsibility in the ghettos (EJ 117) and in the essay 'On Humanity in Dark Times', when she asks: 'To what extent do we remain obligated to a world even when we have been expelled from it or have withdrawn from it?' (MDT 22). Her answer is clear: there is no outside of the world. As such there is no way to refuse taking responsibility for the world.[32]

Nonetheless, Arendt is painfully aware that the space for responsibility in a totalitarian regime is almost nonexistent. However, as her account of the two-in-one and of 'men in dark times' (like Lessing) shows, there is always space for humanity within one's mind. 'When men are deprived of the public space—which is constituted by acting together and then fills of its own accord with the events and stories that develop into history—they retreat into their freedom of thought' (MDT 9). What is striking about Arendt's reflection on Lessing is that she shows, through his exemplarity, that it is possible to remain political, to think and judge from the perspective of plurality and humanity, even when the public realm disappears, by representing it in one's mind and continuing to think, judge and act upon this basis (MDT 9, 26–27). In this vein, the *vita contemplativa* is politicized, as plurality has been introduced as one of its conditions.

ASSESSING ARENDT'S POLITICAL ETHICS

Having focused on the notion of plurality in Arendt's opus—the principle of the political she proposes to counter the destruction of the shared world under totalitarianism, a destructive tendency still present in contemporary democracies—it is now time to do some reflective bookkeeping. Contrary to a common reading of Arendt as hostile to all forms of morality in the political, we identified her appreciation for a particular type of ethics, one that arises from within the *polis* and strengthens its inherent fragility. In her personal correspondence, Arendt confirms that this was indeed her goal: 'It really is important to me to "create the foundations of a new political morality" although out of modesty I never did say so explicitly'.[33] It is now time to judge Arendt's attempts to create a new foundation for political ethics by considering their strengths and weaknesses. The first question to answer is why Arendt believes that the 'resolution' must be first and foremost a political one (as opposed to ethical, for example, as Levinas believes). Second, we can consider what kind of ethics can arise from within her vision of the political. Third, the question is whether her political ethics is enough given the state of contemporary democratic societies.

On what basis does Arendt justify her position that the destruction of the shared world, systematically undertaken by totalitarian regimes, is a political problem? If we can understand the answer to this question, we can appreciate why she claims it requires a political response. Let us recall what the term political, in its most condensed form, means for Arendt. First, 'plurality is specifically *the* condition—not only the *condition since qua non,* but the *condition per quam*—of all political life' (HC 7) and 'action . . . corresponds to the human condition of plurality' (HC 7). In other words something is political if its activity arises from the interaction of people. While Arendt refines this account of the political by introducing notions of publicity, temporality, space and so forth, its fundamental meaning is unaffected. In this vein, one can define an Arendtian political problem as a problem that is shared by those living together and inhabiting the world. It is for this reason that Arendt saw both totalitarianism and the Shoah as political problems that required political responses. A public and worldly reply is needed to a public and worldly problem. While the 'victims', a term that should by no means be understood as a denial of anyone's political agency, were particular people or groups, all of whom were singled out because they were different (such as the Jews, Romas, the disabled and homosexuals among other persecuted groups and individuals), their exclusion from the shared world and eventual elimination from the earth concerned all peoples. This idea is well articulated by rabbis in the Talmud: 'Whoever destroys even a single life . . . scripture regards him as if he had destroyed an entire world'.[34] While suffering is subjective and cannot (and should not) be compared, it is important to recall that everyone suffers when the world is harmed:

> The possibility that extermination of whole ethnic groups—the Jews, or the Poles, or the Gypsies [*sic*]—might be more than a crime against the Jewish or the Polish or the Gypsy people, that the international order, and mankind in its entirety, might have been grievously hurt and endangered. (EJ 275–276)

Arendt, rare among her 'co-religionists' (who were very critical of her on this point), claimed that being attacked as a Jew called for a political rather than an ethical response. In her opinion, one of the greatest problems of Jews, throughout history, is that their factual, often legally justified, exclusion from the *polis* (e.g., as established by church law as of the Fourth Lateran Council in 1215) led Jews to see the world in moral terms at the cost of the political. While she does not deny that the Shoah can be described as an ethical failure on the part of humanity, and would not disagree with Levinas, who views anti-Semitism as an expression of an allergic reaction to alterity, she was acutely aware that ethics was often misunderstood to be a private or purely moral affair, which neither the Shoah nor totalitarianism was. It is only within the political, which of course includes ethics, which is also an interhuman event rooted in plurality, that the public expression of this world-destruction can be challenged.

While in one sense taking the political as our explicit starting point, as Arendt does, means rejecting approaches, such as Levinas's, that view the political from the lens of alterity (rather than plurality), taking the political as our starting point is by no means a rejection of ethics *tout court*. What I hope to have demonstrated in this chapter is that Arendt rejects morality, that is, absolutism and foundationalism, which she defines as external threats to plurality imposed from beyond the *polis*. By contrast, she esteems an ethics that arises from within the *polis* and embraces its plurality—a post-foundational ethics. But ethics means more than post-foundationality for Arendt; it means valuing the gift plurality brings to the shared world—a gift Levinas recognizes in terms of alterity. Prioritizing the political over morality is also a way for Arendt to recognize and appreciate the fact and gift of plurality as well as its paradoxical nature as rooted in both equality and distinction. Defining the political in terms of plurality means viewing difference, and alterity, as a fact, and ideally as an enriching one rather than a stumbling block. Practically, this means questioning our attempts to seek consensus and unity, often by force, and looking for similarities in our interactions with others in the public realm.

While difference can certainly be disorienting, according to Arendt (and Levinas, as we will explore in the next chapter), this difference arises from within the unity I project to others in the public realm. There is a difference inserted into my oneness, which is what makes the two-in-one both possible and desirable (LM 183). Being one, or having an identity in Arendt's account, means that the 'I', or self, is not reducible to the 'me', or myself (LM 184). In this vein the 'I' does not in fact need plurality to create difference; it carries the difference that is plurality within itself. The two-in-one can keep itself company, even in dark times, as long as it does not seek to silence its own difference. The discomfort we might experience in the public realm when interacting with others, who are always different than the self, is a discomfort we must also address in isolation from others. There is no escape from either. While there is no doubt that differences can be difficult to deal with, this may be due to the fact that we assume that this difference is a problem rather than a blessing. Arendt's *amor mundi*, her prioritization of the political, is an expression of gratitude for the plurality of the shared world. However, her gratitude should by no means be understood as naiveté. Arendt understood how much courage and risk it took to engage with and in the world. It is because of the intense fragility of the interhuman realm and the courage required to act that Arendt appreciated all attempts to strengthen the political realm—as long as these attempts do not threaten its fundamental plurality.

Ethics, as long as it arises from within the political and thus shares its condition of plurality, is necessary for the political. In this chapter we have seen how Arendt identifies several forms of political ethics. Forgiveness allows for human errors to be overcome, allowing us to connect the lived and experienced in the present to the past. Promises connect present actions to the future and in so doing give us hope and inspire us to take responsibility for those to come. Thinking, rooted in a represented plurality, is a space for others in one's mind. It is fundamentally ethical, as it continuously tills the soil, preventing banisters from being planted, banisters that lead to the thoughtless that is so dangerous to the world. Judgement, closely connected to the temporality of promises and forgiveness, allows us to reconcile ourselves to the past and to imagine an alternative future. Furthermore, it helps us to be at home in a world that is increasingly becoming inhospitable. Responsibility is the means by which we are each asked to step into the *polis* and to act with others in order to create a shared world in which all forms of difference can feel at home. All of these activities are means to strengthen the unpredictability of Arendt's new post-foundational political principle of plurality and thereby help to make the world more inclusive and hospitable.

However, this Arendtian political ethics rooted in plurality will by no means be an easy balance to achieve. Too much stability and the political disappears, too little stability and it is taken over by those who refuse to recognize plurality as the heart of the human condition. This fundamental instability is a constant reminder of vigilance needed when it comes to human interactions. However, the interhuman realm's fragility and contingency is also part of its potency and appeal. Because of its unpredictability, anything is possible, reality can be changed for better or worse, the world can be transformed and as such each one of us can be transformed. In this sense maybe what Arendt writes when describing thinking, which is equally contingent, can be applied to the political. 'The business of thinking is like the veil of Penelope: it undoes every morning what it had finished the night before' (RJ 166). Perhaps the best means to safeguard the plurality of the political is to recognize that we must never allow ourselves to get too comfortable and to assume that the world does not need to be (re)-repaired. As such, it is up to each of us to find a difficult balance between our desires for stability and for change. Between the way the world is and the way we want (or hope) it to be.

While I believe there is enough evidence in Arendt's writings to justify the claim that she has such an implicit political ethics, it would be incorrect to claim that she ever made this explicit or completed this project. As such, it is important to acknowledge that what I have characterized as Arendt's political ethics is in need of further elaboration. While she implicitly recognized that alterity is fundamental to plurality, she never considers what is central to Levinas's approach, his ethics of alterity. While she refers to *alteritas*, by which she does not mean alterity in Levinas's sense, her only attempt at theorizing alterity is in her rather vague discussions of difference and otherness with regard to the two-in-one or the difference in the self. We can only imagine that if she had lived longer and completed her writings on judgement, she might have filled this lacuna. Perhaps Arendt allowed a banister to prevent her from thinking about the ethics of plurality; she repeatedly limited morality to a Kantian framework rooted in singularity and autonomy.

Inspired by Arendt's political project and the importance of thinking without banisters, I take this opportunity and responsibility to think about the possibility of an ethics of plurality. I do so, as discussed in the introduction, by turning to Levinas's ethics of alterity. While there are certainly many fundamental differences between their projects, which is why we cannot simply reduce alterity to plurality, I believe that Levinas's ethics as first philosophy, like Arendt's rethinking of the political, seeks a new post-foundational guarantee of human dignity rooted in difference.

In other words, I argue that Arendt and Levinas are inspired by the same principle, a principle that arises from their shared background in terms of phenomenology, Heidegger, the experience of the Shoah and the Judaic. As intimated above, this principle has echoes in the Talmudic adage 'whoever destroys even a single life . . . scripture regards him as if he had destroyed an entire world. And whoever saves a single soul in Israel [which means all people and not the State], Scripture regards him as if he preserved the entire world'.[35] While for Levinas the starting point, and focus, is the avoidance of the destruction of the single life, for Arendt, her starting point and focus is preserving the world. Both agree on the principle but not from which perspective to approach it, a truly phenomenological quarrel. Given Arendt's claim that 'our decisions about right and wrong depend upon our choice of company' (RJ 145–146), I feel that my choice to turn to Levinas, and to bring their respective thinking together by way of a staged dialogue, is clearly justified, as my own ambition is develop a political ethics of relationality that embraces both of their perspectives.

NOTES

1. And has now been turned into a film; see www.zeitgeistfilms.com/film.php?directoryname=hannaharendt.
2. A lecture course published in *Social Research* 38, no. 3 (Autumn 1971): 417–446. Reprinted in *Social Research* 51, no. 1 (Spring 1984): 7–37 and in *Responsibility and Judgment* (2003).
3. In agreement with Jacques Taminiaux, there is clearly an ethical preoccupation in Arendt's thought that arises from its very beginnings, between 'Athens and Jerusalem'. In Anne Kupiec et al., *Hannah Arendt, crises de l'Etat-nation: Pensées alternatives* (Paris: Sens & Tonka, 2007), 306.
4. Peg Birmingham, *Hannah Arendt and Human Rights: The Predicament of Common Responsibility* (Bloomington: Indiana University Press, 2006), 131.
5. Oliver Marchart, *Post-Foundational Political Thought: Political Difference in Nancy, Lefort, Badiou and Laclau* (Edinburgh, Scotland: Edinburgh University Press, 2007).
6. Veronica Vasterling on Hannah Arendt in *The Routledge Companion to Phenomenology*, ed. Sebastian Luft, and Soren Overgaard (London: Routledge, 2013), 87.
7. Liisi Keedus, 'Liberalism and the Question of "The Proud": Hannah Arendt and Leo Strauss as Readers of Hobbes', *Journal of the History of Ideas* 73, no. 2 (2012): 319–341, doi:10.1353/jhi.2012.0017; Peter Graf Kielmansegg, Horst Mewes, and Elisabeth Glaser-Schmidt, eds., *Hannah Arendt and Leo Strauss: German Émigrés and American Political Thought after World War II* (Washington, D.C.; Cambridge, England; New York: Cambridge University Press, 1997).
8. Annelies Degryse, 'The Sovereign and the Social', *Ethical Perspectives* 15, no. 2 (30 June 2008): 239, doi:10.2143/EP.15.2.2032369.
9. By explicitly connecting covenants to the act of making mutual promises, Arendt—possibly unknowingly—taps into a rich Jewish tradition based on covenental politics. For more on this see Michael Walzer et al., eds., *The Jewish Political Tradition*, vol. 2, *Membership* (New Haven, Conn.; London: Yale University Press, 2006); Jonathan Sacks, *The Dignity of Difference: How to Avoid the Clash of Civilizations*, 2nd ed. (London: Bloomsbury Academic, 2003); Jonathan Sacks, *To Heal a Fractured World: The Ethics of Responsibility* (New York: Schocken, 2007); Jonathan Sacks, *Covenant & Conversation: A*

Weekly Reading of the Jewish Bible, Genesis: The Book of Beginnings, ed. Koren Publishers Jerusalem (New Milford, Conn.: Koren Publishers Jerusalem, 2009); Jonathan Sacks, *The Home We Build Together: Recreating Society*, 1st ed. (New York: Continuum, 2009).

10. While many Arendt scholars argue that Arendt is a neo-Aristotelian, this reading is often constructed by way of a Habermasian lens in which the agonism and performative aspects of the political are downplayed. Dana R. Villa, 'Beyond Good and Evil: Arendt, Nietzsche, and the Aestheticization of Political Action', *Political Theory* 20, no. 2 (1 May 1992): 274–308; Jacques Taminiaux, 'Bios Politikos and Bios Theoretikos in the Phenomenology of Hannah Arendt', *International Journal of Philosophical Studies* 4, no. 2 (1 September 1996): 215–232. Nonetheless Arendt does on several occasions reaffirm that Aristotle emphasizes praxis, which is essential to her understanding of the political in that it is what lets the actor or agent manifest herself.

11. Dana Villa, *Arendt and Heidegger: The Fate of the Political* (Princeton, N.J.: Princeton University Press, 1995), 52.

12. As she also argues, a good parent should do this, in her essay 'Crisis in Education'; for more on this see Anya Topolski, 'Creating Citizens in the Classroom', *Ethical Perspectives* 15, no. 2 (30 June 2008): 259–282, doi:10.2143/EP.15.2.2032370.

13. Larry May and Jerome Kohn, *Hannah Arendt: Twenty Years Later* (Cambridge, Mass.: MIT Press, 1997), 161.

14. Elizabeth Minnich, 'To Judge in Freedom: Hannah Arendt on the Relation of Thinking and Morality', in Gisela T. Kaplan, *Hannah Arendt: Thinking, Judging, Freedom*, ed. Clive S. Kessler (Sydney: Allen & Unwin, 1990), 139.

15. May and Kohn, *Hannah Arendt*, 174.

16. This point reminds us of Arendt's conception of the public as a place within which to 'deal' with tensions that lie within us but cannot be healed from within.

17. Anya Topolski, '*Tzedakah*: The True Religion of Spinoza's *Tractatus*?' *History of Political Thought* 36, no. 3 (2015).

18. Michael Denneny, 'The Privilege of Ourselves: Hannah Arendt on Judgment', in *Hannah Arendt: The Recovery of the Public World*, ed. Melvyn A. Hill (New York: St. Martin's Press, 1979), 251–252. Arendt also shared, in a letter to Jaspers her own experience as a jury member: 'The whole business is really quite wonderful. You sit together with people from all classes, and the deliberations are very impressive, on the one hand because everyone takes the matter of justice very seriously and on the other because everyone is very happy to be there even if it means a significant loss of money and time for just about everyone. It is a duty of citizenship, and people are happy to assume it. And they perform it without any pretensions'. Hannah Arendt and Karl Jaspers, *Correspondence 1926 –1969* (San Diego: Mariner Books, 1993), 616.

19. Denneny, 'The Privilege of Ourselves',

20. Oliver Marchart, *Post-Foundational Political Thought: Political Difference in Nancy, Lefort, Badiou and Laclau*. Edinburgh: Edinburgh University Press, 2007.

21. As is often the case, Arendt provides her readers with distinctions rather than definitions by referring to the following kinds of responsibility: personal, legal, moral, political, collective and universal. Given her well-known distinction between the private and public, one would assume that this may apply here, but Arendt is quick to refuse mapping responsibility onto the private-public distinction. It is therefore important not to associate personal responsibility with the private realm or to equate the political with either universal or collective responsibility. To demonstrate that personal responsibility can be either private or public, Arendt uses the example of Hitler, who she claims was both personally and politically responsible (RJ 30).

22. Although she does use the term universal responsibility in several essays from the 1940s (EU), in her latter writings she eliminates it, stating that universal responsibility is both an empty term and an oxymoron.

23. She intentionally mistranslates Kant's use of *allgemeine* as general rather than as universal (KL 70–71).

24. Here the distinction between natural and positive law becomes interesting, as the former is clearly grounded in foundational claims, whereas the latter could be said

to have more horizontal or intersubjective grounds, although it would not celebrate its own contingency.

25. Margaret Kohn, *Radical Space: Building the House of the People* (Ithaca, N.Y.: Cornell University Press, 2003); Don Mitchell, 'The End of Public Space? People's Park, Definitions of the Public, and Democracy', *Annals of the Association of American Geographers* 85, no. 1 (1 March 1995): 108–133, doi:10.1111/j.1467-8306.1995.tb01797.xa; Don Mitchell, *The Right to the City: Social Justice and the Fight for Public Space* (New York: Guilford Press, 2003); Simon Springer, 'Public Space as Emancipation: Meditations on Anarchism, Radical Democracy, Neoliberalism and Violence', *Antipode* 43, no. 2 (1 March 2011): 525–562, doi:10.1111/j.1467-8330.2010.00827.x.

26. Hannah Arendt, *Elemente und Ursprünge totaler Herrschaft: Antisemitismus, Imperialismus, Totale Herrschaft.* Neuausg. Auflage. (Zürich: Piper Taschenbuch, 1991), 704.

27. She distinguishes shame from guilt in that the latter is singular and solipsistic.

28. Martine Leibovici, *Hannah Arendt* (Paris: Desclée de Brouwer, 2000), 137.

29. Anya Topolski, 'Relationality as a "Foundation" for Human Rights: Exploring the Paradox with Hannah Arendt and Emmanuel Levinas', *Theoria and Praxis: International Journal of Interdisciplinary Thought* 2, no. 1 (6 August 2014), pi.library.yorku.ca/ojs/index.php/theoriandpraxis/article/view/39373.

30. Birmingham, *Hannah Arendt and Human Rights*, 6.

31. In addition, it is interesting that both Levinas and Arendt refer to saints in relation to responsibility. This is intriguing in that there are no saints in Judaism, and as such this is an example of the influence of Christian culture in their thought.

32. The same is true of Arendt's discussion of participation. Although the issue of voluntary participation becomes a nonissue under tyrannical or totalitarian rule, its inverse, the choice not to participate, remains open to citizens. By contrast, citizens in a democratic state are asked to freely participate. While this request to participate can be made on ethical grounds, Arendt makes it first and foremost on political grounds, arguing that it is for the sake of the world, which is created through the participation of its citizens, through human interaction. While there is clearly a strong ethical argument to be made for participation, Arendt wants to recreate an ethics within the *polis*, one that is based on the particularity of plurality rather than singularity. As such, participation is understood as necessary for the world, for the creation of a shared reality as a means to make the world hospitable and to guarantee human dignity.

33. Hannah Arendt, Letter to Meier-Cronenmeyer, 18 July 1963 (The Hannah Arendt Papers at the Library of Congress), memory.loc.gov/cgi-bin/ampage?collId=mharendt&fileName=03/030100/030100page.db&recNum=20.

34. Rabbi Adin Steinsaltz, *The Talmud*, vol. 15, *The Steinsaltz Edition: Tractate Sanhedrin, Part 1* (New York: Random House, 1996), sec. 37a.

35. Ibid.

III

On Emmanuel Levinas

Before plunging into Levinas's project, a clarificatory caveat is called for. Contrary to most philosophical approaches to Levinas's thought, I do not follow a strict separation between his 'so-called' philosophical and 'so-called confessional' writings.[1] Levinas expressed himself, certainly in his more mature works, in a language particular to his thought, a language that allows for a dialogue between Jewish thought and Greek philosophy and that challenges the symbolic boundaries between Athens and Jerusalem.

> In contrast to many modern exponents of Judaism, and potentially to his credit, Levinas did not understand the Talmud and modernity in mutually exclusive terms; and his attempt to reinterpret the Talmud, rather than reject it, in his reinvention of Judaism for modern times has to be seen as an act of exceptional daring.[2]

I thus see the term Judaic as expressing the unique interaction of two modes of wisdom both of which are vital for Levinas's thought. It is more than a simple translation of 'Greek' to 'Hebrew' (or vice-versa); it is more than a case of two parallel languages, one for Jews, the other for philosophers. For this reason I affirm Ephraim Meir's position that 'there is a clear relation between the two types of writing practiced by Levinas. They are inseparable'[3] What this means is that one cannot fully understand Levinas's unless one is willing to consider how he brings together ideas from Jewish thought and Greek philosophy. Practically, this requires that one read—and take seriously—*both* his so-called confessional and philosophical writings. Levinas uses the terms confessional and philosophical because of the increasingly secularised ethos within which he wrote as well as the expectations of his different audiences.[4] His later writings openly intertwine literary, philosophical and Judaic sources, a style which was less evident in the earlier works that were published at a time when religion and philosophy were seen to be at odds with each other.[5] The fact that he refers to these as so-called (*dits* in French) indicates that it was an artificial separation that played only a secondary role in his thought. For this reason, I move freely between all of LevinasMeir's essays.

Caveat completed, let us now consider the structure of part 3 dedicated to the work of Levinas. Parallel to part 2 on Hannah Arendt, part 3 is composed of two chapters dedicated to Levinas's ethics and the notion of alterity. It is specifically his notion of alterity that I seek to engage in dialogue with Arendt's notion of plurality as a means to strengthen the political from within. In chapter 4, I consider how Levinas develops his own answer, in terms of ethics, to the same question that inspired Arendt to turn to the political. In this vein, I trace the genealogy of his response to Heidegger from a critique of ontology to his claim that ethics is first philosophy. Levinas persuasively demonstrates in his early writings that our common sense approach to ethics need to be questioned and is thus equally critical of what Arendt defines as a morality rooted in singularity. With this critical resonance as a basis for dialogue, I consider the meaning of responsibility in Levinas as a bridge to Arendt's thought. In chapter 5, I focus on Levinas's notion of the political, a topic often overshadowed by his discussion of ethics. While we do not deny the many difficulties related to Levinas's politics, it is equally necessary to consider that his politics is by no means a tangential reflection, especially if one considers the discussions in so-called Judaic writings. The goal of this chapter is to see how Levinas himself transforms the notion of alterity when it is introduced into the political, and secondly to consider whether it has a place in Arendt's *polis*.

NOTES

1. Anya Topolski, "Listening to the Language of the Other," in *Radical Passivity*, ed. Benda Hofmeyr, Library of Ethics and Applied Philosophy 20 (Springer Netherlands, 2009), 111–31, link.springer.com/chapter/10.1007/978-1-4020-9347-0_8.

2. Samuel Moyn, "Emmanuel Levinas's Talmudic Readings: Between Tradition and Invention," *Prooftexts* 23, no. 3 (2003): 11, doi:10.1353/ptx.2004.0007.

3. Danielle Cohen-Levinas and Shmuel Trigano, *Emmanuel Levinas: Philosophie et judaïsme* (Paris: In Press, 2002), 127.

"Il existe cependant une relation claire et nette entre les deux sortes d'ecriture pratiquee par Levinas. Ells sont inseparables."

4. Based on his own admission (RTB 37) and related by Marc-Alain Ouaknin, one of Levinas' students (in a lecture series held at the Martin Buber Centre of the Université Libre de Bruxelles, 2006) Levinas initially was not confident that the Talmudic tradition was an appropriate source for philosophical reflection. Later, he realised there was no reason to exclude a source which was so important to Western thought as long as it was not used, unchallenged, to prove an argument. He later clarified that while he often found his inspiration in a verse, he felt that it was important to complement it with a philosophical, and more specifically a phenomenological, line of inquiry. It is this affirmation that led him to state that "philosophical discourse must therefore be able to embrace God—of whom the Bible speaks" (1998, 56).

5. Jeffrey L. Kosky, *Levinas and the Philosophy of Religion* (Bloomington: Indiana University Press, 2001).

FIVE

Levinas's Ethics

From Ontology to Alterity

In this chapter I trace the genealogy of Levinas's ethics from a critique of the ontological tradition defended by Heidegger to his claim that ethics is first philosophy (and precedes ontology). While this was a gradual process, there are certain decisive moments to investigate. As with Arendt, Levinas was fascinated by Heidegger's variation of the phenomenological tradition and began his career by introducing French intellectuals to the work of Husserl and Heidegger. Precipitated by historical events, which Levinas seems to have grasped very early on (see his 1934 essay on Hitlerism), he felt it necessary to challenge and question Heidegger's ontological project, without rejecting the phenomenological methodology. In light of the rise of anti-Semitism and Heidegger's rectoral address, both Arendt and Levinas felt called to question what they had learned from Heidegger and the philosophical tradition upon which his thought had been developed. Arendt chose to reinterpret the tradition from within by means of innovative readings of figures such as Socrates and Kant, whereas Levinas, having taken this approach in his initial post-Shoah writings, later chose to both complement and challenge the 'Athenian' tradition from the perspective of 'Jerusalem' (whether Jewish thought is part of the Western tradition or its 'other' is a much larger discussion[1]). Levinas was familiar with Judaism (the religious practice) from childhood, but only discovered its full riches—in terms of the Talmudic tradition—after the war. While it is possible to separate his notion of alterity from this latter Judaic source, it would be unfaithful to the genealogy of Levinas's notion of ethics and lead to an impoverished understanding of his distinctly Judaic ethical-phenomenological approach.

FROM ONTOLOGY TO ETHICS

The importance of Levinas's debt to Heidegger, Husserl and the phenomenological tradition is evident from some of his earliest published essays which include the 1929 'Sur les "Ideen" de M. E. Husserl'[2] and the 1932 'Martin Heidegger et l'ontologie'.[3] This inheritance is still very much present in several of his earliest works written prior to the 1950s, such as *Théorie de l'intuition dans la phénoménologie de Husserl* (1930), *De l'évasion* (1935), *De l'existence à l'existent* (1947), *Le Temps et l'Autre* (1948), and *En Découvrant l'existence avec Husserl et Heidegger* (1949).[4] In these early writings, Levinas defines ontology as 'the science of the *being of a being*. . . . It is the study of man which is going to reveal to us the horizon within which the problem of being arises, for it is here that *the understanding of being comes about*'.[5] Although Levinas does distance himself from Heidegger's ontological project, it is important not to lose sight of the fact that his intellectual debt to Heidegger is inestimable. Both Levinas and Arendt were inspired by Heidegger to challenge the abstract and theoretical approaches, which were prevalent in the tradition they had studied prior to their interaction with Husserl and Heidegger.[6] While Levinas and Arendt eventually redirect the phenomenological method to subjects in relation (in terms of the face-to-face or plurality[7]) rather than to *Dasein*, certain fundamental Heideggerian presuppositions (see chapter 1) continue to play a pivotal role in their thinking. Take for example Levinas's claim that 'the analysis of the World thus becomes the central component of the *Analytic of Dasein*, for it allows us to rejoin subjectivity to finitude, the theory of knowledge to ontology, and truth to being'.[8]

In some ways Arendt and Levinas did precisely what they understood Heidegger to be doing by studying what it means to be a human being; where they disagreed with Heidegger was with regard to the fact that human beings could be understood in their singularity. Rather than presenting their early writings as a rejection of Heidegger's project, they can be understood as an alternative approach, in which forms of *mitsein*, are prioritized over *Dasein*. The trace of *mitsein* fades, but its trace certainly remains in their respective notions of plurality and alterity, which eventually take priority over ontology, the study of *Dasein*. Levinas first announces this change in the introduction to *Existence and Existents*: 'If at the beginning our reflections are in large measure inspired by the philosophy of Martin Heidegger . . . they are also governed by a profound need to leave the climate of that philosophy'.[9] In the 1979 English reprinting of the 1935 *On Escape*, Levinas claims he took his first steps away from Heidegger by presenting his position as an enhancement of Heidegger's ontology. This development continues in *Time and the Other* in Levinas's threefold approach to subjectivity, the 'third' part that clearly goes beyond Heidegger, although there is not yet an explicit relation to a phenomenology of alterity. 'The mastery of the Ego over being's anonymous *there is* (*il y a*), forthwith the reversal of the Self over the Ego. . . . Next there is what is said of the world . . . knowledge . . . enjoyment . . . absorbing every *other*. . . . Finally, there is what is said of the relationship with the Other, the feminine, the child, of the fecundity of the Ego'.[10] While this threefold account of subjectivity is never denied in Levinas's later writings, it is rarely reiterated. Instead, the relationship with the Other and its role in constituting the self takes centre stage.

Additional evidence of Levinas's taking distance from both Husserl and Heidegger is evident in his account of knowledge in the 1940s. His criticism of both thinkers is based on his conclusion that their philosophy gives priority to knowledge over alterity. Studying and knowledge are now characterized as part of the absorption of the other. 'It must be understood that morality comes not as a secondary layer, above an abstract reflection on the totality and its dangers; morality has an independent and preliminary range. First philosophy is an ethics' (EI 77). Levinas's bold claim that ethics precedes ontology is first declared, and later fully articulated, in the essays published just prior to his doctoral dissertation *Totality and Infinity*, although its full meaning and connection to the Shoah only becomes explicit in his later writings. This does not mean that references to the Shoah are not already present in this period. Evidence of this is his notion of the *il y a*, an aspect of his earlier account of subjectivity that fades into the background, was written during the war. The *il y a* is associated with darkness, turmoil, nausea and insomnia and clearly tied to Levinas's horrifying war experiences.[11] In this vein, understanding Levinas's early writings, like those of Hannah Arendt from the 1950s, one must consider them as responding to both Heidegger's ontological project and the horrors of World War II.

Levinas's 1951 publication, 'Is Ontology Fundamental?' (BPW), not only explicitly criticizes the ontological tradition; it also presents the central argument of *Totality and Infinity*. Although he realized that it was 'reckless to question the primacy of ontology' (BPW 2), Levinas felt compelled to do so. It is thus our task to consider why Levinas felt it was necessary to challenge the ontological tradition. Undoubtedly, the main problem with Heidegger's ontology was its equating of being, the horizon from which all beings are understood, with a concept. The consequence of this equation is that all beings, including every particular human being, the self as well as other, are reduced to the status of a concept, an object of knowledge:

> Existence is interpreted as comprehension. From now on the transitive character of the verb *to know (connaître)* is attached to the verb *to exist*. . . . It turns out that the analysis of existence and of what is called its *haecceity* (*Da*) is only the description of the essence of truth, of the condition of the very understanding of being. (BPW 4–5)

Levinas declares this reduction of the other to an object or concept to be *ethically* unacceptable. Yet what the term ethics means for Levinas is not yet clear from this essay. What he does develop is an analytic that does not begin with *Dasein* but with a transformation of *mitsein*, a self-other relation that he asserts is prior to knowledge. Levinas claims to be criticizing Heidegger for the same failure that Heidegger criticized in Husserl—the blurring of the distinction between knowing and existing. Knowledge takes a secondary role to the relation to the existing other to whom we are in relation and whom we must first welcome. He presents this relation and welcoming in terms of responsibility, a notion that later becomes central to his thinking (BPW 3). Yet Levinas's challenge to Heidegger and the ontological tradition has much broader repercussions, as it also applies to many of the same canonical figures of the philosophical tradition that Arendt criticizes (i.e., Plato, Aristotle, Mill, Hobbes, etc.). While Arendt argues that they fail to think about the interhuman realm from the perspective of plurality, Levinas frames his far-reaching criticism in terms of a reduction of the human being, and especially the other, to an object (of knowledge).

He structures this initial challenge to the primacy of ontology by questioning the Heideggerian link between language and reason. In reply to Heidegger's claim that universal reason is necessary for the understanding of the particularity of language, Levinas argues that language is always first a response to a particular other. Speech is always addressed to another person; it is thus prior to both reason and universality. Language thus interrupts the universality of reason and ontology, an interruption that allows the other to appear (phenomenologically not literally). While Heidegger writes about letting the other be (*gelassenheit*), for both Arendt and Levinas the other appears—it has its own centre and activity and is not a passive object. By challenging the priority of reason and the universal on behalf of the other, Levinas is also contesting the priority of the ontological difference, which views *a* being through the lens of Being. Reason, knowledge and ontology have all allowed for such a reduction, and according to Levinas, language can challenge this. While Arendt does not present language as a means to go beyond reason, speech, as we saw in chapter 3, is indispensable for political action. For both thinkers speech takes priority over appearances, as the former is the basis for our relation to the other.[12] While both distance themselves from the importance of language, Levinas after *Totality and Infinity*, Arendt in her post-Eichmann writings, this connection is both an important shared critique of Heidegger and a basis for thinking about their respective projects in terms of a dialogue.

Levinas further develops the importance of language in terms of its ability to express an appeal made by an interlocutor; the other thus invokes me without naming me. Language expresses the uniqueness of this relation. 'The relation with the other (*autrui*) is not therefore ontology.

This tie to the other (*autrui*), which does not reduce itself to the representation of the Other (*autrui*) but rather to his invocation, where invocation is not preceded by comprehension, we call *religion*' (BPW 7). With reference to this calling, Levinas attempts to name this unique relation, struggling between the terms *religion* and *the ethical*. To avoid misunderstanding Levinas's project as a theological one, it is worth noting that the root of the term religion means, on the one hand, relation, which for Levinas is a link to the ethical relation, and on the other hand to bind oneself (to gather together, to create bonds between or to place a shared obligation upon), pointing towards the notion of responsibility in Levinas's project. Thus rather than conceiving of the term religion theologically (which is specifically a Christian science), the term religion should be read in light of the Judaic as well as in relation to its etymological roots, *religare*. Another sense in which Levinas uses the term religion (and prayer, which also entails 'imploring' in French) is with reference to Comte's definition in *Politique Positive*, which he explicitly qualifies as neither theological nor mystical (BPF 8). What is noteworthy about his justification of the term religious in the final paragraphs of 'Is Ontology Fundamental?' is that he simultaneously uses the term 'religion' as the ethical relation in his so-called confessional writings.[13]

Levinas problematizes the term theology for its reduction of God to human logic, a reduction he implicitly connects to the reduction of the other to an object. For this reason he prefers the term religion, which he assumes (incorrectly) to be free from such Christian logic. For Levinas theology is the 'act of naming the other' in which one, intentionally or otherwise, falls prey to a form of ethical violence. In the act of naming, one negates the call of the other and thus instrumentalizes the other—much like the relation of work does in Arendt's *Human Condition*. In his own terminology, Levinas calls this negation of the particularity of the other 'murder'. Given the foresight of his more mature thought, we know that he is here referring to the biblical commandment 'thou shall not kill'—a commandment that is central to what Levinas refers to as the ethical or the religious. Naming is thus a negation of the particularity of the other, whom Levinas claims needs no universal light or reason to speak. To approach this relation through the lens of universality is to deny the particularity of this relation. It is for this reason that 'from this first contestation of the primacy of ontology' (BPW 10), Levinas calls for a return to the ethical as the ground for a relation to the other. Arendt makes a similar argument with regard to the political realm. Rather than seek unity or universality, the political is a relational realm in which the distinctness of every unique being must have priority. Singularity is problematic for Arendt, as it fails to appreciate the paradox of plurality and particularity that characterizes the interhuman realm. Arendt would thus agree with Levinas that *mitsein* cannot be reduced to *Dasein*, yet she would certainly not agree with his absolute prioritization of the other.

For Arendt, the public realm is one that responds to all forms of inequality by imposing an artificial equality. While Levinas recognizes this as necessary in terms of justice, this is not the case for the ethical relation, which is the main focus of his early writings. What this comparison helps to establish is how Levinas's thought has a depth in terms of the self-other relation, a depth that Arendt's thought lacks because of its attention to plurality.

ETHICS AS FIRST PHILOSOPHY

Totality and Infinity, Levinas's *Doctorat d'État* published in 1961, defends the bold thesis that ethics, and not ontology or epistemology, is first philosophy. Moreover, the content of his ethics is equally audacious; it is 'radically different . . . [and] appears to be in contrast to the ethical discourse dominant in contemporary philosophy . . . [he] does not seem to speak of generally binding norms and ethical foundations'.[14] While this certainly leaves his thought open to the criticism that it fails to provide a normative theory or to be applicable, neither claim denies the strength of his challenge to the philosophical tradition. Bernasconi, who appreciates both this radicalism and its shortcomings, described Levinas's ethics as 'an ethics against ethics',[15] or in our terms, an ethics against morality. This is precisely what Arendt seeks to strengthen the political. In order to properly understand what ethics means for Levinas, it is necessary to consider his critique of traditional morality. The fundamental claim of his critique of morality, already present in his writings from the 1950s, is that it justifies the reduction of the other to the same for the sake of knowledge. Rather than understand individuals as their own individual and unique origin of meaning, an epistemological system or totalizing framework, much like the role of an ideology in totalitarianism according to Arendt, is imposed, destroying and reducing all differences, all alterity—in Arendtian terms reducing plurality to multiplicity, many copies of the same. Levinas, like Arendt, accuses Kant of this same quantifiable reduction:

> In the kingdom of ends, where persons are indeed defined as wills, but where the will is defined as what permits itself to be affected by the universal—where the will wishes to be reason, be it practical reason—multiplicity rests in fact only on the hope of happiness . . . [the] identification of will and reason, which is the ultimate invention of idealism, is opposed by the entire pathetic experience of humanity. (TI 217)

Yet as was the case with Arendt, Levinas is both greatly indebted to and highly critical of Kant. The first criticism regards Kant's reliance on universal categories, which Levinas views as a failure to account for the particularity of every human being. The horrors of the camps leave Levinas with a heightened sensitivity to the potential for the universal to be totalizing. However, in tension with this criticism, Levinas—like Arendt—applauds Kant's emphatic claim that human beings are never to be means for another end—a rejection of the instrumentalization that Levinas identified as violence during the Shoah. Second, Levinas faults Kant for his prioritization of reason's universality over the importance of human affectivity, such as need and desire, which are particularizing. A third criticism, which he often claims applies to the vast majority of the Western tradition of moral philosophy, is the fact that the ethical relation to the other is secondary in importance to, for example, that of *ipseity* or autonomy with respect to practical reason. It is this last reason that is certainly the most significant for Levinas, in that any philosophical approach that denies the absolute priority of the ethical relation is at risk of denying alterity. This is precisely why Levinas claims that ethics precedes ontology.

So while Levinas's ethics is to be understood as opposing morality in the Kantian sense—a good indication of the possibility for dialogue with the political in Arendt—it is still far from clear what exactly such an ethics as first philosophy could be. Levinas answers this question in relation to subjectivity in *Totality and Infinity*. His ethics is an ethics of subjectivity; a subjectivity of a subject *subject* to the other. In Levinas's own words, *Totality and Infinity* is 'a defence of subjectivity, but it will apprehend the subjectivity not at the level of its purely egoist protestation . . . but as founded in the idea of infinity' (TI 26). This is also what Bettina Bergo captures in her claim that his ethics is not 'an exploration of conditions of possibility of any interest in good actions of lives. [But] exploring the meaning of intersubjectivity and lived immediacy'.[16] As I hope to have shown in part II, Arendt also engages in such an exploration of intersubjectivity and lived immediacy, but in terms of plurality. Both thinkers began to explore the importance of intersubjectivity and lived immediacy against the horizon of totalitarianism and the Shoah. For Arendt this exploration focuses on the political phenomenon of totalitarianism; for Levinas the focus lies in understanding what, if any, connections there between the Shoah and totality as a philosophical concept in the ontological tradition.

Ethics as a Response to Totalitarianism

Levinas—who is not interested in understanding the historical horrors of the mid-twentieth century politically—uses the terms *tyranny* and *totalitarian* interchangeably, often referring to both as forms of totality (whereas Arendt argues for a political distinction between these on the grounds that in the former regime there is still space for private freedom). In this way, Levinas's ethics can be understood as a response to the hegemony of totality in the ontological tradition and exemplified by totalitarianism. In this vein, Arendt and Levinas both trace the origins of the totalizing impulse, taken to its extreme in the Nazi regime, to the Western philosophical tradition. As we saw in chapter 3, Arendt critiques the tradition of political philosophy that begins with Plato for seeking to destroy that which prevents totality—spontaneity, unpredictability—by trying to control it. Levinas makes a similar claim in terms of ethics. 'Western philosophy has most often been an ontology; a reduction of the other to the same' (TI 43). This reduction is, for Levinas, a form of totalization—a refusal of exteriority, that which is outside my knowledge or understanding because of its fundamental difference or alterity (TI 290). 'Respect for exteriority delineates another structure essential for metaphysics. In its comprehension of being (or ontology) it is concerned with critique. It . . . calls into question the freedom of the exercise of ontology' (TI 43). His ethics, in the form of a critique of ontology, prioritizes this alterity. The aspect of critique is fundamental to Levinas's ethics. Ethics is the calling into question of the prioritization of the same, including the self that aims to reduce the other to the same. Critique here is more than simply being critical; it is a complete calling into question of the 'logic of the same', a logic that Levinas associates with the total domination of the Nazi regime. Ethics is the resistance to the reduction of the other to the same and the prevention of the totalization of being (TI 44). Concretely, by resisting the temptation to approach the other as an object or concept, by entering into relation with the other as other, my interiority or identity is interrupted by exteriority.

According to Levinas this encounter with the other is a form of self-awakening, a breaking open of my identity, which calls me to challenge myself and the logic of the same (that grounds ontology). Interiority is 'the same gathered up in ipseity as an "I", as a particular existent unique and autochthonous in itself' (TI 39). Essentially bound to the first person (TI 57), interiority is within the realm of the same, thereby allowing for personal enjoyment, happiness, egoism and an experience of independence. It is considering oneself, one's freedom, one's pleasure; it is an 'I' that is independent of all others and quite content in itself. Yet this interiority is also absolutely essential for the possibility of an ethical relation to the other, in that it allows for a separation necessary for exteriority. In this vein Levinas claims that the ethical relation to the other in which the other is not reduced to the same is fundamentally constitutive of the self. Not only does this aspect of Levinas's critique signify a direct challenge to Heidegger, it also makes clear the shared grounds with Arendt. Both prioritized *the relation* to the other over the notion of a nonrelational self, or of a self in which interhuman relations are seen as secondary. Both Arendt and Levinas do so phenomenologically, which allows for an account of the experience of this relation. As Levinas expresses this:

> To affirm the priority of *Being* over *existents* is to already decide the essence of philosophy; it is to subordinate the relation with *someone,*

> who is an existent, (the ethical relation) to a relation with the *Being of existents*, which, is impersonal, permits the apprehension, the domination of existents (a relationship of knowing), subordinates justice to freedom. (TI 45)

Framed in terminology heavily influenced by Heidegger and the phenomenological tradition, the above critique can also be found in Arendt's *Origins*. Freedom, as Levinas uses this term, is freedom rooted in singularity (it is not the worldly, shared and plurality-based freedom Arendt seeks to reclaim from the tradition).[17] Arendt also seeks to rid the political of the vertical element of domination and control that Levinas here calls the priority of Being. It is for this reason that she repeats that the political is the realm of people, in the plural, and not persons, in the singular. Her notion of plurality is the affirmation of the priority of this ethical relation over against Being, singularity and freedom (the latter in Levinas's sense of the term).[18] The importance of plurality and particularity in Arendt is expressed by Levinas in his critique of the notion of pluralism, which he takes to be a synonym for multiplicity. 'Pluralism appears in Western philosophy only as a plurality of subjects that exist. . . . The plural, exterior to the existence of beings, is given as a number; to a subject that counts it is already subordinated to the synthesis of the "I think". Unity alone is ontologically privileged' (TI 274). For Levinas, pluralism is the reduction of particularity in the name of unity. This is what Arendt identifies as the modus operandi of totalitarianism—the destruction of plurality for the sake of unity. Levinas does not see the possibility of plurality serving as a principle for the political (as Arendt does), but rather he sees how the Western tradition reduces it to the sum of the same, to a multiplicity. The traumatic image that captures this reduction of individuals to numbers is concretized by means of the tattoos in Auschwitz, the reduction of human particularity to a number, a multiple:

> Levinas is actively working against a notion of politics in which the name of the individual is subsumed—and in the case of the Final Solution, erased, by the name of the universal, where the 'we' of nation, or community, or race eliminates that which resists naming.[19]

Similarly, bureaucratic regimes often fall prey to the tendency to see all individuals as numbers, a tendency that remains tangible in today's liberal democracies. 'The pathos of liberalism, which we rejoin on one side, lies in the promotion of a person inasmuch as he represents nothing further, that is, is precisely a self. The individuals would appear as participants in the totality: the Other would amount to a second copy of the I' (TI 120–121). Liberalism, in Levinas's estimation, refuses to allow for alterity because it threatens totality, the same threat Arendt empowers and celebrates in the political. It thus comes as no surprise that Arendt equally decries liberalism's substitution of plurality for multiplicity. Levinas, like Arendt, seeks to prevent such predetermined scripts in which human beings are pawns. 'They play the role of moments in a system, and not that of *origin*. Political society appears as a plurality that expresses the multiplicity of the articulations of a system' (TI 216–217). Thus while Levinas and Arendt do not agree upon terminology, they do agree that first, the Western philosophical tradition cannot be easily disentangled from the phenomenon of totalitarianism, in that both seek to totalize or control human beings by means of a reduction to singularity; and second, in order to respond to this danger, what must be prioritized is the human *relation* and the *haecceity*, particularity or unicity, of every human being.

Alterity and the Face of the Other

In his attempt to understand and describe the ethical relation of self to other, Levinas struggles with how to do so phenomenologically rather than cognitively, that is, without doing violence to the other. A secondary difficulty is how to describe or express this unique relation, a relation that both requires language but is also limited by language. As developed in *Totality and Infinity*, the answer is to be found in experience of the face-to-face, in the encounter with alterity:

> The effort of this book is directed toward apperceiving in discourse a non-allergic reaction with alterity, toward apperceiving Desire—where power, by essence murderous of the other, becomes faced with the other and 'against all good sense', the impossibility of murder, the consideration of the other. (TI 47)

What does Levinas mean by the peculiar phrase 'to apperceive in discourse a non-allergic reaction with alterity'? To apperceive in discourse means to hear the call (voice) of the other. The other asks me to respond, a response that is the first step towards taking responsibility for the other. For Levinas discourse begins with the experience of being, of the self, being interrupted by the face of the other (TI 66). This experience of the face-to-face is the encounter or non-allergic reaction to alterity. According to Levinas, this encounter affects me, making it impossible for me to murder the other even if this contradicts the ego. Levinas's phenomenological descriptions, in *Totality and Infinity*, of the many ways in which the self encounters alterity each seek to demonstrate that the primary response to the other is not an allergic one (a reaction against or rejection of) but rather an ethical one.

It is worth noting that prior to the attempts to describe the face-to-face in *Totality and Infinity*, the face first appeared in Levinas's 1952 essay 'Ethics and Spirit', published in *Difficult Freedom*, which was intended for a primarily Jewish audience.[20] This audience had a clear advantage, as the term for face in Hebrew, *panim*, is a linguistic key to understanding Levinas's notion of ethics. The Hebrew term *panim* is quite exceptional in that it does not exist in the singular (the suffix '*im*' in Hebrew signifies the plural). Levinas, as well as his audience, was certainly aware of this fact, both because it is a basic aspect of Hebrew grammar but also because of its importance in the Torah, in many Talmudic discussions, and from Maimonides's lengthy commentary on its different meanings (presence of a person, the hearing of a voice, care for the other) in the *Guide to the Perplexed*.[21] Thus *panim*, unlike its English translation as 'the face', already carries with it a great deal of the ethics Levinas wishes to make first philosophy. *Panim* is always already in the plural; the face is always in relation. In the face-to-face, it is always making an appeal, interrupting, always heteronomous. It is also a 'concept' that cannot be detached from God, whose *panim* can never be seen but only heard. *Panim* also calls to mind the importance of externality, as it can never be 'seen' from within. This latter association with externality is enriched by the root of *panim*, *panah*, which means to turn towards someone, to respond to the call of the other. Levinas discusses this at length in several of his Talmudic readings on Yom Kippur, the Day of Atonement and judgement, and *teshuvah* (forgiveness). The Judaic notion of forgiveness, which is very demanding and similar to Arendt's politically significant ethic of forgiveness, linguistically means to return but also literally asks that the one explicitly asking for forgiveness must 'turn' or change her ways. Arendt does also explicitly discuss the Judaic notion of *teshuvah*, demonstrating her knowledge of how it differs from the Christian notion of forgiveness (JW 42). With this in mind, it is understandable why Levinas said: 'One can forgive many Germans, but there are some Germans it is difficult to forgive. It is difficult to forgive Heidegger' (NTR 25), as Heidegger never asked to be forgiven, nor did he change his ways (according to Levinas).

The entirety of the third section of *Totality and Infinity* is dedicated to a phenomenological analysis of the face, an analysis that touches upon all the meanings of *panim*. Given the lack of a singular form of *panim*, it is clear that the face can never be possessed; it is not a singularity that can be grasped and reduced like other concepts, it is a relation (or a between in Arendt's terminology) that forces me to (re)turn (*panah)* and to respond. In addition, according to Levinas it has command over me and possesses me. *Panim*, which is perhaps best translated as the face-to-face (given its nonsingularity), already points towards an asymmetrical relation that challenges my freedom by confronting me with my own egoism. In an interview, Levinas stated, 'the face is a fundamental event';[22] it is not an appearance or representation, it is an event in which I am transformed by the experience of encountering alterity.

Levinas's also seeks to describe this non-allergic relation, experienced in the face-to-face, by turning to the classroom.[23] 'The establishing of this primacy of the ethical, that is, of the relationship of man to man—signification, teaching, and justice—a primacy of an irreducible structure upon which all the other structures rest . . . is one of the objectives of the present work' (TI 79). The other is my teacher, and I am her student—an asymmetrical relation (unlike in Buber's *I and Thou*). 'To have meaning is to teach or to be taught, to speak or to be able to be stated' (TI 97). The meaning of the other does not come from me; I do not know the other—to have such knowledge of another is already to reduce the other to the same. Furthermore, the other is my teacher both in relation to alterity but also with regard to the self. For Levinas, who only began to study the Talmud in 1947, the experience of learning from his teacher, Monsieur Chouchani, and with his study partner, Dr. Nerson, was such a transformational experience.[24] It is from the signification the other gives to my world that I can learn and discern meaning. The other for both Arendt and Levinas, unlike a thing, is its own source of meaning (signification). This is a unique form of signification in that the face does not require a context; it breaks through all form (TI 23). Unlike objects or things that cannot be encountered without a horizon, which provides them with meaning, the face requires no external source of meaning. To accept this in one's encounter with the other is to appreciate the other's alterity; a non-allergic reaction is the refusal to reduce the other—to force the face into a form. 'The face, still a thing among things, breaks through the form that nevertheless delimits it. This means concretely: the face speaks to me and thereby invites me to a relation incommensurate with a power exercised, be it enjoyment or knowledge' (TI 198). This encounter, much like learning, is not a painless one. On the contrary—it is a violent interruption; the ego's safety blanket is being ripped away. According to Levinas, ethics 'begins when freedom [rooted in singularity and the self], instead of being justified by itself, feels itself to be arbitrary and violent' (TI 84). In other words, ethics is born from the experience of being questioned by alterity. Arendt also doesn't minimize the agonism and courage needed to interact with others. While we may 'act in concert' with others in the *polis*, one should not presume that this concert is harmonious or congenial. For both thinkers this experience of encountering the other is both the most fulfilling and challenging for the self.

The ethical relation is one in which the other teaches me and through discourse creates a network of meaning. 'Speech is thus the origin of all signification—of tools and all human works—for through it the referential system from which every signification arises receives the very principle of its function' (TI 98). Conversation creates a world; the ethical relation between two individuals initiates a shared world filled with meaning. By means of the Heideggerian notion of the world, it is clear that Arendt and Levinas are both engaged in a similar project of grounding the world in intersubjective discourse, discourse that creates meaning. This is precisely the role Arendt defines for the political realm in which actors speak to each other and in so doing create a shared world and shape reality by confirming each others' perspectives. For Arendt action—in the form of speech—creates a horizontal transcendence that forms a web-of-relations, a web that is the 'ground' of meaning. Yet Arendt fails to engage in further reflection on the meaning of speech, this web or the meaning it creates. I would claim that Levinas's understanding of speech (which does change after *Totality and Infinity*) brings him directly into conversation with Arendt. Like Levinas, she puts a great deal of emphasis on speech as the 'ground' for a network of relations that have the potential, although not the purpose, to share meaning. Levinas clearly suggests the other is the source of this signification, whereas Arendt claims that meaning arises both from 'in the between' as well as from the storytellers who observe these interactions. In this way it could be said that the ethical relation created by discourse in Levinas is the relation that constitutes the interactions fundamental to Arendt's *polis*. However, Levinas's conclusion goes further and potentially adds depth to the role of language in Arendt's analysis of speech in the political realm. For Levinas, through speech 'the other remains transcendent to the same' (TI 39). Language prevents the formation of a totality, as the signified is never completely present, maintaining an asymmetry that allows alterity to be respected. The interactions between people in the *polis* can never be totalized; each relation—according to Levinas—is an infinite form of horizontal transcendence. This insight into the ethical relation between self and other, absent in Arendt's analysis, is certainly one that strengthens the claim she makes about the political being uncontrollable and unpredictable. By considering how speech challenges totality, Levinas supports Arendt's claim that action can prevent totalitarianism, as it is constituted by a non-allergic response to alterity that strengthens the fundamental plurality of the *polis*.

The Constraints of Philosophical Language

Soon after the publication of *Totality and Infinity*, which was received with great applause, Jacques Derrida's 'Violence and Metaphysics'[25] confronted Levinas with a serious problem. He realized that language, the language he claimed the other spoke with, was contaminated by the ontological desire for totality. As Michael Bernard-Donals writes: 'To obey the obligation to speak and act, both ethically and politically, one may have to find another language. Lyotard and Blanchot suggest something similar, that after Auschwitz, the disaster which has ruined everything, the language of history and politics may not do justice to the future'.[26] Levinas recognized and appreciated Derrida's criticism and spent the following decade in search of a new language for the ethical relation. This search is apparent in his 1972 collection of essays *Humanism of the Other*. In the interview 'Bible and Philosophy' with Philippe Nemo he expressed his initial conclusion that 'at no moment did the Western philosophical tradition in my eyes lose its right to the last word; everything must, indeed, be expressed in its tongue; but perhaps it is not the place of the first meaning of beings, the place where meaning begins' (EI 25). It is thus 'the first word', the source or origin of meaning, and the words to express this meaning that Levinas seeks in this collection. Levinas's struggle for the proper means to express his ethics without recourse to the language of ontology parallels Arendt's frustration with the limitations of the language of political philosophy. Her solution, which makes comparisons with other thinkers much more difficult, was to introduce distinctions as well as to redefine the traditional terms of political philosophy (e.g., by redefining power in terms of plurality and horizontality and as opposed to violence, strength and force).

Levinas takes this linguistic limitation as an opening to slowly introduce terms with roots in the Judaic into his so-called philosophical writings. He begins by using terms such as hostage, election, trace and responsibility (terms which are central in his 1974 *Otherwise Than Being).* Part and parcel of this new language is the use of expressions that have been shunned in recent philosophical discourse because of their religious significance, such as that of being infinitely responsible. While Levinas makes recourse to explicitly religious orientation, he does not want it to be alien to an atheistic Greek paradigm. An example of this is his reference to 'entering the Promised Land' in the same paragraph in which he asks us to bracket God, if only temporarily (HO 27–28).[27] This atheistic-religious tension in Levinas's thought, most visible in these transitional essays, is worth noting because of the issues surrounding the philosophical significance of the so-called confessional writings. What this tension makes evident is that for Levinas, while philosophy may have 'the last word', it is perhaps incapable of expressing 'the first word'. Nonetheless this does not mean that the first word is theological and relies on either dogma or belief in God; neither dogma nor belief is part of the Judaic. According to Levinas, the Judaic is actually closer to secularism than to Christian theology and is thus a space in which there is a spirit of atheism (UH 117).[28]

Another marked shift in Levinas's thinking in this period is the focus on the relation between the same and the other rather than on the meaning of the other for the self, as was the case in *Totality and Infinity*. In this vein, Levinas seems to follow Arendt's step into the between, into the space of intersubjectivity. The essay 'Signification and Meaning' (also referred to as 'Sense and Meaning') is the first glimpse of the shift toward the relation itself as central. Meaning is discovered in the relation itself, in the movement, which originates from the other's appeal. 'Does not sense, as orientation, indicate a thrust, an outside of self toward the *other than self*' (HO 25). Levinas here suggests that the 'ground' for meaning is not in objects, or the self (consciousness), but is the relation to the other. Thus according to Levinas without the other, neither judgement nor ethics would be possible, as meaning is the ground for both. This claim has strong Arendtian echoes, especially as it concerns intersubjectivity as the post-foundational standard for judgement. Like Arendt's embracing of contingency, Levinas's 'grounding' of meaning in the relation offers no guarantees or stability; it does provide hope and promise, which are both vital in a world marked by contingency. In other words, rather than resort to universality, reason or the self, Levinas's approach embraces the contingency that defines the post-foundational by 'grounding' ethics as first philosophy in the relation to the other.

This text, 'Signification and Meaning', foreshadowing *Other Than Being*, emphasizes the notions of responsibility and substitution in the ethical relation. Again this reveals a shift from the self to the ethical relation itself. 'Consciousness loses its first place' (HO 32); however, the self is not forgotten in her encounter with the other (a conclusion that some of Levinas's readers have come to). On the contrary, the self becomes unique and un-exchangeable in this relation. 'The uniqueness of the Ego is the fact that no one can answer in my stead' (HO 33). Not only does this speak to the critique that Levinas denies the self, it also addresses Arendt's concern expressed in *The Origins of Totalitarianism* (as well as her later writings) about the danger of making individuals superfluous. This paradoxical situation, in which I am absolutely irreplaceable because of my relation to the other, is central to the development of Levinas's thought in this period. It is also the source of a tension that Levinas is never able to resolve. It is impossible to find a *just* 'balance' between the self and the other without denying the value of either, and it is often in the search for such 'justice' that justice is lost. It is partially because of this irresolvability that I argue that we must limit Levinas's ethics within a notion of the political as conceived by Arendt, creating a virtuous circle between alterity and plurality. Without such a frame, the notions of substitution and responsibility are in danger of playing a foundational role and coming at the cost of justice for others and plurality.

Another new linguistic development that occurs in this period is the notion of the trace, which is both an example of the opening to the Judaic and a step into the between. According to Adriaan Peperzaak, Levinas's 1963 essay 'The Trace of The Other' is his 'first attempt to answer a fundamental question left open in that book [T&I]: how is it possible that the alterity of "the Other" (l'Autre) is understood as alterity of the human Other (Autrui) and as alterity of the Most High (du Très Haut)' (BPW 34). The trace does not appear; it is not a phenomenon and yet it signifies a past presence—it thus has an aspect of temporality that is phenomenologically significant. The trace can only be known from the perspective of presence because of its lack of presence, its interruption of presence as it were. Yet how it comes to signify without appearing differs from its signification, which is that of an order that is part of an inaccessible past that is beyond being. Levinas also coins the neologism *illeity* to refer to the trace of God that is experienced in the relation to the other. Yet God is not a theological notion or dogma for Levinas; God is the condition for responsibility.[29] Levinas's search for 'the first word', for the origin, thereby leads him to connect the trace to an order beyond being from which responsibility arises.

Levinas also begins to refer to 'the Third' as an indirect relation to God; the question this raises is how *or if* this reference to 'the Third' connects to his later political usage of this term in relation to justice (to be discussed in the next chapter). In the ethical relation, the trace of *illeity* left by the past presence of 'the Third' is experienced. By way of the trace of *illeity*, experienced in the face-to-face encounter with the other, 'the Third' invests me with responsibility for an other. In this way Levinas distinguishes between the alterity of the other and the alterity of 'the Third'. What is most significant is that the latter is only experienced through the former. This is a claim that Levinas has already repeatedly made in his so-called confessional writings, stating that the relation to God is never outside of the relation to the other person (UH 117). Levinas concludes the essay by explicitly naming the revealed God of monotheism, who is present in his absence through the trace of *illeity*. This trace is the source of the face that speaks enabling 'being [to have] . . . sense' (HO 44). This marks a turning point in Levinas's thought. With the introduction of the notion of the trace, Levinas makes explicit the Judaic source of his ethics as first philosophy while at the same time justifying the more religious terminology that begins to appear in his so-called philosophical essays.

In an essay from the same period, entitled 'Humanism and An-Archy', Levinas begins with a reference to the Shoah, explicitly reaffirming its connection to his ethics:

> The unburied dead of wars and death camps accredit the idea of death with no future, making tragicomic the care for one's self and illusory the pretensions of the *rational animal* to a privileged place in the cosmos, capable of dominating and integrating the totality of being in a consciousness of self. (HO 45)

Before considering the meaning of this citation within the context of this essay, it is worth once again noting the presence of an engagement with Heidegger and an implicit connection between the ontological tradition and the horrors committed by totalitarian regimes. Although Levinas does not equate the death of the camps with the centrality of *Dasein*, and the meaning of his death, he is certainly trying to lead his readers to consider precisely such an association (a similar method is used by Arendt with reference to Plato's need to control the *polis*). The camps as well as the hundreds of unmarked graves scattered throughout Europe are an inexpressible reminder of the danger of privileging the self. The dead, who have no name, remind us of our failed responsibility to care for the other. By criticizing Heidegger's focus on death, Levinas is reminding us of ontology's failure to prioritize the other and ethics. This is a critique shared by Arendt, who focuses on life beyond survival, and natality.

Moreover, a new term Levinas introduces in this essay, that of being held hostage by what comes from beyond, is also an implicit reference to the Shoah.[30] Based on this, he develops 'a new concept of passivity, . . . *beneath* consciousness and knowledge . . . a passivity referring beyond being, prior to the ontological plane . . . referring to the anteriority of creation' (HO 50).[31] Struggling to find the words to describe this new source or origin, one that is meant to be preconceptual and precognitive, Levinas uses the term *beneath* to express the separation between the realms of ontology and consciousness and this preliminary, pre-original or beyond (HO 51). Other expressions he uses for similar purposes are *beyond*, or *an-archical, the wrong side of being,* and *saying* (although each expresses something in addition to being prior to ontology). The uncertainty and awkwardness of the language he chooses to use clearly expresses the difficulty he faced when trying to escape language that is haunted by the spectre of the ontological tradition.[32] In addition, the Judaic is no longer limited to scattered references; it now plays a significant role in the account of his ethics.

In the third essay in *Humanism of the Other*, 'Without Identity', Levinas's further explores the potential of this new ethical language:

> That politics and an administration guided by the humanist ideal maintain the exploitation of man by man, and war—these are singular reversals of reasonable projects, disqualifying human causality and, as a result, transcendental subjectivity understood as spontaneity and action. (HO 60)

The last part of this quote is interesting because of its Kantian and Arendtian subtext. Although perhaps less explicitly supportive of the 1968 student movement (than Arendt), Levinas was in favour of their demonstrations and political protest. The final section of this essay speaks of the youth of 1968 as the other. 'This is the perfect occasion to ask, in closing, if the aspirations of today's youth, despite the violence and irresponsibility in which these aspirations degenerate, can do without thought devoted to subjectivity defined from responsibility and against the notion of being' (HO 68). In Levinas's brief reference to the events of 1968, he recognizes a humanism of the other in the words of the youth, in the *saying* that is prior to the *said* (which is on the level of language and ontology). Unfortunately, as soon as this *saying* becomes a *said*, it is 'quickly extinguished by a language just as wordy and conformist as the one it was supposed to replace' (HO 69). Levinas clearly had hoped for another type of revolution, one that would have rejected the prioritization of politics over justice that is rooted in ethics. In this sense, his disappoint with the events of 1968 is rooted in his dream of an ethical revolution, one in which the *saying* is not reduced to *the said*. What he observed in 1968 struck him as an unfortunate failure of the humanist movement because of its denial of the spontaneity for action that characterizes the human condition, the same spontaneity Arendt sought to rescue with the political realm. Arendt's emphasis on political change as opposed to the institution of this change (or its stabilization) expresses a similar tension between *the saying* and *said*. This essay is also significant in that it foreshadows Levinas's interest in connecting the political to his ethics. If the political were reoriented by alterity, rather than its present form as a humanism of the self, Levinas might no longer claim that 'politics is opposed to morality', as he did in *Totality and Infinity*.

With this glimmer of political hope, let us turn to the essay 'Subjectivity and Vulnerability'. As part of his new ethical vocabulary, Levinas makes recourse to several powerful metaphors in order to describe the vulnerability of subjectivity exposed by the encounter with the other. It is these metaphors that allow Levinas to move beyond the language of ontology. A few examples from this essay are the pain and suffering of an open wound, a nakedness so complete that one shivers at the thought of such vulnerability and a city so desperately defenceless that it welcomes an enemy incursion, motivated by the hope that the enemy will show mercy. In each of these cases, the encounter with the other is meant to be transformative of the self 'into an "otherwise than being" . . . the subject is *for the other*: substitution, responsibility, expiation' (HO 63–64). In addition to these terms, Levinas also makes recourse to explicitly Judaic terms, as if to express his lack of complete satisfaction with the more philosophically established terms. He does so rhetorically by asking whether Western society is as nourished by Jerusalem as it is by Athens, his way of asking whether 'we' have forgotten the Bible (the 'we' referring to Europe or the West). While Levinas is clear that he is not asking philosophy to consider the biblical tradition to be its equal, he does want its voice to be heard. 'Biblical verses do not function here as proof but as testimony of a tradition and an experience. Don't they have as much right as Hölderlin and Trakl to be cited?' (HO 66).

For Levinas the experience of a beneath, or of the beyond, which he struggles to express philosophically, is the experience central to the Judaic. It is only at the tail end of this transitional period that Levinas first begins to openly intertwine the two traditions that nourish his ethics. What is fundamental to this intertwinement is that it is by no means a parallelism or translation. Levinas makes recourse to the language of the biblical tradition because he seeks to express something he believes philosophy does not have the tools to express. The Judaic helps him to discover a means to express the inexpressible. Furthermore, Levinas's choice to allow these two traditions to interact is his way of reminding us that they have always interacted, influencing each other throughout history, and ought to continue to do so in the present. While this calls for a commitment to rediscovering the biblical tradition, which has lost its prominence among intellectuals, Levinas claims that without such a commitment 'the first word' cannot be spoken. The following quotation is a fine example of how Levinas brings these two traditions together to express the condition of humanity after the experience of exile from Egypt (which for Levinas seems to also relate to Europe after the Shoah):

> Echo of the permanent *saying* of the Bible: the condition—or incondition—of strangers and slaves in the land of Egypt brings man closer to his fellow man. Men seek one another in their incondition of strangers. No one is at home. The memory of that servitude assembles humanity. The difference that gaps between ego and self, the non-coincidence of the identical, is a thorough non-indifference with regard to men. (HO 66)

The experience of being a stranger, having no home, no certainty, of being absolutely vulnerable is the condition that binds the ego to the other. It is a condition the Bible cannot prove through logic or reason but can testify to. It is also the condition that Arendt identifies as the most dangerous after the Shoah, the condition of not being at home in the world both literally, in terms of the refugee problem, and figuratively, in terms of an alienation from the shared world. It is worth recalling that Arendt also appeals to the biblical tradition, in the name of plurality, as necessary given the reality of the condition both she and Levinas experienced and are trying to describe phenomenologically:

> If philosophers, despite their necessary estrangement from the everyday life of human affairs, were ever to arrive at a true political philosophy they would have to make the plurality of man, out of which arises the whole realm of human affairs—in its grandeur and misery—the object of their *thaumadzein*. Biblically speaking, they would have to accept—in speechless wonder the miracle for the universe, of man and of being—the miracle that God did not create Man, but 'male and female created He them.' They would have to accept in something more than the resignation of human weakness the fact that 'it is not good for man to be alone.' (PhP 103; PP 39, 60)

While Arendt was neither as familiar with nor as educated in terms of the Judaic as Levinas, she does share the view that insights from Jerusalem might speak to the lacuna of traditional Western philosophy. Likewise, both Arendt and Levinas recognize that the Judaic has much to say when it comes to the meaning of responsibility.

RESPONSIBILITY FOR THE OTHER

What makes Levinas's 1974 *Otherwise Than Being or Beyond Essence* so important to the politics of relationality that I develop in the final chapters is that it is in terms of responsibility, the central concern of this work, that I bring together Arendt's notion of the political rooted in plurality and Levinas's ethics of alterity. This book is also considered by many to be Levinas's most important contribution because of its goal to free itself from the logic and language of ontology. The core of Levinas's project in *Otherwise Than Being* centres on the notion of substitution, a notion that grounds responsibility. 'It is a justifiable simplification to say that substitution is responsibility'.[33] Following upon his reflection in the period between his first two so-called philosophical works, Levinas now takes a radical step and rethinks subjectivity as born in the relation of responsibility. He thus relocates 'the possibility of the subject in the interruption of the other'.[34] The-other-in-me is the basis of my subjectivity, and substitution is 'the means' by which I experience this. The other is my source of meaning in the me-for-the-other that is the ground of responsibility. My subjectivity is constituted in alterity. What Levinas aims to show by means of substitution is that subjectivity is constituted by alterity, a claim Arendt affirms in terms of plurality.

The Judaic Roots of Responsibility

Otherwise Than Being is refreshingly unapologetic in its use of biblical and Talmudic terms as well as its explicit engagement with God and the Judaic. According to Bernasconi, the reason for this is that '"Substitution", as Levinas understands it, cannot be accounted for by the Western philosophical tradition [because] . . . a radical challenge to the subject is excluded by it from the outset'.[35] In support of this claim, let us consider the first references to substitution, which like the face and the trace, are not to be found in the so-called philosophical works but in the so-called confessional writings. Levinas first connects substitution and responsibility to the notion of *teshuvah*—Judaic forgiveness (which Arendt writes about in JW 42). In a Talmudic reading, Levinas declares that substitution is fundamental for justice. In referring to substitution he makes clear that 'no one can take my place', claiming this is equally true of *teshuvah* (NTR 17). In its Judaic praxis, forgiveness is a turn towards the other, which is the first step in accepting responsibility for harming another or the world. It must be followed by a change in my actions, which demonstrates to the other that I have been transformed by this encounter. 'The effort the moral conscience makes to re-establish itself as moral conscience, *Teshuvah,* or Return, is simultaneously the relation with God and an absolutely internal event' (NTR 17). Although Levinas does not further develop the concept of substitution in this Talmudic reading, it is clear that it is connected to the transformative encounter formative for the praxis of *teshuvah*.

The connection between substitution and *teshuvah* is illuminating in another sense. *Teshuvah* is—contrary to 'common-sense' understanding—not a solitary undertaking; it is a communal or collective process. I am always responsible for the wrongs (not sins, a word too imbued with

Christian theology to be used in this context) committed by my community. As Levinas often explains, I am also responsible for the intentions of the other. In the Judaic, a position echoed by Arendt, responsibility arises from the web-of-relations, from being part of a community. While Levinas affirms this in his so-called philosophical writings by referring to Dostoyevsky—'we are all guilty of all and for all men before all, and I more than the others' (EI 98)—its origin is Talmudic, which he acknowledges in 'Ideology and Idealism'. Referring to the Talmudic *Sotah* tractate, 37b, Levinas reminds us: 'What is the issue between them [the different rabbis debating this issue]?—R. Mesharsheya said: "The point between them is that of personal responsibility and responsibility for others because it is held according to the Rabbis that each Israelite is responsible for the conduct of the rest".'[36] While Arendt does not refer to the Talmud or the Judaic when discussing responsibility, this idea is clearly present in her notion of responsibility, as we all share responsibility for the world. The weight of responsibility, following the Judaic, is the unbearable weight of the world inscribed at the heart of subjectivity.[37] For Levinas, 'each individual . . . is called to leave in his turn, or without awaiting his turn, the concept of the ego . . . to respond with responsibility: *me,* that is, *here I am for the others*' (OB 185). I am irreplaceable (thereby challenging the superfluousness totalitarianism seeks to create); I cannot be substituted for by another because only I can be responsible for the other.

The link Levinas here first makes between responsibility and the other might seem a stretch to some readers; nonetheless to a Jewish audience it was almost redundant. In Hebrew 'the word "responsibility" comes from the word "response". It implies existence of an other who has legitimate claims on my conduct, for, or to, whom I am accountable. The Hebrew equivalent, *achrayut,* derives from the word *acher,* meaning "an other". Responsibility is intrinsically relational'.[38] Although the two most important terms in Levinas's thought are responsibility and the other, he never offers his philosophical audience this connection, which is taken for granted by any reader familiar with Hebrew or the Judaic. It is impossible, whether reading a biblical text or in dialogue, to forget the bond between responsibility and the other. It is so firmly imprinted in the Judaic that it is often taken for granted. By looking closely at these terms, let us consider the subtle distinction in meaning. Responsibility is your ability to respond, to answer and to account for your actions. *Achrayut* (אחריות) has as its root *acher* (אחר), which means other. Its meaning in Hebrew is more of a commitment to the other, a commitment that is not limited to a particular situation or condition. In this sense it is much more than a response to a particular action; it is a commitment to the other as a person. *Achrayut* contains the respect for the absolute alterity of the other; it is to alterity that we have a responsibility. Because of the unicity of the other in the world, I am responsible for the other as part of my responsibility to the world. It is the fact that every person is other, *acher*, that makes us responsible, *achrayut*.

Responsibility in Terms of Substitution

While Levinas's notion of responsibility is clearly connected to the Judaic, this does not imply that he abandons a philosophical approach to responsibility—the two approaches are mutually inclusive. In *Otherwise Than Being*, he introduces two new terms, *proximity* and *anarchy*, neither of which has a Judaic reference. Proximity is an an-archic relation, a relation prior to the order of ontology. It is a summons to responsibility that comes from another order, from beyond being. Proximity describes how the relation to the other affects and disturbs the self. This disturbance is transformative and leaves an affective rather than a visible trace (BPW 100). These terms also clarify that Levinas does not seek to create a new foundation for ethics.[39] In terms that allow for a parallel to Arendt, Levinas's ethics is post-foundational. He does not attempt to found ethics in responsibility as such; rather it is the anarchic appeal to responsibility that is a reminder of the rupture of foundationalism. What remains is its trace. His goal is to describe the trace of another order, a trace experienced from within the order of being, yet originating from alterity. Responsibility is a response to an-archic relation that constitutes subjectivity.

However, this an-archic appeal is stifled by ontology. Due to the philosophical tradition's focus on concepts and ideas, on consciousness, this order—because it cannot be thematized—is discounted. 'The me[ta]-ontological and meta-logical structure of this Anarchy is outlined, undoing the logos framing the apology through which consciousness still recovers itself and commands' (BPW 82). It is thus essential to disconnect the relation to things from the ethical relation. While both people and things appear, proximity can only be experienced to another human being (OB 81). We can only experience proximity by its limits, contours or margins. To think beyond being means to think on the margin of being, to question its limits. It is thus only on the hither side of the tradition that one can begin to approach the ethical relation. The self cannot consciously experience proximity; likewise knowledge of proximity is impossible. This attempt to describe what is beyond being, beyond ontology, is greatly impeded because of the limitations imposed by a language that is so rooted in Western metaphysics. As such, Levinas tries to find a new vocabulary to describe the trace left by this summons to responsibility. To do so Levinas begins to use several of the new terms explored after *Totality and Infinity*, such as recurrence, hostage, obsession and persecution.

To provide 'evidence', an impossibility as evidence belongs to the domain of knowledge science and ontology, of this beyond from within the realm of being and through the language of being, Levinas must use the language of *the said* without erasing the trace of *the saying*. Given that the trace is an affective experience, a transformative encounter for the self, Levinas focuses on how this demand affects me. He does so in terms of an analysis of identity by showing how the self is a 'me' (*moi*) in the accusative prior to being an 'I' (an ego, *le Moi*). In order to establish the anarchy (or temporal priority) of the 'me', Levinas introduces another term, *recurrence*. Recurrence is the 'means' by which the positive meaning of the ethical relation can be illuminated (OB 103). However, in order to understand how this occurs, it is necessary to grasp the link between recurrence and identity. First, for the self to be aware of itself, it must disclose itself to itself. This self-awareness is 'evidence' of the 'process' of recurrence. For the self to recognize itself in recurrence, there must be a distinction within the self; the self thus 'rests on a "subjective condition", an identity that one calls an ego or I' (OB 102). Next Levinas challenges the notion of identity and consciousness so closely connected to the ontological tradition. He claims that the failure to distinguish between the two terms of recurrence results in subjectivity's reduction to consciousness. Concretely, Levinas challenges the position Sartre inherited from Hegel that the oneself (the identity of the I) is based on the for-itself. According to Levinas, the oneself is a restless unity and therefore cannot be the basis of the for-itself. This restlessness is testified to by proximity, persecution (and obsession), which all bear witness to the 'presence' of a weight of suffering within the self. 'The oneself is "in itself" as one is in one's own skin' (BPW 85). One cannot escape one's own skin, and yet one is never truly completely comfortable in one's own skin. There are moments, such as shame or embarrassment, when one wishes one could crawl out of one's skin. This leads Levinas to conclude that while the oneself may be the basis of what we call identity, it is in fact a unity riddled by an internal tension.

For Levinas, this internal tension is essential, as it points towards the hither side of being. The fact that one can speak of oneself as being uncomfortable in one's own skin leads him to ask whether recurrence is possible if there isn't something 'other' causing it. 'For there to be a return, must not the knot of *ipseity* be tied at some point?' (BPW 83). Thus, Levinas does not, like Sartre, seek the oneself within the same order as the for-itself—that of *ipseity* within identity. *Ipseity*, for Levinas, is at odds with itself when it returns to itself. It is this 'at odds with', already experienced in proximity and persecution, that is the 'evidence' of a trace of an otherwise than being within the self. Another metaphor Levinas uses to express this otherness within the self is that of maternity. While less present in *Otherwise Than Being*, maternity remains a significant metaphor in Levinas's opus, much like that of natality for Arendt. Here, maternity 'suggests to us the proper sense of the oneself. The oneself cannot form itself; it is already formed with absolute passivity' (OB 104). It is clear that for Levinas the separation within the oneself—within *ip-*

seity—is 'evidence' of the impossibility of positing the oneself on the for-itself.

While Arendt does not explore the constitution of the self with the same depth as Levinas, quite a bit can be construed based on her reflections on the two-in-one and the activity of thinking. As presented in chapter 4, Arendt agrees with Levinas that a difference arises from within the presupposed unity of the oneself (LM 183). In her words, the I/self is irreducible to the 'me'; this is precisely what Levinas claims when he says the oneself cannot be posited on the for-itself. Arendt also acknowledges how discomforting the experience and awareness of this difference can be for the self. She sees the public realm as a means to address this disunity, because when others see and hear us we appear to have an identity. In other words, while I appear to the other as one, I never do so to myself. Nonetheless Arendt does acknowledge that what we call consciousness is 'the curious fact that in a sense I also am for myself, though I hardly appear to me, . . . I am not only for others but for myself, and in this later case, I clearly am not just one. A difference is inserted into my Oneness' (LM 183). While she does not explore the nature or source of this difference, saying only that this difference is part of the fundamental plurality of the earth, it is clear that her views of identity and unity are similar to Levinas's. For Arendt this difference is essential because of its importance for thinking. This difference allows for the intercourse both between me and myself (two-in-one) and between the self and others (LM 186). Actualizing consciousness occurs by means of a thinking dialogue or dialectic between me and myself, an actualization that allows me to keep myself company and keeps loneliness at bay (LM 187). What Arendt then suggests is critical, as it justifies the engagement between Levinas's alterity and her plurality that I pursue here. 'Difference and otherness, which are such outstanding characteristics of the world of appearances as it is given to man for his habitat among a plurality of things, are the very conditions for the existence of man's mental ego as well' (LM 187). In other words, Arendt acknowledges that otherness and difference, alterity in Levinas's terminology, is the basis not only for the thinking self or two-in-one; it is also the basis of the plurality in the world that is the condition for the political. She rephrases this claim a few paragraphs later: '[T]he Socratic two-in-one heals the solitariness of thought; its inherent duality points to the infinite plurality which is the law of the earth' (LM 187). Alterity, understood by Arendt in terms of otherness and difference, is the condition for plurality. Moreover, this otherness disrupts the unity of the self. While Levinas goes beyond Arendt in trying to find the source of this alterity, I hope to have established that Arendt acknowledges this alterity as fundamental for both thinking and acting.

Levinas—rejecting the approach taken by the ontological tradition—suggests that we seek the second term of recurrence beyond being:

> The term of recurrence will be sought . . . in itself as in exile. It will be found under the effect of an expulsion. . . . Under the effect of such an expulsion outside of being, it is in itself. There is an expulsion in that it assigns me before I show myself, before I set myself up. I am assigned without recourse, without fatherland, already sent back to myself, but without being able to stay there, compelled before commencing. (BPW 103)

While it might seem strange to link Levinas's analysis of recurrence with the Shoah, he makes this association explicit in an interview, which also helps to explain his usage of the terms exile, expulsion and fatherland in this context.[40] He claims, in response to Sartre, who associates hell with the other, that the oneself does not find peace within itself, as a for-itself. In negative terms, the oneself expels or exiles itself from itself, creating a space for the difference within oneself that Levinas posits in recurrence. This space of alterity is a fundamental space with regard to both Levinas's and Arendt's intersubjective approaches. It is fundamental to combat totalitarianism—whether internal or external—by safeguarding this space of difference within the self. Only outside of itself is it in-itself. Yet the oneself is in exile in-itself because in expulsion I am assigned, that is, I am summoned to responsibility. Thus only by going beyond essence is there a positive meaning for the in-itself. Yet the oneself cannot remain in exile; it is sent back to itself, and all that is left behind is the trace of the expulsion, experienced as the uneasiness at the heart of *ipseity*. Being or the self, in relation to the other, experiences this trace as persecution.

The self (the 'I' that flows to the 'me') has come to this hither side by being assigned, by being marked, singled out prior to any choice. This passivity is so radical that the persecuted self is also responsible for the persecutor—the other who calls me (OB 111). Persecution means to put oneself in the place of one's persecutor—to put oneself into question. Ethical responsibility means to take responsibility for the other with whom one is in relation. Yet 'it has meaning only as an upsurge in me of a responsibility prior to commitment. . . . There I am one and irreplaceable, one inasmuch as irreplaceable in responsibility' (BPW 103). In responsibility, I am one, unique and irreplaceable. I am in a position where no one can replace me; the other has called me and no one can respond in my name or place. Substitution is not possible. Responsibility makes me utterly unique and irreplaceable. Levinas calls this recurrence of the self in response to the other an *obsession* (OB 109). It is an undesirable obsession that cannot be escaped; it is a self-accusing finger that never tires of pointing. The self is a *hostage* to the other. While recurrence endlessly provokes, or persecutes, the self to recognize itself in the past—anarchically—the an-archic past marked by its responsibility for the other holds the self hostage. 'A subject is a hostage' (OB 112).

'The responsibility of the other, the responsibility in obsession, suggests an absolute passivity of a self that has never been able to diverge itself from itself' (OB 114). The recurrence of the self, and the persecution it undergoes, leads the self to its infinite responsibility for the other. In its recurrence the self can no longer limit itself to being a for-itself; having been exiled beyond being, the self can no longer limit its concern to itself. It is through the condition of being a hostage that proximity is possible. It is not presence, but proximity that comes from being a hostage, a proximity that leaves a trace of transcendence. The trace is inscribed in me; it is other to me. All this arises in radical passivity; it is prior to consciousness. The response of the self is a turning—ideally a transformation—it is the first act of a subject who has heard an an-archic call to responsibility. I can either turn towards the other or away from the other—this is already the realm of ontology, the realm of choice. By taking responsibility, I substitute myself for the other in me, I respond to this inscription. Although the idea that my identity is based on my substitution for the other may seem quite alienating, it is in fact what defines me as unique, singular, and irreplaceable. No one else can take my place with regard to substitution. 'I exist through the other and for the other, but without this being alienation: I am inspired' (OB 114). Given the complexity of the notion of substitution, Levinas attempts from a variety of perspectives to further explain how this experience is not one of loss or misfortune.[41] Being a subject is to be hostage to the other, to take responsibility for the other via substitution, but it is also much more than persecution, *it is a gift,* it allows the 'I' to be more than an ego. Thus one no longer begins from the 'I' (or ego), but from alterity. It is not the 'I' that comes to the other, but the other who calls and *elects me,* transforming me into an 'I' that can respond. It is because of my responsibility that I am able to have a non-allergic reaction to alterity. Rather than relate to the other as another self, substitution creates an 'I' who can engage the other without reducing her.

Many of Levinas's readers have claimed his notion of responsibility, as developed by way of substitution, is too extreme. While framed in another manner, the same criticism is launched against Arendt in response to her equally radical notion of responsibility in relation to the *Judenrate* during the Shoah. Developed after the Eichmann trial, Arendt asks herself whether Eichmann was capable of seeing himself from the eyes of the accusers—from the perspective of the others who wanted him to take responsibility for his deeds. These others, the witnesses in the trial, were survivors of the Shoah. Was Eichmann able to question himself and call his actions into question from the position of the persecuted, or was he only capable of seeing himself as the persecuted? Responsibility in terms of an active praxis is this ability to be questioned and to call oneself into question. While Levinas takes ethics to be an asymmetrical relation, Arendt views responsibility in terms of plurality and thus asks whether the survivors were able to imagine themselves in the shoes of Eichmann, or did they refuse to do so by defining him as a monster and denying their own agency? For Arendt the world is shared; whether one is persecuted or the persecutor, both need to understand each other to act together to repair the world. For this reason she stresses the political importance of 'training one's imagination to go visiting', of putting oneself in the shoes of the other as other (as opposed to another self). Only if one is able to imagine the world according to the other can one take responsibility for it. This brings to light how responsibility and solidarity are inextricably intertwined for Arendt.

Returning to the Judaic

Still unsatisfied with his account of responsibility, Levinas returns once again to the Judaic tradition in the latter sections of *Otherwise Than Being*. What he realizes here is that it is not only in terms of language that his account of ethics is limited, it is also in terms of an underlying philosophical anthropology. While Levinas never explicitly distinguishes between a Judaic and a non-Judaic philosophical anthropology in *Otherwise Than Being* (he does in the Talmudic reading 'When God Created Women')—he does so implicitly by differentiating his view from what he defines as Christianity. In this final section on responsibility, I consider this aspect of the Judaic, which also makes clear how Levinas and Arendt both reject the underlying ethos in Heidegger's project, one that embraces a non-Judaic philosophical anthropology by focusing on death and singularity.

In Levinas's final attempt to express the rich meaning, both positive and negative, of responsibility in terms of substitution, he turns to the notion of *hineni*. He defines the term as follows: '[T]he word *I* means *here I am*, answering for everything and everyone' (OB 114). *Hineni* (הנני) comes from a Hebrew phrase that cannot be defined as either a noun or a verb, as הנה is closer to a responsorial (in the accusative) predicator of existence that also emphasizes presence and immediacy.[42] *Hineni* (הנני) has the first-person singular suffix added onto it and so means 'here I am' and is used in biblical Hebrew to connote that one is present and ready to respond. Levinas, following a rich Talmudic tradition, interprets *hineni* (הנני) in a variety of ways. For Levinas, *hineni* is 'a sign made to another . . . a sign of this impossibility of slipping away and being replaced, of this identity, this uniqueness' (OB 145). It is the only possible ethical response to the face of the other. This is the response of a persecuted self; it is the hostage as 'a witness of the Infinite . . . an exception to the rule of being, irreducible to representation, only of the Infinite. It is by the voice of the witness that the glory of the Infinite is glorified' (OB 146). It is by responding with the words *hineni* (הנני) that we are witness to the ethical relation, to the infinity that transcends any totality and to God. Although *hineni* does mean belief in God, it recognizes that it signifies 'here I am' in the name of God; I am a witness to the glory of God and it is this glory that is the source of my response (OB 149). Thus the sign of the Infinite, of the Other, is testified to by the words *hineni*; these words are the present response to a trace, that is the face of the other, that came from the past and is already withdrawn.

In addition to the use of the term *hineni*, Levinas concludes *Otherwise Than Being* by citing a famous medieval Jewish scholar, Yehuda Halevi, who was said to have claimed, 'God speaks to each man in particular' (OB 184). This idea resonates with Levinas's exposition in *Otherwise Than Being* in that substitution singularizes me; it is an election that holds me hostage. 'This book interprets the subject as a hostage and the subjectivity of the subject as a substitution breaking with being's essence' (OB 184). He added, in an interview, 'There is a Hebrew expression: "Here am I" [*hineni*]; it's used by Abraham. And the word which sums up this positioning is *responsibility*'.[43] It is quite likely that Levinas always had the notion of *hineni* in mind when he introduced the notions of substitution and responsibility into his ethics. This biblical notion exemplifies the paradox Levinas seeks to express. Responsibility is both a gift and a burden, I am elected—particularized—while at the same time I am a hostage, persecuted by the other. 'Each individual . . . is called to leave in his turn, or without awaiting his turn, the concept of the ego . . . to respond with responsibility: *me,* that is, *here I am for the others*' (OB 185). The presence of language of election here is clearly a reference to the Judaic notion of election. While often misunderstood or misrepresented as a claim to superiority, Levinas and other Judaic scholars define the Judaic notion of election as a call to responsibility. Although Levinas does not provide the readers of *Otherwise Than Being* with the underlying Judaic narrative, I will briefly do so here based on his discussion of election or choseneness in *Unforeseen History* (113–124).

Election, like the call, can be either affirmed or denied. The latter leaves one in the realm of ontology, where ethics is reduced to morality. However, by affirming my election, I choose the *yetzer tov* over the *yetzer ra,* I affirm that goodness is prior to freedom (NTR 163). To welcome being summoned by the other is to verify that goodness precedes being, that ethics precedes ontology. *Yetzer,* which means impulse or inclination, indicates that humanity was formed with two impulses: a worldly impulse (*the yetzer tov*) and a selfish impulse (*the yetzer ra*). The *yetzer tov* is the ethical voice that reminds us of our relation to others and to God. The *yetzer ra* is clearly more difficult to define. Unlike many Christian-inspired philosophical views, or the Kantian notion of evil, the *yetzer ra* is not interpreted as a desire to do wrong. By contrast, it is usually conceived of as the selfish nature, the desire to satisfy personal needs without regard for ethics and the law—that is, for the other, others or God. The *yetzer ra* is not a bad thing. The Talmud makes clear that without the desire to satisfy personal needs, we would not build a house, get married, have children, and so forth—much of what Levinas describes as part of the self prior to the ethical encounter in *Totality and Infinity*. Being is by no means evil in a Christian sense; rather, being is being for oneself, is being selfish, which is both good and bad, often depending on the circumstances.

While many of Levinas's readers see his discussion of being as overly polemical and critical of Heidegger's reading of being, it is equally affected by the Judaic philosophical anthropology of *yetzer ra*. What is perhaps most fundamental to this anthropology is that the *yetzer ra* needs to be tempered or interrupted by the *yetzer tov* (and vice versa). We are clearly marked by these two impulses and thus always have the ability to choose which impulse to follow. Jonathan Sacks writes about 'a concept that ought to exist in ethics but doesn't: *original virtue*. Sin is rarely original, but a good deed sometimes is'.[44] This exemplifies a Judaic philosophical anthropology based on hope and an explicit rejection of the egoism driven by fear. Levinas explicitly writes about the two inclinations in several of his Talmudic readings, and at length in 'God Created Women' (NTR). Furthermore, Levinas suggests that there is a link between the negativity and fear, which arise from the notion of original sin and Hobbes's account of the state of nature. In *Entre Nous*, Levinas critiques the doctrine of original sin as a grand narrative used by Christians to justify suffering (96–97). Levinas argues, in opposition to thinkers such as Hobbes, that people are not by nature egotistic.[45]

Arendt never explicitly refers to either the *yetzer ra* or *tov*. Nonetheless, based on her comments on Augustine and Hobbes, she clearly rejects both of their philosophical anthropologies. In her doctoral dissertation, she has to reconcile Augustine's negative philosophical anthropology with her own.[46] She interprets Augustine, and implies that this view is upheld by all Christian theologians,[47] as follows: '[H]umanity's common descent is its common share in original sin. This sinfulness, conferred with birth, necessarily attaches to everyone. There is no escape from it. It is the same in all people'.[48] While in her dissertation she accepts Augustine's position and connects it to Heidegger's thinking, in her later political writings she develops what she takes to be a contradiction in his thinking. She writes that 'the decisive fact determining man as a conscious, remembering being is birth or "natality", that is, the fact that we have entered the world through birth [not yet political]. The decisive fact determining man as a desired being was death or mortality'.[49] From *Origins* onward, it is clear that Arendt rejects this Augustinian view as well as that of Heidegger in relation to death. A similar rejection of fear and control as the underlying principles of humanity is apparent from her comments on Hobbes (discussed in chapter 3 in relation to totalitarianism), which she also develops in *The Life of the Mind*. According to Arendt, Hobbes denies any meaningful notion of freedom, claiming that it 'signifieth properly the absence of . . . external impediments of motion' (LM 24), equating it with necessity. She equally disdains his assumption that without a sovereign the essence of life is based on fear, violence, solitude and poverty. Thus while one cannot claim that she embraces a Judaic view of the *yetzer,* she does clearly reject its alternative. Her hope in the interhuman realm also embodies a certain optimism with regard to human potential, one that is central to the Judaic. 'In certain Jewish interpretations of the tale the Fall was seen as a rise, a gaining status for humanity'.[50] The difference fundamentally comes down to whether one believes that human beings are born inclined towards good or towards evil, a belief that is often 'imprinted' by one's 'religion' (even though it may no longer play a visible role in one's life). The Judaic position is that we are born with both but by turning towards the other, we come closer to the good. Closely connected to a grounding of one's view of the human person in *tov* rather than *ra,* is a choice between 'grounding' society, the interaction of human persons, in *tov* or *ra,* or as Sacks describes it in '*a politics of interests* or a *politics of principle*'.[51] While we have not yet considered Levinas's politics, it is clear that he—like Arendt—seeks to rescue this relational subjectivity, constituted by responsibility for the other.

The explicit religious engagement in the final pages of *Otherwise Than Being* is significant because it makes clear that Levinas's 'search' for that which is beyond essence cannot be described in purely philosophical terms and without recourse to an openness towards transcendence that is religious, in the sense of relational and binding (as opposed to theological or dogmatic). It makes clear that at the basis of the notion of substitution is a claim for the goodness of the subject in relation, a claim that is affirmed by a Judaic philosophical anthropology. This goodness is associated with a particular vision of the good, that of alterity, and as such is central to Levinas's claim that ethics is first philosophy. He says this explicitly: 'One must not conceive it [persecution] to be in the state of original sin; it is, on the contrary, the original goodness of creation' (OB 121). He claims that the substituted self is goodness (OB 118). What this entails for Levinas is an understanding of the human being as a being called, from beyond being, by goodness. While this claim has certainly been contested by those thinkers who believe in the doctrine of original sin, the latter is not present in the either Levinas's or Arendt's approaches. Although she only rarely uses such theology-laden terms, this is the same 'goodness' Arendt sees in plurality and the reason that she wishes to ground a new principle to guarantee human dignity in it.

> Has not the Good chosen the subject with an election recognizable in the responsibility of being hostage, to which the subject is destined, which he cannot evade without denying himself, and by virtue of which he is unique? . . . This antecedence of responsibility to freedom would signify the Goodness of the Good; the necessity that the Good choose me first before I can be in a position to choose, that is, welcome its choice. (OB 122)

From this passage it is clear that Levinas associates the other with goodness. Yet this goodness is beyond being, in the realm prior to responsibility, and can only be experienced by its trace in the present. This unbridgeable gap between being and the Good is very important to Levinas's ethics. The trace marks us as open to goodness but does not give us access to the saying of the Good. The first act of goodness is being capable of 'doing', accepting the responsibility for the other, of responding to the call or face of the other. This is done by means of substitution. 'The ego . . . is this original expiation' (OB 118). Taking responsibility means to apologize for prioritizing my being over that of the stranger, widow or orphan. Reversing this ontological prioritization means to recognize how the other transforms 'me' into an 'I', allowing the call of the other to be constitutive of my subjectivity.[52] While Arendt, unfortunately, never delves this deeply into the significance of subjectivity, the political is the space of intersubjectivity, of the between, the space in which the relation to the other is prioritized—it is a space that rejects the ontological reduction and the instrumentalization of the other. Is it possible that a Levinasian view of subjectivity could underline and strengthen her notion of personal responsibility for the world, a responsibility that is necessary if the political is to thrive? Arendt does not offer an account of why the self takes responsibility, of why the self feels called to act and to repair the world. Given the agonism of the *polis* and the courage it takes to participate, why would anyone enter the *polis*? Furthermore, Arendt—contrary to almost all other writers in the post-Shoah period—continues to view the political as a realm of freedom, as a space of hope and discovery. Where does this overwhelmingly positive vision come from? Certainly not from the past—Arendt knew firsthand what crimes humanity was capable of committing. The following quote, which reveals a side of her thought often unnoticed, certainly points towards a Judaic philosophical anthropology:

> Biblically speaking, they would have to accept—in speechless wonder the miracle for the universe, of man and of being—the miracle that God did not create Man, but 'male and female created He them.' They would have to accept in something more than the resignation of human weakness the fact that 'it is not good for man to be alone.' (PhP 103; PP 39, 60)

After all the horrors Arendt had examined and experienced, she did not lose faith in the miraculous potential for human beings—in the plural—to create a shared world together, and this by means of the political. The question we will now consider is whether Levinas shared Arendt's faith in the political.

NOTES

1. David Nirenberg, *Anti-Judaism: The Western Tradition* (New York: W. W. Norton, 2013); Simon Schama, *The Story of the Jews: Finding the Words 1000 BC–1492 AD*, 1st ed. (New York: Ecco, 2014).

2. Emmanuel Levinas, 'Sur Les "Ideen" de M. E. Husserl', *Revue Philosophique de La France et de l'Étranger* 107 (1 January 1929): 230–265.

3. Emmanuel Levinas, 'Martin Heidegger et L'ontologie', *Revue Philosophique de La France et de l'Étranger* 113 (1 January 1932): 395–431.

4. Emmanuel Levinas, *Théorie de l'intuition dans la phénoménologie de Husserl* (Paris: Librairie Philosophique Vrin, 2000); Emmanuel Levinas, *De l'évasion* (Paris: Le Livre de Poche, 1998); Emmanuel Levinas, *De l'existence à l'existant*, 2nd ed. (Paris: Librairie Philosophique Vrin, 2002); Emmanuel Levinas, *Le temps et l'autre*, 11th ed. (Paris: Presses Universitaries de France—PUF, 2014); Emmanuel Levinas, *En découvrant l'existence avec Husserl et Heidegger* (Paris: Librairie Philosophique Vrin, 2002).

5. Levinas, 'Martin Heidegger et L'ontologie', 15–16. A better translation of the French 'L'être de l'étant est l'objet' de l'*ontologie*' is 'The being of Being is the "object" of ontology'.

6. Raoul Mortley, *French Philosophers in Conversation: Levinas, Schneider, Serres, Irigaray, Le Doeuff, Derrida* (London; New York: Routledge, 1991); Jacques Derrida and Elisabeth Weber, *Questioning Judaism: Interviews by Elisabeth Weber* (Stanford, Calif.: Stanford University Press, 2004).

7. Both Levinas and Arendt share the view Nancy articulates in *Being Singular Plural* (Stanford, Calif.: Stanford University Press, 2000). *Mitsein* is constitutive of *sein*, rather than Heidegger's position that *sein* is constitutive of *mitsein*. Another way to phrase this would be to say that intersubjectivity constitutes subjectivity.

8. Levinas, 'Martin Heidegger et L'ontologie', 18.

9. Emmanuel Levinas, *Existence and Existents*, trans. Alphonso Lingis (Pittsburgh, Pa.: Duquesne University Press, 2001), 19.

10. Emmanuel Levinas, *Time and the Other*, trans. Richard A. Cohen (Pittsburgh, Pa.: Duquesne University Press, 1990), 35.

11. Emmanuel Levinas, *Existence et Existents*, translated by Alphonso Lingis (The Hague: Springer Science & Business Media, 1978), 54.

12. This prioritization of speech, or sound/listening, over appearing or visual/sight is also typically attributed to the Judaic, as Jerusalem is identified by its rejection of images (especially when it is contrasted to Athens or Christianity).

13. To summarize: he shows a preference for the term ethical in his early so-called philosophical writings, and for the term religion in his so-called confessional writings, although this distinction disappears in all his later writings.

14. Antje Kapust, Kent Still, and Eric Sean Nelson, eds., *Addressing Levinas*, 1st ed. (Evanston, Ill.: Northwestern University Press, 2005), xi.

15. Gary Brent Madison, *The Politics of Postmodernity: Essays in Applied Hermeneutics* (Dordrecht, Netherlands; Boston: Kluwer Academic Publishers, 2001), 34.

16. Bettina Bergo, 'Emmanuel Levinas', in *The Stanford Encyclopedia of Philosophy*, ed. Edward N. Zalta, Fall 2014, 2, plato.stanford.edu/archives/fall2014/entries/levinas/.

17. Anya Topolski, 'On Freedom in Athens and Jerusalem: Arendt's Political Challenge to Levinas' Ethics of Responsibility', in *The Awakening to the Other: A Provocative Dialogue with Emmanuel Levinas*, ed. R. Burggraeve (Leuven; Dudley, Mass.: Peeters Publishers, 2008), 215–240.

18. While, as forewarned, their distinct terminology makes it difficult to show this shared perspective, it is clear that they are both critical of the same elements of the tradition and that both seek to respond by focusing on the relationship to the other.

19. Michael F. Bernard-Donals, '"Difficult Freedom": Levinas, Language, and Politics', *Diacritics* 35, no. 3 (2005): 2, doi:10.1353/dia.2007.0019.

20. According to Gibbs, it is 'as if' Levinas spent a decade trying to 're-found' his Judaic idea in philosophical terms. *Correlations in Rosenzweig and Levinas* (Princeton, N.J.: Princeton University Press, 1994).

21. Robert Bernasconi and David Wood, eds., *The Provocation of Levinas: Rethinking the Other* (London; New York: Routledge, 1988).

22. Ibid., 168.

23. In addition to the teaching metaphor, Levinas provides a phenomenological account of the experience of the face by means of Descartes's idea of infinity, an idea that overflows or goes beyond the concept of infinity, which itself is infinite and thus cannot be bounded.

24. Salomon Malka, *Monsieur Chouchani: L'enigme d'un maitre du XXe siecle; entretiens avec Elie Wiesel, suivis d'une enquete* (Paris: J. C. Lattes, 1994). In addition, it is worth noting that when studying Talmud one can never study alone. Studying usually takes the form of a heated exchange between two students sitting face-to-face, a method referred to as *pilpul*. In this way, one is always both learning from a teacher, from the other and from what both bring out of the self.

25. Jacques Derrida, *Writing and Difference* (Chicago: University of Chicago Press, 1978).

26. Bernard-Donals, '"Difficult Freedom",' 5.

27. For those of Levinas's readers who were also present at his Talmudic readings in 1965, entitled 'Promised Land or Permitted Land', a few months after the publication of this essay, the allusion to promised land immediately calls to mind his thorough discussion of the relation among identity, peoples and geography.

28. See especially the essay 'Secularism and the Thought of Israel', 113–124.

29. Claire Elise Katz and Lara Trout, eds., *Emmanuel Levinas: Levinas, Phenomenology and His Critics* (London: Taylor & Francis, 2005), 51.

30. Michaël de Saint-Cheron, *Du juste au saint: Ricoeur, Rosenzweig et Levinas* (Paris: Desclée de Brouwer, 2013), 31.

31. This is my translation. The original French is: 'Il s'agirait d'un nouveau concept de la passivité, d'une passivité plus radicale que celle de l'effet dans une série casuale, d'*en deçà* la conscience et le savoir . . . une passivité référée à l'*envers* de l'être, antérieure au plan ontologique . . . référée à l'antériorité encose sans dehors de la création' (73).

32. This is similar to a more recent claim made by Jean-Luc Nancy in *Being Singular Plural,* in which he tries to find the means to express this relation (as the between or as singular plurality). For Nancy, the struggle itself to find a means to express this notion is emblematic of the ontological tradition's failure to properly thematize this relation. Thus, for both Levinas and Nancy, overcoming this linguistic difficulty is a major obstacle. Nancy, *Being Singular Plural.*

33. Bergo, 'Emmanuel Levinas', 17.

34. Philip J. Maloney, 'Levinas, Substitution and Transcendental Subjectivity', *Man and World* 30, no. 1 (1 January 1997): 55, doi:10.1023/A:1004228124719.

35. Simon Critchley and Robert Bernasconi, *The Cambridge Companion to Levinas* (Cambridge, Mass.; New York: Cambridge University Press, 2002), 236.

36. Lévinas, *Of God Who Comes to Mind*, 245.

37. David Banon, *Emmanuel Levinas: Philosophe et pedagogue* (Paris: Editions du nadir de l'Alliance israelite universelle, 1998), 25.

38. Jonathan Sacks, *To Heal a Fractured World: The Ethics of Responsibility* (New York: Schocken, 2007), 144.

39. Critchley and Bernasconi, *Cambridge Companion to Levinas*, 238; Jeffrey Bloechl, *The Face of the Other and the Trace of God: Essays on the Philosophy of Emmanuel Levinas* (New York: Fordham University Press, 2000); Jeffrey Bloechl, *Liturgy of the Neighbor: Emmanuel Levinas and the Religion of Responsibility*, 1st ed. (Pittsburgh, Pa.: Duquesne University Press, 2000).

40. Saint-Cheron, *Du juste au saint*, 31.

41. For example, he returns to the metaphor of 'being in one's own skin' now suggesting a new paradigm, that of 'having-the-other-in-one's-own-skin' (BPW 115).

42. There is nothing like this in English grammar. We translate it as 'being' even though it is neither a verb nor a noun. 'After the death of a certain god inhabiting the world behind the scenes, the substitution of the hostage discovers the trace, the unpronounceable inscription, of what, always already past, always "he", does not enter into any present, to which are suited not the nouns designating beings, or the verbs in which their essence resounds, but that which, as a pronoun, marks with its seal all that a noun can convey' (OB 185).

43. Mortley, *French Philosophers in Conversation*, 16; Hilary Putnam, *Jewish Philosophy as a Guide to Life: Rosenzweig, Buber, Levinas, Wittgenstein* (Bloomington: Indiana University Press, 2008).

44. Sacks, *To Heal a Fractured World*, 61.

45. It is worth clarifying, to avoid any confusion, that this critique of Hobbes's naturalism implies that Levinas's philosophy espouses a naturalist or essentialist position. See Oona Ajzenstat, *Driven Back to the Text: The Premodern Sources of Levinas's Postmodernism* (Pittsburgh, Pa.: Duquesne University Press, 2001), 57.

46. Arendt, *Love and Saint Augustine*, ed. Joanna Vechhiarelli and Judith Chelius Stark, 1st ed. (Chicago: University of Chicago Press, 1998), 102–108.

47. Ibid., 52.

48. Ibid., 102.

49. Ibid., 51.

50. Mortley, *French Philosophers in Conversation*, 18.

51. Sacks, *To Heal a Fractured World*, 124.

52. Levinas reminds his interviewer, Phillipe Nemo, that the goal in *Totality and Infinity* was to explore 'the problem of the intersubjective relationship's content' (EI 79).

SIX

An Ethical Politics

While Levinas is recognized as one of the twentieth century's most influential ethical thinkers, his many essays on politics are often completely overlooked. According to Simon Critchley, the question of politics is Levinas's Achilles heel.[1] While this claim has led to more interest in the question of politics in Levinas, it has also reinforced the claim that he fails to see the potential of the political and as such does not find it necessary to properly develop its relation to his ethics.[2] In this vein, one could compare criticisms of Levinas's political lacuna to those of Arendt's ethical lacuna—in both cases their focus is assumed to come at the cost of another aspect of the interhuman realm. However, as I have demonstrated in chapter 4, it is a fundamental misconception with regard to Arendt's writing that it is unethical. It is now time to challenge the position held by the vast number of Levinas scholars that his writing is either nonpolitical or even worse, antipolitical. The latter claim is all too often justified by citing the following quote from *Totality and Infinity*: 'The art of foreseeing war and of winning it by every means—politics—is henceforth enjoined as the very exercise of reason. Politics is opposed to morality' (TI 21). It is the goal of this chapter to correct these misunderstandings and to bring to light Levinas's ambiguous understanding of politics, the political and justice.

Levinas, like Arendt, felt called to rethink the philosophical tradition because of the dehumanization, injustice and horrors that ultimately led to the Shoah. The world he witnessed called for a radical change, and specifically with regard to its failure to care for the other. Thus his ethics can, and should, be read in relation to totalitarianism, a political regime.[3] For Levinas, ethics is about radical subjectivity, a subjectivity that is experienced and expressed in all forms of human interaction—including the interactions Arendt would describe as political. This is most clear from the connection, in his writings, between responsibility and justice. Justice, for Levinas among other Jewish thinkers, is what the political is for Arendt. It is thus essential to consider the relationship between Levinas's ethics and his conception of justice to understand his views on the political. Levinas is aware, although he does not always make this point explicit, that while ethics may be first philosophy, it is always in the world in which we must consider the question of justice—in a space where there is not only an other but also always and already a third person. In this vein, Levinas's ethics delimits the political. This is precisely the danger of Levinas's ethical politics (as opposed to Arendt's political ethics), in that his ethics is imposed upon justice rather than being immanent to the political. This was a great concern for Arendt, for 'if we knew what justice was, then theoretically we could construct a great grid to lay over all possible human actions, informing us whether they are just or not. A certain amount of calculation might still be necessary, but we would no longer have to think about the meaning of justice'.[4] Yet it would be unjust to Levinas to read his ethics in terms of a normative prescription. There is no direct, unthinking path from ethics to justice that is from the other to the third or from responsibility to justice. The purpose of this chapter is thus first to show how Levinas understands the separation between ethics and politics; second, to show that Levinas was always concerned with politics; and third, to consider several Arendtian echoes in his political reflection. Last but not least, I intend to consider some of the main debates concerning Levinas's political potential as well as the limits of his notion of an ethical politics or a messianic politics.

THE CRITERION FOR LEVINAS'S POLITICS

In 1972, at an academic conference organized in her honour, Arendt was asked (by Hans Morgenthau): 'What are you? Are you a conservative? Are you a liberal? Where is your position in the contemporary possibilities'?[5] She replied:

> I don't know and I've never known. And I suppose I never had any such position. You know the left think that I am conservative, and the conservatives think that I am a maverick or God knows what. And I must say I couldn't care less. I don't think that the real questions of this century will get any kind of illumination by this kind of thing.[6]

While there is no public record of Levinas's answering such a question, many of his readers have sought to categorize his political writings into the same categories rejected by Arendt. As students of Heidegger they followed in his footsteps in terms of trying to rethink the entire Western tradition of philosophy, and as phenomenologists, it is necessary to recognize that their thought cannot be forced into the standard categories of

Western politics. In order to avoid making this mistake, let us consider the range of positions Levinas's politics is said to fill in order to show why his notion of justice needs to be understood—much like his ethics—as beyond categorization. William Paul Simmons defends the position that 'Levinas calls for a liberal state'.[7] As is clear from our analysis of Levinas's ethics in the previous chapter, this conclusion is the product of a problematic oversimplification[8] and, as we show in this chapter, will find no support in his politics. C. Fred Alford advances the thesis that Levinas 'does not fit into any of the categories by which we ordinarily approach political theory',[9] but then quickly goes on to categorize him as an 'inverted liberal'. By focusing more closely on the ethical and political importance of his notion of fraternity, as Catherine Chalier does,[10] one can try to connect his notion of justice to the school of French republicanism, a tempting interpretation that leads to a rapprochement with Arendt's republican interests. It is also a reading supported by Howard Caygill in *Levinas & the Political* (2002), which considers the relationship between Levinas's life, his thought (although the Talmudic writings are too quickly passed over) and his understanding of the political.

Although I acknowledge that these responses have helped to bring the question of Levinas and the political to the foreground, they have also, unfortunately, led us astray. Many of these scholars have allowed themselves to get caught up in the game of politics that Levinas so clearly criticizes, the game that leads to the totalization of the other. Thus, rather than struggling through Levinas's complex and contradictory reflections on the political, with the aim of understanding their contradictions and trying to distil their meaning, many of these scholars have focused on categorizing Levinas's thought according to criteria delineated by contemporary political theory. The danger of such readings is a flattening of Levinas's claims and neglect of the originality of his potential contribution to the political. Just as Levinas's ethics has challenged the entire Western ontological tradition, we ought not to presume his political reflection is less radical. It is my contention that part of the problem is rooted in the fact that many of the readers interested in the question of Levinas and the political fail to consider the importance of the so-called confessional writings in this area, which, as I intend to demonstrate, are rich with insight. Setting aside this task for the following section, let us first look at Levinas's political contribution from within the so-called philosophical writings.

Justice as a Model of Ethical Politics

The question fundamentally at stake for Levinas is: Is society rooted in the principle of fear (and of war against all), or in hope (and in the-one-for-the-other)? While he initially associates the former with politics and the latter with ethics, he soon begins to rethinks this dichotomy in terms of justice. It is this latter rethinking that brings his thought closer to that of Arendt. Let us begin by considering the meaning of the term justice in his earlier writings:

> In political life, taken unrebuked, humanity is understood from its works—a humanity of interchangeable men, of reciprocal relations. . . . Justice consists in again making possible expression, in which in non-reciprocity the person presents himself as unique. Justice is a right to speak. It is perhaps here where the perspective of a religion opens. It diverges from political life, to which philosophy does not necessarily lead. (TI 298)

Much like the distinction Arendt introduces in *The Human Condition* between work and action, Levinas's position here is that humanity is erroneously being reduced and understood from its works. Like Levinas, Arendt emphasizes the non-superfluousness of every person, her non-interchangeability, arguing that because of our absolute alterity and unicity, the other must be prioritized. While Levinas is attacking politics, his understanding of politics is precisely that which is not political for Arendt. Both see a politics that denies the particularity of every subject as dangerous. Arendt responds by developing a new notion of the political rooted in plurality; Levinas chooses to use another term, that of justice, in order to respond to Western politics.

As we saw in *Totality and Infinity*, language is ethics' mouthpiece. Likewise, justice is also expressed by means of speech. Justice is only possible through an encounter with the other that occurs via language. However, justice—like ethics—cannot be 'known'; it is beyond epistemology, a phenomenon to be experienced rather than calculated. It is the latter temptation to define justice that makes Levinas apprehensive with regard to theories of justice (such as Rawls's), which have a tendency to seek totality; this is analogous to Arendt's position. Justice for Levinas is not a theory—like ethics it originates in the other's right to speak and my responsibility to respond; it however goes beyond the face-to-face relation and enters the realm of sociality in which ethics' exclusivity is limited by justice's inclusivity. Ethics is a relation between self and other; justice is a relation that is not limited to a twosome, as the other always has a third, as does the self. According to Levinas, 'the third party looks at me in the eyes of the Other' (TI 213). The third, as some readers have suggested, is by no means an afterthought in Levinas's writings. An essay from 1954, written seven years prior to *Totality and Infinity*, clearly shows otherwise. 'Earthly morality invites one into the difficult detour that leads to third parties that have remained outside of love. Justice alone satisfies its need for purity'.[11] Justice in this vein enters Arendt's realm of plurality. What makes this comparison interesting is how both compare it to the phenomenon of love, a comparison that has many echoes in the writings of other Jewish thinkers. Arendt defines the political in terms of friendship and as opposed to love (HC 51–52). Likewise, Levinas defines justice in opposition to love. In *Totality and Infinity*, he describes responsibility as harsh love or love without reciprocity. Love can be exclusive, and justice is by definition inclusive (which is not to be equated with universal). This distinction between exclusive and inclusive separates responsibility from justice as well as ethics from the political. While ethics is exclusive, justice must aim—but will always fail—to be inclusive. In a late interview from 1986, Levinas further clarified this point:

> The word 'justice' applies much more to the relationship with the third party [*autrui*] than to the relationship with the other [*autre*]. But in reality, the relationship with another is never uniquely the relationship with the other: from this moment on, the third is represented in the other; that is, in the very appearance of the other the third always regards me. And this nevertheless, makes the relationship between justice and responsibility with regard to the other extremely narrow.[12]

From the perspective of the ethical relation, justice is an interruption, and yet according to Levinas, the third is always already present in the ethical relation. In this reading, which differs from that of *Totality and Infinity*, justice has priority over ethics—just as ethics interrupts the ego, justice must constantly interrupt the self-other relation to create space for the relation to the third. Justice cannot be as blind as love. Arendt makes an analogous claim in her political critique of love: 'Love, by reason of its passion, destroys the in-between which relates us to and separates us from others. . . . [I]t is by its very nature unworldly, and it is for this reason rather than its rarity that it is not only a political but antipolitical' (HC 242). What both Levinas and Arendt are trying to express is the danger of limiting the intersubjective relation to any love-based relation that destroys the possibility of creating an inclusive solidarity.

According to Levinas, this distinction between love and justice has political implications in yet another sense. Love, unlike the law in liberal states, arises from within. Law is externality, whereas love remains rooted in the relationship between the self and the other. Thus, while for both Arendt and Levinas an externally imposed law is not sufficient for justice, it is nonetheless a necessary minimum. It is in this vein that both see the limits of liberalism. Like Arendt, Levinas emphasizes the importance of putting oneself into question, of being questioned and of responding (by means of judgement and responsibility). It is not sufficient to allow the state or government to do this in one's name—there is no place for representation, as one is irreplaceable and no substitutions are possible, a claim to which Arendt—a staunch supporter of direct democracy—would strongly agree. Substitution is as impossible with regard to justice as it is with regard to responsibility. According to Levinas, liberalism all too often creates a situation in which we justify ignoring the call to responsibility from within subjectivity because we defer to an appeal from the state:

> Man is also in this sense a political animal. . . . Then no one can find the law for his action in the depths of his heart. The impasse of liberalism is in this exteriority of my consciousness to itself. The subject of the faults awaits the meaning of being from the outside; he is no longer the man who confesses his sins, but the one who acquiesces to the accusations.[13]

Levinas's notion of justice, which like responsibility arises from within the intersubjective relation and thus from within subjectivity, offers a perspective on justice other than that of liberalism. This intersubjective notion of justice is much closer to Arendt's notion of the political, which arises from 'in the between.' There is no relation to another person in the singular. The third is always already present in the face of the other. While this is deeply destabilizing if one wants to read Levinas's notion of ethics as foundational, it is also evidence of his post-foundational approach—one that enables a further engagement with Arendt's post-foundational notion of the political. The face-to-face is always in fact a face-to-faces (which is already clear from the Hebrew term *panim*). Justice, or in Arendt's terms the political, is always 'present' in the ethical. While an ethical relation is theoretically possible, in reality it is always interrupted by a, or many, third(s).

As is evident from the above, the relationship between ethics and justice for Levinas is clearly complicated. Can one choose to refuse the third and only respond to the other, or is this inhuman? Is humanity to be found in ethics or justice? Would it not be unethical to deny others for the sake of the other? Likewise, wouldn't Levinas's ethics of infinite responsibility be totalizing if it were not interrupted by the third? This is precisely the question posed in a 1987 interview with Levinas, to which he responded: 'I don't know if this situation is intolerable. It is not what you would call agreeable, surely, it is not pleasant, but it is the good'.[14] The good Levinas refers to here is the goodness beyond being; it is good even if it is impossible. While I have immense respect for Levinas's position, I wonder if his ideals are politically irresponsible, an accusation Derrida has also explored.[15] It is for this reason that I take his answer to be an important reason to opt for the priority of the political, as Arendt does. Levinas, aware of how impossible and painful ethics is, remains tied to the ideal of absolute justice rather than the real hope of some more justice. Instead of beginning from the reality of plurality and the limitations it imposes on absolute justice, Levinas prioritizes the good beyond being—an unattainable good. Rather than fully embrace the contingency and uncontrollability of the human realm, as Arendt does, Levinas sets humanity up to fail by setting an impossible standard for justice. The question is, why does he do so?

Difficult Freedom

'Ontology as first philosophy is a philosophy of power, does not call into question the same, a philosophy of injustice . . . and leads inevitably to another power, to imperialist domination, to tyranny. The terms must be reversed' (TI 17). While ontology inspires a politics rooted in freedom by establishing the self as the centre of the world, thereby prioritizing the ego's freedom over all others, it is an oversimplification to state that Levinas is opposed to freedom. Clearly limited by his own assumptions about what politics is and can be, Levinas fails to consider a paradigm of the political not rooted in ontology or singularity (in a similar manner to Arendt's failure to consider an ethics not rooted in ontology or singularity). Nonetheless, he repeatedly points towards such an alternative notion of the political, not only when speaking about justice, but also with relation to a freedom he describes as difficult.

> Totalitarianism is the . . . demented pretension to the invisible, when the acute experience of the human in the twentieth century teaches that the thoughts of men are borne by needs which explain society and history, that hunger and fear can prevail over every human resistance and freedom! There is no question of doubting this human misery, this dominion the things and the wicked exercise over man, this animality. But to be a man is to know that this is so. Freedom consists in knowing that freedom is in peril. (TI 35)

This citation clearly complicates any reading of freedom in Levinas that reduces its meaning to either egoism or ontology. He, like Arendt, recognizes that totalitarianism was a threat to humanity because it denied the importance of freedom. *Difficult Freedom*, the title of the first published collection of so-called Jewish writings, is about seeking a life beyond an existence defined by egoism, instincts and need; freedom for freedom's sake is meaningless. Arendt, in her collection of Jewish writings (written mostly between the 1930s and 1950s), expresses a similar position by claiming that a life for the sake of survival or work, the experience of being instrumentalized, is not worth living. To live means to do more than survive—it means to experience the interhuman realm, its empowerment and freedom. Levinas also refers to the phenomena of fear and hunger, experiences that reduce human beings to animals (as does labour for Arendt) and thereby destroy the possibility to protest and to express one's freedom. What this makes clear is that Levinas is equally aware of the fragility of such difficult freedom. When he calls for a reversal of the priority of ontological freedom, he does not mean that freedom cannot be meaningful. Freedom rooted in ontology justifies injustice towards others and has the potential to be murderous to the life and dignity of the other.

A freedom detached from the ethical relation is ontological egoism; it is not difficult freedom. 'In European thought the spontaneity of freedom is not called into question, its limitation alone is held to be tragic and to constitute a scandal' (TI 55). The notion of 'calling into question' is essential for both ethics and justice; it is likewise essential for Arendt in terms of responsibility and judgement. Implicitly, Levinas is addressing thinkers who defend the concept of negative freedom, such as Isaiah Berlin, arguing that only negative freedom is robust enough to prevent totalitarianism. For Levinas, such unquestioned support of freedom, freedom from interruption, a freedom to be 'left alone', is unethical and contrary to the human condition. Although Berlin's support of negative freedom can certainly be understood as a valid response to the Shoah, according to both Arendt and Levinas it is reactionary rather than responsible.[16] Negative freedom in Berlin is similar to Heidegger's notion of *Dasein*; both fail to prioritize the relation to the other and in so doing equally deny that the self is constituted by the other (a form of self-denial). While I can choose to deny this part of myself, just as I can choose not to respond to the other, in so doing I am silencing a part of myself. This silencing, in Arendt's terms, is politically irresponsible and dangerous, as it leads to the thoughtlessness she decries in Eichmann. While this is by no means a crime, I am nonetheless responsible for this other whom I have harmed by prioritizing myself and refusing to call myself into question.

What is intriguing is that Levinas seems to limit reflexivity—questioning oneself—to an internal process, albeit one awoken by an external other, whereas Arendt sees reflexivity as something that is created both within the self by way of the *vita contemplativa,* and within the public sphere by means of action. In this vein, Levinas is no different than many of the thinkers Arendt criticizes for following Plato's lead in terms of originating politics in fear (rather than allowing hope to reign). Levinas is highly suspicious of what Arendt takes to be the heart of the political—spontaneity. His fear is that spontaneity prevents both responsibility and reflexivity. 'Political theory derives justice from the undiscussed value of spontaneity; its problem is to ensure, by way of knowledge of the world, the most complete exercise of spontaneity by reconciling my freedom with the freedom of others' (TI 55). Levinas here refers to—with disdain—what many political theorists deem acceptable. What is wrong with a political theory that aims to reconcile the freedom of individuals? For Levinas, this ontological freedom is in tension with ethics and he fears that such a reconciliation will justify the precedence of the self in such 'calculations'—implicitly affirming a non-intersubjective understanding of the self as constituted by the other. It is thus not freedom, in itself, that is problematic, but rather the prioritization of my freedom over that of the other. For Levinas, there are two types of freedom: one negative, exemplified by Hobbes and rooted in fear and the self, and the other positive, rooted in responsibility and the other, which he refers to as difficult freedom. The latter is similar to Arendt's freedom rooted in plurality (with the exception of its connection to spontaneity). Arendt expresses a similar criticism of ontological freedom rooted in the will, in ego-logie, and tries instead to reintroduce a notion of positive political freedom, much as Levinas reintroduces a notion of difficult freedom, or as he refers to it in his later writings, a freedom beyond being.[17]

Justice and the Third

As shown in the previous chapter, one of the marked changes between *Totality and Infinity* and *Otherwise Than Being* is the introduction of several new terms, many of which have explicit Judaic sources. A similar change occurs on the level of justice and the third is now most often referred to in terms of the neighbour, emblematic of the central role of the stranger, widow and orphan in the Torah:

> To be sure—but this is another theme—my responsibility for all can and has to manifest itself also in limiting itself. The ego can, in the name of this unlimited responsibility, be called upon to be concerned also with itself. The fact that the other, my neighbour, is also a third party with respect to another, who is also a neighbour, is the birth of thought, consciousness, justice and philosophy. (OB 128)

Levinas once again affirms that while responsibility for the other is theoretically unlimited, in reality the world is shared by a plurality of others, and as such my responsibility has to limit itself so that it can be for-the-others and not just for-one-other. In order for this to be possible, the self, constituted by the ethical relation, must limit its infinite relation to the other for the sake of all others. 'It is the third party that interrupts the face-to-face of a welcome of the other man, interrupts the proximity or approach of the neighbour, it is the third man with which justice begins' (OB 150). When confronted, questioned or faced by a third to which I *also* have infinite responsibility, I am challenged to reconcile my different responsibilities. Who to respond to first? How? How much to give? These are the difficult questions that must be considered time and again with regard to justice. How can I be infinitely responsible to more than one individual other, how can I possibly limit my responsibility, how can I compare what is incomparable—these are the questions that are born from the third party that interrupts the ethical relation and that gives rise to the ethical dilemmas that distinguish justice from politics. 'Justice is necessary, that is, comparison, coexistence, contemporaneousness, assembling, order, thematization, the visibility of faces, and thus intentionality and the intellect' (OB 157).

What makes Levinas's account of justice difficult to reconcile is the question: If there is always already a third, why does Levinas focus so much on the self-other relation? Or, in other words, why present justice as having its origin in ethics? Does ethics impose itself on justice, and if so, doesn't this implicitly diminish justice, making it always an impure or compromised ethics? Arendt clearly refuses such a secondary status to the political. The world is not impure or compromised; its complexity is not something to be shunned. It is for this reason that she refuses to grant priority to morality. Arendt embraces the anarchism and dynamism of community, which Levinas is more reticent to accept for fear that the other, the widow, stranger and orphan, might be persecuted—might be lost in the calculation of totality. It is for this reason that Levinas envisions a politics that must always be interrupted, as this interruption is a constant reminder of one's responsibility. Nonetheless, it would be unjust to reduce Levinas's position on politics to one of disdain for sociality or community. In the end, Levinas accepts—with trepidation—that there are no guarantees. Thus rather than settle for a lesser, but more secure, alternative (that of liberalism and politics), Levinas suggests that—without instrumentalizing ethics—we must strive for justice by prioritizing the ethical interruption of the *polis*. In this sense, the aim of justice is always to recall this original relation in its ethical memory. Concretely, this means that justice is never considered to be complete or comprehensive (hence the aversion for theories of justice that often seek such ends). A space, or gap, is always necessary in order to prevent universalization or totalization, which is the trap that politics falls into. In this way justice is a double struggle: it requires space within the self for the ethical relation but also a space within the relation to the other for a third. Justice, which is the guiding principle of a political sphere in which there are more than two individuals, is the birth of a responsibility that must consider the self, the other and the third, a responsibility that requires consciousness, synthesis and synchrony (OB 16).

Levinas thus neither desires to nor can he offer a prescriptive or normative notion of either ethics or justice. His account of justice must be read in terms of critique of the current approach to politics and to create space for another origin for the political. How this alternative is actually to be realized is not ever systematically addressed. Nonetheless, it is clear that justice cannot follow the asymmetrical model of responsibility. The law cannot be different from one person to another. Yet based on Levinas's discussion of law and judgement in his Talmudic writings, it is clear that particularity must always have priority over universality in order to prevent the latter from being totalized. This is precisely the same choice Arendt makes in her writings on judgement with regard to the relation between particular, universal and general. It is also the same methodology embraced by the authors of the Talmud:

> The Talmud never limits itself to the concept, which, however, is important to it. When it uses concepts, it never forgets the example from which the concept was drawn. '*Here is the law—it is perfectly good, but what will happen if . . .*' is a particular case. The discussion never drops it, and often the concept is reversed.[18]

Although there is space for alterity within the legal system, it is secondary to the laws that are applied universally. It is for this reason that Levinas notes that justice is always violent (a claim that is similar to that developed in his first Talmudic readings). He also makes clear that the equality that must be presupposed for politics is always in danger of erasing the asymmetry of the ethical relation. This is one of his fundamental reproaches towards liberal democracies that are founded upon an abstract notion of equality. While traditionally justice is associated with equality between individuals, Levinas challenges this position because of equality's potential to create inequality among people.[19]

What Levinas seeks is paradoxically a notion of equality based on asymmetry, which he finds in the Judaic. The idea behind this notion of asymmetrical equality is that of unicity, particularity and alterity, rather than a universal and abstract equality. Difficult freedom, difficult in that it is rooted in responsibility, is asymmetrical freedom. What makes it even more difficult is that it is like ethics, nonreciprocal (unlike, for example, the ethics of Martin Buber). My responsibility is to ensure that all others are treated justly regardless of my own rights. While this leaves me vulnerable, it is this vulnerability that is the 'ground' for the ethical relation. I have a responsibility to all others regardless of the duties, actions or words of others. 'The equality of all is borne by my inequality, the surplus of my duties over my rights' (OB 159). I cannot ask that justice be conditional upon the other acting justly, I must assume that I alone act justly—a great risk in the realm of the political. For Levinas this is a necessary risk. To deny the individualizing 'hostage-like' demand of ethics and justice is to deny the externality of the other. What Levinas wants is for this asymmetry not to be denied as it enters the realm of justice. Not all others are the same; some others need more and some have more than others. This cannot be overlooked. Levinas thus calls on those defining the law to consider these differences. This is not to say that the asymmetrical equality associated with difficult freedom is not in favour of individuals being treated with equal rights; it is simply a question of challenging the nature of a blind, blanket-like form of equality (such as liberalism, according to Levinas). What is implicit in Levinas's model is still a state-centred, top-down approach to justice, whereas—as we saw with Arendt—there is a refusal to understand the political as defined by such hierarchy. For Arendt the political is a space of horizontal transcendence and not one of passive acceptance of vertical authority, as it seems to be for Levinas. This is yet another reason to criticize Levinas's notion of justice, which fails to appreciate the importance and potential of horizontality.

POST-FOUNDATIONAL JUDAIC POLITICS

So many citizens in the period after the Shoah, among them intellectuals from all walks of life, were emotionally besieged by the question: How could it have happened? The fact that the death camps emerged from what had once been a liberal democratic state created an overwhelming feeling of disbelief. For the vast majority of Jews (especially for those who considered themselves integrated), the liberal state had held with it the promise of justice, equality and rights, and as a result the end of the war also came to symbolize the end of a dream, an escape from the burden of being Jewish, an escape from the pain of particularity. This dream had led millions of Jews to assimilate in hopes of being granted the rights that ought to have saved them from the gas chambers. The reality of the capricious nature of this political promise was a harsh reminder that equality and rights needed to be rethought. Levinas takes up this task in many of his Talmudic readings, presented to an audience most of whom had miraculously survived the Shoah and as such were, for the most part, searching for new guarantees of justice.

The Rights of the Other

Even before World War II officially began Arendt was aware of the looming refugee crisis and its paradoxical relation to the notion of rights. She dedicates perhaps the most frequently cited chapter of *Origins of Totalitarianism* to the paradox of rights captured in the 1789 Declaration of the Rights of Man and of the Citizen. The question she poses, which has yet to be answered satisfactorily, is: Are persons entitled to rights as human beings or as citizens?

> Arendt had long known that universal human rights are a chimera for those who lack the power to defend them. She knew from her own experience that despite any proclamation of their universality such rights are *not* 'independent of human plurality' and are *not* possessed by human beings 'expelled from the human community'. . . . She spoke, therefore, of 'a right to have rights,' a right 'to live in a framework where one is judged by one's actions and opinions,' and it was that right, denied by totalitarianism, that she hoped would be seen by all as the basic principle of human solidarity. The right to have rights, the right of a plurality of people 'to act together concerning things that are of equal concern to each', was for Arendt the minimum condition of a common human world.[20]

For Arendt, rights are rooted in the state and as such are beyond the reach of those who most need rights—the stateless. Without community, without plurality, these rights remain abstract universal ideals. For this reason, she sought to ground rights in terms of the solidarity, the web-of-relations that arises from plurality. While Arendt rethinks the notion of rights in terms of the right to have rights (to be part of a community or polity), Levinas rethinks rights in terms of the rights of the other. Neither finds the current human rights discourse satisfactory, and both question the 'ground' of human rights.[21]

In order to appreciate Levinas's analysis of human rights discourse, it is necessary to consider several essays, as his position developed and changed over time. In some of his earliest writings on rights, he explores the meaning of being a stranger, or foreigner, in terms of the meaning of rights. He explicitly connects this to the status of Jews during the Shoah as aliens or political refugees or rightless. According to Levinas, human rights cannot be granted by the state. In agreement with Arendt, he appreciates that the state is not a secure enough guarantor for rights, as is clear from the manner by which Jews, in many European states, were denied rights. Rather than 'ground' rights in plurality, Levinas tries to 'ground' rights in alterity. In this sense, both thinkers seek an alternative 'ground' for rights. While they differ in their response, their differences reveal an underlying agreement as well as the importance of considering the intertwined meanings of alterity and plurality:

> By locating 'original right' in proximity and substitution—in what he also called the 'humanism of the other man'—Levinas rigorously distinguished human from natural rights. While the early modern rights tradition used the adjective 'natural' to validate the *a priori* character of human rights, Levinas insists they transcend nature.[22]

While Levinas's later essays directly address the issue of human rights, or 'the rights of man,' many of his Talmudic readings provide a preview of his position. In *Beyond Memory* he writes: 'The government surveyor challenges your title to the land you [referring to the minor prophet *Amos* (5:19)] are working, the tax collector always finds you owe money—these are civil servants or states questioning your illusory rights as a citizen' (TN 85). The impersonal nature of civil servants and technocrats—visible in all bureaucratic states—resists the consideration of every human as a particular and unique person. While we elect, recognize and support our governments because they promise to uphold our rights, Levinas expresses an Arendtian position by describing these rights as 'illusory'. Yet in addition to the political connotations of this claim, Levinas defines these rights as 'illusory' because they are tools of power masked in ethical attire. Thus Levinas, like Arendt, feels the need to challenge the basis of these rights on the ground that they are a source of false hope for the excluded of the world that need them most.

Neither Levinas nor Arendt denies the fact that human rights have improved the lives of many people across the globe; nonetheless both identify dangers at the foundational level. In search for an alternative ground for human rights, Levinas turns to the Judaic tradition, grounding rights in the notion of responsibility. Let us recall that for him, Athens—which speaks on behalf of my rights as well as those of the other—must constantly be interrupted and challenged by Jerusalem, by my responsibility for the other. According to Levinas, the state serves as a surrogate substitute for our own relations to the other. In other words, we excuse ourselves from taking responsibility by relying on the state to do it for us. But as Levinas reminds us, we are irreplaceable, and as such the state cannot care, in the way we can, for the other. By allowing the government to be the supplier (and likewise the revoker) of our rights, we deny our relation to the other, which is based on responsibility and not on rights. As a result we substitute a relation of the face-to-face with one of abstract impersonal alienation—a loss for both the other and the self—and which as Arendt has shown destroys the fabric of the shared world. It is also for this reason that she emphasizes the importance of participation in the *polis* and direct democracy.

A similar position is to be found in Levinas's interpretation of the Talmud based on the notion of *tikkun olam*—which is our unique contribution to the shared responsibility to repair the world and in so doing bring about justice:

> It is as if the multiplicity of persons—and is this not the very meaning of personal?—were the prerequisite for the fullness of 'absolute truth' as if each person, by his uniqueness, endured the revelation of a unique aspect of truth, and that some of its aspects would never be revealed if some members of humanity were missing. This suggests that the totality of truth is made up of the contribution of multiple persons: the uniqueness of each reaction bearing the secret of the text. (NTR 20)

This view directly opposes that of negative freedom, which sees responsibility in terms of a burden. By contrast, Levinas views what Arendt would describe as participation as a form of taking responsibility for the world, which is fundamental to our humanity; it is a form of caring for the other and a means to create community. In addition, both view responsibility and participation in the creation of a shared world as a means to combat alienation. Through our contributions we come to feel valuable to others; we realize we are irreplaceable, keeping the isolation and alienation of modern society at bay. While this requires commitment and can be taxing, it is seen as a blessing for Arendt and Levinas (as well as for the rabbis of the Talmud) because it affirms that to be human is to be in relation to the other, a freedom for the world or other, and thereby rejects the notion of a freedom from (the other or world).

Levinas further develops this position in the 1985 essay 'The Rights of Man and the Rights of the Other':

> A freedom in fraternity, in which the responsibility of one-for-the-other is affirmed, and . . . for which I am answerable. Their original manifestation as rights of the other person and as duty for an *I*, as my fraternal duty—that is the phenomenology of the rights man. . . . My freedom

> and my rights, before manifesting themselves in my opposition to the freedom and rights of the other person, will manifest themselves precisely in the form of responsibility, in human fraternity. . . . Immutable significance and stability, better than guaranteed by the state. (OS 125)

Fraternity, which Levinas refers to in many of his writings, has an explicitly political meaning. Like Arendt, Levinas was greatly inspired by the principles of republicanism (although Arendt clearly preferred the American to the French Revolution, while Levinas preferred the latter). Fraternity, which is more problematic for Arendt because of its familial origin, is related to her notion of solidarity (removing the familial reference), which arises from responsibility for others that is the 'ground' upon which communities are formed. Catherine Chalier, a Levinas scholar, reinterprets fraternity in terms of plurality: 'Fraternity, irreducibly plural, is from then on never a total amalgamation (*fusionelle*) afraid of falling into a dangerous misinterpretation, and thus precedes the different types of community or of societies thought or imagined by people in order to live together without destroying themselves'.[23] While republicanism certainly emphasizes participation, responsibility and citizenship, these concepts are world-oriented rather than other-oriented and thus closer to Arendt's notion of plurality than to Levinas's notion of alterity. Could Levinas's claim that fraternity is present in the spirit of republicanism possibly connect alterity to plurality?

According to Caygill, Levinas's reading of the Rebulican motto *liberté, egalité, fraternité* was greatly influenced by his republican professors at Strasbourg. His references to fraternity are thus to be read as attempts to connect their republican ideals to his own thought and to find a means to relate Greek political thought to the notion of fraternity he knows from the biblical tradition. What remains questionable is whether these two are reconcilable. While Chalier argues convincingly that they are in her book *La Fraternité, Un Espoir en Clair-Obscur*, Arendt, among others, is quite critical of the familial, private and hierarchical roots of fraternity. The latter make the notion of fraternity more difficult to incorporate into a political context based on 'equality', whether symmetrical or asymmetrical, and freedom, whether positive or negative. Without acknowledging any such tension, Levinas reads a commitment to the other into the republican notion of fraternity, one that seems to fall between the boundaries of duty and responsibility. What is implied here is that I experience fraternity through the rights of the other and not my own rights; fraternity thus comes from the other rather than the self. Like Arendt, Levinas makes recourse to the notion of humanity (a less problematic term than that of fraternity), yet he seems to go much further by suggesting that the other has more rights than I do. While this suggestion may be ethically justifiable (as Levinas has shown), it is questionable whether it is politically judicious or justifiable.

This concern has been raised by many of Levinas's readers. Isn't there a danger that no one will look out for my rights? While this is a legitimate question, it is not a Levinasian question, for the following reasons. First, the Buberian symmetry sought is ethically problematic for Levinas, as it requires that one attribute responsibility to another person. Levinasian responsibility arises from within; it is not something that can be ascribed or imposed upon another. There is only one scenario in which responsibility can be attributed: when it is self-attributed—I am responsible. It is for this reason that he seeks a form of asymmetrical responsibility. Second, given the constitutive role the other plays with regard to my subjectivity, especially after *Otherwise Than Being*, there is no absolute separation between my rights and the rights of the other from a phenomenological, ethical or political perspective. My rights, just like the self, arise from the relation to the other whose rights I defend. In terms of the political, this is supported by Arendt's account of the Dreyfus affair. While (some) Jews may have had rights as early as 1789, it was not until non-Jews were publicly willing to defend them, as during the Dreyfus case, that these rights were political, or in Aristotelian terms, these rights were actualized. Without denying that an ever-increasing and infinite responsibility for the other, which Levinas calls for, is absolutely foreign to the current human rights discourse, one can argue that in light of the events of the previous century, Levinas's position may be justified, even though it is extreme. One can also try to find a middle ground between right discourse and responsibility for the other, which would ideally lead to a shift in the present paradigm of the autonomous liberal self.[24]

Let us now consider the last phrase of the essay 'The Rights of Man and the Rights of the Other', seemingly added as an afterthought: 'immutable significance and stability, better than guaranteed by the state'. This claim is noteworthy in that it reaffirms both Levinas's critique of the state, which as a series of intertwined institutions failed the Jewish people and thus humanity during the Shoah, and his claims that grounding human rights in fraternity, a post-foundational form of alterity, is a better guarantor than the state. While Levinas is certainly justified in his claim that the state cannot provide the security and guarantee necessary for human rights, a position Arendt shares, his claim that alterity can provide a 'guarantee' is quite radical. Levinas here expresses an immense faith in human beings and in their sense of solidarity, a faith that some of the best readers of Arendt also see as her 'weakness.'[25] According to both Arendt and Levinas, it is the state that has eroded this solidarity by imposing vertical relations instead of allowing horizontal relations to flourish between individuals:

> The order of politics (post-ethical or pre-ethical) that inaugurates the 'social contract' is neither the sufficient condition nor the necessary outcome of ethics. In its ethical position, the *I* is distinct both from the

> citizen born of the city and from the individual who precedes all order in his natural egotism, but from whom political philosophy, since Hobbes, has tried to derive—or succeeded in deriving—the social or political order of the city.[26]

More recently, such claims have been taken up by thinkers such as Roberto Esposito, who in a manner similar to both Arendt and Levinas, focuses on Hobbes's destruction of this *communitas* (horizontality) by means of contract theories of the state.[27]

Another interpretation of Levinas's comment is that the only alternative to the illusory human rights (grounded in the singularity of the autonomous self) is to 'found' rights in alterity and responsibility. This is precisely the suggestion Levinas advances in the essay 'The Rights of the Other Man' (AT). He develops the argument that the only hope for peace is one rooted in justice—an ethical politics. According to Levinas, the alternative—a political peace—is basically a Bismarckian preparation for war. In this essay, Levinas returns to the language of hope already present in his first Talmudic reading on the notion of prophecy as a form of messianic politics.[28] In addition, he develops the claim that human rights are grounded in the natural rights tradition, but yet have been too strongly reinterpreted in light of the Enlightenment's focus on free will, autonomy and reason. This reinterpretation has led to the loss of the roots of the natural law tradition, which in itself is not a problem; what is, however, deeply problematic is that this tradition was the only link to Jerusalem its original inspiration and the commandment to care for one's neighbour. Accordingly, it is the loss of this biblically rooted ethical connection that has enabled the rise of a liberal interpretation of rights as almost inimitable. The law is seen as a limitation rather than as a source of freedom. As seen above, rights are for-the-other, and as such I need to put my rights into question, which calls for limitation. Yet rather than using reason to limit oneself, reason—in a liberal paradigm—is a tool to agree upon common limitations to impose on the other in the name of autonomy and at the cost of heteronomy. In such a framework, rights continue to promote the politics of war rather than justice, and as such Levinas calls for a re-evaluation of rights in light of the need for greater political responsibility.

The Crisis of Europe

Levinas commences "Peace and Proximity" with the following enigmatic claim: 'The problem of Europe and peace is precisely the one posed by the contradiction of our European consciences' (AT 131). Because of a contradiction internal to Europe itself, in the idea of Europe itself, Europe has not had a lasting peace. Kant's dream of perpetual peace is impossible, according to Levinas, because of 'the idea of Europe' itself—what could this possibly mean? Europe's peace is inspired by Athens; it is a peace based on the search for the Truth and 'attained' by commanding, convincing and mastering people, it is a totalizing peace (AT 131). Levinas thus, similar to Arendt in her critique of Plato, associates violence, domination and war with the quest for Truth, the sort of truth that prevents discourse, interaction and a relationship to the other. Truth that *prima facie* rejects the value of *doxa*, preventing alterity from being expressed, is by definition unethical and unjust. Levinas thus questions whether it is truly peace if it can only be maintained by denying alterity. Arendt makes an analogous claim with regard to truth's silencing of *doxa* as a sign of its antipolitical nature. Likewise, she asks, how can (negative) freedom require the destruction of the plurality of the world?

Yet tranquillity and rest do not typify Levinas's alternative proposal for peace, much as Arendt's notion of the political is one rooted in agonism. Tranquillity and rest are part of political peace, not justice. Subjectivity must constantly be put into question and be attentive to the call of the other. According to Levinas this is precisely what the peace of Europe has failed to achieve; it is peace that justifies negative freedom and thus aims to liberate individuals from disturbances, failing to appreciate the importance of being disturbed, or taken hostage, by the other—of being responsible for an other.[29] According to Levinas, Europe's guilt when it looks at its own past has led to 'the shattering of the universality of theoretical reason' (AT 132).[30] After the horrors of the Shoah, Europe's bad conscience could not be eased by grand meta-narratives, dogmatic faith or any philosophical position that sought a singular all-encompassing truth (what Arendt refers to as ideologies in *Origins*). The Shoah is the political event that symbolizes the absolute end of metaphysics and the ontological tradition, a claim affirmed by Arendt.

The Shoah destroyed the shaky foundations of European thought, both theoretical and practical. These foundations could not, and more important should not, be re-established. Levinas and Arendt accept the end of foundationalism but not the end of contingent foundations. In this vein, both Arendt and Levinas are post-foundational thinkers, as defined by Marchart. 'Assumption of the impossibility of a *final* ground, which is something completely different as it implies an increased awareness of, on the one hand, contingency and, on the other, . . . the moment of partial and always, in the last instance, unsuccessful grounding'.[31] Post-foundationalism takes the form of a contingent and fragile horizontal intersubjectivity for Levinas and Arendt:

> What for Heidegger was still a project, namely the 'deconstruction' of European metaphysics, became for Levinas's thinking an empirical datum, given in the Hitlerian realization of simple, literal *destruction*. To be precise, the destruction of every metaphysic of morals, empirically and ontically accomplished in Auschwitz, became the levelled ground and 'space' of Levinas's thought.[32]

While some thinkers do not place as great an emphasis on the Shoah as the event that radically challenges the philosophical tradition, Western thought has been ineffably affected by this political and historical trauma. One of the clearest signs of this change is the reception Levinas's work has received in the past few decades. Would philosophy have been open to such a radically new ethical approach had Europe not experienced such horrors in the twentieth century?[33] While many of Levinas's critics have argued that his ethics is too radical, his response was that only such an extreme reversal of the dominant and powerful Greek logic is enough to allow for the ethical interruption of the other. Nothing less than a radical challenge can create space for alterity, for the weak, excluded, downtrodden and forgotten.

In the second part of this essay, Levinas returns to Europe's bad conscience, which 'expresses more than just a contradiction between a certain project of culture and its result' (AT 134). By exploring the contradictions manifest in our modern desire for peace, Levinas shows why and how such moral ideals can result in such devastation. One such example is the concept of freedom tied to the notion of peace; it is a freedom rooted in a self who desires to be 'free from' impediments such as those posed by the presence of others in a shared world. By connecting this notion of freedom to the dangers of politics presented by unchecked egoism and individualism, it is possible to understand the bad conscience which Levinas claims grounds so many concepts central to politics. We should not be surprised that a peace based on freedom from others can lead to a politics that excludes otherness. This exemplifies the contradiction of European conscience. For Levinas, the only way to address Europe's bad conscience is to listen to the voice of the other excluded by our politics. No excuses, rational or other, can possibly justify silencing the other that forces the self to look into the shameful mirror of history. The heaviness of our responsibility for the suffering and death of others, such as was experienced by those who lived through the atrocities of the twentieth century, is greater than our right to what Levinas describes as the pleasures of being, or 'enjoyment'. Allowing ourselves to be accused by the disfiguring mirror of history forces us to grapple with the reality of our bad conscience; 'Greek' peace comes at the cost of the other. This realization is at the source of the contradiction that Levinas defines as 'the ethical moment of our European crisis' (AT 135).

While Levinas finds ample resources for this 'more urgent call' in the Talmud, in 'Peace and Proximity' it is to its phenomenological roots that he turns:

> I have thought that the uniqueness and the alterity of the unique is concretely the face of the other man, the original epiphany of which is not in its visibility as a plastic form, but in 'appresentation'. The thought awakened to the face of the other man is not a thought of . . . a

> representation, but from the start a thought for . . . a non-indifference for the other. (AT 139)

It is from the experience of the vulnerability of the other—in the face-to-face encounter—that the challenge or demand to respond awakens us to our (guilt) and responsibility. He also provides a concrete example of such an encounter that helps to clarify the meaning of appresentation. In Vasily Grossman's *Life and Fate,* it is 'the human back [that is] so expressive and transmits states of mind do penetratingly . . . [it] seemed to shout, to cry, to sob' (AT 140). This experience awakens a call in me that is expressed by the commandment 'thou shall not kill'. This seemingly negative commandment is interpreted by Levinas as the need to take responsibility for the neighbour, the widow and the orphan. Thus the concrete encounter with another awakens a voice within me that challenges me to question the tranquil and self-affirming peace that comes at the cost of the other.

In 'Peace and Proximity', Levinas emphasizes the importance of responding with non-indifference. Much like the notion of a non-allergic reaction to alterity, this non-indifference is the openness to being questioned by the other, an openness that constitutes my subjectivity. Arendt also reflects on this indifference and recognizes how politically and ethically problematic it is. 'Morally and even politically speaking, this indifference [the refusal to take responsibility], though common enough, is the greatest danger. And connected to this, only a bit less dangerous, is another very common modern phenomenon, the widespread tendency to refuse to judge at all' (RJ 145f). For both thinkers, being questioned and questioning is fundamental to keeping oneself open to the other and the world. The interhuman realm is one constituted by a challenging openness to difference that demands us to take responsibility for the fragility of the other and the shared world. Non-indifference demands that one limit one's ego. It is this limitation that creates a space for the horizontal bond with others that 'founds' community. This is in clear contrast to Hobbes's vision, in which one transfers one's freedom to the sovereign out of fear for one's life. While it may appear to be 'easier' to give up one's autonomy—to become the subject of the sovereign, autonomy—for both thinkers—is an illusion. As heteronomous subjects, Hobbes's contractual solution destroys any possibility of horizontal relations with the other, thereby preventing any real peace or community.

A Judaic Politics?

What remains unclear is whether the possibility of an ethical politics, for Levinas, is internal or external to Europe itself. Does this reversal of Greek logic come from within 'Europe against Europe' (AT 133)—or from the rebirth of a voice outside of Europe? Is there no other solution than to reject this rich philosophical history and to replace it with the voice of the Judaic, or is this latter voice always already part of Europe itself? While in previous essays Levinas certainly leaned towards the former conclusion, he is much less polemical in 'Peace and Proximity'. Greek thought is appreciated for its past contribution and future potential. The European heritage has two essential roots that are in tension—that of Jerusalem and that of Athens. To further explore this clash, he turns to Rashi, a celebrated Talmudic rabbi. In the same vein that Hobbes is Levinas's symbolic representative of 'all that is Greek'[34] as the *Leviathan* embodies the absolute justification for the egoism of politics, Rashi means 'all that is Talmudic' or all that is the Judaic. In this essay, Levinas returns to Rashi's analysis of fear and anguish in relation to the biblical story of Jacob and Esau. Rashi's account of the intensity of Jacob's anguish, which is much greater than his fear of Esau, is that although '[Jacob] was fearful for his death, [he was] anguished at possibly having to kill' (AT 135). The core of the message is that responsibility trumps fear. It is better to be killed than to kill. It is better to give up one's rights than to deny those of another. Precisely what Arendt argues is one of the few ethical lessons we can learn from Socrates's thinking. The commandment 'do not kill' ethically outweighs the instinct to survive. Hobbes's analysis presupposes the inverse. Levinas demands that we listen to the biblical message, which rejects a meaningless and violent existence for humanity. Life is not 'nasty, brutish, and short'. The only way to rupture this prophecy is to rupture the self that creates it by making space for the other. Levinas asks us to consider whether 'peace must not respond to a call more urgent than that of truth and initially distinct from the call of truth'? (AT 136).

Despite Levinas's harsh criticism of the Hobbesian-inspired liberal tradition, he does not completely reject this approach to politics.[35] One reason for this more detailed consideration of politics was Levinas's engagement with questions related to the state of Israel. In this vein, in the final section of 'Peace and Proximity', Levinas affirms that the Greek tradition does indeed have an essential role to play with regard to peace. His alternative, which could perhaps be designated as political alterity, is not to be seen as a replacement but as a partner in the peace process. Although many have understandably interpreted Levinas's work to be a blanket criticism of all politics, a justified reading given his highly polemical and hyperbolic style of communication, a more careful reading shows the necessity to create a space for the marginalized voice of the Judaic tradition within the dominant tradition of politics. Levinas thus concludes that Jerusalem is part of Europe's heritage that has been often overlooked or silenced:

> Europe: its biblical heritage implies the necessity of the Greek heritage. Europe is not a simple confluence of two cultural currents. It is the concretization in which the wisdoms of the theoretical and the biblical

> do better than converge. The relation with the other and the unique, which is peace, comes to require a reason that thematizes and synchronizes and synthesizes, that thinks the world and reflects on being. (AT 142)

Here Levinas, perhaps for the first time, unambiguously clarifies the structure of the relationship between the two roots of Western thought. Neither is meant to replace the other; both are essential for a just political peace. This is quite a different claim than that argued for in the 'Messianic Texts' of the 1960s.[36] This recognition of the value of Greek politics also reiterates Levinas's respect for many of the elements of our current democracies, such as the rule of law as well as the theoretical equality and dignity conferred on citizens by means of constitutions and charters.

> The extreme importance in human multiplicity of the political structure of society under the rule of law, and hence institutions in which the for-the-other of subjectivity—in which the I—enters with the dignity of the citizen into the perfect reciprocity of political laws that are essentially egalitarian or held to become so. (AT 143)

The Greek tradition has the ability, by means of reason, to develop and disseminate the ethical principle symbolically rooted in Jerusalem, but it cannot take precedence. A Greek-centred peace is dangerous, as it presents itself as the totalization, or completion, of truth, thereby excluding all other voices. For this reason, Levinas claims that the message of the Bible must have priority in that it creates a space that cannot be closed. It is clear that the Judaic tradition must be the guiding principle.

In addition, by reaffirming his defence of ethics as first philosophy in terms of justice, Levinas provides a political justification for the priority of the Judaic. While Levinas acknowledges that unity, singularity and truth are to have priority in the realms of math, music or philosophy (by which I assume Levinas means epistemology and logic, etc.), he reaffirms that alterity must be the principle of ethics and the political. Levinas's claim is that in relation to justice (as with the ethical relation that is the guiding principle of justice), the ontological or traditional Greek-inspired philosophical approach in which the self or singularity is prioritized is not acceptable. For Levinas ethics must precede politics; he does not see an Arendtian alternative—a political ethics—as possible. The prioritization of alterity is necessary so that the ethical relation is not neglected during the necessary political processes of 'thematization, synchronization and synthesis'. Levinas—who because of his Lithuanian heritage was in many ways more familiar with Stalinism than Arendt—understood that this neglect of the other was a common occurrence within the administrative and bureaucratic realms of politics.

By advocating the primacy of alterity over singularity with regard to interhuman relations, Levinas is in fact making the same argument Arendt made with regard to the primacy of plurality over singularity with regard to the political. In this vein both Levinas and Arendt claim that a fundamental lesson that must be learned from totalitarianism is that liberal democracies can easily be manipulated, a reality that continues to ring true today, and as such political responsibility demands that we do not simply accept our contemporary political system because of a supposed lack of alternatives. The Third Reich was not an exception, and it would be naïve to assume that it was a 'one-time' historical aberration. What happened could happen again if we do not take responsibility for the other and the shared world. Levinas's justification for this position is that the possibility of tyranny or totalitarianism, as well as less obviously evil or violent forms of government, is still present within the origins of liberalism itself. This is a claim he develops in his 1934 essay 'Reflections on Hitlerism', which is almost prophetic in its ability to understand the dangerous implications of a liberalism driven by racism.[37] Arendt expresses a similar concern, as both totalitarianism and liberalism are political 'regimes' rooted in distinct forms of singularity, the former in loneliness and the latter in individualism. For Levinas, liberalism, in its many forms, always has the potential to be manipulated, either by the state or by the people in the case of democracies and is an inherently contingent and fragile system. 'At every moment, [a liberal democracy is] on the verge of bearing within [itself its] centre of gravity and weighing in [its] own right on the fate of men, as a source of conflict and violence' (AT 143). Liberalism, in some measure defined by its goal to promote 'freedom from' through the rule of law, and the value it sees in what Levinas claims is an illusory neutrality, has the potential to become ethically vacuous—a vacuum that is easily filled by force and fear. According to Kearney:

> The norm that must continue to inspire and direct the moral order is the ethical norm of the interhuman. If the moral-political order totally relinquishes its ethical foundation, it must accept all forms of society, including the fascist or totalitarian, for it can no longer evaluate or discriminate between them. The state is usually better than anarchy—but not always. In some instances,—fascism or totalitarianism, for example—the political order of the state may have to be challenged in the name of our ethical responsibility to the other. This is why ethical philosophy must remain first philosophy.[38]

Levinas's conclusion also enigmatically encapsulates his post-foundational position on the political.[39] While it might be tempting to interpret Levinas's claim that ethics is first philosophy (or that ethics is metaphysics) as a foundational claim, a substitute for traditional ethics or metaphysics, Levinas recognized that such absolute foundations are a threat to the absolute priority that must be given to the ethical relation. Nonetheless he does not entirely dismiss all forms of grounding, claiming: 'It is not unimportant to know—and this is perhaps the European experience of the twentieth century—whether the egalitarian and just State in which the European realizes himself . . . proceeds from a war of all against all—or from the irreducible responsibility of one for the other' (AT 144/TI 247). What is possible (and what Levinas argues for in this essay and is expressed so poetically in this quotation) is the recognition of these two roots, one Greek and one Judaic, at the heart of Europe (which sadly, given Levinas's Eurocentrism, can be interpreted as being the two roots for all humanity). Yet more than this, Levinas here defends the priority of alterity, symbolized by the Judaic root, as the post-foundational ground for both ethics and the political. In a nutshell, responsibility and justice are to be 'grounded' in alterity. What this entails, contrary to the tradition, whether as defined by Hobbes or by Kant, is that autonomy, freedom and reason are, as it were, second to heteronomy. Levinas's move from subjectivity to alterity is a move from freedom to responsibility, from autonomy to heteronomy. 'Heteronomy is somehow stronger than autonomy here, except that this heteronomy is not slavery, is not bondage' (EN 111). In terms of the political, this 'move' is similar to the one Arendt makes in the name of the plurality, which is also a space of intersubjective responsibility.

Levinas's post-foundationalism is also evident in his aim to find a balance between Athens and Jerusalem. In these later political texts, Levinas understands that ethics and the political will always be in tension with each other. 'Politics must be able in fact always to be checked and criticized starting from the ethical. This second form of sociality would render justice to that secrecy which for each is his life . . . a secrecy which holds to the responsibility for the Other' (EI 81). For Levinas, ethics must have a voice in the *polis*, and if the priority of this voice is denied, it will have the final word in terms of responsibility. In other words, if we neglect to consider every individual person as irreplaceable within the political, we cannot evade responsibility for such atrocities as the Shoah, in which people were tattooed and counted like cattle. If we are not willing to recognize the miracle that every new life brings, then we are participants in the injustice of politics that treats other human beings as superfluous. For Levinas, the Judaic tradition of Talmudic interpretation of the Bible, a central part of Europe's heritage, serves as a reminder of this wisdom through stories such as that of Cain and Abel, which warns us of the dangers of failing to respond affirmatively to the question, 'Am I my brother's keeper?' While Arendt clearly does not use the same religious metaphors (except that of miracles in relation to natality), she does present a similar argument in her analysis of the equation of plurality with multiplicity. In this vein, she affirms Levinas's claim that alterity and heteronomy are the 'foundation' of humanity, a form of alterity that should never be instrumentalized.

In addition, Levinas approaches the relationship between singularity and alterity in terms of Athens and Jerusalem, respectively. Those who take the road of singularity directed towards Athens share Hobbes's perception of life as 'brutish and short' and human interaction as 'a war of all against all', leading them to advocate for freedom, equality and the rights of the self—all of which denies space for alterity.[40] If we accept Hobbes's picture of human nature as the origin of politics, why are we surprised that the history of humanity is violent? Isn't this exactly what we should expect from a contract enforced by fear? According to Levinas, such a notion of freedom can only come at the cost of the other. This same tension arises in terms of human rights, which fail to recognize their origin in responsibility.

His solution, comparable to Arendt's, is to seek an intersubjective perspective from which to think of the *polis*. It is this point of view that demands a reflection upon the individualism now ruling politics and the dangers of an unethical politics. Equality, in its abstract and universal form, can be as unjust as the greatest inequalities of the twentieth century, even more so since it may be blind to 'the tears of the other'. This leads Levinas to make a sweeping generalization, which he—like Arendt—learned to do from Heidegger: the philosophical tradition is willing to sacrifice the other if this sacrifice provides security, certainty and control for the self (EN 157). While this 'sacrifice of the other' is justified as a demand for rights and freedoms in response to oppression, it potentially leads to the destruction of humanity. As such, the self must constantly be held in check by ethics. Arendt was well aware of this fact and sought to create a place, from within the *polis*, for such ethics. Sadly, it came too late to be properly developed. Is Levinas's alternative of an ethical *polis* a better option? Or is there a third option—somewhere between alterity and plurality?

IS LEVINAS'S ETHICAL *POLIS* ENOUGH?

While Levinas clearly did not construct a normative political theory, the essays considered in this chapter (which are only a small fraction of all those written on political topics) indicate his interest in the idea of an ethical politics rooted in alterity. Levinas, like Arendt, understood the urgent need to rethink the grounds of the political. For Levinas this ground is to be found in the ethical relation. Levinas expresses this *Never Again* outlook in the dedication to *Otherwise Than Being*:

> To the memory of those who were closest among the six million assassinated by the National Socialists, and of the millions on millions of all confessions of all nations, victims of the same hatred of the other man, the same anti-semitism. . . . תנצבה [May their souls be bound together in the bond of life].

The Shoah epitomized the danger of 'the same hatred of the other man' that Levinas had already identified this danger in the distortion of liberalism (in his 1934 essay). It is the hatred of the other characterized by an allergic reaction to alterity that Levinas wants to confront. He scrutinizes this hatred—just as Arendt does in order to reconcile herself to this world—and concludes by identifying its roots in a particular ontological paradigm. By means of both the phenomenological and Judaic traditions, he challenges this paradigm by means of a subjectivity constituted by alterity. By understanding ourselves as relational beings, created by and responsible for the other, we can affirm and strengthen the bonds of solidarity. While this challenge is no guarantee of its success, it does force the self to face itself. This interruption of the self, making space for the other, is critical for Levinas's ethics. The question we must now consider is whether this is enough for the political realm.

Levinas's political paradigm is presented in terms of justice—justice, like ethics, is the relentless interruption of totality and reminder of the priority of the other. Justice is not a model to be imposed on the ethical relation; it is an ideal defined by the ethical relation. The question is, what motivates the empowerment and enactment of justice? *Tikkun olam*, the Judaic notion of repairing the world, is not just an ideal; it must be realized collectively both by means of small acts of kindness and on a larger scale. Given the potential of the political to further strengthen the horizontal bonds that are essential to both alterity and plurality, as described by Arendt, is Levinas's transposition of ethics into the political a sufficient solution? While ethics accomplishes its 'end' every time it challenges injustice or interrupts the ego by means of a question, the political does not 'succeed' when such an ethics is realized. Levinas's ethics is not a project, law or set of normative principles that can be inscribed within a certain system. Ethics, to repeat, is precisely that which challenges the boundaries of all systems. We are indeed a step closer to justice every time the political is interrupted, but that is ethics or justice—not the political as defined by Arendt. The step from justice to the political is greater than Levinas realized. In the space between justice and the political there are many questions to be addressed, including those concerning collective action, empowerment, participation and community.

Likewise, Levinas's ethics fails in its political form with regard to the transformation of responsibility from the other to the third. Ethics can respond responsibly to the other. The political can never respond responsibly to all others. As discussed above, if politics could do so, it would no longer be able to maintain the space necessary to prevent totalization, to ensure that it does not become tyrannical. This is the inverse danger of liberalism, which by seeking neutrality creates too great a space from the other. Furthermore, while a certain form of unlimited, or infinite, totalization—in terms of responsibility—is desirable in ethical terms, it is precisely such lack of limits, or boundaries, that the political must prevent on ethical grounds. This is precisely what both Levinas and Arendt recognize, with reference to love. While love is one of the most wondrous human experiences, it is also exclusive and irresponsible. This is why love cannot 'ground' the political (as some Christian thinkers have suggested). Given that Levinas's ethics is potential as exclusive even if he claims that the third is always already present in the other, it too cannot 'ground' the political. Ethics should inspire, not define or limit, the political. Reversing the terms we approach this same limitation in Levinas's ethical *polis*. If the political is guided by ethics, how can ethics interrupt it? Love itself is not difficult, what is difficult is the experience of being torn by one's commitments to the other, whom one loves, and to the world. Returning this romantic analogy to the realm of the political, one only has to consider the reality of limited resources in order to understand that the responsibility of the political is quite unlike that of the ethical relation. The latter is infinite and must remain open to externality to remain ethical. This last point brings us to three related tensions, all of which further problematize Levinas's move from ethics to the political: first, the relation between theory and practice; second, ethics' lack of limits; and third, Levinas's political naïveté.

While I do not wish to reduce Levinas's move from ethics to justice to one between theory and practice, many of the problems with the latter relationship, certainly as presented by Arendt, apply to Levinas's approach. As Arendt establishes in her critical reading of Plato, there is a danger of approaching the realm of the political by means of an ideal or model if one wishes to respect its plurality, which Levinas, unlike Plato, does. While it is not fair to reduce the ethical relation, the face-to-face, to the status of either an ideal or model, it takes on this role in relation to justice, which it is meant to guide. If unlimited, a theoretical impossibility, the ethical relation is potentially totalizing, requiring the absolute sacrifice of the self for the other. The self must allow itself to be continuously challenged and must never ask for reciprocity. Again, while this is an 'ideal' worth aspiring to, it is incredibly dangerous. To avoid this danger, Arendt prioritizes enactment, performance and judgement—excluding theories and truth from the interhuman realm. Both thinkers strive for justice, Levinas by means of an ideal that can never be attained, Arendt by enabling moments of justice to appear in the world. In this vein, while Levinas's 'model' of an ethical *polis* is not a theory of justice, at times it comes very close, which as Arendt is right to remind us is always potentially totalitarian.

The second problem of Levinas's move from ethics to justice concerns limits in relation to the notion of the third. While Levinas's ethics is to be praised for its ability to test limits and to challenge boundaries, this experimentation is politically irresponsible. Levinas himself acknowledges the need for limits with regard to justice, and yet these same limits are contrary to his ethics. 'We need laws, and—yes—courts of law, institutions and the state to render justice' (TN 174). Albeit reluctantly, Levinas admits that if responsibility is at the heart of ethics, and justice is to be inspired by ethics, justice must limit ethics. Justice needs to be limited to be just. This is a contradiction that Levinas fails to resolve. If ethics cannot be limited and justice must be limited, another 'framework' is needed to limit justice. This is a problem recognized by Annabel Herzog, who concludes that the only 'solution' is to limit the ethical encounter by means of a political context, which is precisely what I argue Arendt offers for a Levinasian ethics.[41] For the political to be ethical, it must be bounded. In Arendtian terms, just as the *polis* needs the walls of the city, the laws to provide stability and limits, ethics also needs to be bounded. While the political comes with no guarantees, the uncertainty of a political ethics without internal support or structure seems to be a poor substitute for at least the basic certainty provided by laws, institutions and the state.

This brings us to a third criticism of Levinas's ethical politics. While Levinas certainly experienced the horrors of politics, his understanding of both politics and the political remained at times surprisingly naïve. This is perhaps most evident from some of the shocking comments he made in interviews. In relation to the atrocities committed by the Israeli army at Sabra and Shatilla in 1982 he stated, on French radio, in dialogue with Schlomo Malka and Alain Finkielkraut:

> My definition of the other is completely different. The other is the neighbour, who is not necessarily kin, but who can be. And in that sense, if you're for the other, you're for the neighbour. But if your neighbour attacks another neighbour or treats him unjustly, what can you do? Then alterity takes on another character, in alterity we can find an enemy, or at least then we are faced with the problem of knowing who is right and who is wrong, who is just and who is unjust. There are people who are wrong.[42]

Or his comment, in relation to the Soviet-Chinese conflict in 1960: 'The yellow peril! It is not racial, it is spiritual. It does not involve inferior values; it involves a radical strangeness, a stranger to the weight of its past, from where there does not filter any familiar voice or inflection, a lunar or Martian past' (DF 293).

Yet Levinas was also politically naïve in another sense. While he certainly makes a persuasive case for the commandment 'thou shall not kill', he understands that there are always people who will choose to ignore this commandment and to follow in the footsteps of Cain (EN 110). While murder is an ethical impossibility, it is not a real or ontological impossibility. Levinas's means to address this is to declare that 'a place has to be foreseen and kept warm for all eternity for Hitler and his followers' (NTR 87)—but is this sufficient? It is politically naïve to assume that an ethical impossibility is a sufficient guarantee for the political. While Levinas's later writings shy away from such naïve claims, he continues to fail—as is evident from his interviews in the final years—to understand the harsh reality of politics. While Levinas's notion of prophetic politics is certainly a powerful vision for the political, it offers even less—in terms of a safety net—than that provided by laws, institutions and the state. As Bettina Bergo writes, 'Levinas offers a principle of hope—realising that principles function as grounds, so that further appeals to "found" them in a prior logic are vain—a sort of superbience'.[43] Arendt, who has a much better grasp of the reality of politics, maintains a principle of hope and positive philosophical anthropology, both of which are present in Levinas's model of ethical *polis*, without this naïveté.

The conclusion that needs to be drawn here is that a responsible means to ensure that the Shoah *never* happens *again* is to combine hope in humanity with political pragmatism. While the latter is certainly lacking in Levinas's thought, it is not only the result of naïveté; it is also the result of the trauma of the Shoah and, without wanting to engage in psychological factors anathema to phenomenology, part and parcel of the history of the Jewish people. As Arendt states, with great controversy, Judaism lacks an understanding of politics, which was one of the reasons that when Jews were attacked politically they failed to understand that only a political response was appropriate. Levinas seems also to fall into this Judaic trap by seeking to respond to the Shoah by means of ethics. Trigano is very critical of Levinas's failure to appreciate the importance of reflecting on the relationship between the Judaic and the political:

> The capacity to be 'for the other'. This is why I emphasise the importance of the political that is the field itself in which the disjunction between singularity and universality has to be installed . . . and this disjunction is the condition itself of the possibility of the other. . . . If Jewish philosophy has a future, it will only come at the cost of a radical reversal in which it will rediscover the question of the political as it is of another nature than the dimension of subjectivity, interiority and the inter-personal.[44]

While Levinas's analysis of the Shoah, written between the lines in every one of his works, makes clear that it was as a result of the hatred of alterity that such atrocities could occur, it is not by combating this hatred, in the name of ethics or morality, that it can be prevented. *Alterity needs to make its appearance in the political realm by becoming its principle.* This is, with the help of Arendt's notion of plurality, what I develop in the next chapter by way of the notion of relationality.

NOTES

1. Simon Critchley, 'Five Problems in Levinas's View of Politics and the Sketch of a Solution to Them', *Political Theory* 32, no. 2 (1 April 2004): 172–185.

2. By far the best text to read on this topic is Howard Caygill, *Levinas and the Political* (London; New York: Routledge, 2002). See "Works Cited" and "Related Works" for writings on Levinas's politics.

3. Simon Malka, *Emmanuel Levinas: His Life and Legacy*, trans. Michael Kigel and Sonja M. Embree (Pittsburgh, Pa.: Duquesne University Press, 2006).

4. Mordechai Gordon and Maxine Greene, *Hannah Arendt and Education: Renewing Our Common World* (Boulder, Colo.: Westview Press, 2002), 230.

5. Melvyn A. Hill, ed., *Hannah Arendt: The Recovery of the Public World* (New York: St. Martin's Press, 1979), 333.

6. Ibid. For an excellent analysis of this discussion, see Dana Villa's chapter on Arendt and Heidegger in *Heidegger's Jewish Followers: Essays on Hannah Arendt, Leo Strauss, Hans Jonas, and Emmanuel Levinas*, 1st ed., ed. Samuel Fleischacker (Pittsburgh, Pa.: Duquesne University Press, 2008).

7. William Simmons, 'The Third: Levinas' Theoretical Move from an-Archical Ethics to the Realm of Justice and Politics', *Philosophy & Social Criticism* 25, no. 6 (1 November 1999): 98.

8. William Paul Simmons, *An-Archy and Justice: An Introduction to Emmanuel Levinas's Political Thought* (Lanham, Md.: Lexington Books, 2003).

9. C. Fred Alford, 'Levinas and Political Theory', *Political Theory* 32, no. 2 (1 April 2004): 146.

10. Catherine Chalier, *La Fraternité: Un espoir en clair obscur* (Paris: Buchet Chastel, 2004).

11. Emmanuel Levinas, *Collected Philosophical Papers* (Pittsburgh, Pa.: Duquesne University Press, 1998), 33.

12. Levinas, *Of God Who Comes to Mind* (Stanford, Calif.: Stanford University Press, 1998), 82.

13. Emmanuel Levinas, *Entre Nous*, trans. Michael B. Smith and Barbara Harshav (New York: Columbia University Press, 2000), 20.

14. Ibid., 175.

15. For more on this see Judith Butler, *Parting Ways: Jewishness and the Critique of Zionism* (New York: Columbia University Press, 2012), 39.

16. Isaiah Berlin, *Two Concepts of Liberty: An Inaugural Lecture Delivered before the University of Oxford on 31 October 1958* (Oxford: Clarendon Press, 1966).

17. Anya Topolski, 'On Freedom in Athens and Jerusalem: Arendt's Political Challenge to Levinas' Ethics of Responsibility', in *The Awakening to the Other: A Provocative Dialogue with Emmanuel Levinas*, ed. R. Burggraeve (Leuven; Dudley, Mass.: Peeters Publishers, 2008).

18. Levinas, *Entre Nous*, 175.

19. Contemporary discussions of equality, such as that of Ronald Dworkin in *Sovereign Virtue: The Theory and Practice of Equality* (Cambridge, Mass.: Harvard University Press, 2000), distinguish between compensatory and distributive justice in order to address the inherent inequality of liberal concepts of equality, which is precisely what Levinas does in his Talmudic readings.

20. Jerome Kohn, 'Evil: The Crime against Humanity', in *Three Essays: The Role of Experience in Hannah Arendt's Political Thought*, n.d., 8, memory.loc.gov/ammem/arendthtml/essayc1.html.

21. Anya Topolski, 'Relationality as a "Foundation" for Human Rights: Exploring the Paradox with Hannah Arendt and Emmanuel Levinas', *Theoria and Praxis: International Journal of Interdisciplinary Thought* 2, no. 1 (6 August 2014), pi.library.yorku.ca/ojs/index.php/theoriandpraxis/article/view/39373.

22. Caygill, *Levinas and the Political*, 153.

23. Chalier, *La Fraternité*, 13. My translation.

24. Sadly, this is not the case, as is patent by the fact that we have a panoply of charters of human rights but very few charters of human responsibilities, as only a very select few political communities have created such documents. See for example the African Charter of Human Rights and Responsibilities.

25. Dana Villa, *Arendt and Heidegger: The Fate of the Political* (Princeton, N.J.: Princeton University Press, 1995).
26. Robert Bernasconi and David Wood, eds., *The Provocation of Levinas: Rethinking the Other* (London; New York: Routledge, 1988), 165.
27. Roberto Esposito, *Communitas: The Origin and Destiny of Community*, trans. Timothy Campbell (Stanford, Calif.: Stanford University Press, 2009).
28. Anya Topolski, 'Universal Political Messianism: A Dialogue with Emmanuel Levinas' First Talmudic Reading', in *On the Outlook Figures of the Messianic.*, ed. Thomas Crombez and Katrien Vloeberghs (Cambridge, England: Cambridge Scholars Publishing, 2007), 141–50.
29. According to Levinas, the source of this bad conscience is events such as Europe's bloody history in the twentieth century (see the quote cited at the beginning of this section), even those that occurred prior to our birth.
30. This is a claim made by Franz Rosenzweig, another Jewish thinker, in his World War I trench letters, later published as the *Star of Redemption*. Franz Rosenzweig, *The Star of Redemption*, trans. William W. Hallo (Notre Dame, Ind.: University of Notre Dame Press, 1985).
31. Oliver Marchart, *Post-Foundational Political Thought: Political Difference in Nancy, Lefort, Badiou and Laclau* (Edinburgh, Scotland: Edinburgh University Press, 2007), 2.
32. Malka, *Emmanuel Levinas*, xix–xx.
33. Caygill, *Levinas and the Political*, 3.
34. Simmons, 'The Third', 92.
35. As he did previously in 'The State of Israel and the Religion of Israel' (DF) or 'Secularism and the Thought of Israel' (DF) or in 'Zionisms', 'The State of Caesar and the State of David', 'Politics After!', 'Assimilation and New Culture' (BV) and 'The Rights of Man and the Rights of the Other' (OS).
36. Topolski, 'Universal Political Messianism'.
37. Emmanuel Levinas and Seán Hand, 'Reflections on the Philosophy of Hitlerism', *Critical Inquiry* 17, no. 1 (1 October 1990): 63–71, doi:10.2307/1343726.
38. Richard A. Cohen, *Face to Face with Levinas* (Albany: State University of New York Press, 2012), 30.
39. Marchart, *Post-Foundational Political Thought*.
40. Cheryl L. Hughes, 'The Primacy of Ethics: Hobbes and Levinas', *Continental Philosophy Review* 31, no. 1 (1 January 1998): 79–94, doi:10.1023/A:1010089805428.
41. Annabel Herzog, 'Is Liberalism "All We Need"? Lévinas's Politics of Surplus', *Political Theory* 30, no. 2 (1 April 2002): 204–227.
42. Seán Hand, *Emmanuel Levinas* (London: Routledge, 2008), 105.
43. Bettina Bergo, 'What Is Politics in Emmanuel Levinas' Ethics? How Did Schmitt's Political Enter Levinas's Totality?' (Montreal: Université de Montreal, 1995), 1; Bettina Bergo, *Levinas Between Ethics & Politics: For the Beauty That Adorns the Earth*, 1st ed. (Pittsburgh, Pa.: Duquesne University Press, 2003).
44. Danielle Cohen-Levinas and Shmuel Trigano, *Emmanuel Levinas: Philosophie et judaïsme* (Paris: In Press, 2002), 176–177. The original French quotation is: 'La capacite d'etre "pour autrui". C'est pourquoi, je souligne l'importance du politique qui est le champ meme ou doit s'instaurer la disjunction entre l'universel et le singulier . . . et cette disjunction est la condition meme d'une possiblite de l'autre. . . . Si la philosophie-juive a un avenir, ce sera uniqument au prix d'un renversement radical dans lequel elle redecouvrira la question du politique en tant qu'il est d'une autre nature que la dimension de la subjectivite, de l'interiorite et de l'inter-personne'.

IV

From Plurality and Alterity to Relationality

SEVEN

From Arendt and Levinas to Relationality

This chapter is both a conclusion to the previous chapters, in which we explored the importance of plurality for Arendt's notion of the political and alterity for Levinas's ethics, and also an introduction to the notion of relationality that was envisioned based on these two post-Shoah phenomenological explorations of intersubjectivity. While my intention, in the previous chapters, was to accurately represent the thought of Arendt and Levinas while at the same time pointing towards the potential for a rich engagement of their respective projects, it is now time to part ways and to develop my own project. In this vein, I have certainly been inspired by other thinkers, among them many feminist philosophers, who have also sought to explore what lies between the 'I' and the 'we', between the individual and the collective or group, as a means to approach the political. With the concept of relationality, I intend to revise some of the limitations uncovered in both Arendt's and Levinas's respective projects. In addition, these revisions will also enable me to develop an Arendtian- and Levinasian-inspired political ethics—what I refer to as a politics of relationality. In what follows, I focus on what I consider to be 'the pearls of great wisdom' in Arendt's and Levinas's writings. In this vein, I follow Arendt, who uses this metaphor of pearl diving when introducing Walter Benjamin's posthumous writings: to 'descend to the bottom of the sea, not to excavate the bottom and bring it to light but to pry loose the rich and the strange, the pearls and the coral in the depths, and carry them to the surface'.[1] It is also worth repeating that my goal is not to harmonize Arendt's and Levinas's projects or to deny the difference between ethics and the political; rather—by means of the concept of relationality—I want to consider how alterity can strengthen the political without destroying its principle of plurality. With this in mind, as well as the insights investigated in the previous chapters, I can begin to sketch a post-foundational political ethics of relationality.

The pearls and coral I seek are those that speak to our current political reality. Those of us fortunate enough to live in the richest and most stable countries nonetheless live in fragile democracies. The past decades have been defined by a string of crises ranging from economic and political concerns such as the problem of representation and democratic deficit, inclusion and exclusion (such as those concerning refugees, immigration and racism) problems both authors were all too familiar with. It is my contention that in addition to institutions, what is necessary is a new principle for democratic politics. For Arendt this principle was plurality; my enhancement—relationality—calls for a plurality strengthened by an ethics of alterity. In addition, relationality distances itself from the notion of intersubjectivity, developing instead a relational approach, which refuses the priority of either the 'I' or the 'we', thereby inhabiting the paradoxical space between both. The most indispensable aspect of relationality is to be found in Arendt's notion of plurality, its implicit inclusion of all those who share the world, an implicit ethics of alterity that is justified politically. As Butler demonstrates, by applying it to the current asymmetrical conflict between Israel and Palestine, through her reading of Arendt's *Eichmann in Jerusalem*, plurality is a principle that reminds us that no one has a right to decide with whom to cohabit the world.[2] Every human being, in her unicity or distinction, is an essential part of the world and cannot be excluded. Another way to express this idea is that a relational approach allows for one to be at home in a community or in the world not in spite of, or out of tolerance for, difference, but because one's alterity is essential to the plurality of this community. By promoting such an *ethos* of alterity from within the political, the alterity of plurality and the importance of plurality for the political are prioritized. This principle also contests the roots of the hatred that enabled the systematic destruction of one of the world's most fragile peoples and sadly continues to manifest itself in Europe today (e.g., the most common targets are Muslims, Romas and refugees).

I assemble relationality's building blocks in two parts. First, I return to the four background elements announced in the introduction and developed throughout this project: the Shoah, phenomenology, Heidegger and the Judaic. I dedicate more time and care to the notion of the Judaic as it has not, in the previous chapters, been explicitly thematized.[3] The Judaic plays an important inspirational role with regard to relationality because of the emphasis it places on hope, responsibility and a relational approach. Second, after this synthetic step, I turn to a more analytic endeavour: loosening the notions of plurality and alterity from the grips of intersubjectivity. This is necessary to free the relational approach from an ontology and epistemology inhabiting the shadow of the subject. With this post-foundational ground as our starting point, I focus on several other aspects of relationality: its contingency, the importance of hope and the priority of the political.

INTRODUCING BACKGROUND ELEMENTS INTO RELATIONALITY

Never Again

As is palpable from their respective oeuvres, the horrors of the Shoah are never far from either Arendt's or Levinas's thinking. Yet neither author accepts the view that the Shoah should be understood as a one-time, exceptional, unrepeatable historical aberration. The lessons each learns from the Shoah are as relevant today as they were seventy years ago when the world first discovered what had happened in the camps and mass graves of Nazi-occupied Europe. For Arendt, traces of totalitarianism remain present in the contemporary practice of violence and terror as well as the escalating numbers of people experiencing homelessness, loneliness and rootlessness (OT vii). For Levinas, *Never Again* requires combating all forms of exploitation caused by rampant unchecked egoism, racism or 'the same hatred of the other man', as well as inequality and poverty (AT 32). What both conclude, a conclusion that was already partially developed by their teacher, Heidegger, is that many of the policies essential during the Shoah have 'origins' or 'roots' in the Western philosophical tradition. For Levinas, it is the tradition's ontological obsession with the self, while for Arendt it is the Platonic-inspired rejection of plurality and the *polis*. In this vein, the Shoah is a historical event that expresses a crisis already present in the Western tradition that fails to guarantee the dignity of difference. Embracing the post-foundational notion of relationality is a means to reject this tradition. I, inspired by both Arendt and Levinas, who refused to give up hope after such horror, refuse to be part of what James Watson describes as the '"we" [who] will place this accumulated mass of Holocaust "facts" quite naturally in the same rational, metaphysical framework whose point of completion was the murder of six million *others* and their memory'.[4] The 'philosophical' lesson to be learned from the Shoah calls for a radical rethinking of the priority of the self and its expression in terms of a morality based in the doctrine of autonomy and a hierarchically constructed, control-oriented politics.

The notion of relationality is thus 'born' from the ashes, both literal and metaphorical, of the Western metaphysical tradition as exposed by the horrors of the Shoah. Relationality is not a new type of metaphysics; seeking truth, reason or control is no longer a priority. Rather, the lesson to be learned from the Shoah is precisely that there is an inherent danger to such foundational philosophical projects when unchecked. For this reason I define relationality as a post-foundational project. Concretely this means its fragility and contingency, which mirror those of the interhuman realm as described by both Arendt and Levinas, are embraced. In his book *Post-Foundational Political Thought*, Marchart traces the post-Heideggerian trend of left-leaning thinkers (such as Nancy, Lefort, Badiou, and Laclau and in the German version Arendt), of engaging in a 'constant interrogation of metaphysical figures of foundation—such as totality, universality, essence, and ground'.[5] While it is possible to read Arendt (as Marchart does) and Levinas (as I have done) as post-foundational thinkers, relationality explicitly defines itself as post-foundational. As such relationality is neither a form of foundationalism nor a form of anti-foundationalism, it does not aim to affirm a particular foundational claim but rather to question the possibility of certainty with regard to all forms of foundationalism. First and foremost, what characterizes a post-foundational approach is the recognition of, and the refusal to fear, its own limitations and contingency. Second, post-foundationalism differs from anti-foundationalism in that it does recognize the human need for partial 'foundations', all the while recognizing the contingency and questionability of these 'grounds'. Post-foundationalism is, in many ways, strengthened by its ability to recognize its limitations and to engage in debate about these to increase awareness and understanding. This is ideal given the reality of life in the twenty-first century, with its increased understanding and awareness of its own contingency and limits. In terms of the principle of relationality, the recognition of the priority of alterity and plurality justifies embracing the contingency and fragility that are inherent to both.

In addition to defining relationality in terms of post-foundationalism, the lesson of the Shoah also affects my project in a broader sense. What both Arendt and Levinas seek to recover, in terms of the political and ethics, respectively, is a means to embrace difference, both as part of the self and as part of the world. The Shoah symbolizes the desire to erase difference, often in order to create a fictitious unity or identity. While the guilt and shame of the Shoah are still present—at least in terms of rhetoric and the rejection of anti-Semitism—it seems that the broader lessons, as expressed by Arendt and Levinas, have only been partially learned. Without denying that anti-Semitism still exists today, which by no means is to be confused with the rise in anti-Israel political sentiments (often poorly or incorrectly articulated and thus interpreted as anti-Semitism), it would be absurd to deny that 'the West' has scorned 'the same hatred of the other person' (or more generally racism). Antizyganism, which has been part of Europe's legacy for over a millennium, continues;[6] Islamophobia—now that there is a growing presence of Muslims and Arabs in Europe (and not as before the Shoah, when their presence was outside of Europe's 'geographical' borders)—is on the rise;[7] and the treatment of migrants, refugees and sans-papier all serve as evidence of 'the same hatred of the other person'. What now exists is at best a temporal tolerance, a tolerance that is not strong enough to withstand economic hardship; this tolerance still embodies a priority of the self over the other and a rejection of the principle of plurality.[8] What Levinas calls for is a radical change with regard to the past and present allergic reaction to alterity. Arendt appeals for a similarly radical change in attitude in terms of plurality that requires that we all accept, and embrace, the fact that all differences make up the plurality of our shared world, which all people have the right to inhabit. It is this 'pearl of wisdom' that I wish to retain in terms of the principle of relationality.

EXPERIENCE AND THE PHENOMENOLOGICAL APPROACH

While Husserl approached phenomenology by means of the conscious experiences from the first-person point of view, Arendt and Levinas—influenced by Heidegger's method of doing phenomenology—were most interested in Husserl's later writings on intersubjectivity as a means to understand 'the interhuman realm'. While their distinct uses of the phenomenological tradition are often debated, both Arendt and Levinas can be categorized as 'existential phenomenologists' interested in understanding how meaning arises from concrete human interactions. This shared interest has been a point of research for those interested in this third wave of phenomenology. 'In post-Husserlian phenomenology, the human life-world and relationality constitute two important areas of investigation. They are interrelated by the fact that the life-world is an intersubjective world commonly given to all men'.[9]

A significant insight both drew from the phenomenological tradition is that one should not compare intersubjective relations to the relations between a subject and an object, as each subject is unique and cannot be reduced to an object.[10] Closely connected to the phenomenological pearl of intersubjectivity is the importance of the phenomenological notion of world. Levinas, who was often criticized for not being a philosopher of the world, rejects this claim: 'They say that in my view—I am often criticized for this—there is an underestimation of the world. In Heidegger, the world is very important. In the *Feldwege*, there is a tree; you don't find men there'.[11] When one reads Levinas in relation to the phenomenological understanding of world, it is clear that he understands it and values it as much as Arendt does as a space for humanity to disclose itself—a space of interhuman interaction in which reality and meaning are co-created. While relationality goes beyond the notion of intersubjectivity, it could not do so without the work done by these and many other thinkers to break out of the subject-object paradigm that dominated much of Western philosophy (especially prior to the Shoah).

Arendt and Levinas, as part of the third wave of phenomenologists, help to transform the phenomenological tradition in which previously 'ethics has been on the horizon of phenomenology . . . [and] political theory has remained on the borders of phenomenology'.[12] By approaching ethics and the political by means of the phenomenological tradition, Arendt and Levinas are able to open new avenues of reflection and consider new approaches to both ethics and the political. These are essential to the notion of relationality I am developing. It is the intersection of the phenomenological approach, with its emphasis on intersubjectivity, meaning, experiences, action and the need to prioritize ethics and the political, that I take from their thought. In addition, I share their understanding that the world (or life-world) is an intersubjective world created between people. Bringing together the importance of Husserlian and Heideggerian phenomenology, Arendt and Levinas both arrive at an appreciation of the intersection between a social ontology and the phenomenological method. Starting from intersubjectivity and focusing on the relations between people that create the world, both go beyond phenomenology, as outlined by Husserl, yet neither ever rejects or abandons the insights this approach allows one to access. While relationality goes beyond this tradition—and specifically its ties to the notion of the subject, implicit in the notion of intersubjectivity—I remain indebted to the importance of experience and understanding, acting and sharing, as a means to make the world more hospitable for all.

WRESTLING WITH HEIDEGGER

While there is no doubt that Heidegger's convoluted relationship to his many Jewish students, as well as his romantic relationship with Arendt, provide rich material for idle chatter among philosophers,[13] it cannot be denied that most of these thinkers recognize him as one of the most brilliant thinkers of the twentieth century and an essential influence in their own intellectual journeys. Heidegger's thought and actions, which often conflicted, were the ground upon which Arendt and Levinas developed their original and brilliant philosophical contributions. As Levinas, who never met with Heidegger after the Shoah, wrote: '[O]nly M. Heidegger dares to confront deliberately this problem, considered impossible by all of traditional philosophy, the problem that has for its object the meaning of the existence of Being . . . and we believe we are entitled to take our inspiration from him.'[14] For both Arendt and Levinas, Heidegger's choice to focus on the meaning of Being, on *Dasein*, is not a step in the wrong direction—it is just too small of a step towards the other. Heidegger prioritizes the meaning of *Dasein*, which limits the other to a 'letting be' in the horizon of the self. For Heidegger there is 'no correlation of "I" and "Thou" or of "we" and "you", that is, no *community*, can ever reach the level of selfhood; instead, every correlation of this kind misses that level and remains excluded from it—unless it manages to ground itself first of all on *Dasein*'.[15]

Having created a space for a phenomenological consideration of the meaning of the existence of *Dasein*, it is possible to appreciate the importance of the other for *Dasein*. While Arendt and Levinas may not have formulated this as such, *Dasein* paved the way for a phenomenological approach to the meaning of the human being, a being who is always in relation to the other. What expresses the human condition is not her *being* but her ability to experience and create a world with the other. It is not coincidental that both Arendt and Levinas felt the need to take a step towards intersubjectivity, a step not taken (or insufficiently taken) by Heidegger.[16] Both Arendt and Levinas realized the limits of Heideggerian ontology, and yet both wrestled—Arendt more publicly and Levinas more privately—with the many attempts to dismiss all of Heidegger's writing because of his anti-Semitism. While his unpublished correspondences and writings from this period are still being edited (see Peter Trawny's *Black Notebooks*[17]), many critics have already firmly concluded that Heidegger's ethics and politics are without promise.[18] Take, for example, Smith's claim that 'aside from some considerations of a "Mitsein" or being with, Heidegger's main consideration of the other is in the negative, inauthentic and impersonal guise of "Das Man", which represents a betrayal of our ownness'.[19] Regardless of how one responds to the question of Heidegger's problematic political views or equally problematic political silence, dismissing his influence on an entire generation of thinkers, including many Jewish thinkers, does injustice to their source and inspiration. Jean-Luc Nancy, a thinker who remained much closer to Heidegger, recognized this lacuna in Heidegger's writings—'[D]espite the presence of the terms *Mitsein* and *Mitdasein* in the text, no lengthy or rigorous analyses of the concepts are provided as in the case of the main concepts—far from it'[20]—and yet goes on to develop a rich appreciation of community based on his reading of Heidegger. While Arendt and Levinas clearly distanced themselves from Heidegger, especially in the years directly after the Shoah, this estrangement prevented neither from recognizing the inheritance each had received from their teacher.

Predictably there are certainly similarities between my concept of relationality and Jean-Luc Nancy's notion of *être singulier pluriel*. Nancy also aims to understand a form of plurality, or a 'we', that is not reducible to singularity. He does so by arguing, by means of Heideggerian existentials, that there is no *Dasein* without *mitsein* so that the self, or I, cannot precede or have priority over the being-with others. 'There is no meaning if meaning is not shared, and not because there would be an ultimate or first signification that all beings have in common, but because meaning is itself the sharing of Being'.[21] While Nancy's effort to rethink the political and refuse the common approach of prioritizing the individual or the collective is to be applauded, his closeness to Heidegger is intellectually limiting—seemingly preventing the radical rethinking of the tradition that Heidegger promoted. Nancy's *être singulier pluriel,* by relying on Heideggerian existentials, stills has its roots in a foundationalist metaphysical project as well as a strong conception of the subject. While the former is what differentiates Nancy's work from that of Arendt and Levinas, the latter is also problematic for relationality. It is with regard to the notion of the subject that my notion of relationality differs from the echoes of phenomenological intersubjectivity present in both Arendt and Levinas.

Not only are there significant differences between Heidegger's *mitsein* and Arendt's plurality or Levinas's alterity; there is also a different underlying philosophical anthropology that Nancy inherits from Heidegger that runs against the alternative Judaic-inspired philosophical anthropology I identified in Arendt's and Levinas's writings. In addition, in as much as Arendt and Levinas criticize Heidegger for his failure to pay proper respect to thinking with regard to ethics and the political, Arendt also failed to explicitly acknowledge the importance of ethics for the sake of the political, and in so doing prevented the political from being as strong and stable as possible while remaining grounded in post-foundationalism. Likewise, Levinas failed to appreciate that the hatred he sought to prevent manifests itself in the political and thus must be challenged in the *polis*. His own allergic reaction to the political displays his lack of faith in plurality, a lack of faith that led him to keep a trace of totality within an ethics of infinity. In this vein, a trace of Heidegger's inheritance is present in the lacunae I have identified in Arendt's and Levinas's respective oeuvres.

THE JUDAIC CONTRIBUTION TO RELATIONALITY

The Talmudic saying 'to save one life is to save the world; to destroy one life is to destroy the world' is an ethic that has strong resonances with both Levinas's ethics of alterity and Arendt's notion of plurality. Sadly, if we only consider the twentieth century, the world, created by means of bonds between people, has been (and continues to be) destroyed. If we are (ever) to be at home in the world, we must take responsibility for the world and begin to repair it. However, one of the preconditions for such repairing, *tikkum olam,* is the possibility of collective action—public actions in which plurality appears and 'acts in concert'. As identified by Arendt in her analysis of the rise of the social and expanded upon by Pitkin in her book *Attack of the Blob,*[22] such spaces and possibilities of collective action are increasingly rare in our modern democracies. While there have been hopeful signs at the beginning of the twenty-first century, such as the Arab Spring, the Occupy movements, the Indigniados,

Tahir Square, Gezi Park and the Brazil bus protests and so forth, these are exceptions that are by no means promoted by our governments, which prefer to govern (rule) docile subjects. Furthermore, collective manifestations such as protests are now increasingly being—either implicitly or explicitly—criminalized.[23] In addition, the rise of individualism, part and parcel of post–World War II liberal democracies, and the increasing gap between rich and poor, exponentially rising in the current neo-liberal economic regime that dictates the policies of many of the richer nations, further stifles the emergence of such collective actions.

Relationality provides an empowering model of human interaction in which collective action is prized. Without sacrificing particularity or alterity, relationality puts a great deal of emphasis on collective undertakings meant to care for the shared world. Lest one consider this the return of 'religion' to the political, let me clarify. Consider the following:

> One cannot separate political and religious: The philosopher finds himself [*sic*] in a different position. When he thinks of the principles that generate society and names them political, he automatically includes religious phenomena within his field of reference. This does not mean that in his view the religious and the political can coincide. It does, however, mean that one cannot separate the elaboration of the political form . . . from the elaboration of a religious form.[24]

While Claude Lefort here refers to Christianity in relation to the political, there is no reason that the Judaic cannot also be a source of political principles in a society of non-Jews. Having clarified, let us not forget that in relation to the idea of Europe, the Judaic is a trope for the excluded or otherwise unwanted elements of a society.[25] Until the Shoah, the presence of Jews was an ethical litmus test of the particular society. 'The critical test of any order is: does it make space for otherness? Does it acknowledge the dignity of difference?'[26] The world, and different societies, can and ought to be judged by how they 'treat the other', the stranger, widow and orphan in terms of the Judaic. Such a test should now be applied to groups currently being excluded, groups such as Romas, Muslims, refugees and immigrants as well as Palestinians in Israel. In this vein, relationality's Judaic inspiration aims to promote a non-allergic reaction to alterity (as Levinas) and a principle of inclusiveness. While some societies have a welcoming ethos and are thus open to alterity in the private realm, this openness is not always mirrored in terms of the public or political.[27] Likewise, many societies claim to be politically welcoming, often pointing to the legal structure as evidence of this fact, but are hostile to difference in both the private and social realms.[28] In search of a political ethics that would pass this hypothetical test, I wish to consider three elements from the Judaic tradition that might be of service: hope, responsibility and the relational approach.

Judaic Hope

While I have examined the role of hope in both Arendt's and Levinas's writings, I now wish to explicitly connect hope, understood as an attitude or outlook about life, which is fundamental to my notion of relationality, to its roots in the Judaic. Many Jewish thinkers have written extensively on the significance of hope, both in its more 'secular' manifestations and in relation to the messianic (e.g., Martin Buber, Walter Benjamin, Ernest Bloch). For so many people struggling to make sense of the world after the Shoah, which calls neither for forgiveness nor for forgetting, this activity of thinking and understanding is confronting, in that it challenges us to make a choice, to choose one's attitude or outlook with regard to the future and its possibilities in light of the horrors of the past. While in some sense it is more rational, as so many did after the Shoah, to 'give in' to the totality of despair, a sensible position when one is drowning in pain, there are others who—seemingly against all reason—struggled to hold onto hope and to continue to believe in a better future for humanity.

For Tony Judt, a 'secular' Jewish historian born in 1948, who could not 'recall a time when I did not know about what was not yet called the Holocaust', this latter choice was the only possible response to 'a collective history of Jewish suffering'.[29] What for Judt was an almost banal fact of history, is in fact a principle reaffirmed by many Judaic sources both medieval and modern. 'Rabbi Nachman of Bratislava (1772–1810) declared, "It is forbidden to despair". Hope—no less than monotheism itself—is a normative and non-negotiable pillar of the Jewish mandate'.[30] While I would distance myself from any notion of normativity, hope is undoubtedly a central pillar of Jewish thought. Hope is a principle or commitment, disclosed in an attitude towards the future and based on faith in humanity, to keep believing, often against all odds. Jonathan Sacks, a philosopher and former Orthodox chief rabbi of the Commonwealth, who has written extensively on the notion of hope, explains that it 'is born in the belief that the sources of action lie within ourselves. . . . Hope is the knowledge that we can choose; that we can learn from our mistakes and act differently next time'.[31] It is precisely this attitude that characterizes the first element of the Judaic that I wish to include in the notion of relationality.

Levinas affirms such a position in one of his first writings after the Shoah, in which he expresses concern that Western philosophy might not have the resources within its own tradition to recover from such a world-shattering event, and that without hope it might crumble under the weight of its responsibility to repair the world destroyed by violence and hatred:

> It is nonetheless necessary to begin from the sources of Judaism. Judaism is not a religion. The word does not even exist in Hebrew. It is

> much more than this. It is a way of being, of living. The Jew introduced into history the idea of hope and the idea of a future. Moreover, the Jew has the feeling that his obligations with respect to the other come before his obligations to God, or more precisely that the other is the voice of high places. . . . Ethics is an optics vis-à-vis God. The only voice of respect vis-à-vis God is that of respect toward one's fellow human beings. (DF 130)[32]

First, it is worth noting that Levinas wants to separate the notion of Judaism from that of a 'religion'. As Masuzawa establishes, theologians invented the notion of 'religion' when Christianity lost its role as the central organizational principle for society.[33] Judaism is not a religion if one takes Christianity, with its focus on dogma and faith, as the model for religions. Judaism is a praxis and ethics, and in this sense Levinas takes it to be closer to philosophy than it is to Christianity. Judaism is not a religion—it does not fit neatly into the space of the private sphere carved out by the separation of church and state (which of course was still ruled by Christians). Judaism has no official dogma (although one cannot deny that Maimonides would have preferred this to be otherwise); rather, it is a call to action, for deeds oriented towards others and the world. Martha Nussbaum, who studied Judaism extensively from a philosophical perspective before making the choice to convert, described it as 'a this-worldly religion, a religion in which the primacy of the moral, and of this-worldly justice, inform[s] not only judgements but also, or so it seemed to me, the entirety of the tradition'.[34]

Second, according to Levinas, the Judaic introduces the idea of hope into human history. While this is undoubtedly evidence of Levinas's monotheistic Eurocentrism, one might qualify his claim by saying that the Judaic introduced the idea of hope into Western European thought. With regard to Europe's theological legacy, this claim can be justified. Without delving too deeply into centuries of theological debates, including the staged disputations of the Middle Ages in which these questions were 'debated', the Judaic does not have a notion of original sin. The notion that humans are sinners or are 'fallen' and must find external salvation is not part of a Judaic narrative (in its place is an 'immense' weight to take responsibility for the other and the world). The importance of hope can also be accounted for historically, as Jews, who have been exiled and dispersed since the sixth century BCE (with notable interludes), have needed hope to 'keep going', often in the face of almost total extermination. The Judaic offers an alternative philosophical anthropology, one driven by hope and the commitment not to give up on the world by giving in to fear. While this is often dismissed as being too simplistic, it is worth considering as an alternative to the politics of fear that directed our shared past.[35]

A commitment to hope also affects the fundamental concepts and questions a thinker focuses on. An example of this is the focus by certain thinkers on death, and others on life. Contrary to Nietzsche's incorrect characterization of the Judaic as life negating, which is the result of his subsumption of Judaism into Christianity (and hence abuse of the signifier Judeo-Christian[36]), Arendt and Levinas explicitly focus on birth and life—whether as natality, fecundity, maternity or in terms of miracles. With each new life, there is an infinite number of possibilities open for an individual and for the world in which this individual will participate. Birth is a relational experience, with roots in a mixture of vertical (between parent and child) and horizontal (between parents) transcendence, and is a source of hope, as it is future related.

Another reason for embracing a Judaic notion of hope in relation to relationality is that its future orientation is a symbolic refusal to celebrate death, to accept suffering and to justify any form of theodicy. It is this same refusal that underlines the choice to use the term Shoah and the rejection of the term Holocaust, which is a theological term with Greek roots that means 'burnt offering' (which implicitly suggests its victims sacrificed themselves). Choosing to affirm life, choosing to be guided by hope rather than by fear (and death) is in itself a choice that is not easily made, but one that according to the Judaic is necessary for humanity. Hope, both in terms of the Judaic and relationality, is a collective commitment. Sadly, according to Linda Alcoff, postmodern thinkers all too often close off the paths both to hope and to the other, paths that of course are clearly connected in the Judaic paradigm:

> The difference between modern and postmodern accounts is simply in their degree of optimism about the extent to which the individual can negate the given and resist an external power. But in both cases negation, resistance, and destabilisation are the privileged tactics because what comes to the individual from the Other is assumed to be ultimately both inaccurate and oppressive.[37]

Contrary to Alcoff's pessimistic appraisal of postmodern thought, Jewish thought—in the aftermath of the Shoah—continues to embrace hope. This Judaic inspiration is also essential for relationality, which also rejects the assumption described by Alcoff that the other is dangerous or threatening; difference is celebrated as an enriching challenge to the self that not only allows one to better understand oneself and the other, it allows one to make the world one's home—it provides roots for those without roots—roots in the other(s).

The Priority of Responsibility

Like the principle of hope, responsibility is a central Judaic concept. As discussed in relation to Levinas's ethics, the Hebrew term *acher*, which means other, shares the same root as the term *achrayut*, which means responsible. In terms of the Judaic, to be responsible is to be responsible for the other. Responsibility is in this sense like hope, a commitment or principle. Relationality also calls for such a promise, as it recognizes that by always already being in relation to others, I am always already also responsible for these others and the shared world we create, or destroy, together. While concepts like hope and responsibility are rooted in plurality, the paradox of plurality as Arendt demonstrates it is that it arises from distinction—from a particular agent or actor. Relationality is also a concept that is rooted in this paradox between plurality and particularity. Both aspects are always present, and yet one can be more accentuated. This is also evident from the two seemingly different manners in which we can speak of Judaic responsibility.

On the one hand, we can speak of responsibility in terms of 'collective or shared'—this comes very close to Arendt's claim that we are all responsible for the creation of reality or the world. This usage is actually the recognition of our fundamental relationality and says less about responsibility in terms of a commitment to act. Levinas also speaks of such a responsibility in his Talmudic messianic readings:

> The messianic dream, and even the simple dream of justice that so delights human foolishness, promises a painful awakening. Men are not only the victims of injustice; they are also the perpetrators. The biblical text rebels against the idyllic messianism of universal pardon and reminds us of the stark severity entailed in justice and judgment. (DF 91–92)

Albeit to differing degrees, I am both a victim of injustice and responsible for this injustice—this is what it means to always be in relation to others. This type of absolute victimization, which Arendt rejects in *Origins*, that the Shoah was caused by the eternal unavoidable anti-Semitism and that Jews played absolutely no role in their own history, is a denial of any form of agency, and fosters further depoliticization and disempowerment. Taking responsibility means accepting that every actor or agent has a role to play in the web-of-relations. In addition, the Judaic notion of responsibility is one that requires action in the sense of words or deeds. While there is no requirement of publicity, to take responsibility seriously means to attempt to 'repair the world' and as such, in most cases, action is required. Concretely, it means I must act and not allow others to simply do so in my place—whether in terms of political representation (hence Arendt's choice for direct democracy) or by waiting for the messianic era to bring about a universal pardon for all people and crimes.

On the other hand, the Judaic also refers to a seemingly different yet complementary notion of responsibility as self-assigned. This calls for the acknowledgement that I am always responsible for the other—an idea we find central in Levinas's work. Responsibility, in this latter sense, is connected to particularity. *I* am responsible. But particularity, and hence responsibility, makes no sense without plurality. I am responsible *for* the other, *for* the world. While by no means limited to Arendt and Levinas, both provide ample evidence of these intertwined meanings of Judaic responsibility. In the context of a discussion of responsibility in relation to the Shoah, part of the Talmudic reading 'Damages Due to Fire', Levinas makes the following peculiar statement: Auschwitz is the source of war (NTR 182). How can Auschwitz be the source of war? The answer is to be found in Levinas's interpretation of the Judaic notion of responsibility. 'The righteous are responsible for evil before anyone else is. They are responsible because they have not been righteous enough to make their justice spread and abolish injustice' (NTR 186). Here it is important to stress that responsibility for Levinas is not a legal category, it is ethical. He is not saying that the Jews who survived should have been tried in the stead of the SS soldiers. What he is saying is that the source of war, 'the madness of extermination', stems from the tension between the politics of the exterminators and the political preachers of justice whose voices they wish to silence. Those fighting for justice are required never to stop fighting. The omnipresence of language related to the Shoah in this text reminds us that for Levinas politics reeks of war and the gas chambers.

While Arendt does not develop this kind of self-assigned responsibility, a fundamental aspect of the political is that action always arises from a particular agent or actor. Thus while responsibility is always shared, it is shared by actors who must each take responsibility for the concrete manifestation of the invisible, yet tangible, web-of-relations that characterizes the human realm they are co-creating. Likewise, any action I initiate or participate in has a consequence, positive or negative, not only for myself but also for other human beings with whom I interact—it is thus important to recognize the political and ethical repercussions of every action and not to seek to separate them in order to 'justify' oneself. Justification is often a first form of evading responsibility. 'The price of setting an example is responsibility, that one will be judged not as a self which might exist outside its relations with others, but as a person whose words and deeds make up the world, that is, the space between human beings'.[38]

Arendt and Levinas, as phenomenologists, also add a temporal dimension to responsibility. Responsibility, not only in the present but also by reaffirming its connection to the past and by inspiring hope in the future, has a temporal continuity. 'Morality [ethics] anchors two vital elements of responsibility: our readiness to commit ourselves to the future, and to be identified with past actions'.[39] Thus not only spatially—by means of its support for the web-of-relations—but also temporally, responsibility connects the political to ethics. As exemplified by Arendt and Levinas, responsibility is both about the self and other(s), enacted by a self who is therefore taking responsibility for the other and thus acts to strengthen and support the shared world. This concept of responsibility is central to the Judaic, which places a great deal of importance on responsibility in relation to *mitzvahs*, good deeds.

While the connection to *mitzvah* is particular to Judaism, the Judaic message is directed towards humanity; it is a message that arises from the particularity of the Judaic but has a universal audience. Levinas writes: 'Violence is no longer a political phenomenon of war and peace, [it is] beyond all morality. It is the abyss of Auschwitz or the world at war. A world which has lost its "very worldliness". . . . Does [it] not have its full meaning because it applies to all humanity. . . . [This] is the suffering of Israel as universal suffering' (NTR 191). While the Jews, Romas and many other marginalized groups were the 'victims' of the Shoah, the world was destroyed and so everyone suffers from its stain. The tragedy of the Shoah is one that unites the world; it is the loss of a shared world for which we are all responsible. According to Levinas, the only possible means to prevent its repetition is for both its 'victims' and 'perpetrators' to learn the same lesson, which is a 'call to man's infinite responsibility, to an untiring wakefulness, to a total insomnia' (NTR 193). While Arendt's terminology is very different from Levinas's and was unappreciated by the Jewish community during her life, her message is quite similar:

> She insisted on intellectual consistency at any price. If Eichmann had no right to deny his moral responsibility for his crimes, the victims who served as his unwilling accomplices, in the Judenrat, had no right to deny their responsibility either. She defended, with vehemence and clarity, the proposition that both victims and perpetrators had their responsibilities.[40]

Arendt argues for a very unpopular position: I must take responsibility and stop trying to deny my responsibility by attributing it to others. Arendt also shares Levinas's view that it is only by taking responsibility for the world that I can prevent its further destruction. They do, however, disagree with regard to the exemplary power of responsibility. For Levinas, while I might act as a model for others by taking responsibility, this is not why I take responsibility; I do so because I am responsible for the world. Arendt does not agree and writes in her *Denktagebuch*: 'Every actor wishes that people will follow him. The act is always also an example. Political thought and judgement is exemplary (Kant), because acting is. Responsibility in fact means: to know that one sets an example, that others will "follow"; in this way one changes the world'.[41] This difference is a reminder of the different frameworks within which each writes. For Levinas ethics is about the self taking responsibility for the other; it is not about publicity and plurality. For Arendt responsibility is political; it is a public deed or commitment to take responsibility that requires an audience:

> If politics is impossible without the factuality of human freedom, then freedom is inconceivable outside the order of *ultimate responsibility* which politics establishes. Thus totalitarianism is in essence not distinguished by its mere abuse of freedom—as in the case of tyranny—but by its immoral discovery that freedom can be used to eliminate its own conditions of existence: plurality and individuality.[42]

While we can be held accountable for our labour and work, which leads to the incorrect impression that responsibility applies in these realms, Arendt's notion of responsibility is limited to the realm of action in which we each act as free agents in relation with others. In this vein, Arendt's notion of responsibility is also easier to connect to the broader debates on rights and responsibility in our current democracies.

According to Jung, a phenomenologist, 'the concept of responsibility lives in the shadow of the hagiographic life of rights in the modern West. Western morality has privileged rights while handcuffing and marginalizing responsibility?'[43] While this claim is overstated, it is fair to say that the post-Shoah Western political arena has been dominated by rights discourse and that the notion of responsibility is often marginalized. This is perplexing in that in the aftermath of the Shoah responsibility should have been the most important political discourse, so why did rights became the priority? Was the rise to prominence of rights discourse Europe's means to further evade taking responsibility for the Shoah, as Tony Judt suggested?[44] It seems absurd, especially given the analysis of the paradox of rights developed by Arendt in *Origins*, to suggest that human rights could prevent what was the product of centuries of exclusion and persecution. The assumption seems to be that had the rights of Jews and other persecuted minorities been respected, the Shoah would not have occurred. Responsibility is externalized and put onto a legal system rather than, as in the Judaic, self-applied. While this is undoubtedly easier then turning the gaze upon oneself, it is sadly an evasion of the lessons both Arendt and Levinas claim must be learned from the Shoah.

Another explanation of why rights discourse was so popular after the Shoah is that it was made possible by the growing gap between people, power and the political (a gap that is now an infinite chasm). 'Amid the turmoil of revolutionary activity in the nineteenth century, one of the less-noticed effects of the historical and sociological theories invented at that time was a weakening of man's sense of direct responsibility for politics'.[45] The less one feels engaged in the political, the less one feels responsible for the world, and sadly in our individualizing neo-liberal climate, there is a growing discontent and disconnect from the political. Furthermore, for those who need rights most, there is no one willing to take up his or her cause, no one whose voice is heard. By grounding human rights discourse in a form of ontological singularity, rights are torn from the web-of-relations that sustains them, a web that is created not by rights but by relations of responsibility. In other words, the 'foundation' for rights affirms an ontology that prioritizes singularity at the cost of the other. In order to challenge this inhuman ontology, responsibility, in its Judaic particularizing or personalizing form, must take priority. Rights do not make sense without responsibilities, as rights need a community to be meaningful, a community that is willing to take responsibility for the other whose rights are being denied.[46]

A Relational Approach

The third Judaic element I wish to import into my concept of relationality is the most difficult to characterize, as it is developed by many different Judaic thinkers, although each in subtly different ways. In this sense some understandings are very close to notions of intersubjectivity, while others focus more on the communicative or dialogical aspect of human relations. As a starting point to better understand what a relational approach entails, we can build upon the fact that both Arendt, in terms of plurality and the between, and Levinas, in terms of alterity and substitution, embrace a Judaic relational approach. To further clarify what it occasions, consider how it relates to the elements of hope and responsibility. If one asks the question—Is there a source for Judaic hope?—the answer points towards a relational approach. There is hope because we are always in relation; we are not alone. Why are we always in relation and never alone? Because we are responsible for each other. A Judaic relational approach is the recognition of both the hope discovered in relation to the other and the weight of the gift of responsibility. As explored in previous chapters, this triangle of Judaic hope—responsibility—and a relational approach are all expressions of a particular philosophical anthropology that runs counter to several currents in both politics and philosophy.

This relational approach combats the loneliness that Arendt identifies as one of the greatest dangers both in totalitarian regimes and also in our modern, depoliticized liberal democracies. It helps us to realize that while we may feel lonely and live in a society where we are told we are autonomous, independent individuals, in reality we are heteronomous, dependent beings, and moreover this is our strength and not a weakness. This ethos, or philosophy, is barely tangible in our post-Christian (or 'secular'), neo-liberal-driven democracies. While nation-states that define themselves as Jewish are by no means an exception to this trend, the Judaic does embrace such an ethos or philosophical anthropology. Rather than asking what makes someone recognize this relation to the other, the Judaic poses this question in terms of a choice between two inclinations. On the one hand is the *yetzer tov* (*tov* means good or ethical), and on the other hand is the *yetzer ra, ra* meaning erroneous or egoism. What is important to retain is that both inclinations, *ra* and *tov*, are essential for humanity—according to the Judaic, what is critical is always striving to find the suitable balance. Without the *yetzer ra*, it would be impossible to satisfy personal needs such as providing shelter for oneself, having children, and so forth. It is only when these are done at the cost of the *yetzer tov* that there is a serious problem. For Jonathan Sacks what a Judaic outlook makes clear when used to analyse some of the major moral writings of Western philosophy is the predominance of the *yetzer ra*, a form of individualism or egoism that if unchecked and disassociated from responsibility is dangerous. While the 'first question asked in lectures and books on ethics is usually: "Why be moral?"—as if the greatest roadblock on the way were selfishness, egocentricity, indifference. I suspect, however, that the real question is "Why me?" Who am I to do the noble deed, the courageous act? I am just an ordinary person'.[47] According to Sacks, the assumption of Western philosophy is that morality requires a motivation that is not already present in human beings, an assumption that is further problematized by setting the standard for morality by means of saints who are willing to completely sacrifice themselves. By contrast, according to Sacks, the Judaic model is one that presents human beings as always in relation and as having to choose, in every situation, whether the appropriate response is to prioritize care for the self or other(s), but that this prioritization never permits one to deny that we are always in relation to others and that our choice will affect others. What a Judaic relational approach demonstrates is that I cannot simply embrace egoism and make life easier for myself, as we are not ever only 'a myself'. The self is a construction that allows us to bracket the fact that we are fundamentally relational creatures. This 'bracketing' allows us to lose sight of the fact that our interdependence is our greatest treasure and resource. If we deny this heteronomy, we have also tragically destroyed the roots of hope and responsibility.

The relational approach is so central to Judaic thought that one could say that it defines how the human condition, or even further human nature, is understood. While a being may not need to be in relation, to be a *human* being is to be in relation to others. While being in relation does not contradict the fact that the idea of autonomy is important to our self-constitution, it recognizes that autonomy arises from an already existing heteronomy. The Judaic relational approach puts the relation to other(s) as prior to any possible form of autonomy or singularity. Unfortunately, the Judaic relational approach does not often get explored, except when developed by a thinker, like Levinas or Arendt, who brings it into dialogue with a broader philosophical tradition:

> The Neo-Kantian philosophers—for example, Buber, Marcel, Rosenstock and Rosenzweig—presented these ideas in terms of 'the dialogical principle', which involved the relationship between 'I' and 'Thou', that is, the relation of co-authors in communication. In addition to

> Hegelian philosophy, their dialogical principle came also from Judaism. . . . It was part of the Old [*sic*] Testament as the cultural and communal spirit.[48]

Many of the academic discussions of the communicative or dialogical approaches do take note of the Judaic roots of this tradition, but seem to reduce a fundamental claim about the human condition as relational to a claim concerning the source of meaning for the self in dialogue with others. It is in this sense that a relational approach and dialogicality are often seen as synonyms.

In order to further elucidate the conceptually nebulous notion of a Judaic relational approach, it is necessary to acknowledge that the relational approach is often connected to God. While I do not import this connection into the notion of relationality, which as I will demonstrate with regard to Arendt's writing is possible, it would be dishonest to deny that for many thinkers of the Judaic, a relational approach is a connection to a transcendent God. Rather than conceive of this relational approach as having two components, imagine it in terms of a triangle. The triangle is made up of the self or subject, the other subject or others (or as Levinas sometimes refers to it—Israel—which means the people) and God or the Other (who is also symbolized by the Torah). Each of the corners of the triangle is in relation and cannot be thought of apart from the others except in abstraction for the purpose of a formal exercise. The self is thus constituted by its relation to the two other poles, as is the other, and strangely enough, as is God. It is human beings, in dialogue and relation to each other, who give God meaning:

> The prophets warned against a rift between the *holy* and the *good*, our duties to God and to our fellow human beings. It still exists today. There are those for whom serving God means turning inwards—to the soul, the house of worship and the life of ritual and prayer. There are others for whom social justice has become a substitute for religious observance or God. The message of the Hebrew Bible is that serving God and our fellow human beings are inseparably linked, and the split between the two impoverishes both.[49]

Many conceptions of a Judaic relational approach are based on this image of a relational triangle. This is also the reason for the affinity between the Judaic and social justice, an affinity that is present in most Judaic writers. What Sacks here strives to communicate is the importance of finding a balance and always keeping a space open for interruptions.

In relation to Arendt's work, which is clearly less influenced by Judaism than that of either Levinas or Sacks, this relational approach is no less present. In some sense Arendt can be argued to have replaced God or the Other with the Heideggerian notion of the world or the phenomenological notion of reality, that which cannot arise without both particularity and plurality. While Arendt has no interest in a vertical transcendence, she acknowledges a horizontal transcendence in the public space and the importance of natality and miracles. Although many of Arendt's readers have claimed that her interest in the notion of miracles is not to be read in relation to the Judaic, or religion more broadly, she does explicitly connect the significance of the political question 'who am I?' to its biblical meaning. The most famous reference to this question is that of Moses, who asks God 'who am I?' when they meet at the burning bush. Arendt was certainly aware of this, as she discussed this biblical story at length in her 1942 article in *Aufbau*, 'Moses or Washington' (JW 149–150). These same words are repeated throughout the *Tanakh* by the greatest of Jewish leaders—Rebekah, Jakob and David—and prophets: Isaiah, Jeremiah and Jonah. As Arendt states a dozen times in *The Human Condition*, the self cannot answer this question without the other—it is what motivates the self to enter the public sphere. For Arendt the core of the political is appearing in word and deed in a public space in which the question 'who am I?' can be answered. The relational triangle is certainly in the horizon of the question 'who am I?'; it is the question that brings us into a space of responsibility and into dialogue with others. In Arendtian terms, 'who am I?' is the question that embodies the paradox of plurality. It is a singularizing question that calls out to the other(s) and with whom the world can be created. For Arendt, the third corner of the triangle is reality, and the shared world for which I am responsible, which is evidence that while for many Judaic thinkers God is a part of this relation, this is by no means a necessity.

As a partial conclusion to this chapter, let us consider an ancillary claim that has been disclosed. While the goal of introducing the Judaic was to familiarize readers with this tradition in order to develop its inspirational role in the project as a whole, a 'by-product' of this endeavour was the considerations of the importance of the Judaic for Arendt and Levinas, respectively. In a direct challenge to the common reading of Arendt as a philosopher nostalgic for the Greeks, I hope to have shown not only that Arendt was more interested in the Judaic than previously thought, but also how her project, clearly critical of the Western political philosophy tradition, has many Judaic resonances. Although underdeveloped in her work, I do think that Arendt's message remains true today, at a time when there are more refugees than ever before. Her message, which for too long was ignored by persecuted Jewish communities, was to stop hiding from the political realm. Appear, act and speak. The political is the community of the world in which all, even if it often seems otherwise, are entitled to participate. It is only on the political stage that injustice can be fought and change brought about. Do not hide in the shadows, to which the marginalized are often pushed. It is this message, which arose from the intersection between the political and the Judaic, that Arendt both experienced in her life and was able to share, with such passion, through her writings.

By returning to the four background elements—the Shoah, phenomenology, Heidegger and the Judaic—which I identified as the horizon upon which Arendt's and Levinas's respective projects can be brought together in dialogue and which have been developed in the previous chapters, I now focus on those aspects that I wish to introduce (or in the case of intersubjectivity to partly leave behind) into the concept of relationality. I have spent more time developing three aspects of the Judaic—hope, responsibility, and a relational approach—which were discussed in previous chapters but not always explicitly in relation to the Judaic, all of which are essential to the concept of relationality. With these aspects of relationality in mind, it is now time to consider the core of relationality, the rapprochement between alterity and plurality.

FROM ALTERITY AND PLURALITY TO RELATIONALITY

With so many potential fruitful intellectual intersections between Arendt and Levinas, many of which I have only been able to point towards in the preceding chapters, it is surprising that their respective post-Shoah Heideggerian-inspired phenomenological projects have hardly been brought into dialogue.[50] While there are numerous routes deserving of further reflection, my main focus has been on their respective notions of plurality and alterity. What I hope to have shown is the rich potential for dialogue between an ethics of alterity, as conceived of by Levinas, and a political realm rooted in plurality, as depicted by Arendt, both of which were inspired by a phenomenological notion of intersubjectivity. It is now necessary to consider which aspects of alterity and plurality can be brought together in order to conceptualize relationality in terms of a post-foundational political ethics.

While I recognize that alterity and plurality are distinct philosophical concepts, I will draw freely from both in order to develop the notion of relationality. My goal is to introduce a Levinasian-inspired notion of alterity into Arendt's political notion of plurality in order to ethically strengthen the *polis* from within. As argued in chapter 4, this is what Arendt sought with her search for a new principle of the political but did not do sufficiently because of her anti-morality bias. In addition, by introducing aspects of Levinas's ethics into Arendt's model of the *polis*, it is possible to revise her at times ambiguous notion of the subject. If we keep in mind that both alterity and plurality, as conceived of by Levinas and Arendt respectively, were meant to challenge the ontological tradition and its prioritization of singularity as transmitted to them by Husserl and Heidegger, it is possible to consider both alterity and plurality as forms of social ontology (or what some theorists refer to affirmatively as weak ontologies).[51] I have also shown that drawing too sharp a distinction between a Levinasian ethics and an Arendtian notion of the political, which makes sense if one assumes the definitions of morality and politics as conceived of by thinkers such as Plato or Kant, is problematic given that both sought to challenge this tradition. If we take these concepts directly from Levinas and Arendt without adapting them, there is a tension between alterity and plurality. The rapprochement that I develop in terms of relationality therefore introduces several revisions. The first revision requires that we consider to what extent Arendt and Levinas retain the notion of subject often associated with forms of intersubjectivity. The second revision seeks to make the post-foundational aspect of relationality explicit. These two revisions, in addition to the Judaic inspiration developed above and the shared horizon developed with regard to the four background elements, form the concept of relationality.

The Subject of Relationality

While I have often presented Arendt and Levinas as thinkers of intersubjectivity, and in this way connected them to an intellectual space opened by Husserlian phenomenology, this title is both appropriate and misleading, depending on how it is understood. Neither thinker stays very close to Husserl's notion of intersubjectivity (as discussed in the *Cartesian Meditations*[52]), which focuses primarily on how the self's relation to the other (and the world) affects its own constitution.[53] One of the problems both Arendt and Levinas have with regard to this conception of intersubjectivity is evident from their respective distanciation from the notion of empathy. Neither alterity nor plurality can be understood in terms of empathy, as intersubjectivity is for Husserl. For Arendt, who discusses empathy in relation to Eichmann and in the *Kant Lectures*, empathy—like psychology—attempts to go beyond the phenomena and into the minds of others and thus presumes knowledge of the other, and in so doing destroys the possibility of critical thinking, which is based on judgement (KL 43). For there to be an 'in between' in the *polis*, there must be space between actors, and empathy tries to minimize or erase this space; imagination and thinking are what maintain this space and respect for plurality. Levinas also clearly associates empathy with psychology and makes explicit in his ethics that it is not based on empathy for the other. Like Arendt, he wants to prevent the self from projecting itself—in the form of knowledge—onto the other. The other is radically different. The self must let the other speak and not try to speak for the other or assume that the self has knowledge of the other. As the case of empathy makes clear, neither Arendt nor Levinas accepts a Husserlian interpretation of intersubjectivity that gives both ontological and epistemological priority to the subject.

To distinguish this Husserlian form of intersubjectivity from the notion of subjectivity that is part of relationality, I will use the term *relational subjectivity* or *relational subject*. This term intentionally echoes many of the projects of postmodern and post-structural thinkers,[54] who seek to problematize the notion of the subject and as such aim to decentre the Cartesian subject central to much of the philosophical tradition. A relational subject is neither ontologically prior to the other nor defined by a prefixed notion of human nature—there is no essential nature to the subject. A relational subject, which I claim Levinas develops in *Otherwise Than Being*, is constituted by means of relations. Relational subjectivity is constituted, enacted and performed, by means of relations to itself, to the other and to the world. There is no foundational subject for either the political or ethical; there are only relations and relational subjects—hence the post-foundational nature of relationality (to be concretized in the next section). Relationality embraces a Judaic philosophical anthropology (of hope), which has both egoist and ethical inclinations, that understands the human condition (not human nature) to be constituted by relational subjects who are themselves constituted by particular relations. There is no presupposed essential human nature, as was the case with Hobbes's subject, which was the basis of his assumption that human beings are by nature selfish or violent.

Levinas's notion of the self, certainly as developed in response to Derrida's ontological critique, is undoubtedly a relational self. The same cannot be said of Arendt's subject, although there are many indications that such a relational subject is being presupposed, specifically with regard to her notions of a web-of-relations, her rejection of human nature and her distinction between agents/actors and authors. For the purpose of relationality and with the assistance of Levinas's notion of alterity, I wish to develop a reading of a relational subject that can act or perform in an Arendtian *polis*. While I do think Arendt's notion of the political allows for such a relational subject, it is not conceptualized as such. However, the point is not whether this possibility exists within Arendt's opus, but rather to argue for its necessity in terms of the concept of relationality. Nonetheless, I wish to begin by building on what is already present in her work. As she writes in *The Life of the Mind*:

> In brief, the specifically human actualization of consciousness in the thinking dialogue between me and myself suggests that difference and otherness, which are such outstanding characteristics of the world of appearances as it is given to man for his habitat among a plurality of things, are the very conditions for the existence of man's mental ego as well, for this ego actually exists only in duality. This original duality, incidentally, explains the futility of the fashionable search for identity. (LM 187)

While Levinas writes about the other's alterity or difference, which constitutes the self, for Arendt this difference or otherness remains a part of the self's mind. Based on this, Arendt does not yet embrace the notion of relational subjectivity. However, according to Arendt, in order to think one must recognize this difference or alterity (she equates these terms in LM 183/RJ 184); that is, each of us must 'do something to actualize the difference within himself' (RJ 186). Given her phenomenological roots, she considers this difference in spatial terms. First, there is a space, or gap, within one's self, within identity; this is the space that allows alterity to manifest itself; second, there is a space between myself and the other—a relational space; third, there is a space of interaction between people, which is the space of plurality; and last, there is the space for the political defined by 'the walls of the city' (or the laws), a space within which the world is prioritized and private interests are set aside. This last space, in which we create a world together, is supported by each of the prior fragile relations. This fragility is experienced phenomenologically at each level: within the self, between the self and other and between selves; each level has the possibility to strengthen or empower the other levels, and analogously each level can also further destabilize the others. This is part of the post-foundational contingency of the political. According to Arendt, a community cannot be defined by sameness; it must maintain a space for difference, whether for the alterity within us or between us. Without this space a community is forced to construct itself by means of a fictitious and equally unstable identity (LM 187).

Yet the question is whether the differences within the self and between the self-other are radically different for Arendt. She was convinced that it is the world, the plurality of others, that allows one to form an identity. In this vein, the other whom I encounter in the interhuman realm assists the self who lacks unity or identity. Likewise, a community is not forced to create an illusionary, and often exclusionary, identity for itself when it has an active *polis*. At times she suggests the plurality of the world is the same as the plurality within the self, which would justify reading her as having a concept of relational subjectivity. For example, Arendt asserts that 'whenever there is a plurality—of living beings, of things, of Ideas—there is difference, and this difference does not arise from the outside but is inherent in every entity in the form of duality, from which comes unity as unification' (LM 184) or 'everything that exists among a plurality of things is not simply what it is, in its identity, but it is also difference from others; this being different belongs to its very nature . . . we must take this otherness (*altereitas*) or difference into account' (RJ 184). This inherent difference is much closer to what Levinas refers to as alterity. In terms of relationality, Levinas's radical alterity is the 'difference [that] is inserted into my Oneness' (LM 183), and as such plurality is constituted by alterity. If, as presupposed by my concept of relationality, alterity constitutes plurality, how are we to interact with this difference—either in relation to others or to the self? This is where the concept of relationality must reconnect with an ethics and the political.

While Arendt certainly does not develop this 'difference' with the same attention as Levinas, she does engage with the importance of embracing plurality in relation to the political. That I am aware of myself indicates that there is a difference within me between the self and the observer of the self. Furthermore, she seems to imply that this difference can never be overcome and that no unity is possible. It is in the search for an impossible unity in the form of an identity that a great deal of suffering, existential as well as political, arises. As such she suggest quite ironically, 'Our modern identity crisis could be resolved only by never being alone and never trying to think' (LM 187). The way to make this pain bearable is, according to Arendt, to enter the political realm. It is only there that one has access, from the perspective of the other and the world, to a 'united' picture of oneself (an idea that should strike Lacanians as familiar, although Arendt has an utter distaste for psychoanalysis). Thus rather than spend our lives trying to deny or escape the difference that marks us from within, as does alterity, or a difference that we equally experience in the plurality of the world, we need to recognize and embrace it by engaging others, including the other within. Only in doing so can this difference become part of who we are, allowing us to better understand ourselves and the world as fundamentally in relation. Arendt develops this insight in response to Eichmann, who refused to accept that he had to share the world with all others. It also allows authors, such as Judith Butler in *Parting Ways*, to use Arendt's notion of plurality to argue for the political importance of a notion of cohabitation as a possible resolution to the asymmetrical conflict in Israel and Palestine.[55]

While Levinas also recognizes the discomfort caused by this inner alterity, he does not consider how the self, or other, should respond to it other than by accepting its weight and responsibility. Given how violent and dangerous 'the hatred of the other man' is, this strikes me as politically irresponsible. Levinas seems to believe that, perhaps after some form of epiphany, we will simply no longer experience an allergic reaction to alterity. This is a reminder of why his ethics are admirable and yet politically problematic. For Arendt, the political is both a space of agonism and a space of freedom. The discomforting difference and conflict within is externalized and shared with others and in this way temporarily alleviated. For Levinas it seems acceptable to define freedom as difficult and simply to leave it at that. He fails to consider that the other as different can help me to understand 'who I am' and help the world understand itself.

The 'coping mechanism' that is available in the political realm is also politically beneficial, as it helps the self to have other perspectives of the shared world and reality. Like the notion of perspective developed by phenomenology, each particular agent, by means of action and judgement, offers a unique perspective of the world, and together these help all those interacting to better understand the shared world as well as to reconcile themselves to the reality that there is no unity either within the self or within society. By means of these perspectives, hearing other points of view (and sharing stories), one acquires this understanding of the intertwinement of identity and difference, *ipseity* and alterity. While we may wish to escape the latter for the ersatz comfort of the former, a desire that has been abused by a variety of political regimes (including totalitarian regimes), Arendt—in a language familiar to the Judaic—implies that this is a denial of the human condition. It is thus a 'crime against humanity',[56] to reduce difference to sameness—an ethical crime for Levinas and a political one for Arendt. This is precisely the point Levinas also makes with regard to the importance of thinking ethically after the Shoah. What is tragic is that even after the Shoah, victims—such as the Romas—continue to be persecuted. Moreover, with the rise of Islamophobia in the twenty-first century, which can be interpreted as a new form of anti-Semitism,[57] there seems to be no end to 'the hatred of the other man' that Levinas speaks of in his dedication in *Otherwise Than Being*.

Relationality is proposed as a means to challenge this obsession with the same that is dangerous for the self, the other and the world. Arendt and Levinas have provided the basis upon which to develop a notion of alterity that is constitutive of plurality. While there are many indications that Arendt and Levinas both appreciated this, their disciplinary divide inhibited this type of rapprochement. The notion of relationality can now be 'defined' in terms of a plurality that is constituted by alterity. By conceptualizing relationality as alterity that arises and strengthens the plurality of the political from within, it is also possible to benefit from the strong ethical contribution provided by Levinas to post-Shoah thought within the framework of an Arendtian conception of the political, which has many advantages over other conceptions of the political in that it is democratic, horizontally constituted (bottom-up), empowering rather than alienating, inclusive and thrives upon publicity (a transparency demanded by many denizens today) and participation.

Before considering relationality in terms of a post-foundational political ethics, let us consider how several other authors have sought to connect alterity and plurality:

> The inner duality of origin is the first phenomenon of alterity within identity: it shows the opening of identity, its originary opening to that alterity, irreducible and external to identity, which presents itself to human plurality. This alterity, in human plurality is irreducible to the ontological alterity immanent to identity, but is already implied in the inner duality of origin, which prepares it.[58]

While Ciaramelli begins from the alterity within the self, he seems to be aiming at a notion similar to that of relationality, which can also be understood as a political ethics (assuming an Arendtian notion of the political and a Levinasian notion of ethics). At the origin of our 'identity', constructed dynamically by means of performativity, is an alterity (I would not reduce this to duality as Ciaramelli does). While the other interacts with the self in terms of 'identity', this identity is already open to the other because of its own alterity. Nonetheless this 'internal' alterity is not identical to the 'otherness' of human plurality, although it does contribute to the richness of this plurality. Plurality is the difference between selves, each of whom is already constituted by an internal difference. When interacting with others, an appreciation for the alterity of their identities leads to an awareness and appreciation that this alterity is also within me. Likewise, an awareness of the alterity of all selves helps us to appreciate the plurality of the world, a plurality that we have also learned to embrace as part of our 'identity'.

If we consider the notion of relationality from the perspective of the political (rather than from the perspective of the self as Ciaramelli does) and theoretically 'zoom in', this would lead us to the type of interaction central to Levinas's ethics—the face-to-face. Whether in terms of the face-to-face, which is always already a space of plurality inhabited by the third, or the political, it is fundamental that one encounters another person as other. This encounter, which is first and foremost experience prior to knowledge, must create space for difference or alterity, which means it cannot be a means towards another end. The face-to-face experience is a transformative encounter that prepares the possibility for all other reflective processes. Only once one has been affected by this encounter, by the face of the other, is one able to keep oneself open to difference and to the type of thinking necessary for political judgements and the ability to think from the standpoint, or perspective, of the other (this is precisely what Eichmann could not, or chose not to, do). The 'Other can only reach me if I create a space for other within me'.[59] What makes relationality so demanding is that it must be constantly repeated, for it is 'like the veil of Penelope: it undoes every morning what it had finished the night before' (RJ 166). This transformative experience must be repeated in every encounter. It is also for this reason that an ontological appreciation of alterity is not sufficient for relationality; relationality must be conceived of as a praxis. In addition, relationality is not a consoling praxis. It, like the challenge presented by the other or the agonism of the political, forces us to confront ourselves and calls for a rather difficult reflection upon our narrative identity, the place it creates for alterity, forcing us to question the grounds upon which we fear the other; it can equally create a space, from within, for difference. While the greatest escape from the latter is to direct this discomfort by means of violence at another (a discomfort that I would venture to suggest has been promoted by a hegemonic, negative philosophical anthropology obsessed with unity and purity), perhaps a less violent option is to deal with our own alterity. This is the avenue pursued by relationality, which seeks to make us aware and understand that the relationship to the other is constitutive of the world and the self.

Post-Foundational Relationality

What does it mean to claim that relationality is a post-foundational political ethics? It means that relationality is an ethics of alterity that manifests itself in political interactions motivated by a principle of plurality without presupposing any foundational or anti-foundational claims. Post-foundationalist projects reject both foundational and anti-foundational claims, such as those that justify a certain version of human nature or the subject, while still acknowledging the need for stability by means of post-foundational 'grounds' that recognize their own contingency. Several such post-foundational 'grounds' have already been explored in previous chapters, such as the notion of horizontality, a web-of-relations and solidarity, all of which offer some stability while still clearly partial, contingent and fragile. While there is undoubtedly a strong appeal to forms of foundationalism, which seemingly offer us stability and certainty, what Arendt and Levinas have made amply evident is that neither stability nor certainty are possible in the interhuman realm without the reduction of the other to the same or of plurality to singularity. Only upon a post-foundational ground can alterity and plurality be respected. For this reason relationality is conceived of in terms of a post-foundational political ethics.

Many of us cannot live without certainty, perhaps more so in 'the West', where we are not confronted with dangers and death on a daily basis; our obsession with statistics and predictions and our desire to be in full control of our lives are but examples of the luxurious illusion of certainty we hold onto. With regard to our interactions with others, whether in the form of ethical encounters or political performances, we expect this same certainty, striving to avoid spontaneity and surprises at all costs. What both Arendt and Levinas have demonstrated is that this desire to control is contrary to the human condition; furthermore, this desire is destructive—it can transform a democracy into a totalitarian regime (or as in this case at present, bring out the totalitarian characteristics of a liberal democracy). While it may be extremely difficult to accept that we are not in control, and that we cannot have absolute certainty, this is the risk we must face—but not alone. We must abandon all foundational projects and yet not give up hope—not an easy task. It is for this reason that many post-foundational thinkers seek to uncover contingent, dynamic sources of *potentia*. Arendt does so most notably with her notion of power that needs no foundation, as it arises from the between, a horizontal form of post-foundationalism. Freedom, in Arendt's approach, is also possible only between people; it is intersubjective, strengthened by the web-of-relations—a further stabilizing post-foundational element.

Her appeal to thinking without banisters can also be translated as thinking without foundations. This is equally the case for judgement, which cannot rely on fixed banisters or rules but must instead result from a mixture of subjective and objective tools that all require publicity:

> Even though we have lost yardsticks by which to measure, and rules under which to subsume the particular, a being whose essence is beginning may have enough of origin within himself to understand without preconceived categories and to judge without the set of customary rules which is morality. (EU 321)

The one institutionalized stabilizing element, introduced by both Arendt and Levinas, is that of the law—often taken to be the bridge between ethics and the political. Both thinkers recognize its importance, and yet both underplay the role of the law, which as the Nuremberg Laws demonstrated, can also be used to stabilize a totalitarian system. Thus while the law may potentially bridge ethics and the political, it is not a substitute for relationality.

Relationality, as a post-foundational project, allows for that which was insupportable under a totalitarian regime—spontaneity and contingency. It recognizes and tries to find a balance between the need for stability and the reality of contingency. Both of these elements are critical to relationality. Unfortunately, with the rise of modern liberal democracies we have become convinced that we are entitled to an increased sense of (false) control over our lives (often at the cost of lives of others, who are made invisible), which, when seemingly under threat, opens the door to a culture and politics of fear.[60] This combination—with regard to politics—is an open invitation for economists, technocrats and sadly populist leaders to offer their expertise and guarantees to a populace in need of greater certainty and reassurances. It is for this reason that post-foundationalism may seem to some to be a leap of faith. This is also why hope is essential for relationality. Post-foundationalist politics inhabits the fragile space between hope and fear. Hope is critical for the ability of relationality to bring stability to the political realm. Without hope, the lack of absolute stability introduced by a post-foundational approach, such as one rooted in relationality, can all too easily, whether by means of a nondemocratic leader or due to economic hardship, become a fertile ground for a violent exclusionary regime.

While such a philosophical anthropology of hope sits comfortably within a Judaic paradigm, this is less so in the case of Western politics. Sadly, even those thinkers who themselves seem to embrace a positive philosophical anthropology do not consider importing this outlook into the *polis*. An exception to this is Viktor Frankl, an Auschwitz survivor, who argued:

> If we are to bring out the human potential at its best, we must first believe in its existence and presence. Otherwise man will 'drift,' he will

> deteriorate, for there is a human potential at its worst as well. We must not let our belief in the potential humanness of man blind us to the fact that humane humans are and probably always will be a minority. Yet it is this very fact that challenges each of us to join the minority: things are bad, but unless we do our best to improve them, everything will become worse.[61]

He claimed that his inspiration was none other than Goethe, whom he quotes as follows: 'When we treat man as he is, we make him worse than he is; when we treat him as if he already were what he potentially could be, we make him what he should be'.[62] This is a type of pragmatic hope—the willingness to act as if one has hope—necessary for relationality. While hope can be found both in brief 'revolutionary' moments, such as those experienced by the many participants in protests across the globe between 2011 and 2013, and over a longer period of peaceful time, both of which are rare, there is one pragmatic argument for hope. Fear has failed. It has proven, whether in this century or in any before, to fail to bring about humanity's potential. Fear only leads to more fear. Assuming the worst not only prepares us to expect the worst, it prevents us from realizing the best. While this claim is undoubtedly idealistic, to continue to think politically in terms of 'the lowest common denominator' given what we know about history is quite frankly absurd. Explicitly influenced by the Judaic, Leo Strauss makes a similar point. 'It is safer to try to understand the low in the light of the high than the high in the light of the low. In doing the latter one necessarily distorts the high, whereas in doing the former one does not deprive the low of the freedom to reveal itself as fully as what it is'.[63] According to Strauss, liberalism's failure arises from its inability to embrace the power of hope. Modernity is designed for the lowest common denominator, according to Strauss. For this reason Strauss argues that liberalism and democracy are not compatible.

Given the problems of liberalism as developed by both Arendt and Levinas, I focus on democracy, which if inspired by hope rather than fear has the potential to transform reality. While this promise offers no individual guarantees, neither does fear. The alternative, as history shows, is further destruction of humanity and the shared world. It is for this reason that I do not appeal to the 'rulers' and a typical vertical structure of politics, but horizontally to all people to take on the responsibility of participating as 'rulers', or in Arendtian terms, as new beginnings, and in Judaic terms, as co-creators of the world. The unpredictable and the spontaneous are resources full of possibility that arise from a post-foundational ground. Relationality cannot offer certainty or predictability, but it can offer hope, miracles, and a world of possibilities as yet unexplored. Closely connected to the hope that a post-foundational approach to political ethics can bring is the invisible but tangible support and strength provided by relationality itself. The web-of-relations, the bond between the self and the other and solidarity are all forms of relationality. These stabilize and sustain the political realm and the ethics that arises from within these interactions. This is the horizontal transcendence of hope; relationality surpasses the singular self and creates an invisible 'network' that supports human interaction and 'grounds' new beginnings. A political ethics of relationality affirms hope as an alternative to the fear-driven need for certainty of traditional politics.

The significance of the connection between hope and relationality is one of the reasons I define the political in Arendtian terms. 'If Arendt is right about the inescapable plurality of men in politics, then the first implication that follows is that theory is no substitute for practice. . . . It is a lie, writing the script for a conversation that has yet to take place'.[64] From the perspective of more vertical forms of politics, plurality represents chaos; it is unpredictable, unmanageable, and as a result theorists are all too often obsessed with finding a means to organize and control the political, and thus people, thereby reducing plurality to singularity. While it is much easier to 'design' a model of the political from the basis of singularity, it is also these models that often fail to safeguard the reality of plurality or to keep a space open for the agonism of the political. While there is much more to relationality than its post-foundationalism, the need for control is quite possibly the greatest threat to the success of any democratic experiment. While liberalism has no explicit desire to totalize its citizenry, its overemphasis on autonomy and individualism leads to atomization and political alienation, opening the door to the loneliness Arendt describes as so dangerous for the political as it makes controlling much easier for any government, whether democratic or totalitarian. Seeing such potential connections between totalitarian elements and democracy, many of which arise in reaction to plurality, leads Arendt to develop her notion of the political as rooted in the human condition of plurality. It is this fundamental link between plurality and the political that makes her project unique in the Western philosophical canon. What's more, as I have shown by engaging her work with that of Levinas, her notion of the political creates a space for an ethics of alterity from within the political, which is essential given the diversity that currently characterizes and, according to many, is problematic for, democracy.

Just as the notion of the political as plurality is crucial for relationality so is Levinas's unique notion of ethics. What is quintessential is that the ethics of relationality embraces difference while being anti-dogmatic and non-normative. Neither dogma nor norms belong in the political realm. This is precisely why Arendt connects the political to *doxa* rather than truth. The latter is hostile to dialogue and debate, that which keeps the public realm alive. Furthermore, norms and dogmas prevent the type of thinking and judgement that is necessary for a political ethics that is post-foundational. Without a foundation, all norms and beliefs are without absolute grounding, and this fact must not be hidden from society. It is precisely because of this groundlessness that people are called to take up their responsibility to each other and to the world. If not them, then who? It is also for this reason that the ethics that is called for is closely related to the notion of responsibility. While this responsibility is a far cry from Kant's deontological ethics, as there are no imperatives, whether categorical or hypothetical, an ethics of alterity nonetheless asks the self to take responsibility for the other. Whereas Levinas makes this responsibility absolute (as does Arendt at times), this is not the case for relationality. By circumscribing an ethics of alterity within the political realm, a limit is set on this responsibility for the other. In this way a politics of relationality inspires and guides without providing a script. Humanity must write its own story, embracing its alterity and plurality in the process (making for even more intertwining stories).

Arendt, in line with the Judaic, stresses the difference between principles and rules, covenants and contracts. While the former are flexible and personal, the latter have a tendency to be absolutely determined as well as universalistic and impersonal. It is this distinction that also is retained by the meaning of the terms politics and the political. In *On Revolution* she discusses the Mayflower compact (OR 88/168) as truly political and rooted in the principle of solidarity. Her preference for principles is based on the fact that they are dynamic and allow the political to remain a space of spontaneity, beginnings and change. Furthermore, principles allow space for responsibility and judgement that laws cannot guarantee. Laws lead to legal judgements, implicitly demotivating citizens from making their own judgements and taking responsibility for actions that are not deemed legally problematic. Principles are thus for Arendt political, as opposed to laws and contracts, which—while essential—are a part of politics that is meant to stabilize and support the political without reducing or replacing it. It is also for this reason that I see Levinas's ethics of alterity to be compatible with an ethos or principle of the political; it inspires and helps us to appreciate difference without setting any clear rules or absolute imperatives.

Adriana Cavarero, who is explicitly influenced by Arendt and Levinas (among others), appreciates the fact that what they can offer in terms of the political and ethics must be accepted in its post-foundationalism. Without using Marchart's notion of post-foundationalism, she makes a similar argument by creating a distinction between the term *political* theory, which she differentiates from Arendt's approach, and *politicizing* theory, which begins from a sceptical appreciation of theory with regard to the political realm:

> Obviously, political theory does not coincide with politics [the political in our terms]; it does not consists in acting politically. Political theory is theory: its disciplinary status consists in observing, seeing and imagin-

> ing. Inaugurating it, Plato constrained political theory to look upward, that is, to free itself from the *proprium* of politics to remedy its constitutive contingency with the security of order. . . . [Arendt] facilitates the gesture of looking at the contingency of an agency in which plurality is the disclosure of a uniqueness that presents itself as absolute, unclassifiable, and non orderable difference. This difference appears as disorder and chaos only from the perspective of the traditional obsession with order.[65]

By refusing to approach the political from the perspective of *political* theory, Cavarero realizes the potential dialogue between Levinas's ethics and Arendt's approach to the political as well as their shared understanding of the necessity of accepting the post-foundational 'anarchy' in the human realm. 'This is, after all, the radical challenge of a political theory that, abandoning the traditional vision of fictitious entities, finally politicises theory and, as Levinas would say, compels it to look in the face of the other'.[66] She also develops this into an alternative model of the political, but without explicitly making space for a Levinasian notion of alterity. 'The public realm is a "relational space—contextual, contingent and groundless—that opens everywhere for everyone", and this combination of plurality and relation building gives the political public realm a means of creating citizenship in terms of membership and publicity'.[67]

Cavarero, as well as Butler and Ciaramelli, have begun to consider what is to be learned from the many intersections between Arendt's and Levinas's respective projects. I do hope that this detailed analysis of their respective projects in a dialogical fashion contributes to further reflection on what is to be learned by bringing their thought together. Furthermore, not only should it make us consider the restrictive nature of the traditional categories of Western philosophy, it should also lead us to consider the wealth of traditions (as well as thinkers excluded because of their race, religion or gender, etc.) excluded by the canon—resources that ought to be included in a dialogue about the shared world. Rather than dodge the plurality of intellectual traditions, as we 'dodge' the other (out of fear), we should accept that we all share this world and that this 'sharing' requires facing our greatest fear: our own alterity. Rather than trying to suppress alterity by violently excluding and silencing it, let us face it—this is precisely what the dialogue between Arendt and Levinas should inspire us to do.

NOTES

1. Walter Benjamin, *Illuminations: Essays and Reflections*, ed. Hannah Arendt, trans. Harry Zohn, English language ed. (New York: Schocken, 1969), 50.
2. Judith Butler, *Parting Ways: Jewishness and the Critique of Zionism* (New York: Columbia University Press, 2012), 166.

3. While Levinas implicitly turns to the Judaic, seeing it as a synonym for an ethics rooted in Jerusalem, as opposed to a traditional philosophical ethics rooted in Athens, I wish to make explicit that the Judaic is not to be reduced either to being Jewish or to Judaism, the practice.

4. Alan Rosenberg and Alan Milchman, *Postmodernism and the Holocaust,* Value Inquiry Book Series 72 (Amsterdam; Atlanta, Ga.: Rodopi Bv Editions, 1998), 113.

5. Oliver Marchart, *Post-Foundational Political Thought: Political Difference in Nancy, Lefort, Badiou and Laclau* (Edinburgh, Scotland: Edinburgh University Press, 2007), 2.

6. Huub van Baar, *The European Roma: Minority Representation, Memory, and the Limits of Transnational Governmentality* (Amsterdam: F & N Eigen Beheer, 2011).

7. S. Sayyid and Abdool Karim Vakil, eds., *Thinking Through Islamophobia: Global Perspectives* (New York: Columbia University Press, 2011); John L. Esposito and Ibrahim Kalin, *Islamophobia: The Challenge of Pluralism in the 21st Century* (New York: Oxford University Press USA, 2011).

8. Wendy Brown, *Regulating Aversion: Tolerance in the Age of Identity and Empire* (Princeton, N.J.; Woodstock: Princeton University Press, 2008).

9. Hwa Yol Jung, 'The Political Relevance of Existential Phenomenology', *Review of Politics* 33, no. 4 (October 1971): 558, doi:10.1017/S0034670500014108.

10. Both also connect this insight to Kant's, who emphasizes the importance of not instrumentalizing human beings by reducing them to a means to an end that denies the dignity of every subject as in end in herself.

11. Emmanuel Levinas, *Entre Nous,* trans. Michael B. Smith and Barbara Harshav (New York: Columbia University Press, 2000), 116.

12. David Woodruff Smith, 'Phenomenology'," in *The Stanford Encyclopedia of Philosophy,* ed. Edward N. Zalta, n.d., plato.stanford.edu/archives/win2013/entries/phenomenology.

13. Richard Wolin, *Heidegger's Children: Hannah Arendt, Karl Löwith, Hans Jonas, and Herbert Marcuse* (Princeton, N.J.: Princeton University Press, 2003); Samuel Fleischacker, ed., *Heidegger's Jewish Followers: Essays on Hannah Arendt, Leo Strauss, Hans Jonas, and Emmanuel Levinas,* 1st ed. (Pittsburgh, Pa.: Duquesne University Press, 2008).

14. Emmanuel Levinas, *The Theory of Intuition in Husserl's Phenomenology* (Evanston, Ill.: Northwestern University Press, 1990), 218.

15. Friedrich-Wilhelm von Herrmann and Martin Heidegger, *Gesamtausgabe 3. Abt.* Bd. 65, *Beiträge zur Philosophie,* 3rd ed. (Frankfurt am Main: Klostermann, Vittorio, n.d.), 172.

16. Marlene Zarader, *The Unthought Debt: Heidegger and the Hebraic Heritage,* trans. Bettina Bergo, 1st ed. (Stanford, Calif.: Stanford University Press, 2006).

17. Peter Trawny, *Heidegger und der Mythos der jüdischen Weltverschwörung,* 1st ed. (Frankfurt am Main: Klostermann, Vittorio, 2014).

18. Berel Lang, *Heidegger's Silence,* 1st ed. (Ithaca, N.Y.: Cornell University Press, 1996); Rosenberg and Milchman, *Postmodernism and the Holocaust;* Richard Wolin, *The Heidegger Controversy: A Critical Reader* (Cambridge, Mass.: MIT Press, 1992); Jean-Francois Lyotard and David Carroll, *Heidegger and 'the Jews',* 1st ed., trans. Andreas Michel and Mark Roberts (Minneapolis: University of Minnesota Press, 1990).

19. Michael B. Smith, 'Emmanuel Levinas's Ethics of Responsiblity' (paper presented at the Mike Ryan Lecture Series, Kennesaw State College, 7 October 2003), sites.google.com/site/philosophystudentassociation/Home/mike-ryan-lecture-series-1.

20. Jean-Luc Nancy, *The Sense of the World,* 2nd ed. (Minneapolis: University of Minnesota Press, 2008), 2.

21. Jean-Luc Nancy, *Being Singular Plural* (Stanford, Calif.: Stanford University Press, 2000), 2.

22. Hanna Fenichel Pitkin, *The Attack of the Blob: Hannah Arendt's Concept of the Social,* 1st ed. (Chicago: University of Chicago Press, 2000).

23. Don Mitchell, *The Right to the City: Social Justice and the Fight for Public Space* (New York: Guilford Press, 2003).

24. Claude Lefort, *Democracy and Political Theory*, 1st ed., trans. David Macey (Cambridge, England: Polity, 1991), 221–222.
25. R. I. Moore, *The Formation of a Persecuting Society: Authority and Deviance in Western Europe 950–1250*, 2nd ed. (Malden: Wiley-Blackwell, 2007).
26. Jonathan Sacks, *The Dignity of Difference: How to Avoid the Clash of Civilizations*, 2nd ed. (London: Bloomsbury Academic, 2003), 61.
27. Ibid., 2.
28. Ibid.
29. Tony Judt and Timothy Snyder, *Thinking the Twentieth Century*, repr. ed. (New York: Penguin Books, 2013).
30. Anita Diamant, *Pitching My Tent: On Marriage, Motherhood, Friendship, and Other Leaps of Faith* (New York: Scribner, 2005), 196.
31. Sacks, *Dignity of Difference*, 206–207.
32. 'Il faut quand meme partir des sources du judaisme. Le Judaism n'est pas une *religion*. Le mot n'existe pas en hebreu. Il est beaucoup plus que cela. Il est une comprehension de l'être. Le Juif a introduit dans l'histoire l'idee d'esperance. . . . L'ethique est une optique vers Dieu. . . . Le seule voie du respect envers Dieu est celle du respect envers le prochain' (DF 15).
33. Tomoko Masuzawa, *The Invention of World Religions: Or, How European Universalism Was Preserved in the Language of Pluralism* (Chicago: University of Chicago Press, 2005).
34. Ruth E. Groenhout and Marya Bower, eds., *Philosophy, Feminism, and Faith* (Bloomington: Indiana University Press, 2003), 13.
35. Frank Furedi, *Culture of Fear Revisited*, 2nd ed. (London; New York: Bloomsbury Academic, 2006); Frank Furedi, *Culture of Fear*, rev. ed. (London; New York: Continuum International Publishing Group, 2002).
36. Anya Topolski and Emmanuel Nathan, eds., *Is There a Judeo-Christian Tradition? A European Perspective* (Berlin: De Gruyter, 2015).
37. Linda Martín Alcoff, *Visible Identities: Race, Gender, and the Self* (New York: Oxford University Press, 2005), 71.
38. Hannah Arendt, Ursula Ludz, and Ingeborg Nordmann, *Denktagebuch*. Bd. 1, *1950–1973*. Bd. 2, *1973–1975* (München: Piper, 2002), Denktagebuch XXIV/56 March 65, 641; XXV/54 May 68, 682.
39. Gareth Williams, 'Ethics and Human Relationality: Between Arendt's Accounts of Morality', *HannahArendt.net* 3, no. 1 (2007): 6.
40. Michael Ignatieff, 'Arendt's Example' (Hannah Arendt Prize Ceremony, Bremen, 28 November 2003), 8, www.hks.harvard.edu/cchrp/pdf/arendt.24.11.03.pdf.
41. Arendt, Ludz, and Nordmann, *Denktagebuch*. Bd. 1, XXIV/60, January 1966, 644.
42. Shiraz Dossa, 'Human Status and Politics: Hannah Arendt on the Holocaust', *Canadian Journal of Political Science/Revue Canadienne de Science Politique* 13, no. 2 (June 1980): 317.
43. Kevin Thompson and Lester E. Embree, *Phenomenology of the Political* (Dordrecht, Netherlands: Springer Science & Business Media, 2000), 147.
44. Tony Judt, 'The Past Is Another Country: Myth and Memory in Postwar Europe', *Daedalus* 121, no. 4 (1992): 83+.
45. Margaret Canovan, 'Arendt, Rousseau, and Human Plurality in Politics', *Journal of Politics* 45, no. 2 (May 1983): 288, doi:10.2307/2130127.
46. Topolski, 'Relationality as a "Foundation" for Human Rights: Exploring the Paradox with Hannah Arendt and Emmanuel Levinas', *Theoria and Praxis: International Journal of Interdisciplinary Thought* 2, no. 1 (6 August 2014), pi.library.yorku.ca/ojs/index.php/theoriandpraxis/article/view/39373.
47. Jonathan Sacks, *To Heal a Fractured World: The Ethics of Responsibility* (New York: Schocken, 2007), 252.
48. Ivana Marková, 'Constitution of the Self: Intersubjectivity and Dialogicality', *Culture & Psychology* 9, no. 3 (1 September 2003): 255, doi:10.1177/1354067X030093006.
49. Sacks, *To Heal a Fractured World*, 9.

50. Here are a few exceptions (excluding my own previously published articles), some of which are doctoral theses and others more general considerations of post-Shoah Jewish thought in which both Arendt and Levinas are studied (but not in dialogue with each other): Paul Matthew Ott, 'The Politics of the Present: A Relational Theory of the Self as a Basis for Political Theory: Dewey, Arendt, and Levinas' (PhD diss., State University of New York at Buffalo, 2010), gradworks.umi.com/34/07/3407936.html; Fred Poché, *Penser Avec Arendt et Levinas: Du mal politique au respect de l'autre* (Lyon: Chronique Sociale, 1998); Mylène Botbol-Baum and Anne-Marie Roviello, *Levinas et Arendt: De L'arrachement À L'évasion* (Paris: Vrin, 2013); Fleischacker, *Heidegger's Jewish Followers*; Marc H. Ellis, *Encountering the Jewish Future: With Wiesel, Buber, Heschel, Arendt, Levinas* (Minneapolis, Minn.: Augsburg Fortress Publishers, 2010); Aurore Mréjen, *La Figure De L'Homme: Hannah Arendt et Emmanuel Lévinas* (Paris: Editions du Palio, 2012).

51. Butler, *Parting Ways*; Stephen K. White, *Sustaining Affirmation* (Princeton N.J.: Princeton University Press, 2000).

52. Edmund Husserl, *Cartesian Meditations: An Introduction to Phenomenology*, 5th ed. (Dordrecht: Netherlands: Klewer Academic Publishers, 1973).

53. Rudolf Bernet et al., *An Introduction to Husserlian Phenomenology*, 1st ed., Northwestern University Studies in Phenomenology and Existential Philosophy (Evanston, Ill.: Northwestern University Press, 1993); Alfred Schutz, 'The Problem of Transcendental Intersubjectivity in Husserl', in *Collected Papers III*, ed. I. Schutz, Phaenomenologica 22 (Dordrecht, Netherlands: Springer Netherlands, 1970), 51–84, link.springer.com/chapter/10.1007/978-94-015-3456-7_4.

54. Judith Butler, *Gender Trouble: Feminism and the Subversion of Identity* (London: Routledge, 2011); Rudi Visker, *Truth and Singularity: Taking Foucault into Phenomenology* (Dordrecht; Boston: Springer, 1999); Michel Foucault, *Discipline & Punish: The Birth of the Prison*, 2nd ed., trans. Alan Sheridan (New York: Vintage Books, 1995); William E. Connolly, *Identity Difference: Democratic Negotiations of Political Paradox, Expanded Edition*, rev. ed. (Minneapolis: University of Minnesota Press, 2002).

55. Butler, *Parting Ways*.

56. While this term predates the Shoah, its publicity, acquired by its central role in the Nuremberg trials, arose from these 'events'. Although the term originated in 1907 (Preamble to the Hague Convention) and was applied in 1919 to both the Germans and the Turks, it was only after the Shoah, during the Nuremberg trials, that it was concretized and took on its present form. For more, see Cherif Bassiouni, *Crimes Against Humanity in International Criminal Law* (The Hague: Martinus Nijhoff, 1988).

57. Anya Topolski, 'How Jews and Muslims Became Races: A Genealogy of Anti-semitism and Islamophobia', in *Philosophy of Race: Introductory Readings*, ed. Nathan Nobis, (2015), 7–15. Available at www.philosophyofrace.com.

58. Fabio Ciaramelli, 'Comparison of Incomparables', in *Levinas and Politics*, ed. Simon Critchley and C. Coyle (London: Routledge, 2002), 73.

59. Rudi Visker, 'Dissensus Communis: How to Keep Silent "after" Lyotard', in *Dissensus Communis Between Ethics and Politics*, ed. P. Birmingham and P. Van Haute (Kampen: Peeters, 1995), 28–29.

60. Frank Furedi, *Culture of Fear*, rev. ed. (London; New York: Continuum International Publishing Group, 2002); *Culture of Fear Revisited*, 2nd ed. (London; New York: Bloomsbury Academic, 2006).

61. Viktor Emil Frankl, *Unheard Cry Meaning*, 1st ed. (New York: Simon & Schuster, 1978), 31. He continues: 'Let me here repeat an illustration that has often shown to be didactically helpful. In aviation there is a business called "crabbing". Say there is a crosswind from the north and the airport where I wish to land lies due east. If I fly east I will miss my destination because my plane will have drifted to the southeast. In order to reach my destination I must compensate for this drift by crabbing, in this case by heading my plane in a direction to the north of where I want to land. It is similar with man: he too ends at a point lower than he might have unless he is seen on a higher level that includes his higher aspirations'.

62. As quoted in ibid., 33.
63. Leo Strauss, *Spinoza's Critique of Religion* (Chicago: University of Chicago Press, 1997), 6.
64. Canovan, 'Arendt, Rousseau, and Human Plurality in Politics', 298.
65. Adriana Cavarero, 'Politicizing Theory', *Political Theory* 30, no. 4 (1 August 2002): 528–529, doi:10.1177/0090591702304004.
66. Ibid., 530.
67. Adriana Cavarero, *For More Than One Voice: Toward a Philosophy of Vocal Expression*, trans. Paul Kottman, 1st ed. (Stanford, Calif.: Stanford University Press, 2005), 69.

EIGHT

The Promise and Pitfalls of Relationality

Hopeful that I have inspired more future engagements between the thought of Arendt and Levinas, I conclude this staged conversation between the Arendtian notion of plurality and the Levinasian ethics of alterity by focusing on what remains: the notion of relationality and its potential political actualization. Given that 'storytelling reveals meaning without committing the error of defining it' (MDT 104), the best way to provide an account of relationality is by trying to connect the different threads of the dialogue I have constructed. Second, I will consider a few arguments in favour of relationality, arguments that are meant to motivate others to take the relational turn and in so doing accept the precarious reality of post-foundationalism and the fragile stability introduced by relationality. I will thus indicate four points of potential within the notion of relationality, points that have already been demonstrated but are worth repeating here. Third, while I wish there were no pitfalls to relationality, it is necessary to acknowledge these briefly. Finally, I explore the promise and importance, for today, of relationality in our contemporary democracies.

RELATIONALITY: PUTTING THE PIECES OF THE PUZZLE TOGETHER

For Adorno, the Shoah called for a rethinking of the entire process by which we raise and educate children. Elie Wiesel, who survived the camps, calls for all to recognize the radical rupture of reality introduced by the horrors of the Shoah—thinking and politics can never be the same. For those trying to make sense of the world after its almost complete destruction, all previous categories, assumptions and dogmas need to be rethought—if thinking after the Shoah is even possible. In this vein, Arendt and Levinas are no exceptions. Both, exceptionally, managed to survive the Shoah, Arendt by way of three courageous escapes, from a German prison and then Germany, from the French detention camp in Gurs and then through the mountains of the Pyrenees onto a boat to America. Levinas, having become a French citizen, was captured as a Jewish prisoner of war rather than just as a Jew, which would have been a direct death sentence. What both experienced and observed affected their thinking for the rest of their lives. While it would be much easier to claim that the Shoah was the responsibility of a small group of monsters, neither thinker accepted this 'explanation'. Both sought to understand how what enabled the destruction of the shared world is something we are each responsible for, a daily form of violence that continues today by way of a rejection of difference. Arendt saw this most clearly in the rejection of plurality, both in the *vita activa* and in the *vita contemplativa*. Levinas saw this in terms of an allergic reaction to alterity. In this sense, the Shoah came to symbolize a type of seemingly benign evil, an appearance that makes it all the more dangerous, that is constitutive of our daily social interactions rooted in an ontological framework based on singularity. In other words, Arendt and Levinas both came to the conclusion that in order to prevent such horror from repeating itself, a horror that neither took to be limited in form by anti-Semitism, change—of a radical sort—was necessary at the level of the foundations of human interaction.

By bringing together these horrifying experiences and their prewar studies in phenomenology, Arendt and Levinas both sought a new means to make the best of what they had learned. Husserl's interest in intersubjectivity may have actually been the spark that both needed to begin to deconstruct the dangers of putting Heidegger's *Dasein* onto a pedestal. Moreover, both Arendt and Levinas remained true to the spirit of the phenomenological tradition all their lives. It is from this tradition that both learned to appreciate the link between thinking and experience and the importance of events and perspective. This is most clear from their distinct analysis of the world, which for Arendt is to be found in *The Human Condition* and for Levinas in *Totality and Infinity*, texts published within three years of each other.

Without wanting to simplify either Arendt's or Levinas's personal and philosophical relation to Heidegger's life and work, this is undoubtedly a starting point for their dialogue. Both thinkers were rightfully awestruck by Heidegger's philosophical brilliance, so much so that their disillusionment with his words and deeds during the war was all the more unbearable. Both responded to Heidegger in the way he had taught them to—by writing and thinking—by trying to make sense of the world. After doing so, and with their experiences of the Shoah, neither could simply follow in his path, a path with only enough space for *Dasein*, leaving *mitsein* to trail behind in the horizon. Both Arendt and Levinas appreciated, and this is their first intellectual intersection, that Heidegger's personal failings were closely tied to his scholarly approach. Their first dialogical encounter is their shared rejection of the ontological tradition, with its priority for singularity and the Greek desire for unity. Yet their response to Heidegger took diverging forms: for Arendt it was the turn to the political—a realm she was completely new to—and for Levinas it was a turn to ethics, to be refounded in terms of first philosophy. The first chapter of this story thus ends with the appearance of two notions, each tied to a seemingly different domain, that of plurality and alterity, and yet both arising as a direct challenge to Heidegger's prioritization of ontology and singularity.

The next piece of the relationality puzzle is one in which I, as the narrator, become an actor. By introducing the notion of the Judaic, a notion I have shown to arise from their respective opuses, I wish to highlight the Judaic contribution to relationality. While the importance of hope can be connected to other sources, it is to a shared Judaic source that I attach it here. While so many living during these darkest times gave up hope—choosing either to end their lives or to give up thinking about its meaning—Arendt and Levinas refused to believe that humanity could not learn from its inhumanity and sought to help achieve this by affirming both responsibility and intersubjectivity. While this struck me as particularly Judaic, most likely because of my own background, it is important to emphasize that I neither take the Judaic to be exclusive nor do I think it has sole ownership rights on the relationship among a relational approach, hope and responsibility.

One of the greatest social dangers I seek to overcome by means of relationality is the individualistic approach to responsibility, which while it understandably guides our legal system, is certainly problematic with regard to the shared world. By understanding the world as relationally created, a creation whose responsibility is shared by all participants, responsibility can no longer be defined in the singular. A similar position is defended by other scholars also inspired by Levinas and Arendt, such as Cavarero, Ciaramelli, Jung and Butler:

> By virtue of its relation to others . . . those relations to others are precisely the venue for its ethical responsibility. . . . I cannot think the question of responsibility alone, in isolation from the Other, or if I do, I have taken myself out of the mode of address that frames the problem of responsibility from the start.[1]

Responsibility is an affirmation of this fundamental relationality. It expresses care for the other and the world and in so doing strengthens the bonds of 'solidarity' that 'ground' the political. It is in this sense that responsibility is both ethical and political. It is an ethics that arises from within the political and also contributes to the strengthening of the political itself. Jung also connects responsibility to the horizontal transcendence that occurs within an intersubjective space, a transcendence that encourages hope: '[R]responsibility is self-transcendence'.[2] Taking responsibility for myself, for the other and for the world connects me to myself, the other and the world—it creates a home for humanity in which I can relationally root myself and help others to do the same. Furthermore, responsibility rooted in relationality does not permit one to escape responsibility for any harm to the other or to the world, an escape that is made easier by way of ontological singularity or liberal individualism.

Responsibility, however, when connected to the Judaic rather than to phenomenology (as with Jung), exits the paradigm of intersubjectivity. As Markova correctly assesses, '[post-Husserlian] intersubjectivity is supposed to express the idea of closing the gap between I and Other(s)—so as to theoretically create the sphere of "in-between" to think of the I and the Other'.[3] However, it is because of the possibility to interpret intersubjectivity as still giving priority to the subject, ontologically or epistemologically, that relationality takes the Judaic relational approach as its starting point to reconsider the relationship between self and other and self and world. As I showed in the previous chapters, I believe Arendt and Levinas—to different degrees—pursue this path. Relationality thus inhabits the relational space between the 'I' and 'we' and thereby treasures the alterity that constitutes both the self and the plurality of the home. Relationality denies the autonomy of the subject, seeing the other as constitutive of the self, a position explicitly supported by Levinas and implicitly endorsed by Arendt in her last writings.

By clarifying the notion of the subject of relationality, I created a space for the rapprochement of the Arendtian notion of plurality and the Levinasian notion of alterity. The connection is equally rooted in the historical context and the relation to the dominant philosophical paradigm. Yet the connection is not seamless. There is a leap from alterity and plurality to relationality, and the chasm must not be denied. It is precisely this desire for certainty, often amplified by fear, that is rejected by relationality. This gap defines relationality as a form of post-foundationalism, thereby ensuring its contingency. In this sense, relationality rejects any attempt to eliminate the gap and close itself off from externality.

Putting all these elements together—the post-foundational approach, the political rooted in plurality and hope and an ethics of alterity and responsibility—leads us to relationality. Relationality is an ethics that is bounded by the political and that arises from within the political, which finds its standard from within (it does not have an external source or legitimating authority). While I am not claiming that all ethics must be bounded by the political, an ethics that can speak to the political must be politically bounded. Alterity is an ethics that is born from within the political, resulting from interactions rooted in relationality. This also means that it is a dynamic ethics rather than fixed. It changes as times and people do. While this prevents us from clearly outlining the ethics of the political, it is precisely this ambiguity that we must accept as part and parcel of the reality, and spontaneity, of human interactions. While this clearly opens it up to the critique that it is relativism, this charge does not hold the same weight (as it traditionally did), as relationality embraces the contingency of the post-foundational 'Our endeavour must be to think the political from within, neither as an object confronting us nor as a system of signifiers linked to a pure signified'.[4] Ethics in this sense is defined by the principle of alterity, a principle that inspires rather than rules or legislates. A political ethics is the ethos created by the *polis* from within. In opposition to alternative approaches that seek to reconcile ethics and the political, I affirm that 'from the ethical to the political there is no deduction, but a spring or a leap'.[5] Nonetheless, as I hope to have shown, this leap is a fruitful one, although not without risks, when one considers the many intersections between alterity and plurality and the need for some internal stability in all post-foundational political projects. An ethics of alterity is the ideal means to strengthen and stabilize the distinction that is the root of plurality without at the same time threatening the post-foundational character, as it, like plurality, is always open to externality—the unpredictable in political terms—as a means to prevent its totalization.

The Promise of Relationality

Relationality is a response to the world we live in—a world seemingly perpetually in crisis—a world in which we can no longer find security in the false promises of absolute foundations. Yet the end of metaphysics need not be the end of a meaningful existence; on the contrary, it may symbolize new opportunities for the shared world:

> The omnipotence of man makes men superfluous (just as monotheism is necessarily the consequence of the omnipotence of God), then totalitarianism's power to destroy humans and the world lies not only in the delusion that everything is possible, but also in the delusion that there is such a thing as man. . . . But man exists only as God's creature. The power of man is limited by the fact that he has not created himself, whereas the power of men is limited not so much by nature as by the fact of plurality—the factual existence of my kind. It does not help me, as the humanists would have it, that I see man in every human being, as this by no means necessarily leads to respect or recognition for human dignity, but can equally well mislead us into believing in a surplus and in superfluity.[6]

While there may be no absolutes, no certainties and no guarantees in life, there is something potentially more meaningful and rewarding: the interactions and relationships we have with others and ourselves and the immense power that can arise from these; this is the basis of relationality.

What relationality entails is that we choose to turn to the other, rather than choosing to turn away from the other and further into ourselves. The latter choice, one we have pursued without much promise, seemingly offers nothing more than a fearful and lonely, seemingly autonomous existence self-driven by consumerism and competition.

It may be possible to learn to turn towards the other, or it might only require that we unlearn the alternative: the allergic reaction to alterity. It is possible to learn to appreciate this alterity as positive or enriching, as is clear from once successful attempts to do so as part of the multicultural education in countries such as Canada. Human beings do not encounter each other in a 'neutral fashion', but it is not clear whether this encounter is one that is originally experienced, preconsciously, as positive or negative, given that society has already formed our views of the other before this question could ever be considered. While the former seems more likely to me given human curiosity, a 'natural inquisitiveness', I believe that our response to alterity is more something determined by our lifeworld and education. Nonetheless, both experience and education can help us discover the richness of difference. This encounter allows us to ask the question 'who am I', thereby helping us to understand ourselves and our relation to the world. These interactions also help to strengthen the web-of-relations that supports human action and allow us the time and space to find meaning in life and in each other. In other words, the struggle to appreciate alterity is beneficial both for the self and for the world, a rare political case of win-win. While relationality is only one particular post-foundational perspective, it has the potential to offer much more, both for the self and for the world. Let us therefore begin by answering the questions: Why choose relationality? Why turn toward the other rather than turning away from the other and the world?

Much of political theory, both past and present, finds vertical 'power' in autonomy, unity and singularity. The alternative relationality offers is empowerment by reaffirming the plurality of the world and alterity within me. This type of power is rooted in heteronomy, interdependence, community and relationality. Seemingly the former type of 'power' offers more certainty and control—the individual finds power in himself or herself. Relationality calls this type of vertical 'power' an illusion and a threat to the world. While relationality does involve taking a risk—acknowledging the alterity of the self and the plurality of the world, as well as fighting fear with hope—its rewards are real. While there is no denying that taking such a risk is a 'leap of faith' given the plurality and unpredictability of strangers—both hostile and hospitable—that inhabit the earth, it is the only option if we accept the principle of plurality, which declares that everyone has the right to be part of the shared world. Once again, plurality means embracing the fact that we live in this world with others—both with whom we agree and with whom we disagree. While individualism, nihilism and a variety of other 'isms' may allow us to survive, relationality might actually allow humanity to flourish. While there are no guarantees that we won't fail, given the horrors of the past century and those of the first decade of the twenty-first century, there is very little left to lose. Relationality is thus a post-foundational ground that seeks to make us aware that not only beneath our feet, but also within us, the ground is crumbling, and the only possible way to flourish is to engage the other both within ourselves and within the world. While relationality requires courage, as it challenges one to take a risk that is countercultural (given the dominance of the capitalist-promoted individualism of many Western societies), the potential rewards—which I now present—outweigh the potential risks.

First, relationality acknowledges our human need for some sense of stability, even if only partial, in a world where we can no longer rely on the illusion of certainty previously provided by tradition, religion and authority (BPF 142). We have all experienced, during moments of instability or after a destabilizing traumatic event, a certain comfort and strength provided by means of the 'reality-check' provided by others with whom we have either shared these experiences or to whom we relate them in the form of stories. As reality is created by interacting with others, it is only by appearing, speaking and hearing that we ever have any certainty about our shared world. Action, in terms of either words or deeds, cannot 'resolve' the instability created by a lack of absolute foundations. Nonetheless, the empowerment of knowing and experiencing that one is not alone does provide some with a sense of partial stability. In this vein the experience of relationality helps to diminish the potentially overwhelming emotion of fear that arises at such moments and empowers one to remain more hopeful. Fear and anxiety feed off isolation, as Arendt showed in *Origins* in her analysis of loneliness. Hope is reinforced by sharing our concerns with others; the web-of-relations is thus a sort of affective safety net.

Second, at a time when so much of our daily existence is occupied with seemingly senseless trivialities (e.g., consumerism), relationality is an elevating source of meaning. While much enjoyment or pleasure, as described by Levinas in *Totality and Infinity*, is to be found in egoism, relationality—much like the ethical encounter according to Levinas—offers the self, without harming the other or the world, a real sense of fulfilment and a joy (without the guilt that often accompanies egoism). Every interaction we experience with another—great or small—leaves its 'traces' on the self as well as in the shared world by means of a story. These stories provide a level of temporal stability to our world, connecting past and present and providing inspiration and hope for the future. Our experiences, by means of stories, become part of something that goes beyond the self—a horizontal form of transcendence. In addition, they also provide us with a sense of meaning beyond the self when weaved together with other stories forming a shared 'history'. Shared experiences also allow us to develop and strengthen our bonds to others, encouraging us to take greater risks with regard to others whom we might otherwise perceive as hostile (because of certain implicit bias or explicit prejudices, etc.). Relationality, both as it is experienced and as a form of awareness, provides us with a sense of meaning by making us aware of how interdependent we are, how interrelated our lives are and our potential, together with others, to change and co-create others and the shared world. While the feeling of being connected to others, responsible for others, needed by others, can by no means erase our feelings of alienation, superfluousness or melancholy, it can prevent us from wallowing in self-pity and getting 'lost in our heads'. The best solution for such 'states of being' is often simply to be pulled out of one's self, and this can only be done by means of relationality. A politics of relationality is thus a praxis that makes this awareness tangible and discernible, often in the form of an empowering solidarity that has great political promise for democratic societies struggling to combat rampant individualism.

Third, relationality also helps us to answer a question that is never far from one's mind (assuming one already has the luxuries of sustenance and shelter): Who am I? This is the political question par excellence for Arendt, which can only be answered by others with whom we interact. Her rejection of the notion of a fixed human nature also requires that we abandon the false illusion of a static identity, whether for the self or for a community (e.g., nationalism, racism). The yearning for such identities is the same craving that motivates totalitarian ascription to ideologies; it is a denial of our agency and responsibility for the world. Relationality provides an alternative means to respond to this desire by offering a partial answer in terms of a dynamic relational identity, a product of a narrative web-of-relations in terms of our relationships to others and the narratives we share with others. While the answers relationality provides to the question 'who am I?' are neither fixed nor final, these answers each help us to better understand ourselves as agents in our own and the world's constitution.

Fourth, by providing partial answers to some of the existential questions that can lead us to feel frustrated, bewildered and anxious, feelings reinforced by the contingency of post-foundationalism, relationality promotes a certain form of 'internal' reconciliation that on the level of the political might translate into a form of 'partial' peace. In contrast to the Kantian aspiration for perpetual peace that inspired the Enlightenment, a peace that can only be rooted in a foundational approach, the partial peace of relationality has the more modest goal of transforming potentially violent and antagonistic conflicts into more verbal and agonistic interactions. The latter, as developed by many theorists of radical democracy, is the ideal of a performative and participatory *polis*, as opposed to forms of consensus-based politics that maintain the possibility, also clearly rooted in a Kantian paradigm, of an ideal-speech situation. While no post-foundational approach could offer the type of guarantees promised by perpetual peace, the greatest stumbling block to such peace is an us versus them frame.[7] This highly polarizing binary approach to the other, which is by no means easy to escape, fails to recognize that while inclusion and exclusion will always play a role in human interactions, frames based on us versus them are constructions that are always partial and contingent and as such need to be constantly challenged and changed. It is this need and space for contestation and change that characterizes a politics of relationality, which rejects any fixed identities or us versus them frames.

Finally, a politics of relationality promotes a praxis of responsibility that is fundamentally necessary as a complement to (rather than substitute for) the current hegemonic rights culture, which often endorses the egoism and individualism of neo-liberal democracies. Relationality, rooted in a relational approach and responsibility, provides a framework within we are much more aware of how our actions, or lack thereof, affect the other and the world, and also helps us to appreciate that many of our problems are not ours alone and that only collective action, rooted in a shared sense of responsibility, can appropriately address these problems. In the past decade, certain global problems have begun to be recognized as being fundamentally rooted in relationality, such as the environmental or economic crisis. While there are, and will continue to be, many people who reject the underlying principle of relationality and who thus explicitly deny the shared dangers of global warming or the interconnectedness of national and global financial crashes (by rejecting demonstrations of financial solidarity with Greece, Spain, and many developing nations), these so-called experts—at least with regard to these two political problems—are slowly being contested. Relationality, with its emphasis on the alterity and plurality constitutive of the self and world, is a call to each of us to take responsibility for addressing and participating in the resolution of our shared problems.

The Pitfalls of Relationality

While there are certainly hazards to all approaches to the political, these should not be used as a justification to not take the risk of relationality. Life, which is much more than biological survival, and the political are characterized by contingency—this is the approach embraced by post-foundationalism. Furthermore, until one has tried all alternatives, we can never be certain of what will succeed or fail. For those more pragmatic in character, another, less hopeful, question to consider is: What are the alternatives to relationality? The world seemed to hold so much promise for peace and humanity at the outset of the twentieth century and yet, in the end, as Arendt and Levinas sought to share with us, we need to radically rethink what was then taken for granted. Nonetheless, it is worth considering three of the most serious threats to relationality: its fragility, the foe and fear.

While I listed responsibility as a potential argument in favour of relationality, it is equally the site of immense fragility. The connection between responsibility and a relational approach demonstrates how immensely fragile all forms of post-foundational horizontalism are—and also why hope is such a necessary source of support. This fragility is a vulnerability that post-foundationalism does not try to hide; it arises from the contingency of human relations, and the only means we have to counter this fragility is to strengthen the bonds between people. Yet as the expression goes, one bad apple can spoil the bunch. The 'free rider' problem, if one makes more of it than necessary, is a threat to relationality. A presupposition of relationality (based on hope) is that these 'bad apples' or 'free riders' will decrease in numbers as the web strengthens. The latter, it is assumed, will empower more and more people to turn towards the other and recognize that relationality is the best option available for modern democracies that are 'grounded' in post-foundationalism. While traumatic events and bad news are never easy to accept, the stronger the web-of-relations, the less relationality is disputed in times of crisis.[8]

This brings us to the second limitation of relationality: the danger of falling into the Schmittian trap of reducing all others into the rigid category of friend or foe. Relationality, in refusing the option of either an 'I' or 'we' origin for the political, equally seeks to deny the notion that relations to others can ever be simplified to this degree. Even with a hostile other, one remains in relation and thus responsible. While it is not easy to deny one's responsibility for a hospitable other, my responsibility for others and the world cannot end there. I am equally responsible for those others I have no interaction with as for those whom I experience as being hostile. While this can certainly be extremely difficult, especially in situations of war, the alternative is to deny relationality. This would mean to deny that which I dislike within me and in the other and to set out to destroy it and in so doing destroy the other, the shared world and myself. Relationality pushes me to focus on my relationships to all others and the responsibility this carries with it. As such I must commit to refusing a completely comprehensible desire to seek revenge, to act aggressively or cruelly towards those who have hurt me. The question relationality, in these situations, pushes one to ask is: How am I responsible for the harm an other has chosen to enact (against me or my community, etc.)? While this is undoubtedly a question that should first and foremost be asked by those in 'power', economically and politically, it must also be asked by those who are most excluded, most forgotten and most vulnerable to victimhood—as all persons are political agents and must commit together to perform *tikkun olam*.

Yet the greatest danger to relationality, the one that has been mentioned throughout this book but cannot possibly be overstated, is fear. Fear is the greatest challenge to relationality. Fear is what motivates us to accept the reduction of the world into friend and foe. Fear is what justifies our retreat from responsibility. Fear is what exposes the fundamental fragility of post-foundationalism and forces many to retreat into the illusion of certainty offered by absolutes. Fear is what enabled the destruction of the other and the shared world during the Shoah. Let us not forget that totalitarianism and democracy are, contrary to what many wish to believe, intimately intertwined. Fear is what continues to destroy our democracies today. According to both Arendt and Levinas, albeit to a lesser extent, fear and the desire for security have led many societies, certainly those driven by capitalism, to settle for a (neo-liberal) politics rather than risk a better alternative, such as that presented by relationality.

TOWARDS A POLITICS OF RELATIONALITY

Relationality is a post-foundational political ethics inspired by an Arendtian notion of plurality as the principle for modern democratic *polis* and a Levinasian ethics of alterity that strives to combat an ontologically justified allergic reaction to the other. Yet this ethics is not like other moral theories (e.g., deontology), as it is bounded by and arises from within the political space of human interactions. It thus strengthens plurality without trying to control it. It is an ethics that does not threaten the spontaneity, unpredictability and freedom of human interactions. A politics of relationality thus points towards a new empowering and life-affirming perspective on the political in light of a relational understanding of the human condition with regard to our responsibility for others and the shared world. It is the latter perspective that has the potential to speak to the lack of interest and engagement in contemporary democratic politics. By inhabiting a paradoxical space between agency and community, relationality strives to promote participation—challenging the widespread feeling that one person cannot make a difference in the political realm—while at the same time denying that one person can ever be the sole author of change, which is always connected to a larger web-of-relations. An ethics of alterity reminds us that every individual actor has a unique role to play and story to share. The other is a gift and not a threat, unless one refuses to recognize the principle of plurality that reminds us that the world is a shared one and that no one has the right to exclude another from acting in it. Relationality, in terms of a politics, offers this approach as an alternative starting point to notions of the political rooted in ontological singularity, which according to Arendt and Levinas formed the girder for totalitarianism and have left their trace on modern liberal democracies.

By way of conclusion, I would like to indicate some of the possible means by which relationality in terms of a politics has promise for our modern democratic societies. First, starting from the most tangible aspect, relationality can act as a counter to the rising democratic deficit in modern societies. Second, relationality can open up a political spectrum that is too one-dimensional by refusing to define the political in terms of either 'I' or 'we' or in terms of its relation to ethics. It is this opening up that also makes a space for a politics of responsibility to complement a politics of rights. Third, and this is the promise that is equally present in the writings of Arendt and Levinas, a politics of relationality aims to fulfil the hope expressed by the phrase *Never Again*. Relationality, by looking deep into the roots of political regimes, whether totalitarian or liberal democracies, and radically questioning the cost of unity and identity, presents an alternative priority. Relationality has as its goal to begin to repair the world so that it is possible once again *for all* to feel at home in it.

While there is no lack of literature on the increasing reality of and challenges posed by the democratic deficit, particularly in countries that have a long history of democracy, relationality may be a new perspective from which to engage this literature.[9] What Arendt and Levinas establish is that the political must seek to celebrate rather than control alterity and plurality if it is to be a world-building space. The problem this raises for those seeking to understand the causes of this democratic deficit requires a fundamental examination of the nature of contemporary democracies: Are they actually open to the reality of a democracy rooted in relationality? Such a democracy is chaotic, unpredictable and ever changing—it is by no means easy to manage, govern or rule. This entails a radical challenge to the now dominant political system of representative liberal democracy, which try to organize and categorize plurality as a means to tame its uncontrollability. This is one of the reasons for the focus on the individual. The individual is much easier to analyse and predict (than plurality), making it easier for liberal rulers to continue to rule. It is not possible to rule over plurality without destroying it, as totalitarianism did. Liberal governments all too often prefer the certainty of a *polis* controlled by means of representation and limited input on behalf of the citizenry.

Yet what appears as an alternative to liberalism, in our current one-dimensional political spectrum, is communitarianism or republicanism. Neither of these alternatives fare much better with regard to the test of relationality: Do these political approaches make space for alterity and plurality? Unlike some forms of liberalism centred on the individual, some forms of communitarians refuse to grant the individual, in his or her alterity, the space to appear by putting the group or common good above all else. In this vein, group-based political theories refuse to allow the alterity of a plurality to appear and thereby reduce plurality to multiplicity. The democratic deficit could thus be said to be a product of its own fear of the *demos*. Relationality seeks to empower the *demos* by prioritizing alterity and plurality, knowing that the price of this empowerment is a loss of control and governance. A politics of relationality does not believe people are meant to be managed or ruled, but rather that they are born to surprise, create and transform the world.

The second promise of relationality is that it introduces another dimension to the way we think, and speak, about politics. By refusing to define the political in terms of either 'I' or 'we', relationality introduces a new perspective to the political spectrum, specifically with regard to its relation to ethics. Habermas, in his essay 'Three Normative Models of Democracy' (1996), defines his discourse theory on democracy in comparison to two paradigms, the liberal and the republican (associating communitarians with the latter), because of their shared conception of politics as connected to a substantial ethical life.[10] In other words, the two paradigms differ in that while the liberals seek neutrality[11] by completely separating ethics, a private affair, from politics, the republicans and communitarians claim that the public sphere cannot be divorced from competing notions of the good life. Thus, while 'the republicans' 'view citizenry as a collective actor that reflects the whole and acts for it; in the latter [liberal account], individual actors function as dependant variables'.[12]

A politics of relationality refuses this aporetic position on ethics by embracing an ethics that arises from within the *polis*, which in this case is that of alterity, which fortifies the importance of plurality for politics. It is as an alternative to these approaches to the political agent as either an autonomous individual or a heteronymous member of a collective (defined by culture, race, religion, and so forth) with regard to the communitarians or by one's citizenship in a nation with regard to republicans. In this way relationality seeks to overcome Marx's denunciation of the 'asinine hypocrisy' of the split between 'the individual' and 'the citizen' or between self-interest and the common good.[13] A politics of relationality creates a critical distance from this one-dimensional model of the political, in which there are three 'camps', in order to point towards a new perspective on the political in light of a relational understanding of the human condition with regard to our responsibility for others and the shared world. Thus while most political thinkers begin from the individual, the citizen or the group, relationality takes the space 'between', the relational roots of the political, as its starting point.

This dialogue between Arendt and Levinas began in their (and my) shared desire to understand how the Shoah could have happened. It is also in this vein that I conclude it. *Never Again*, a phrase that cannot be detached from the Judaic, has a much broader meaning: embrace the alterity and plurality that constitutes the self and the shared world. Do not run or attempt to destroy it. Do not allow uncertainty to be fed by fear; do not hate what you do not know. Relationality is a political project that calls us to embrace difference within us and in the political realm. It helps us to understand that the desire we may have for unity, for harmony, for consensus and for cohesion comes at a heavy price: that of the other, both within and without. While it would be a lie to say that this is easy to do—in fact it may be the most difficult thing we will ever have to do—relationality emphasizes the fact that we do not need to do it alone.

In this sense, the promise of relationality in terms of a political project goes far beyond what I have developed here. I believe, much like Arendt, Levinas, and so many other thinkers writing after the Shoah, that it is necessary to reconsider the meaning of the political, and that this reconsideration must seek a means to create a relationship between the political and ethics. It is because of this need, which the Shoah exposed as acute, that I have sought to reconsider the political from the perspective of the relational, a perspective that allows for both the plurality of the political and the alterity of the ethical. Moreover, relationality's need for participation and action helps to combat the feelings of superfluousness and rootlessness at the heart of the democratic deficit. Last but not least, relationality is a means to remind us that even without roots one remains forever rooted to the world by being connected to other human beings. Given the events of the twentieth century, let us not forget wisdom that has been with humanity for several thousand years: 'It is not good for man to be alone [*sic*]'. We flourish when we allow ourselves to be in relation, to be responsible for the other and the world, to be inspired by hope rather than fear and to listen and learn rather than strive to evade or eliminate. A political ethics of relationality is a first step towards such a world.

NOTES

1. Judith Butler, 'Giving an Account of Oneself', *Diacritics* 31, no. 4 (2001): 22, 38, doi:10.1353/dia.2004.0002.
2. Kevin Thompson and Lester E. Embree, *Phenomenology of the Political* (Dordrecht, Netherlands: Springer Science & Business Media, 2000), 154.
3. Ivana Marková, 'Constitution of the Self: Intersubjectivity and Dialogicality', *Culture & Psychology* 9, no. 3 (1 September 2003): 255, doi:10.1177/1354067X030093006.
4. Bernard Charles Flynn, 'Political Theory and the Metaphysics of Presence', *Philosophy & Social Criticism* 11, no. 3 (1 July 1986): 256, doi:10.1177/019145378601100303.
5. Fabio Ciaramelli, 'Comparison of Incomparables', in *Levinas and Politics*, ed. Simon Critchley and C. Coyle (London: Routledge, 2002), 57.
6. Hannah Arendt, Ursula Ludz, and Ingeborg Nordmann, *Denktagebuch*. Bd. 1, *1950–1973*. Bd. 2, *1973–1975* (München: Piper, 2002), XXV1/58 July 70, 721.
7. Judith Butler, *Frames of War: When Is Life Grievable?* (London: Verso Books, 2009); Anya Topolski, 'An Ethics of Relationality: Destabilising the Genocidal Frame of Us vs. Them', in *Genocide, Risk and Resilience: An Interdisciplinary Approach*, ed. Bert Ingelaere, Stephan Parmentier, Jacques Haers, and Barbara Segaert, Rethinking Political Violence (New York: Palgrave Macmillan, 2013), ch. 13; Anya Topolski, 'Power, Peace

and the Political: Arendt's Alternative to Perpetual Peace', *Peace Studies Journal* 6, no. 3 (July 2013): 57–68.

8. Consider for example the concrete—and noticeably different—reactions Americans had after 9/11 as compared to the British after 7/7 after being tested by the traumatic events of terrorism.

9. Pippa Norris, 'Representation and the Democratic Deficit', *European Journal of Political Research* 32, no. 2 (1997): 273–282, doi:10.1111/1475-6765.00342; Andrew Moravcsik, 'Is There a "Democratic Deficit" in World Politics? A Framework for Analysis', *Government and Opposition* 39, no. 2 (2004): 336–363, doi:10.1111/j.1477-7053.2004.00126.x; Giandomenico Majone, 'Europe's "Democratic Deficit": The Question of Standards', *European Law Journal* 4, no. 1 (1998): 5–28, doi:10.1111/1468-0386.00040.

10. Jürgen Habermas, 'Three Normative Models of Democracy', *Constellations* 1, no. 1 (1994): 1–10, doi:10.1111/j.1467-8675.1994.tb00001.x; Quentin Skinner, *Liberty before Liberalism* (Cambridge, England; New York: Cambridge University Press, 1998); Philip Pettit, 'Deliberative Democracy, the Discursive Dilemma, and Republican Theory', in *Debating Deliberative Democracy*, ed. James S. Fishkin and Peter Laslett (Malden: Blackwell Publishing Ltd, 2003), 138–162, onlinelibrary.wiley.com/doi/10.1002/9780470690734.ch7/summary; Alasdair MacIntyre, *After Virtue: A Study in Moral Theory*, 3rd ed. (Notre Dame, Ind.: University of Notre Dame Press, 2007); Michael J. Sandel, *Liberalism and the Limits of Justice*, 2nd ed. (Cambridge, England; New York: Cambridge University Press, 1998); Michael Walzer, 'Liberalism and the Art of Separation', *Political Theory* 12, no. 3 (1 August 1984): 315–330.

11. Charles Larmore, 'Political Liberalism', *Political Theory* 18, no. 3 (1 August 1990): 339–360, doi:10.1177/0090591790018003001.

12. Ibid., 28.

13. Nadia Urbinati, *Representative Democracy: Principles and Genealogy* (Chicago; Bristol: University of Chicago Press, 2008), 23.

Works Cited

Adorno, Theodor W. *Prisms*. Cambridge, Mass.: MIT Press, 1982.

Agamben, Giorgio. *Remnants of Auschwitz: The Witness and the Archive*. New York: Zone Books, 2000.

Ajzenstat, Oona. *Driven Back to the Text: The Premodern Sources of Levinas's Postmodernism*. Pittsburgh, Pa.: Duquesne University Press, 2001.

Alcoff, Linda Martín. *Visible Identities: Race, Gender, and the Self*. New York: Oxford University Press, 2005.

Alford, C. Fred. 'Levinas and Political Theory'. *Political Theory* 32, no. 2 (1 April 2004): 146–171.

Anidjar, Gil. *Semites: Race, Religion, Literature*. Stanford, Calif.: Stanford University Press, 2007.

Arendt, Hannah. *Between Past and Future: Six Exercises in Political Thought*. Cleveland, Ohio: Meridian Books, 1963.

———. *Crises of the Republic: Lying in Politics; Civil Disobedience; On Violence; Thoughts on Politics and Revolution*. New York: Mariner Books, 1972.

———. *Eichmann in Jerusalem*. 1st ed. London: Penguin Classics, 2010.

———. *Elemente und Ursprünge totaler Herrschaft: Antisemitismus, Imperialismus, Totale Herrschaft*. Neuausg. Auflage. Zürich: Piper Taschenbuch, 1991.

———. *Essays in Understanding, 1930–1954: Formation, Exile, and Totalitarianism*. New York: Schocken, 2005.

———. 'The Great Tradition: I. Law and Power; Part 2: Ruling and Being Ruled'. *Social Research: An International Quarterly* 74, no. 3 (2007): 713–726.

———. *Hannah Arendt/Heinrich Blucher: Briefe 1936–1968*. München: Piper, 1996.

———. *The Human Condition*. 1st ed. Chicago: University of Chicago Press, 1998.

———. *The Jew as Pariah: Jewish Identity and Politics in the Modern Age*. 1st Evergreen ed. New York: Grove Press; distributed by Random House, 1978.

———. *The Jewish Writings*. New York: Schocken, 2007.

———. *Lectures on Kant's Political Philosophy*. Edited by Ronald Beiner. 1st ed. Chicago: University of Chicago Press, 1989.

———. Letter to Meier-Cronenmeyer, 18 July 1963. The Hannah Arendt Papers at the Library of Congress. memory.loc.gov/cgi-bin/ampage?collId=mharendt&fileName=03/030100/030100page.db&recNum=20.

———. *The Life of the Mind*. San Diego: Houghton Mifflin Harcourt, 1981.

———. *Love and Saint Augustine*. Edited by Joanna Vecchiarelli Scott and Judith Chelius Stark. 1st ed. Chicago: University of Chicago Press, 1998.

———. *Men in Dark Times*. New York: Mariner Books, 1970.

———. *On Revolution*. Harmondsworth, UK: Penguin, 1990.

———. *The Origins of Totalitarianism*. New York: Harcourt, Brace, Jovanovich, 1973.

———. 'Philosophy and Politics'. *Social Research* 57, no. 1 (1 April 1990): 73–103.

———. *The Promise of Politics*. 1st ed. New York: Schocken, 2005.

———. *Rahel Varnhagen: The Life of a Jewess*. Edited by Liliane Weissberg. Translated by Richard Winston and Clare Winston. Baltimore, Md.: Johns Hopkins University Press, 1997.

———. *Responsibility and Judgment*. 1st ed. New York: Schocken, 2003.

Arendt, Hannah, and Martin Heidegger. *Letters: 1925–1975*. Edited by Ursula Ludz. Translated by Andrew Shields. 1st ed. Orlando, Fla.: Harcourt, 2003.

Arendt, Hannah, and Karl Jaspers. *Correspondence 1926–1969*. San Diego: Mariner Books, 1993.

Arendt, Hannah, and Ursula Ludz. *Was ist Politik?: Fragmente aus dem Nachlaß*. München: Piper, 2005.

Arendt, Hannah, Ursula Ludz, and Ingeborg Nordmann. *Denktagebuch*. Bd. 1, *1950–1973*. Bd. 2, *1973–1975*. München: Piper, 2002.

Arendt, Hannah, and Mary McCarthy. *Between Friends: The Correspondence of Hannah Arendt and Mary McCarthy 1949–1975*. Edited by Carol Brightman. 1st ed. New York: Harcourt, Brace, 1995.

Asad, Talal. *Formations of the Secular: Christianity, Islam, Modernity*. 1st ed. Stanford, Calif.: Stanford University Press, 2003.

———. *Genealogies of Religion: Discipline and Reasons of Power in Christianity and Islam*. Baltimore, Md.: Johns Hopkins University Press, 1993.

Aschheim, Steven E., ed. *Hannah Arendt in Jerusalem*. Berkeley: University of California Press, 2001.

Assy, Bethania, and Agnes Heller. *Hannah Arendt—An Ethics of Personal Responsibility*. 1st ed. Frankfurt am Main: Peter Lang International Academic Publishers, 2007.

Astell, Ann W. 'Mater-Natality: Augustine, Arendt, and Levinas'. In *Logos of Phenomenology and Phenomenology of the Logos. Book Two*, edited by Anna-Teresa Tymieniecka, 373–398. Analecta Husserliana 89. Dordrecht, Netherlands: Springer Netherlands, 2006. link.springer.com/chapter/10.1007/1-4020-3707-4_23.

Baar, Huub van. *The European Roma: Minority Representation, Memory, and the Limits of Transnational Governmentality*. Amsterdam: F & N Eigen Beheer, 2011.

Balibar, Etienne. '(De)Constructing the Human as Human Institution: A Reflection on the Coherence of Hannah Arendt's Practical Philosophy'. *Social Research: An International Quarterly* 74, no. 3 (2007): 727–738.

Banon, David. *Emmanuel Levinas: Philosophe et pedagogue*. Paris: Editions du nadir de l'Alliance israelite universelle, 1998.

Bassiouni, Cherif. *Crimes Against Humanity in International Criminal Law*. The Hague: Martinus Nijhoff, 1988.

Beiner, Ronald. *Political Judgement*. Chicago; London: University of Chicago Press, 1984.

Benhabib, Seyla. *'The' Reluctant Modernism of Hannah Arendt*. Lanham, Md.: Rowman & Littlefield, 2003.

Benjamin, Walter. *Illuminations: Essays and Reflections*. Edited by Hannah Arendt. Translated by Harry Zohn. English language ed. New York: Schocken, 1969.

Bergo, Bettina. 'Emmanuel Levinas'. In *The Stanford Encyclopedia of Philosophy Archive*, edited by Edward N. Zalta. Fall 2014. plato.stanford.edu/archives/fall2014/entries/levinas/.

———. *Levinas Between Ethics & Politics: For the Beauty That Adorns the Earth*. 1st ed. Pittsburgh, Pa.: Duquesne University Press, 2003.

———. 'Ontology, Transcendence, and Immanence in Emmanuel Levinas' Philosophy'. *Research in Phenomenology* 35, no. 1 (2005): 141–180.

———. 'What Is Politics in Emmanuel Levinas' Ethics? How Did Schmitt's Political Enter Levinas's Totality?' Université de Montreal, 1995. Lecture.

Berlin, Isaiah. *Two Concepts of Liberty: An Inaugural Lecture Delivered before the University of Oxford on 31 October 1958*. Oxford: Clarendon Press, 1966.

Bernard-Donals, Michael F. '"Difficult Freedom": Levinas, Language, and Politics'. *Diacritics* 35, no. 3 (2005): 62–77. doi:10.1353/dia.2007.0019.

Bernasconi, Robert, and David Wood, eds. *The Provocation of Levinas: Rethinking the Other*. London; New York: Routledge, 1988.

Bernet, Rudolf, Iso Kern, Eduard Marbach, and Lester E. Embree. *An Introduction to Husserlian Phenomenology*. 1st ed. Northwestern University Studies in Phenomenology and Existential Philosophy. Evanston, Ill.: Northwestern University Press, 1993.

Bernstein, Richard J. *Hannah Arendt and the Jewish Question*. Cambridge, Mass.: MIT Press, 1996.

Birmingham, Peg. *Hannah Arendt and Human Rights: The Predicament of Common Responsibility*. Bloomington: Indiana University Press, 2006.

Bloechl, Jeffrey. *The Face of the Other and the Trace of God: Essays on the Philosophy of Emmanuel Levinas*. New York: Fordham University Press, 2000.

———. *Liturgy of the Neighbor: Emmanuel Levinas and the Religion of Responsibility*. 1st ed. Pittsburgh, Pa.: Duquesne University Press, 2000.

Botbol-Baum, Mylène, and Anne-Marie Roviello. *Levinas et Arendt: De L'arrachement À L'évasion*. Paris: Vrin, 2013.

Bradbury, Hilary, and Benyamin M. Bergmann Lichtenstein. 'Relationality in Organizational Research: Exploring *The Space Between*'. *Organization Science* 11, no. 5 (October 2000): 551–564. doi:10.1287/orsc.11.5.551.15203.

Brown, Wendy. *Regulating Aversion: Tolerance in the Age of Identity and Empire*. Princeton, N.J.; Woodstock: Princeton University Press, 2008.

Butler, Judith. *Frames of War: When Is Life Grievable?* London: Verso Books, 2009.

———. *Gender Trouble: Feminism and the Subversion of Identity*. London: Routledge, 2011.

———. 'Giving an Account of Oneself'. *Diacritics* 31, no. 4 (2001): 22–40. doi:10.1353/dia.2004.0002.

———. *Parting Ways: Jewishness and the Critique of Zionism*. New York: Columbia University Press, 2012.

Canovan, Margaret. 'Arendt, Rousseau, and Human Plurality in Politics'. *Journal of Politics* 45, no. 2 (May 1983): 285–302. doi:10.2307/2130127.

———. 'Arendt's Theory of Totalitarianism: A Reassessment'. In *The Cambridge Companion to Hannah Arendt*, ed. Dana Villa. Cambridge, England: Cambridge University Press, 2000.

———. *Hannah Arendt: A Reinterpretation of Her Political Thought*. Cambridge, England; New York: Cambridge University Press, 1994.

Carroll, James. *Constantine's Sword: The Church and the Jews, a History*. Boston: Mariner Books, 2002.

Cavarero, Adriana. *For More Than One Voice: Toward a Philosophy of Vocal Expression*. Translated by Paul Kottman. 1st ed. Stanford, Calif.: Stanford University Press, 2005.

———. 'Politicizing Theory'. *Political Theory* 30, no. 4 (1 August 2002): 506–532. doi:10.1177/0090591702304004.

Caygill, Howard. *Levinas and the Political*. London; New York: Routledge, 2002.

Chalier, Catherine. *La Fraternité: Un espoir en clair obscur*. Édition Buchet/chastel. Paris: Buchet Chastel, 2004.

Ciaramelli, Fabio. 'Comparison of Incomparables'. In *Levinas and Politics*, edited by Simon Critchley and C. Coyle, 45–58. London: Routledge, 2002.

Cohen, G. A. *If You're an Egalitarian, How Come You're So Rich?* Cambridge, Mass.: Harvard University Press, 2009.

Cohen, Richard A. *Face to Face with Levinas*. Albany: State University of New York Press, 2012.

———. 'Levinas: Thinking Least about Death—contra Heidegger'. In *Self and Other: Essays in Continental Philosophy of Religion*, edited by Eugene Thomas Long, 21–39. Dordrecht, Netherlands: Springer Netherlands, 2007. link.springer.com/chapter/10.1007/978-1-4020-5861-5_3.

Cohen-Levinas, Danielle, and Shmuel Trigano. *Emmanuel Levinas: Philosophie et judaïsme*. Paris: In Press, 2002.

Connolly, William E. *Identity Difference: Democratic Negotiations of Political Paradox, Expanded Edition*. Rev. ed. Minneapolis: University of Minnesota Press, 2002.

Cranston, Maurice. 'Notes and Topics: Hannah Arendt'. *Encounter* (March 1976): 54–55. UNZ.org. www.UNZ.org/Pub/Encounter-1976mar-00054. Accessed 7 November 2014.

Crick, Bernard. 'On Rereading 'The Origins of Totalitarianism".' *Social Research* 44, no. 1 (1 April 1977): 106–126.

Critchley, Simon. 'Five Problems in Levinas's View of Politics and the Sketch of a Solution to Them'. *Political Theory* 32, no. 2 (1 April 2004): 172–185.
Critchley, Simon, and Robert Bernasconi, eds. *The Cambridge Companion to Levinas*. Cambridge, England; New York: Cambridge University Press, 2002.
Curtis, Kimberley. *Our Sense of the Real: Aesthetic Experience and Arendtian Politics*. 1st ed. Ithaca, N.Y.: Cornell University Press, 1999.
Dallmayr, Fred. *Being in the World: Dialogue and Cosmopolis*. Lexington: University Press of Kentucky, 2013.
———. *The Promise of Democracy: Political Agency and Transformation*. Albany; Bristol: State University of New York Press, 2011.
———. *Twilight of Subjectivity: Contributions to a Post-Individualist Theory of Politics*. Amherst: University of Massachusetts Press, 1981.
Dallmayr, Fred, Azizah Y. al-Hibri, Yoko Arisaka, John J. Clarke, Ahmet Davutoglu, Manochehr Dorraj, Roxanne L. Euben, et al. *Border Crossings*. Lanham, Md.: Lexington Books, 1999.
Dauenhauer, Bernard P. *Elements of Responsible Politics*. Contributions to Phenomenology. Dordrecht, Netherlands: Kluwer Academic Publishers, 1991.
Degryse, Annelies. 'The Sovereign and the Social'. *Ethical Perspectives* 15, no. 2 (30 June 2008): 239–258. doi:10.2143/EP.15.2.2032369.
Derrida, Jacques. *Writing and Difference*. Chicago: University of Chicago Press, 1978.
Derrida, Jacques, and Elisabeth Weber. *Questioning Judaism: Interviews by Elisabeth Weber*. 1st ed. Stanford, Calif.: Stanford University Press, 2004.
Diamant, Anita. *Pitching My Tent: On Marriage, Motherhood, Friendship, and Other Leaps of Faith*. New York: Scribner, 2005.
Dossa, Shiraz. 'Human Status and Politics: Hannah Arendt on the Holocaust'. *Canadian Journal of Political Science/Revue Canadienne de Science Politique* 13, no. 2 (June 1980): 309–323. doi:10.1017/S0008423900033035.
Drichel, Simone. 'Of Political Bottom Lines and Last Ethical Frontiers: The Politics and Ethics of "the Other".' *Borderlands* 6, no. 2 (2007).
Ellis, Marc H. *Encountering the Jewish Future: With Wiesel, Buber, Heschel, Arendt, Levinas*. Minneapolis, Minn.: Augsburg Fortress Publishers, 2010.
Esposito, John L., and Ibrahim Kalin. *Islamophobia: The Challenge of Pluralism in the 21st Century*. New York: Oxford University Press USA, 2011.
Esposito, Roberto. *Communitas: The Origin and Destiny of Community*. Translated by Timothy Campbell. Stanford, Calif.: Stanford University Press, 2009.
Fleischacker, Samuel, ed. *Heidegger's Jewish Followers: Essays on Hannah Arendt, Leo Strauss, Hans Jonas, and Emmanuel Levinas*. 1st ed. Pittsburgh, Pa.: Duquesne University Press, 2008.
Flynn, Bernard Charles. 'Political Theory and the Metaphysics of Presence'. *Philosophy & Social Criticism* 11, no. 3 (1 July 1986): 245–258. doi:10.1177/019145378601100303.
Foucault, Michel. *Discipline & Punish: The Birth of the Prison*. Translated by Alan Sheridan. 2nd ed. New York: Vintage Books, 1995.
Frankl, Viktor Emil. *Unheard Cry Meaning*. 1st ed. New York: Simon & Schuster, 1978.
Friedman, Susan Stanford. 'Beyond White and Other: Relationality and Narratives of Race in Feminist Discourse'. *Signs* 21, no. 1 (1 October 1995): 1–49.
Furedi, Frank. *Culture of Fear*. Rev. ed. London; New York: Continuum International Publishing Group, 2002.
———. *Culture of Fear Revisited*. 2nd ed. London; New York: Bloomsbury Academic, 2006.
Gibbs, Robert. *Correlations in Rosenzweig and Levinas*. Princeton, N.J.: Princeton University Press, 1994.
Gordon, Mordechai, and Maxine Greene. *Hannah Arendt and Education: Renewing Our Common World*. Boulder, Colo.: Westview Press, 2002.
Grass, Günter. 'Hannah Arendt "Zur Person": Full Interview; An Interview from 1964 with Günter Grass'. Video. plus.google.com/+aliasinkhorn/posts/UJ6UBkutcRU. Accessed 20 November 2014.

Groenhout, Ruth E., and Marya Bower, eds. *Philosophy, Feminism, and Faith*. Bloomington: Indiana University Press, 2003.

Grunenberg, Antonia. 'Totalitarian Lies and Post-Totalitarian Guilt: The Question of Ethics in Democratic Politics'. *Social Research* 69, no. 2 (1 July 2002): 359–379.

Habermas, Jürgen. 'Three Normative Models of Democracy'. *Constellations* 1, no. 1 (1994): 1–10. doi:10.1111/j.1467-8675.1994.tb00001.x.

Halberstam, Michael. *Totalitarianism and the Modern Conception of Politics*. New Haven, Conn.: Yale University Press, 2000.

Hand, Seán. *Emmanuel Levinas*. London: Routledge, 2008.

Hansen, Phillip. *Hannah Arendt: Politics, History and Citizenship*. Stanford, Calif.: Stanford University Press, 1993.

Heidegger, Martin. *Being and Time*. Translated by John Macquuarrie and Edward Robinson. Malden, Mass.: Blackwell, 1962.

———. *Gesamtausgabe. 4 Abteilungen/Überlegungen VII–XI*. Frankfurt am Main: Klostermann Vittorio GmbH, 2014.

Herrmann, Friedrich-Wilhelm von, and Martin Heidegger. *Gesamtausgabe 3. Abt.* Bd. 65, *Beiträge zur Philosophie*. 3. Auflage. Frankfurt am Main: Klostermann, Vittorio, n.d.

Herzog, Annabel. 'Is Liberalism "All We Need"? Lévinas's Politics of Surplus'. *Political Theory* 30, no. 2 (1 April 2002): 204–227. doi:10.1177/0090591702030002002.

Hill, Melvyn A., ed. *Hannah Arendt: The Recovery of the Public World*. New York: St. Martin's Press, 1979.

Hinchman, Lewis P., and Sandra K. Hinchman. 'In Heidegger's Shadow: Hannah Arendt's Phenomenological Humanism'. *Review of Politics* 46, no. 2 (April 1984): 183–211. doi:10.1017/S0034670500047720.

Hofmeyr, Benda. *Radical Passivity: Rethinking Ethical Agency in Levinas*. Dordrecht, Netherlands: Springer, 2009.

Howard, Dick. *The Specter of Democracy: What Marx and Marxists Haven't Understood and Why*. New York: Columbia University Press, 2013.

Hughes, Cheryl L. 'The Primacy of Ethics: Hobbes and Levinas'. *Continental Philosophy Review* 31, no. 1 (1 January 1998): 79–94. doi:10.1023/A:1010089805428.

Husserl, Edmund. *Cartesian Meditations: An Introduction to Phenomenology*. 5th ed. n.p. Dordrecht, Netherlands: Klewer Academic Publishers, 1973. Reprint of 5th ed.

Ignatieff, Michael. 'Arendt's Example'. Hannah Arendt Prize Ceremony, Bremen, 28, November 2003. www.hks.harvard.edu/cchrp/pdf/arendt.24.11.03.pdf.

Ingram, David, ed. *The Political*. 1st ed. Malden, Mass.: Wiley-Blackwell, 2002.

Isaac, Jeffrey C. 'Situating Hannah Arendt on Action and Politics'. *Political Theory* 21, no. 3 (1 August 1993): 534–540.

Jansen, Yolande. *Secularism, Assimilation and the Crisis of Multiculturalism: French Modernist Legacies*. Amsterdam: Amsterdam University Press, 2014.

Judt, Tony. 'The Past Is Another Country: Myth and Memory in Postwar Europe'. *Daedalus* 121, no. 4 (1992): 83+.

Judt, Tony, and Timothy Snyder. *Thinking the Twentieth Century*. Repr. ed. New York: Penguin Books, 2013.

Jung, Hwa Yol. 'The Political Relevance of Existential Phenomenology'. *Review of Politics* 33, no. 4 (October 1971): 538–563. doi:10.1017/S0034670500014108.

Kaplan, Gisela T. *Hannah Arendt: Thinking, Judging, Freedom*. Edited by Clive S. Kessler. Sydney: Allen & Unwin, 1990.

Kapust, Antje, Kent Still, and Eric Sean Nelson, eds. *Addressing Levinas*. 1st ed. Evanston, Ill.: Northwestern University Press, 2005.

Kateb, George. 'Existential Values in Arendt's Treatment of Evil and Morality'. *Social Research: An International Quarterly* 74, no. 3 (2007): 811–854.

Katz, Claire Elise. *Levinas, Judaism, and the Feminine: The Silent Footsteps of Rebecca*. Bloomington: Indiana University Press, 2003.

Katz, Claire Elise, and Lara Trout, eds. *Emmanuel Levinas: Levinas, Phenomenology and His Critics*. London: Routledge, 2005.

Keedus, Liisi. 'Liberalism and the Question of "The Proud": Hannah Arendt and Leo Strauss as Readers of Hobbes'. *Journal of the History of Ideas* 73, no. 2 (2012): 319–341. doi:10.1353/jhi.2012.0017.

Kielmansegg, Peter Graf, Horst Mewes, and Elisabeth Glaser-Schmidt, eds. *Hannah Arendt and Leo Strauss: German Émigrés and American Political Thought after World War II*. Washington, D.C.; Cambridge, England; New York: Cambridge University Press, 1997.

King, Richard H. 'Endings and Beginnings: Politics in Arendt's Early Thought'. *Political Theory* 12, no. 2 (1 May 1984): 235–251.

Kohn, Jerome. 'Arendt's Concept and Description of Totalitarianism'. *Social Research* 69, no. 2 (1 July 2002): 621–656.

———. 'Evil: The Crime against Humanity'. In *Three Essays: The Role of Experience in Hannah Arendt's Political Thought*, n.d. memory.loc.gov/ammem/arendthtml/essayc1.html.

Kohn, Margaret. *Radical Space: Building the House of the People*. Ithaca, N.Y.: Cornell University Press, 2003.

Kosky, Jeffrey L. *Levinas and the Philosophy of Religion*. Bloomington: Indiana University Press, 2001.

Kundnani, Arun. *The Muslims Are Coming! Islamophobia, Extremism, and the Domestic War on Terror*. London; New York: Verso, 2014.

Kupiec, Anne, Martine Leibovici, Géraldine Muhlmann, Etienne Tassin, et al. *Hannah Arendt, crises de l'Etat-nation: Pensées alternatives*. Paris: Sens & Tonka, 2007.

Kupiec, Anne, and Etienne Tassin. *Critique de la politique autour de Miguel Abensour*. Paris: Sens & Tonka, 2006.

Lang, Berel. *Heidegger's Silence*. 1st ed. Ithaca, N.Y.: Cornell University Press, 1996.

Larmore, Charles. 'Political Liberalism'. *Political Theory* 18, no. 3 (1 August 1990): 339–360. doi:10.1177/0090591790018003001.

Lefort, Claude. *Democracy and Political Theory*. 1st ed. Translated by David Macey. Cambridge, England: Polity, 1991.

———. *The Political Forms of Modern Society: Bureaucracy, Democracy, Totalitarianism*. 1st MIT Press ed. Edited by David Thompson. Cambridge, Mass.: MIT Press, 1986.

———. 'Thinking with and against Hannah Arendt'. *Social Research* 69, no. 2 (1 July 2002): 447–459.

Leibovici, Martine. *Hannah Arendt*. Paris: Desclée de Brouwer, 2000.

———. *Hannah Arendt et la tradition juive: Le judaïsme à l'épreuve de la sécularisation*. Geneva: Labor et Fides, 2003.

———. *Hannah Arendt, une Juive: Expérience, politique et histoire*. Paris: Desclée De Brouwer, 1998.

Levinas, Emmanuel. *A l'heure des nations*. Paris: Editions de Minuit, 1988.

———. *Alterity and Transcendence*. Translated by Michael B. Smith. New York: Columbia University Press, 1999.

———. *Autrement qu'être: Ou, Au-delà de l'essence*. Dordrecht, Netherlands: Kluwer Academic Publishers, 1974.

———. *Basic Philosophical Writings*. Bloomington: Indiana University Press, 1997.

———. 'Being Jewish'. *Continental Philosophy Review* 40, no. 3 (1 July 2007): 205–210. doi:10.1007/s11007-007-9052-7.

———. *Beyond the Verse: Talmudic Readings and Lectures*. 1st ed. Translated by Gary D. Mole. Bloomington: Indiana University Press, 1994.

———. *Collected Philosophical Papers*. Pittsburgh, Pa.: Duquesne University Press, 1998.

———. *De Dieu qui vient à l'idée*. Paris: Vrin, 1982.

———. *De l'évasion*. Paris: Le Livre de Poche, 1998.

———. *De l'existence à l'existant*. 2nd ed. Paris: Librairie Philosophique Vrin, 2002.

———. *Difficile liberté*. 4th ed. Paris: Albin Michel, 1996.

———. *Difficult Freedom: Essays on Judaism*. Translated by Seán Hand. Baltimore, Md.: Johns Hopkins University Press, 1997.

———. *Du sacré au saint, cinq nouvelles lectures talmudiques*. Paris: Editions de Minuit, 1977.
———. *En découvrant l'existence avec Husserl et Heidegger*. Paris: Librairie Philosophique Vrin, 2002.
———. *Entre nous*. Paris: Le Livre de Poche, 1993.
———. *Entre Nous*. Translated by Michael B. Smith and Barbara Harshav. New York: Columbia University Press, 2000.
———. 'Ethics and Politics'. In *The Levinas Reader*, 1st ed., edited by Sean Hand. Oxford, England; Cambridge, Mass.: Blackwell Publishers, 1989.
———. *Existence et Existents*. Translated by Alphonso Lingis. The Hague: Springer Science & Business Media, 1978.
———. *God, Death, and Time*. 1st ed. Translated by Bettina Bergo. Stanford, Calif.: Stanford University Press, 2000.
———. *Hors sujet*. Paris: Le Livre de Poche, 1997.
———. *Humanism of the Other*. Translated by Nidra Poller. Urbana; Chicago: University of Illinois Press, 2003.
———. *Humanisme de l'autre homme*. Montpellier: LGF-Livre de Poche, 1987.
———. *In the Time of the Nations*. Translated by Michael B. Smith. Bloomington: Indiana University Press, 1994.
———. *Is It Righteous to Be? Interviews with Emmanuel Levinas*. 1st ed. Edited by Jill Robbins. Stanford, Calif.: Stanford University Press, 2002.
———. 'La Substitution'. *Revue Philosophiques de Louvain* 66 (August 1968): 478–508.
———. *L'au-delà du verset: Lectures et discours talmudiques*. Collection Critique. Paris: Editions de Minuit, 1982.
———. *Le temps et l'autre*. 11th ed. Paris: Presses Universitaires de France—PUF, 2014.
———. *Les imprévus de l'histoire*. Paris: Le Livre de Poche, 1999.
———. *The Levinas Reader*. 1st ed. Edited by Sean Hand. Oxford, England; Cambridge, Mass.: Blackwell Publishers, 1989.
———. 'Martin Heidegger and Ontology'. Translated by Committee of Public Safety. *Diacritics* 26, no. 1 (1996): 11–32. doi:10.1353/dia.1996.0007.
———. 'Martin Heidegger et L'ontologie'. *Revue Philosophique de La France et de l'Étranger* 113 (1 January 1932): 395–431.
———. *New Talmudic Readings*. Pittsburgh, Pa.: Duquesne University Press, 1999.
———. *Nine Talmudic Readings by Emmanuel Levinas*. Translated by Annette Aronowicz. Bloomington: Indiana University Press, 1990.
———. *Noms Propres*. Saint Clement de Riviere: Fata Morgana, 1976.
———. *Nouvelles lectures talmudiques*. Paris: Editions de Minuit, 1995.
———. *Of God Who Comes to Mind*. Stanford, Calif.: Stanford University Press, 1998.
———. *On Escape: De L'évasion*. 1st ed. Translated by Bettina Bergo. Stanford, Calif.: Stanford University Press, 2003.
———. *Otherwise Than Being: Or Beyond Essence*. Pittsburgh, Pa.: Duquesne University Press, 1998.
———. *Outside the Subject*. 1st ed. Stanford, Calif.: Stanford University Press, 1994.
———. *Proper Names*. Stanford, Calif.: Stanford University Press, 1996.
———. *Quatre lectures talmudiques*. Paris: Les Editions de Minuit, 2005.
———. 'Reflections on the Philosophy of Hitlerism'. *Critical Inquiry* 17, no. 1 (1 October 1990): 63–71. doi:10.2307/1343726.
———. 'Sur Les "Ideen" de M. E. Husserl'. *Revue Philosophique de La France et de l'Étranger* 107 (1 January 1929): 230–65.
———. *Théorie de l'intuition dans la phénoménologie de Husserl*. Paris: Librairie Philosophique Vrin, 2000.
———. *The Theory of Intuition in Husserl's Phenomenology*. Evanston, Ill.: Northwestern University Press, 1995.
———. *Time and the Other*. Translated by Richard A. Cohen. Pittsburgh, Pa.: Duquesne University Press, 1990.
———. *Totalité et infini*. The Hague: M. Nijhoff, 1961.

———. *Totality and Infinity: An Essay on Exteriority*. Translated by Alphonso Lingis. Pittsburgh, Pa.: Duquesne University Press, 1969.

———. *Unforeseen History*. Translated by Nidra Poller. Urbana: University of Illinois Press, 2003.

Levinas, Emmanuel, and Philippe Nemo. *Ethics and Infinity*. Michigan: Duquesne University Press, 1985.

Levinas, Emmanuel, and Seán Hand. 'Reflections on the Philosophy of Hitlerism'. *Critical Inquiry* 17, no. 1 (1 October 1990): 63–71, doi:10.2307/1343726.

Lévinassiennes, Institut d'études. *Cahiers d'études levinassiennes*. Paris: Institut d'éudes levinassiennes, 2002.

Lewis, Bernard. *Semites and Anti-Semites: An Inquiry into Conflict and Prejudice*. New York: W. W. Norton, 1999.

Luft, Sebastian, and Soren Overgaard, eds. *The Routledge Companion to Phenomenology*. London: Routledge, 2013.

Lyotard, Jean-Francois. *Phenomenology*. Albany: State University of New York Press, 1991.

Lyotard, Jean-Francois, and David Carroll. *Heidegger and 'the Jews'*. 1st ed. Translated by Andreas Michel and Mark Roberts. Minneapolis: University of Minnesota Press, 1990.

MacIntyre, Alasdair. *After Virtue: A Study in Moral Theory*. 3rd ed. Notre Dame, Ind.: University of Notre Dame Press, 2007.

Madison, Gary Brent. *The Politics of Postmodernity: Essays in Applied Hermeneutics*. Dordrecht, Netherlands; Noston: Klewer Academic Publishers, 2001.

Majone, Giandomenico. 'Europe's "Democratic Deficit": The Question of Standards'. *European Law Journal* 4, no. 1 (1998): 5–28. doi:10.1111/1468-0386.00040.

Malka, Salomon. *Monsieur Chouchani: L'enigme d'un maitre du XXe siecle; entretiens avec Elie Wiesel, suivis d'une enquete*. Paris: J. C. Lattes, 1994.

Malka, Simon. *Emmanuel Levinas: His Life and Legacy*. Translated by Michael Kigel and Sonja M. Embree. Pittsburgh, Pa.: Duquesne University Press, 2006. www.dupress.duq.edu/products/philosophy22-cloth.

Maloney, Philip J. 'Levinas, Substitution and Transcendental Subjectivity'. *Man and World* 30, no. 1 (1 January 1997): 49–64. doi:10.1023/A:1004228124719.

Marchart, Oliver. *Post-Foundational Political Thought: Political Difference in Nancy, Lefort, Badiou and Laclau*. Edinburgh, Scotland: Edinburgh University Press, 2007.

Marková, Ivana. 'Constitution of the Self: Intersubjectivity and Dialogicality'. *Culture & Psychology* 9, no. 3 (1 September 2003): 249–259. doi:10.1177/1354067X030093006.

Masuzawa, Tomoko. *The Invention of World Religions: Or, How European Universalism Was Preserved in the Language of Pluralism*. Chicago: University of Chicago Press, 2005.

May, Larry, and Jerome Kohn. *Hannah Arendt: Twenty Years Later*. Cambridge, Mass.: MIT Press, 1997.

Meir, Ephraim. 'Les Écrits Professionnels et Confessionnels d'Emmanuel Lévinas'. In *Emmanuel Lévinas—Philosophie et Judaïsme*, edited by Shmuel Trigano and Danielle Cohen, 101–114. Paris: Pardes 26, 1999.

Mitchell, Don. 'The End of Public Space? People's Park, Definitions of the Public, and Democracy'. *Annals of the Association of American Geographers* 85, no. 1 (1 March 1995): 108–33. doi:10.1111/j.1467-8306.1995.tb01797.xa.

———. *The Right to the City: Social Justice and the Fight for Public Space*. New York: Guilford Press, 2003.

Mitchell, Stephen A. *Relationality: From Attachment to Intersubjectivity*. Vol. 19. Relational Perspectives Book Series, Vol. 20. Mahwah, N.J.: Analytic Press, 2000.

Montesquieu, [Charles de]. *Montesquieu: The Spirit of the Laws*. Cambridge Texts in the History of Political Thought. Cambridge, England: Cambridge University Press, 1989.

Moore, R. I. *The Formation of a Persecuting Society: Authority and Deviance in Western Europe 950–1250*. 2nd ed. Malden: Wiley-Blackwell, 2007.

Moravcsik, Andrew. 'Is There a "Democratic Deficit" in World Politics? A Framework for Analysis'. *Government and Opposition* 39, no. 2 (2004): 336–363. doi:10.1111/j.1477-7053.2004.00126.x.

Mortley, Raoul. *French Philosophers in Conversation: Levinas, Schneider, Serres, Irigaray, Le Doeuff, Derrida*. London; New York: Routledge, 1991.

Moyn, Samuel. 'Emmanuel Levinas's Talmudic Readings: Between Tradition and Invention'. *Prooftexts* 23, no. 3 (2003): 338–364. doi:10.1353/ptx.2004.0007.

Mréjen, Aurore. *La Figure De L'Homme: Hannah Arendt et Emmanuel Lévinas*. Paris: Editions du Palio, 2012.

Myers, David G., and David B. Ruderman. *The Jewish Past Revisited: Reflections on Modern Jewish Historians*. New Haven, Conn.: Yale University Press, 1998.

Nancy, Jean-Luc. *Being Singular Plural*. Stanford, Calif.: Stanford University Press, 2000.

———. *The Sense of the World*. 2nd ed. Minneapolis: University of Minnesota Press, 2008.

Nirenberg, David. *Anti-Judaism: The Western Tradition*. New York: W. W. Norton, 2013.

Norris, Pippa. 'Representation and the Democratic Deficit'. *European Journal of Political Research* 32, no. 2 (1997): 273–282. doi:10.1111/1475-6765.00342.

Ott, Paul Matthew. 'The Politics of the Present: A Relational Theory of the Self as a Basis for Political Theory: Dewey, Arendt, and Levinas'. PhD diss., State University of New York at Buffalo, 2010. gradworks.umi.com/34/07/3407936.html.

Parekh, Bhikhu C. *Hannah Arendt and the Search for a New Political Philosophy*. New York: Macmillan, 1981.

Peperzak, Adrian T. 'Intersubjectivity and Community'. In *Phenomenology of the Political*, edited by Kevin Thompson and Lester Embree, 55–64. Contributions to Phenomenology 38. Dordrecht, Netherlands: Springer Netherlands, 2000. link.springer.com/chapter/10.1007/978-94-017-2606-1_5.

———. 'Phenomenology—Ontology—Metaphysics: Levinas' Perspective on Husserl and Heidegger'. *Man and World* 16, no. 2 (1 June 1983): 113–127. doi:10.1007/BF01260324.

Pettit, Philip. 'Deliberative Democracy, the Discursive Dilemma, and Republican Theory'. In *Debating Deliberative Democracy*, edited by James S. Fishkin and Peter Laslett, 138–162. Malden: Blackwell Publishing, 2003. onlinelibrary.wiley.com/doi/10.1002/9780470690734.ch7/summary.

Pitkin, Hanna Fenichel. *The Attack of the Blob: Hannah Arendt's Concept of the Social*. 1st ed. Chicago: University of Chicago Press, 2000.

Poché, Fred. *Penser Avec Arendt et Levinas: Du mal politique au respect de l'autre*. Lyon: Chronique Sociale, 1998.

Putnam, Hilary. *Jewish Philosophy as a Guide to Life: Rosenzweig, Buber, Levinas, Wittgenstein*. Bloomington: Indiana University Press, 2008.

Rieff, David. 'The Persistence of Genocide'. *Policy Review*, no. 165 (March 2011): 29–45.

Rosenberg, Alan, and Alan Milchman. *Postmodernism and the Holocaust* (Value Inquiry Book Series 72). Amsterdam; Atlanta, Ga.: Rodopi Bv Editions, 1998.

Rosenzweig, Franz. *The Star of Redemption*. Translated by William W. Hallo. Notre Dame, Ind.: University of Notre Dame Press, 1985.

Roviello, Anne-Marie, and Catherine Temerson. 'The Hidden Violence of Totalitarianism: The Loss of the Groundwork of the World'. *Social Research: An International Quarterly* 74, no. 3 (2007): 923–930.

Ruderman, David B. *Jewish Thought and Scientific Discovery in Early Modern Europe*. Detroit: Wayne State University Press, 2001.

Sacks, Jonathan. *Covenant & Conversation: A Weekly Reading of the Jewish Bible, Genesis: The Book of Beginnings*. Edited by Koren Publishers Jerusalem. New Milford, Conn.: Koren Publishers Jerusalem, 2009.

———. *The Dignity of Difference: How to Avoid the Clash of Civilizations*. 2nd ed. London: Bloomsbury Academic, 2003.

———. *To Heal a Fractured World: The Ethics of Responsibility*. New York: Schocken, 2007.

———. *The Home We Build Together: Recreating Society*. 1st ed. New York: Continuum, 2009.

Saint-Cheron, Michaël de. *Du juste au saint: Ricoeur, Rosenzweig et Levinas*. Paris: Desclée de Brouwer, 2013.

Sandel, Michael J. *Liberalism and the Limits of Justice*. 2nd ed. Cambridge, England; New York: Cambridge University Press, 1998.

Sayyid, S., and Abdool Karim Vakil, eds. *Thinking Through Islamophobia: Global Perspectives*. New York: Columbia University Press, 2011.

Schaap, Andrew. 'Political Theory and the Agony of Politics'. *Political Studies Review* 5, no. 1 (1 January 2007): 56–74. doi:10.1111/j.1478-9299.2007.00123.x.

Schama, Simon. *Story of the Jews, The: Finding the Words 1000 BC–1492 AD*. 1st ed. New York: Ecco, 2014.

Schutz, Alfred. 'The Problem of Transcendental Intersubjectivity in Husserl'. In *Collected Papers III*, edited by I. Schutz, 51–84. Phaenomenologica 22. Dordrecht, Netherlands: Springer Netherlands, 1970. link.springer.com/chapter/10.1007/978-94-015-3456-7_4.

Shults, F. LeRon. *Reforming Theological Anthropology: After the Philosophical Turn to Relationality*. Grand Rapids, MI: Wm. B. Eerdmans Publishing, 2003.

Simmons, William Paul. *An-Archy and Justice: An Introduction to Emmanuel Levinas's Political Thought*. Lanham, Md.: Lexington Books, 2003.

———. 'The Third: Levinas' Theoretical Move from Anarchical Ethics to the Realm of Justice and Politics'. *Philosophy & Social Criticism* 25, no. 6 (1 November 1999): 83–104.

Skinner, Quentin. *Liberty before Liberalism*. Cambridge, England; New York: Cambridge University Press, 1998.

Smith, David Woodruff. 'Phenomenology'. In *The Stanford Encyclopedia of Philosophy*, edited by Edward N. Zalta. n.d. plato.stanford.edu/archives/win2013/entries/phenomenology.

Smith, Michael B. 'Emmanuel Levinas's Ethics of Responsiblity'. Paper presented at the Mike Ryan Lecture Series, Kennesaw State College, 7 October 2003. sites.google.com/site/philosophystudentassociation/Home/mike-ryan-lecture-series-1.

Sokolowski, Robert. *Husserlian Meditations: How Words Present Things*. 1st ed. Evanston, Ill.: Northwestern University Press, 1974.

Springer, Simon. 'Public Space as Emancipation: Meditations on Anarchism, Radical Democracy, Neoliberalism and Violence'. *Antipode* 43, no. 2 (1 March 2011): 525–562. doi:10.1111/j.1467-8330.2010.00827.x.

Steinsaltz, Rabbi Adin. *The Talmud*. Vol. 15, *The Steinsaltz Edition: Tractate Sanhedrin, Part 1*. New York: Random House, 1996.

Strauss, Leo. *Spinoza's Critique of Religion*. Chicago: University of Chicago Press, 1997.

Taminiaux, Jacques. 'Bios Politikos and Bios Theoretikos in the Phenomenology of Hannah Arendt'. *International Journal of Philosophical Studies* 4, no. 2 (1 September 1996): 215–232. doi:10.1080/09672559608570832.

———. *The Thracian Maid and the Professional Thinker: Arendt and Heidegger*. Translated by Michael Gendre. Albany: State University of New York Press, 1997.

Thompson, Kevin, and Lester E. Embree. *Phenomenology of the Political*. Dordrecht, Netherlands: Springer Science & Business Media, 2000.

Topolski, Anya. 'An Ethics of Relationality: Destabilising the Genocidal Frame of Us vs. Them'. In *Genocide, Risk and Resilience: An Interdisciplinary Approach*, ed. Bert Ingelaere, Stephan Parmentier, Jacques Haers, and Barbara Segaert. Rethinking Political Violence. New York: Palgrave Macmillan, 2013. ch. 13.

———. 'Creating Citizens in the Classroom'. *Ethical Perspectives* 15, no. 2 (30 June 2008): 259–282. doi:10.2143/EP.15.2.2032370.

———. 'How Jews and Muslims Became Races: A Genealogy of Antisemitism and Islamophobia'. In *Philosophy of Race: Introductory Readings*, ed. Nathan Nobis. 2015. 7–15. Available at www.philosophyofrace.com.

———. 'Listening to the Language of the Other'. In *Radical Passivity*, edited by Benda Hofmeyr, 111–131. Library of Ethics and Applied Philosophy 20. Dordrecht, Netherlands: Springer Netherlands, 2009. link.springer.com/chapter/10.1007/978-1-4020-9347-0_8.

———. 'On Freedom in Athens and Jerusalem: Arendt's Political Challenge to Levinas' Ethics of Responsibility'. In *The Awakening to the Other: A Provocative Dialogue with Emmanuel Levinas*, edited by R. Burggraeve, 215–240. Leuven; Dudley, Mass.: Peeters Publishers, 2008.

———. "Power, Peace and the Political: Arendt's Alternative to Perpetual Peace." *Peace Studies Journal* 6, no. 3 (July 2013): 57–68.

———. 'Relationality as a "Foundation" for Human Rights: Exploring the Paradox with Hannah Arendt and Emmanuel Levinas'. *Theoria and Praxis: International Journal of Interdisciplinary Thought* 2, no. 1 (6 August 2014). pi.library.yorku.ca/ojs/index.php/theoriandpraxis/article/view/39373.

———. '*Tzedakah*: The True Religion of Spinoza's *Tractatus?*' *History of Political Thought* 36, no. 3 (2015).

———. 'Universal Political Messianism: A Dialogue with Emmanuel Levinas' First Talmudic Reading'. In *On the Outlook Figures of the Messianic*, edited by Thomas Crombez and Katrien Vloeberghs, 141–150. Cambridge, England: Cambridge Scholars Publishing, 2007. public.eblib.com/choice/publicfullrecord.aspx?p=1114276.

Topolski, Anya, and Emmanuel Nathan, eds. *Is There a Judeo-Christian Tradition? A European Perspective*. Berlin: De Gruyter, 2015.

Trawny, Peter. *Heidegger und der Mythos der jüdischen Weltverschwörung*. 1st Auflage Frankfurt am Main: Klostermann, Vittorio, 2014.

Urbinati, Nadia. *Representative Democracy: Principles and Genealogy*. Chicago; Bristol: University of Chicago Press, 2008.

Villa, Dana. *Arendt and Heidegger: The Fate of the Political*. Princeton, N.J.: Princeton University Press, 1995.

———, ed. *The Cambridge Companion to Hannah Arendt*. Cambridge, England: Cambridge University Press, 2000.

Villa, Dana R. 'Beyond Good and Evil: Arendt, Nietzsche, and the Aestheticization of Political Action'. *Political Theory* 20, no. 2 (1 May 1992): 274–308.

Visker, Rudi. 'Dissensus Communis: How to Keep Silent "after" Lyotard'. In *Dissensus Communis Between Ethics and Politics*, edited by P. Birmingham and P. Van Haute, 7–31. Kampen: Peeters, 1995.

———. *Truth and Singularity: Taking Foucault into Phenomenology*. Dordrecht, Netherlands; Boston: Springer Science & Business Media, 1999.

Walzer, Michael. 'Liberalism and the Art of Separation'. *Political Theory* 12, no. 3 (1 August 1984): 315–330.

Walzer, Michael, Menachem Lorberbaum, Noam J. Zohar, and Ari Ackerman, eds. *The Jewish Political Tradition*, Vol. 2, *Membership*. New Haven, Conn.; London: Yale University Press, 2006.

White, Stephen K. *Sustaining Affirmation*. Princeton, N.J.: Princeton University Press, 2000.

Williams, Gareth. 'Ethics and Human Relationality: Between Arendt's Accounts of Morality'. *HannahArendt.net* 3, no. 1 (2007).

———, ed. *Hannah Arendt*. 1st ed. New York: Routledge, 2006.

Wolin, Richard. *The Heidegger Controversy: A Critical Reader*. 1st MIT Press ed. Cambridge, Mass: MIT Press, 1992.

———. *Heidegger's Children: Hannah Arendt, Karl Löwith, Hans Jonas, and Herbert Marcuse*. Princeton, N.J.: Princeton University Press, 2003.

Young-Bruehl, Elisabeth. *Hannah Arendt: For Love of the World*. 2nd ed. New Haven, Conn.: Yale University Press, 2004.

Zahavi, Dan. 'Phenomenology and Metaphysics'. In *Metaphysics, Facticity, Interpretation*, edited by Dan Zahavi, Sara Heinämaa, and Hans Ruin, 3–22. Contributions to Phenomenology 49. Dordrecht, Netherlands: Springer Netherlands, 2003. link.springer.com/chapter/10.1007/978-94-007-1011-5_1.

Zarader, Marlene. *The Unthought Debt: Heidegger and the Hebraic Heritage*. 1st ed. Translated by Bettina Bergo. Stanford, Calif.: Stanford University Press, 2006.

Related Works

Adorno, Theodore. *Kulturkritik Und Gesellschaft*. Frankfurt: Suhr-Kamp, 1951.

Akenson, Donald H. *Surpassing Wonder: The Invention of the Bible and the Talmuds*. Chicago: University of Chicago Press, 2001.

Armstrong, Karen. *A History of God: The 4000-Year Quest of Judaism, Christianity, and Islam*. New York: A. A. Knopf, 1993.

Aronowicz, Annette. 'Jewish Education in the Thought of Emmanuel Levinas'. In *Abiding Challenges: Research Perspectives on Jewish Education*. Edited by Yisrael Rich and Michael Rosenak. Bar Ilan University: Freund Publishing House, 1999.

Assy, Bethânia. 'Hannah Arendt and the Faculty of Thinking—a Partner to Think, a Witness to Act'. *Revisita Ethica & Filosofia Politica* 9, no. 1 (2006). Digital journal.

———. 'Hannah Arendt's Doxa Glorifying Judgment and Exemplarity—a Potentially Public Space'. *Veritas* 50, no. 1 (2005).

———. 'The State and the Jews: Reflections on Difficult Freedom'. *Journal of Jewish Thought and Philosophy* 14, nos. 1–2 (2006): 109–130.

Atterton, Peter, Matthew Calarco, and Maurice S. Friedman. *Levinas & Buber: Dialogue & Difference*. Pittsburgh, Pa.: Duquesne University Press, 2004.

Awerkamp, Don. *Emmanuel Levinas: Ethics and Politics*. Studies in Modern Philosophy. New York: Revisionist Press, 1977.

Barnouw, Dagmar. *Visible Spaces: Hannah Arendt and the German-Jewish Experience*. Johns Hopkins Jewish Studies. Baltimore: Johns Hopkins University Press, 1990.

Batnitzky, Leora Faye. *Leo Strauss and Emmanuel Levinas: Philosophy and the Politics of Revelation*. Cambridge, England: Cambridge University Press, 2006.

———. 'On Reaffirming a Distinction Between Athens and Jerusalem'. *Hebraic Political Studies* 2, no. 2 (2007): 211–31.

Beiner, Ronald. 'Hannah Arendt and Leo Strauss: The Uncommenced Dialogue'. *Political Theory* 18, no. 2 (1990): 238–254.

———. *Liberalism, Nationalism, Citizenship: Essays on the Problem of Political Community*. Vancouver: University of British Columbia Press, 2003.

———. *Theorizing Citizenship*. SUNY Series in Political Theory: Contemporary Issues. Albany: State University of New York Press, 1995.

———. *What's the Matter with Liberalism?* Berkeley: University of California Press, 1992.

Beiner, Ronald, and Jennifer Nedelsky. *Judgment, Imagination, and Politics: Themes from Kant and Arendt*. Lanham, Md.: Rowman & Littlefield, 2001.

Beiner, Ronald, and W. J. Norman. *Canadian Political Philosophy: Contemporary Reflections*. Don Mills: Oxford University Press, 2001.

Benhabib, Seyla. 'Democracy and Identity: In Search of the Civic Polity'. *Philosophy & Social Criticism* 24, nos. 2–3 (1998): 85–100.

———. 'In Defense of Universalism: Yet Again! A Response to Critics of Situating the Self'. *New German Critique* 62 (1994): 173–189.

———. 'Judgment and the Moral Foundations of Politics in Arendt's Thought'. *Political Theory* 16, no. 1 (1988): 29–51.

———. 'The Pariah and Her Shadow: Hannah Arendt's Biography of Rahel Varnhagen'. *Political Theory* 23, no. 1 (1995): 5–24.

Bergo, Bettina. 'Is There a "Correlation" Between Rosenzweig and Levinas?' *Jewish Quarterly Review* 96, no. 3 (2006): 404–412.

———. 'The Return of the Religious, or Reading Ethics Using Religious Categories: Kierkegaard, Levinas, and Recent French Thought'. *Tympanum* IV (2000). www.usc.edu/dept/comp-lit/tympanium/4/bergo.html.

Berlin, Adele, Marc Zvi Brettler, and Michael Fishbane. *The Jewish Study Bible*. Oxford: Oxford University Press, 2004.

Berman, Michael. 'The Situatedness of Judgment and Action in Arendt and Merleau-Ponty'. *Politics and Ethics Review* 2, no. 2 (2006): 202–20.

Bernasconi, Robert, and Simon Critchley. *Re-Reading Levinas*. Studies in Continental Thought. Bloomington: Indiana University Press, 1991.

Bernasconi, Robert, et al. *Ethics and Responsibility in the Phenomenological Tradition*. Annual Symposia of the Simon Silverman Phenomenology Center 9. Pittsburgh, Pa.: Duquesne University, Simon Silverman Phenomenology Center, 1992.

Bernauer, James William. *Amor Mundi: Explorations in the Faith and Thought of Hannah Arendt*. Boston College Studies in Philosophy. The Hague: M. Nijhoff, 1987.

Biesta, Gert. *Beyond Learning: Democratic Education for a Human Future*. Boulder, Colo.: Paradigm Publishers, 2006.

Bloechl, Jeffrey. *The Face of the Other and the Trace of God: Essays on the Philosophy of Emmanuel Levinas*. Perspectives in Continental Philosophy. New York: Fordham University Press, 2000.

Boman, Thorleif. *Hebrew Thought Compared with Greek*. Philadelphia: Westminster Press, 1960.

Borowitz, Eugene B. *Choices in Modern Jewish Thought: A Partisan Guide*. New York: Behrman House, 1983.

Botbol-Baum, Mylène. 'Responsabilité Et Liberté'. In *Lévinas En Contrastes*, edited by M. Dupuis, 157–77. Brussels: De Boeck Université, 1994.

Bradshaw, Leah. *Acting and Thinking: The Political Thought of Hannah Arendt*. Toronto: University of Toronto Press, 1989.

Braembussche, A. A. van den, and Maurice Weyembergh. *Hannah Arendt: Vita Activa Versus Vita Contemplativa*. Budel: Damon, 2002.

Braidotti, R. 'Sexual Difference Theory'. In *A Companion to Feminist Philosophy*, edited by A. M. Jaggar and I. M. Young, 298–306. London: Blackwell Publishers, 1998.

Braiterman, Zachary. 'Joseph Soloveitchik and Immanuel Kant's Mitzvah-Aesthetic'. *Association for Jewish Studies (AJS) Review* (2000): 1–24.

Brunkhorst, Hauke. *Hannah Arendt*. München: C. H. Beck, 1999.

Buckler, Steve. 'Political Theory and Political Ethics in the Work of Hannah Arendt'. *Contemporary Political Theory* 6 (2007): 461–83.

Burggraeve, Roger. *Emmanuel Lévinas: Une Bibliographie Primaire Et Secondaire (1929–1985) Avec Complément 1985–1989*. Leuven: Peeters, 1990.

———. *From Self-Development to Solidarity: An Ethical Reading of Human Desire in Its Socio-Political Relevance According to Emmanuel Lévinas*. Publications of the Center for Metaphysics and Philosophy of God. Leuven: Peeters, 1985.

Burggraeve, Roger, and Jeffrey Bloechl. *The Wisdom of Love in the Service of Love: Emmanuel Levinas on Justice, Peace, and Human Rights*. Milwaukee, Wis.: Marquette University Press, 2002.

Burggraeve, Roger, and Emmanuel Lévinas. *Emmanuel Levinas Et La Socialité De L'argent: Un Philosophe En Quête De La Réalité Journalière, La Genèse De Socialité Et Argent Ou L'ambiguïté De L'argent*. Leuven: Peeters, 1997.

Butler, Judith. *Giving an Account of Oneself*. New York: Fordham University Press, 2005.

Calhoun, Craig J., and John McGowan. *Hannah Arendt and the Meaning of Politics*. Contradictions of Modernity. Minneapolis: University of Minnesota Press, 1997.

Canovan, Margaret. 'Arendt's Theory of Totalitarianism: A Reassessment'. In *The Cambridge Companion to Hannah Arendt*, edited by Dana R. Villa, 25–43. New York: Cambridge University Press, 2000.

———. 'The Contradictions of Hannah Arendt's Political Thought'. *Political Theory* 6, no. 1 (1978): 5–26.

———. 'On Levin's "Animal Laborans and Homo Politicus in Hannah Arendt".' *Political Theory* 8, no. 3 (1980): 403–405.
———. *The Political Thought of Hannah Arendt*. London: Dent, 1974.
Chalier, Catherine. *Judaïsme Et Altérité*. Lagrasse: Verdier, 1982.
———. *La Trace de L'infini: Emmanuel Levinas Et La Source Hébraïque*. Paris: Editions du Cerf, 2002.
———. *Les Matriarches: Sarah, Rébecca, Rachel Et Léa*. Paris: Editions du Cerf, 1985.
———. *What Ought I to Do? Morality in Kant and Levinas*. Ithaca, N.Y.: Cornell University Press, 2002.
Chandler, M. 'Reconceiving the Political: Arendt, Levinas, and the Potential for Politics to Become Otherwise'. Unpublished Conference Paper. Canadian Political Science Association Annual Conference, 2005.
Chanter, Tina. *Feminist Interpretations of Emmanuel Levinas*. Re-Reading the Canon. University Park: Pennsylvania State University Press, 2001.
Ciaramelli, Fabio. 'The Circle of the Origin'. In *Rethinking the Political: Continental Philosophy and Political Theory*, edited by Lenore Langsdorf and Stephen H. Watson. Albany: State University of New York Press, 1998.
———. *Transcendance Et Éthique: Essai Sur Lévinas*. Bruxelles: Ousia, 1989.
Cohen, A. *Everyman's Talmud: The Major Teachings of the Rabbinic Sages*. New York: Schocken Books, 1995.
Cohen, Richard A. '"Political Monotheism": Levinas on Politics, Ethics and Religion'. In *Issues Confronting the Post-European World*, edited by Chan-Fai Cheung, Ivan Chvatik, Ion Copoeru, Lester Embree, Julia Iribarne, and Hans Rainer Sepps. Conference Paper, 2003. Web publication: www.o-p-o.net.
Cohen-Levinas, Danielle, and Shmuel Trigano. *Emmanuel Levinas: Philosophie Et Judaisme*. Lettres Promises. Paris: In Press, 2002.
Congres Juif Mondial, ed. *La Conscience Juive: Donnees Et Debats; Textes Des Trois Premiers Colloque D'intellectuels Juifs De Langue Francaise*. Colloque d'Intellectuels Juifs de Langue Francaise. Paris: Presses Universitaires de France, 1963.
Courtine-Denamy, Sylvie. *Three Women in Dark Times: Edith Stein, Hannah Arendt, Simone Weil, or Amor Fati, Amor Mundi*. Ithaca, N.Y.: Cornell University Press, 2000.
Cranston, Maurice. 'Hannah Arendt'. *Encounter* (March 1976): 54–55.
Critchley, Simon. *The Ethics of Deconstruction: Derrida and Levinas*. Edinburgh: Edinburgh University Library, 1999.
———. 'Ethics, Politics and Radical Democracy: History of a Disagreement'. Special ethico-political issue, *Culture Machine: Generating Research in Culture and Theory* 4 (2002).
———. 'Five Problems in Levinas's View of Politics and the Sketch of a Solution to Them'. *Political Theory* 32, no. 2 (2004): 172–185.
Dallmayr, Fred. *Beyond Dogma and Despair: Toward a Critical Phenomenology of Politics*. Notre Dame, Ind.: University of Notre Dame Press, 1981.
———. 'Cosmopolitanism: Moral and Political'. *Political Theory* 31, no. 3 (2003): 421–442.
———. *Critical Encounters: Between Philosophy and Politics*. Notre Dame, Ind.: University of Notre Dame Press, 1987.
———. *From Contract to Community: Political Theory at the Crossroads*. New York: M. Dekker, 1978.
———. 'Ontology of Freedom: Heidegger and Political Philosophy'. *Political Theory* 12, no. 2 (1984): 204–234.
———. *Polis and Praxis: Exercises in Contemporary Political Theory*. Cambridge, Mass.: MIT Press, 1984.
———. 'Postmetaphysics and Democracy'. *Political Theory* 21, no. 1 (1993): 101–127.
———. 'Toward a Critical Reconstruction of Ethics and Politics'. *Journal of Politics* 36, no. 4 (1974): 926–957.
Dallmayr, Fred, and José María Rosales. *Beyond Nationalism? Sovereignty and Citizenship*. Global Encounters. Lanham, Md.: Lexington Books, 2001.

Dallmayr, Fred, and Stephen K. White. *Life-World and Politics: Between Modernity and Postmodernity; Essays in Honor of Fred R. Dallmayr*. Notre Dame, Ind.: University of Notre Dame Press, 1989.

d'Entreves, Maurizio Passerin. 'Hannah Arendt'. In *The Stanford Encyclopedia of Philosophy*, edited by Edward N. Zalta. 2006. plato.stanford.edu/archives/fall2006/entries/arendt/.

———. *The Political Philosophy of Hannah Arendt*. London: Routledge, 1994.

Derrida, Jacques. *Adieu À Emmanuel Lévinas*. Incises. Paris: Galilée, 1997.

———. *Adieu to Emmanuel Levinas*. Stanford, Calif.: Stanford University Press, 1999.

———. *Margins of Philosophy*. Chicago: University of Chicago Press, 1982.

———. *Politics of Friendship*. London: Verso, 1997.

Derrida, Jacques, and Anne Dufourmantelle. *De L'hospitalité*. Petite Bibliothèque des Idées. Paris: Calmann-Lévy, 1997.

———. *Of Hospitality*. Cultural Memory in the Present. Stanford, Calif.: Stanford University Press, 2000.

Derrida, Jacques, and Gianni Vattimo. *Religion*. Cambridge, England: Polity Press, 1998.

Descombes, Vincent. *Le Même Et L'autre: Quarante-Cinq Ans De Philosophie Française (1933–1978)*. Paris: Éditions de Minuit, 1979.

———. *Modern French Philosophy*. Cambridge, England: Cambridge University Press, 1980.

Dienstag, Joshua Foa. *'Dancing in Chains': Narrative and Memory in Political Theory*. Stanford, Calif.: Stanford University Press, 1997.

Dietz, Mary G. *Turning Operations: Feminism, Arendt, and Politics*. New York: Routledge, 2002.

Dinesen, Isak. *Daguerreotypes, and Other Essays*. Chicago: University of Chicago Press, 1979.

Disch, Lisa Jane. *Hannah Arendt and the Limits of Philosophy*. Ithaca, N.Y.: Cornell University Press, 1994.

Dossa, Shiraz. *The Public Realm and the Public Self: The Political Theory of Hannah Arendt*. Waterloo: Wilfrid Laurier University Press, 1989.

Drabinski, John. 'The Possibility of an Ethical Politics: From Peace to Liturgy'. *Philosophy and Social Criticism* 26, no. 4 (2000): 49–73.

Drichel, Simone. 'On Political Bottom Lines and Last Ethical Frontiers: The Politics and Ethics of "The Other".' *Borderlands: E-Journal* 6.2 (2007). Digital journal

Duyndam, Joachim, and Marcel Poorthuis. *Levinas*. Kopstukken Filosofie. Rotterdam: Lemniscaat, 2003.

Dworkin, Ronald. *Sovereign Virtue: The Theory and Practice of Equality*. Cambridge, Mass.: Harvard University Press, 2000.

Edyvane, Derek. 'A Back-Turning Harmony: Conflict as a Source of Political Community'. *Res Publica* 11 (2005): 27–54.

Eidelberg, Paul. *Beyond the Secular Mind: A Judaic Response to the Problems of Modernity*. Contributions in Philosophy. New York: Greenwood Press, 1989.

Eisen, Arnold M. *Rethinking Modern Judaism: Ritual, Commandment, Community*. Chicago Studies in the History of Judaism. Chicago: University of Chicago Press, 1998.

Ettinger, Elzbieta. *Hannah Arendt/Martin Heidegger*. New Haven, Conn.: Yale University Press, 1995.

Fackenheim, Emil L. *Encounters between Judaism and Modern Philosophy: A Preface to Future Jewish Thought*. New York: Schocken Books, 1980.

———. *A Political Philosophy for the State of Israel: Fragments*. Jerusalem: Jerusalem Center for Public Affairs, 1988.

———. *What Is Judaism? An Interpretation for the Present Age*. Library of Jewish Philosophy. Syracuse, N.Y.: Syracuse University Press, 1999.

Fackenheim, Emil L. *To Mend the World: Foundations of Future Jewish Thought*. Berlin: Schuken Books, 1982.

Fackenheim, Emil L., and International Center for University Teaching of Jewish Civilization. *Jewish Philosophy and the Academy*. Madison, N.J.: Fairleigh Dickinson University Press, 1996.

Fackenheim, Emil L., and Michael L. Morgan. *Jewish Philosophers and Jewish Philosophy*. Bloomington: Indiana University Press, 1996.

Farrelly, Colin. *Introduction to Contemporary Political Theory*. New York: Sage, 2004.

Finkielkraut, Alain. *The Imaginary Jew = Le Juif Imaginaire*. Texts and Contexts. Lincoln: University of Nebraska Press, 1994.

Flynn, Bernard. *The Philosophy of Claude Lefort: Interpreting the Political*. Northwestern University Studies in Phenomenology & Existential Philosophy. Evanston, Ill.: Northwestern University Press, 2005.

———. *Political Philosophy at the Closure of Metaphysics*. Contemporary Studies in Philosophy and the Human Sciences. Atlantic Highlands, N.J.: Humanities Press, 1992.

Flyvbjerg, Bent. 'Habermas and Foucault: Thinkers for Civil Society?' *British Journal of Sociology* 49, no. 2 (1998): 210–233.

Fonrobert, Charlotte Elisheva, and Martin S. Jaffee. *The Cambridge Companion to the Talmud and Rabbinic Literature*. Cambridge Companions to Religion. Cambridge, England: Cambridge University Press, 2007.

Forst, Rainer. *Contexts of Justice: Political Philosophy Beyond Liberalism and Communitarianism*. Philosophy, Social Theory, and the Rule of Law. Berkeley: University of California Press, 2002.

Frank, Daniel H. *The Jewish Philosophy Reader*. London: Routledge, 2000.

Frank, Daniel H., and Oliver Leaman. *The Cambridge Companion to Medieval Jewish Philosophy*. Cambridge, England: Cambridge University Press, 2003.

Frankl, Viktor E. *Man's Search For Meaning*. Rev. ed. New York: Pocket, 1997.

———. *The Will to Meaning: Foundations and Applications of Logotherapy*. Rei Exp. Editions. New York: Plume, 1988.

Gauchet, Marcel. *Le Désenchantement Du Monde: Une Histoire Politique De La Religion*. Paris: Gallimard, 1985.

Gibbs, Robert. *Why Ethics? Signs of Responsibilities*. Princeton, N.J.: Princeton University Press, 2000.

Glatzer, Nahum Norbert. *Essays in Jewish Thought*. Tuscaloosa: University of Alabama Press, 1978.

Glowacka, Dorota. 'Community and the Work of Death: Thanato-Ontology in Hannah Arendt and Jean-Luc Nancy'. *Culture Machine: Generating Research in Culture and Theory* 8 (2006). Open access e-journal.

Goodman, Lenn Evan. *Judaism, Human Rights, and Human Values*. New York: Oxford University Press, 1998.

Gottsegen, Michael G. *The Political Thought of Hannah Arendt*. Albany: State University of New York Press, 1994.

Grant, Ruth W. 'Political Theory, Political Science, and Politics'. *Political Theory* 30, no. 4 (2002): 577–595.

Guignon, Charles B. *The Cambridge Companion to Heidegger*. Cambridge Companions to Philosophy. Cambridge, England: Cambridge University Press, 2006.

Haas, Peter J. *Morality after Auschwitz: The Radical Challenge of the Nazi Ethic*. Philadelphia: Fortress Press, 1988.

Habermas, Jurgen. 'Religion and the Public Sphere'. *European Journal of Philosophy* 14, no. 1 (2006): 353–67.

Halberstam, Michael. 'Totalitarianism as a Problem for the Modern Conception of Politics'. *Political Theory* 26, no. 4 (1998): 459–88.

Halperin, Jean, Eliane Amado Lévy-Valensi, and Colloque d'intellectuels juifs de langue francaise. *Israël Dans La Conscience Juive: Données Et Débats*. Congrès Juif Mondial. Paris: Presses Universitaires de France, 1971.

———. *Tentations Et Actions De La Conscience Juive: Données Et Débats*. Congrès Juif Mondial. Paris: Presses Universitaires de France, 1971.

Halperin, Jean, et al. *La Conscience Juive Face À L'histoire: Le Pardon*. Congrès Juif Mondial. Paris: Presses Universitaires de France, 1965.

Halperin, Jean, and Colloque des intellectuels juifs de langue francaise. *Israel, Le Judaisme Et L'europe: Actes Du Xiiie Colloque Des Intellectuels Juifs De Langue Française*. Paris: Gallimard, 1984.

———. *La Conscience Juive: Donnees Et Debats: Textes Des Trois Premiers Colloque D'intellectuels Juifs De Langue Française*. Paris: Presses Universitaires de France, 1963.

———. *Les Soixante-Dix Nations: Regards Juifs Sur Les Peuples De La Terre; Données Et Débats; Actes Du Xxviie Colloque Des Intellectuels Juifs De Langue Francaise*. Paris: Denoël, 1987.

———. *Mémoire Et Histoire: Données Et Débats; Actes Du Xxve Colloque Des Intellectuels Juifs De Langue Francaise*. Paris: Denoël, 1986.

Halperin, Jean, et al. *Idoles: Données Et Débats; Actes Du Xxiv Colloque Des Intellectuels Juifs De Langue Francaise*. Paris: Denoël, 1985.

Halperin, Jean, Georges Levitte, and Colloque des intellectuels juifs de langue francaise. *Jérusalem, L'unique Et L'universel: Données Et Débats*. Congrès Juif Mondial: Paris: Presses Universitaires de France, 1979.

———. *Jeunesse Et Révolution Dans La Conscience Juive: Données Et Débats*. Congrès Juif Mondial. Paris: Presses Universitaires de France, 1972.

———. *La Bible Au Présent: Actes Du Xxiie Colloque Des Intellectuels Juifs De Langue Française*. Paris: Gallimard, 1982.

———. *La Conscience Juive Face À La Guerre: Données Et Débats*. Congrès Juif Mondial 26. Paris: Presses Universitaires de France, 1976.

———. *La Question De L'etat/Textes Presentes Par Jean Halperin Et Georges Levitte*. Paris: Denoël, 1989.

———. *L'argent: Données Et Débats: Actes Du Xxviiie Colloque Des Intellectuels Juifs De Langue Francaise*. Colloque Des Intellectuels Juifs. Paris: Denoël, 1989.

———. *L'autre Dans La Conscience Juive: Le Sacré Et Le Couple; Données Et Débats*. Paris: Presses Universitaires de France, 1973.

———. *Le Modèle De L'occident: Données Et Débats*. Congrès Juif Mondial. Paris: Presses Universitaires de France, 1977.

———. *Politique et Religion*. Idées 457. Paris: Gallimard, 1981.

Hand, Séan. 'Ab-Originality: Radical Passivity through Talmudic Reading'. In *Radical Passivity: Rethinking Ethical Agency in Levinas*, edited by Benda Hofmeyer, 133–42. Dordrecht, Netherlands: Springer International Academic Publishers, 2008.

Hansel, Georges. *De La Bible Au Talmud: L'itinéraire De Pensée D'emmanuel Levinas*. Paris: Odile Jacob, 2008.

Hartman, David. *Joy and Responsibility: Israel, Modernity and the Renewal of Judaism*. Jerusalem: Ben-Zvi-Posner, 1978.

Heidegger, Martin. *Beiträge Zur Philosophie*. Klostermann: Frankfurt Am Main, 1936–1938.

———. *Identity and Difference*. New York: Harper & Row, 1969.

———. *An Introduction to Metaphysics*. New Haven, Conn.: Yale University Press, 1959.

———. *What Is Philosophy?* New York: Twayne Publishers, 1958.

Heller, Agnes. 'Hannah Arendt on the "Vita Contemplativa".' In *Hannah Arendt: Thinking, Judging, Freedom*, edited by Gisela T. Kaplan and Clive S. Kessler, 144–59. Sydney: Allen and Unwin, 1989.

Hendley, Steve. *From Communicative Action to the Face of the Other: Levinas and Habermas on Language, Obligation, and Community*. Lanham, Md.: Lexington Books, 2000.

Herzog, Annabel. *Penser Autrement La Politique: Eléments Pour Une Critique De La Philosophie Politique*. Paris: Kimé, 1997.

Hilberg, Raul. *The Destruction of the European Jews*. New Haven, Conn.: Yale University Press, 2003.

Hinchman, Lewis P., and Sandra K. Hinchman. 'Existentialism Politicized: Arendt's Debt to Jaspers'. *Review of Politics* 53, no. 3 (1991): 435–468.

———. *Hannah Arendt: Critical Essays*. SUNY Series in Political Theory: Contemporary Issues. Albany: State University of New York Press, 1994.
Hinchman, Sandra K. 'Common Sense & Political Barbarism in the Theory of Hannah Arendt'. *Polity* 17, no. 2 (1984): 317–339.
Holtz, Barry W., ed. *Back to the Sources: Reading the Classical Jewish Texts*. New York: Simon and Schuster, 1984.
Honig, Bonnie. 'Arendt, Identity, and Difference'. *Political Theory* 16, no. 1 (1988): 77–98.
———. 'Difference, Dilemmas, and the Politics of Home'. In *Democracy and Difference: Changing Boundaries of the Political,* edited by Seyla Benhabib, 252–77. Princeton, N.J.: Princeton University Press, 1996.
———. *Feminist Interpretations of Hannah Arendt*. Re-Reading the Canon. University Park: Pennsylvania State University Press, 1995.
———. 'The Politics of Agonism: A Critical Response to "Beyond Good and Evil: Arendt, Nietzsche, and the Aestheticization of Political Action" by Dana R. Villa'. *Political Theory* 21, no. 3 (1993): 528–533.
Horowitz, Asher, and Gad Horowitz. *Difficult Justice: Commentaries on Levinas and Politics*. Toronto: University of Toronto Press, 2006.
Hösle, Vittorio. *Morals and Politics*. Notre Dame, Ind.: University of Notre Dame Press, 2004.
Hull, Margaret Betz. *The Hidden Philosophy of Hannah Arendt*. London: Routledge Curzon, 2002.
Iris Marion, Young. 'Comments on Seyla Benhabib, Situating the Self'. *New German Critique* 62 (1994): 165–172.
Isin, Engin F., and Greg Marc Nielsen. *Acts of Citizenship*. London: Zed Books Ltd, 2008.
Jacobitti, Suzanne. 'Hannah Arendt and the Will'. *Political Theory* 16, no. 1 (1988): 53–76.
———. 'Individualism & Political Community: Arendt & Tocqueville on the Current Debate in Liberalism'. *Polity* 23, no. 4 (1991): 585–604.
———. 'The Public, the Private, the Moral: Hannah Arendt and Political Morality'. *International Political Science Review/Revue internationale de science politique* 12, no. 4 (1991): 281–293.
Jonas, Hans. 'Hannah Arendt'. *Partisan Review* XLII, no. 1 (1976): 13.
———. *The Imperative of Responsibility: In Search of an Ethics for the Technological Age*. Chicago: University of Chicago Press, 1984.
Jordaan, Eduard. 'Affinities in the Socio-Political Thought of Rorty and Levinas'. *Philosophy and Social Criticism* 32, no. 2 (2006): 139–209.
Jung, Hwa Yol. 'Confucianism and Existentialism: Intersubjectivity as the Way of Man'. *Philosophy and Phenomenological Research* 30, no. 2 (1969): 186–202.
———. 'Jen: An Existential and Phenomenological Problem of Intersubjectivity'. *Philosophy East and West* 16, nos. 3/4 (1966): 169–188.
———. 'Leo Strauss's Conception of Political Philosophy: A Critique'. *Review of Politics* 29, no. 4 (1967): 492–517.
Jung, Hwa Yol. 'Taking Responsibility Seriously'. In *The Phenomenology of the Political,* edited by Kevin and Lester Embree Thompson, 147–68. Dordrecht: Kluwer Academic Publishers, 2000.
Kant, Immanuel. *Critique of Judgment*. New York: Prometheus Books, 2000.
———. *Kant's Political Writings*. Translated by H. B. Nisbet. Cambridge Texts in the History of Political Thought. Cambridge, England: Cambridge University Press, 1991.
Kass, Leon. *The Beginning of Wisdom: Reading Genesis*. Chicago: University of Chicago Press, 2006.
Kateb, George. *Hannah Arendt, Politics, Conscience, Evil*. Philosophy and Society. Totowa, N.J.: Rowman & Allanheld, 1984.

Kearney, Richard. *Debates in Continental Philosophy: Conversations with Contemporary Thinkers*. Perspectives in Continental Philosophy. New York: Fordham University Press, 2004.

———. *On Stories*. Thinking in Action. London: Routledge, 2002.

———. *Twentieth-Century Continental Philosophy*. Routledge History of Philosophy. London: Routledge, 2003.

Kearney, Richard, and Mark Dooley. *Questioning Ethics: Contemporary Debates in Philosophy*. London: Routledge, 1999.

Kearney, Richard, and Mara Rainwater. *The Continental Philosophy Reader*. London: Routledge, 1996.

Kearney, Richard, and Paul Ricœur. *Dialogues with Contemporary Continental Thinkers: The Phenomenological Heritage; Paul Ricoeur, Emmanuel Levinas, Herbert Marcuse, Stanislas Breton, Jacques Derrida*. Manchester, England: Manchester University Press, 1984.

Kohn, Jerome, and Arien Mack. *Hannah Arendt's Centenary: Political and Philosophical Perspectives, Part I and II*. New York: New School for Social Research, 2007.

Kristeva, Julia, and Frank Collins. *Hannah Arendt: Life Is a Narrative*. Toronto: University of Toronto Press, 2001.

Kugel, James L. *Traditions of the Bible: A Guide to the Bible as It Was at the Start of the Common Era*. Cambridge, Mass.: Harvard University Press, 1998.

Kymlicka, Will. *Contemporary Political Philosophy: An Introduction*. Oxford: Oxford University Press, 2002.

La Caze, Marguerite. 'At the Intersection: Kant, Derrida, and the Relation between Ethics and Politics'. *Political Theory* 35, no. 6 (2007): 781–805.

Laclau, Ernesto. 'Ethics, Politics and Radical Democracy: Response to Simon Critchley'. Special ethico-political issue, *Culture Machine: Generating Research in Culture and Theory* 4 (2002).

Laclau, Ernesto, and Chantal Mouffe. *Hegemony and Socialist Strategy: Towards a Radical Democratic Politics*. London; New York: Verso, 2001.

Lacoue-Labarthe, Philippe, Jean-Luc Nancy, and Simon Sparks. *Retreating the Political*. Warwick Studies in European Philosophy. London: Routledge, 1997.

Langsdorf, Lenore, Stephen H. Watson, and Karen A. Smith. *Reinterpreting the Political: Continental Philosophy and Political Theory*. Selected Studies in Phenomenology and Existential Philosophy. New York: State University of New York Press, 1998.

Larmore, Charles. *The Morals of Modernity*. Modern European Philosophy. Cambridge, England: Cambridge University Press, 1996.

———. *Patterns of Moral Complexity*. Cambridge, England: Cambridge University Press, 1987.

Lefort, Claude. *Essais Sur Le Politique: Xixe-Xxe Siècles*. Collection Esprit. Paris: Seuil, 1986.

———. 'Hannah Arendt and the Question of the Political'. In *Democracy and Political Theory*, trans. David Macey, 45–55. Minneapolis: University of Minnesota Press, 1988.

———. 'Hannah Arendt on the Law of Movement and Ideology'. In *Complications: Communism and the Dilemmas of Democracy*, trans. Julian Bourge, 146–57. New York: Columbia University Press, 2007.

———. 'Reflections on the Present'. In *Writing, the Political Test*. Translated by David Ames Curtis. Durham, N.C.: Duke University Press, 2000.

Lefort, Claude, et al. *Le Retrait Du Politique*. Cahiers Du Centre De Recherches Philosophiques Sur Le Politique. Paris: Cahiers Galilée, 1983.

Lescourret, Marie-Anne. *Emmanuel Levinas*. Paris: Flammarion, 1994.

Levi, Primo. *Survival in Auschwitz: The Nazi Assault on Humanity*. New York: Collier Books, 1961.

Lilla, Mark. *New French Thought: Political Philosophy*. New French Thought. Princeton, N.J.: Princeton University Press, 1994.

———. *The Reckless Mind: Intellectuals in Politics*. New York: New York Review Books, 2001.

Llewelyn, John. *Appositions of Jacques Derrida and Emmanuel Levinas*. Studies in Continental Thought. Bloomington: Indiana University Press, 2002.

Lyotard, Jean-Francois. "Le Survivant." In *Ontologie Et Politique: Actes Du Colloque Hannah Arendt*, edited by Miguel Abensour, 288–309. Paris: Tierce, 1989.

Martel, James. 'Amo: Volo Ut Sis: Love, Willing and Arendt's Reluntant Embrace of Sovereignty'. *Philosophy and Social Criticism* 34, no. 3 (2008): 287–313.

May, Larry. *Sharing Responsibility*. Chicago: University of Chicago Press, 1992.

McGowan, John. *Hannah Arendt: An Introduction*. Minneapolis: University of Minnesota Press, 1998.

Mendelssohn, Moses, and Alfred Jospe. *Jerusalem, and Other Jewish Writings*. New York: Schocken Books, 1969.

Meyer, Michael A. 'Where Does the Modern Period of Jewish History Begin?' *Judaism: A Quarterly Journal* 24, no. 3.95(1975): 329–38.

Minnich, Elizabeth. 'Teaching Thinking: Moral and Political Considerations'. *Change* 25(5)(2003): 19–24.

———. 'To Judge in Freedom: Hannah Arendt on the Relation of Thinking and Morality'. In *Hannah Arendt: Thinking, Judging, Freedom*, edited by Gisela T. Kaplan and Clive S. Kessler, 133–43. Sydney: Allen and Unwin, 1989.

Morgan, Michael L. *Discovering Levinas*. New York: Cambridge University Press, 2007.

———. *Interim Judaism: Jewish Thought in a Century of Crisis*. Bloomington: Indiana University Press, 2001.

Morgan, Michael L., and Peter Eli Gordon. *The Cambridge Companion to Modern Jewish Philosophy*. Cambridge Companions to Religion. Cambridge, England: Cambridge University Press, 2007.

Mosès, Stéphane. 'Emanuel Levinas: Ethics as Primary Meaning'. *Graduate Faculty Philosophy Journal* 20–21, nos. 2–1 (1998): 13–24.

Mouffe, Chantal. *The Democratic Paradox*. London: Verso, 2000.

———. *Dimensions of Radical Democracy: Pluralism, Citizenship, Community*. London: Verso, 1992.

———. *On the Political*. Thinking in Action. London: Routledge, 2005.

———. 'Politics and Passions: The Stakes of Democracy'. *Ethical Perspectives* 7, no. 2–3(2000): 146–50.

———. *The Return of the Political*. London: Verso, 2005.

Nancy, Jean-Luc. 'The Being-with of Being-There'. Translated by Marie-Eve Morin. *Continental Philosophy Review* 41, no. 1 (2008): 1–16.

———. *Être Singulier Pluriel*. Collection La Philosophie En Effet. Paris: Galilée, 1996.

———. *La Communauté Affrontée*. Collection La Philosophie En Effet. Paris: Galilée, 2001.

Nelson, Eric Sean, Antje Kapust, and Kent Still. *Addressing Levinas*. Northwestern University Studies in Phenomenology & Existential Philosophy. Evanston, Ill.: Northwestern University Press, 2005.

Neusner, Jacob. *Judaism as Philosophy: The Method and Message of the Mishnah*. Baltimore, Md.: Johns Hopkins University Press, 1999.

———. *The Modern Study of the Mishnah*. Studia Post-Biblica. Leiden: Brill, 1973.

———. *Rabbinic Narrative: A Documentary Perspective*. Brill Reference Library of Judaism. Leiden: Brill, 2003.

———. *Rabbinic Political Theory: Religion and Politics in the Mishnah*. Chicago Studies in the History of Judaism. Chicago: University of Chicago Press, 1991.

———. *The Talmud: What It Is and What It Says*. Lanham, Md.: Rowman & Littlefield Publishers, 2006.

Newton, Adam Zachary. *The Fence and the Neighbor: Emmanuel Levinas, Yeshayahu Leibowitz, and Israel among the Nations*. SUNY Series in Jewish Philosophy. Albany: State University of New York Press, 2001.

Ouaknin, Marc-Alain. *The Burnt Book: Reading the Talmud*. Princeton, N.J.: Princeton University Press, 1995.

Peperzak, Adriaan Theodoor. *Beyond: The Philosophy of Emmanuel Levinas*. Northwestern University Studies in Phenomenology & Existential Philosophy. Evanston, Ill.: Northwestern University Press, 1997.

———. *Ethics as First Philosophy: The Significance of Emmanuel Levinas for Philosophy, Literature, and Religion*. New York: Routledge, 1995.

Peperzak, Adriaan Theodoor, and Emmanuel Lévinas. *To the Other: An Introduction to the Philosophy of Emmanuel Levinas*. West Lafayette, Ind.: Purdue University Press, 1993.

Petit, Philip. *Republicanism: A Theory of Freedom and Government*. Oxford: Oxford University Press, 1999.

Pettit, Philip, ed. *Contemporary Political Theory*. Philosophical Topics. New York: Macmillan, 1991.

Pitkin, Hanna Fenichel. 'Justice: On Relating Private and Public'. *Political Theory* 9, no. 3 (1981): 327–52.

Plato. *Theaetetus*. Chicago: University of Chicago Press, 1986.

Poché, Fred. *Penser Avec Arendt Et Lévinas: Du Mal Politique Au Respect De L'autre*. Savoir Penser. Lyon: Diffusion Sofedis, 1998.

Poirié, François. *Emmanuel Lévinas*. Qui Êtes-Vous? Lyon: La Manufacture, 1987.

Polin, Raymond. *Ethique Et Politique*. Philosophie Politique. Edited by Raymond Polin. Paris: Editions Sirey, 1968.

Rabaté, Jean-Michel, Michael Wetzel, and Jacques Derrida. *L'ethique Du Don: Jacques Derrida Et La Pensée Du Don*. Colloque De Royaumont, 1990. Paris: Métailié-Transition, Diffusion Seuil, 1992.

Raz, Joseph. *Ethics in the Public Domain: Essays in the Morality of Law and Politics*. Oxford: Oxford University Press, 1994.

Ring, Jennifer. *The Political Consequences of Thinking: Gender and Judaism in the Work of Hannah Arendt*. SUNY Series in Political Theory: Contemporary Issues. Albany: State University of New York Press, 1997.

Rosenzweig, Franz, and Nahum Norbert Glatzer. *On Jewish Learning*. Modern Jewish Philosophy and Religion. Madison: University of Wisconsin Press, 2002.

Roth, John K. *Ethics after the Holocaust: Perspectives, Critiques, and Responses*. St. Paul, Minn.: Paragon House, 1999.

Roviello, Anne-Marie. *Sens Commun Et Modernité Chez Hannah Arendt*. Bruxelles: Ousia, 1987.

Sacks, Jonathan. *Celebrating Life*. London: Continuum, 2003.

———. *Crisis and Covenant: Jewish Thought after the Holocaust*. Sherman Studies of Judaism in Modern Times. Manchester, England: Manchester University Press 1992.

———. *From Optimism to Hope: Thoughts for the Day*. London: Continuum, 2004.

———. *A Letter in the Scroll: Understanding Our Jewish Identity and Exploring the Legacy of the World's Oldest Religion*. New York: Free Press, 2000.

———. 'Miketz: Faith, Universal and Particular'. In *Covenant and Conversation: Thoughts on the Weekly Parsha fro the Chief Rabbi*. 2003. www.rabbisacks.org, 8 December 2007.

———. *The Politics of Hope*. London: Vintage, 2000.

Saint-Cheron, Michael de. *Entretiens Avec Emmanuel Levinas: 1992–1994*. Paris: Librairie Générale Francaise, 2006.

Samuelson, Norbert Max, and Academy for Jewish Philosophy (U.S.). *Studies in Jewish Philosophy: Collected Essays of the Academy for Jewish Philosophy, 1980–1985*. Studies in Judaism. Lanham, Md.: University Press of America, 1987.

Sandel, Michael J. *Public Philosophy: Essays on Morality in Politics*. Cambridge, Mass.: Harvard University Press, 2005.

Sarna, Nahum M. 'The Authority and Interpretation of Scripture in Jewish Tradition'. In *Understanding Scripture: Explorations of Jewish and Christian Traditions of Interpreta-*

tion, edited by Clemens Thoma and Michael Wyschogrod, 9–20. New York: Paulist New York, 1987.

Schmiedgen, Peter. 'Polytheism, Monotheism and Public Space: Between Levinas and Arendt'. *Critical Horizons* 6, no. 1 (2005): 225–37.

Schmitt, Carl, et al. *The Concept of the Political*. Chicago: University of Chicago Press, 1996.

Seeskin, Kenneth. *Autonomy in Jewish Philosophy*. Cambridge, England: Cambridge University Press, 2001.

Seidler, Victor J. *Jewish Philosophy and Western Culture: A Modern Introduction*. London: I. B. Tauris, 2007.

Sibony, Daniel. *Don De Soi Ou Partage De Soi? Le Drame Lévinas*. Paris: Jacob, 2000.

Sims, Jesse. 'Absolute Adversity: Schmitt, Levinas and the Exceptionality of Killing'. *Philosophy and Social Criticism* 31, no. 2 (2005): 223–252.

Skinner, Quentin. *Visions of Politics,* Volumes I–III. Cambridge, England: Cambridge University Press, 2002.

Smith, Barry, and David Woodruff Smith. *The Cambridge Companion to Husserl*. Cambridge, England: Cambridge University Press, 1995.

Smith, Michael B. *Toward the Outside: Concepts and Themes in Emmanuel Levinas*. Pittsburgh, Pa.: Duquesne University Press, 2005.

Srajek, Martin C. *In the Margins of Deconstruction: Jewish Conceptions of Ethics in Emmanuel Levinas and Jacques Derrida*. Pittsburgh, Pa.: Duquesne University Press, 2000.

Steinsaltz, Adin. *Talmud: Sanhedrin*. Vol. XVII. New York: Random House, 1998.

Stone, Ira F. *Reading Levinas/Reading Talmud: An Introduction*. Philadelphia: Jewish Publication Society, 1998.

Stout, Jeffrey. *Democracy and Tradition*. New Forum Books. Princeton, N.J.: Princeton University Press, 2004.

Strauss, Leo. 'Jerusalem and Athens'. In *Jewish Philosophy and the Crisis of Modernity: Essays and Lectures in Modern Jewish Thought*, edited by Kenneth Hart Green, 377–408. Albany: State University of New York Press, 1997.

———. *Liberalism Ancient and Modern*. Ithaca, N.Y.: Cornell University Press, 1989.

———. *What Is Political Philosophy? And Other Studies*. Chicago: University of Chicago Press, 1988.

Strauss, Leo, and Kenneth Hart Green. *Jewish Philosophy and the Crisis of Modernity: Essays and Lectures in Modern Jewish Thought*. SUNY Series in the Jewish Writings of Leo Strauss. New York: State University of New York Press, 1997.

Taylor, Charles. 'Ontology'. *Philosophy* 34, no. 129 (1959): 125–141.

———. *A Secular Age*. Cambridge, England: The Belknap Press of Harvard University Press, 2007.

———. 'Two Theories of Modernity'. *The Hastings Center Report* 25, no. 2 (1995): 24–33.

Tocqueville, Alexis de. *De La Démocratie En Amérique*. Paris: Flammarion, 1981.

Tolle, Gordon J. *Human Nature under Fire: The Political Philosophy of Hannah Arendt*. Washington, D.C.: University Press of America, 1982.

Tracy, David. *Dialogue with the Other: The Inter-Religious Dialogue*. Louvain Theological & Pastoral Monographs. Louvain: Peeters Press 1991.

Tsao, Roy T. 'Arendt against Athens: Rereading the Human Condition'. *Political Theory* 30, no. 1 (2002): 97–123.

Tsongo Luutu, Vincent. *Penser Le Socio-Politique Avec Emmnanuel Lévinas*. Lyon: Profac, 1993.

Van Haute, Philippe, and Peg Birmingham. *Dissensus Communis: Between Ethics and Politics*. Edited by Albert W. and Paul J. M. van Tongeren Musschenga. Morality and the Meaning of Life. Kampen: Kok Pharos Publishing House, 1995.

Villa, Dana R. *Politics, Philosophy, Terror: Essays on the Thought of Hannah Arendt*. Princeton, N.J.: Princeton University Press, 1999.

———. 'Postmodernism and the Public Sphere'. *American Political Science Review* 86, no. 3 (1992): 712–721.

———. *Public Freedom*. Princeton, N.J.: Princeton University Press, 2008.

———. 'Public Sphere, Postmodernism and Polemic'. *American Political Science Review* 88, no. 2 (1994): 427–33.
———. *Socratic Citizenship*. Princeton, N.J.: Princeton University Press, 2001.
Villa, Dana R., and Joke J. Hermsen. *The Judge and the Spectator: Hannah Arendt's Political Philosophy*. Morality and the Meaning of Life. Leuven: Peeters, 1999.
Visker, Rudi. 'The Core of My Opposition to Levinas: A Clarification for Richard Rorty'. *Ethical Perspectives: Journal of the European Ethics Network* 4, no. 3 (1997): 154–170.
———. 'Dispossessed: How to Remain Silent after Levinas'. *Tijdschrift voor Filosofie* 57, no. 4 (1995): 631–666.
———. *The Inhuman Condition: Looking for Difference after Levinas and Heidegger*. Dordrecht, Netherlands: Kluwar Publisher, 2004.
———. 'Is Ethics Fundamental? Questioning Levinas on Irresponsibility'. *Continental Philosophy Review* 36, no. 3 (2003): 263–302.
———. 'Levinas, Multiculturalism and Us'. *Ethical Perspectives: Journal of the European Ethics Network* 6, no. 2 (1999): 159–169.
———. 'Philosophy and Pluralism'. *Philosophy Today* 48, no. 2 (2004): 115–127.
———. 'Pluralisme, Participatie En Vertegenwoordiging: Hannah Arendt Herlezend'. *Tijdschrift voor Filosofie* 69 (2007): 419–65.
———. 'The Strange(R) within Me'. *Ethical Perspectives: Journal of the European Ethics Network* 12, no. 4 (2005): 425–441.
Wall, Thomas Carl. *Radical Passivity: Lévinas, Blanchot, and Agamben*. New York: State University of New York Press, 1999.
Walzer, Michael. 'The Communitarian Critique of Liberalism'. *Political Theory* 18, no. 1 (1990): 6–23.
———. *Exodus and Revolution*. New York: Basic Books, 1985.
———. *Law, Politics, and Morality in Judaism*. Ethikon Series in Comparative Ethics. Princeton, N.J.: Princeton University Press, 2006.
———. *Spheres of Justice: A Defense of Pluralism and Equality*. New York: Basic Books, 1983.
Walzer, Michael, and David Miller. *Thinking Politically: Essays in Political Theory*. New Haven, Conn.: Yale University Press, 2007.
Walzer, Michael, et al. *The Jewish Political Tradition*. New Haven, Conn.: Yale University Press, 2000.
Weber, Elisabeth. *Questioning Judaism*. Translated by Rachel Bowlby. Cultural Memory in the Present. Stanford, Calif.: Stanford University Press, 2004.
William, Gareth. 'Love and Responsibility: A Political Ethic for Hannah Arendt'. *Political Studies* 46, no. 5 (1998): 937–50.
Wolff, Ernst. *De L'éthique À La Justice: Language Et Politique Dans La Philosophie De Lévinas*. Phenomenologica. Dordrecht, Netherlands: Springer Science & Business Media, 2007.
Wolin, Sheldon S. *Politics and Vision: Continuity and Innovation in Western Political Thought*. Princeton, N.J.: Princeton University Press, 2004.
Wright, Tamra. *The Twilight of Jewish Philosophy: Emmanuel Lévinas' Ethical Hermeneutics*. Amsterdam: Harwood Academic Publishers, 1999.
Wygoda, Schmuel. 'A Phenomenological Outlook at the Talmud: Levinas as Reader of the Talmud'. 2005. ghasel.free.fr/wygode.html.
Wyschogrod, Edith. *Emmanuel Levinas: The Problem of Ethical Metaphysics*. Perspectives in Continental Philosophy. New York: Fordham University Press, 2000.
Wyschogrod, Edith, and Gerald P. McKenny. *The Ethical*. Blackwell Readings in Continental Philosophy 5. Oxford: Blackwell, 2003.
Yates, Melissa. 'Rawls and Habermas on Religion in the Public Sphere'. *Philosophy and Social Criticism* 33 (2007): 880–91.
Young-Bruehl, Elisabeth. *Why Arendt Matters?* New Haven, Conn.: Yale University Press, 2006.

Zetterbaum, Marvin. 'Self and Subjectivity in Political Theory'. *Review of Politics* 44, no. 1 (1982): 59–82.

Ziarek, Ewa Plonowska. *An Ethics of Dissensus: Postmodernity, Feminism, and the Politics of Radical Democracy*. Stanford, Calif.: Stanford University Press, 2001.

Zuckerman, Ian. *Power: Communicative or Political? On the Successful Failure of the Discourse Theory of Power*. Chicago: The Midwest Political Science Association, 2004.

Index

Made in the USA
Lexington, KY
22 August 2016